Extreme Hermeneutics Presents:

The Full Character of God

Recovering the Whole Biblical Vision of Who He Is

Written By: Jeff C. Edwards

Published by: Extreme Hermeneutics

Disclaimer

This work is a theological study and reflects the author's interpretation of scripture. Readers are encouraged to examine the scriptures for themselves. "…they received the word with all readiness of mind, and searched the scriptures daily, whether those things were so" -Acts 17:11

Contact the Author: ExtremeHermeneutics@gmail.com

Copyright © 2026 by Jeff C. Edwards
All rights reserved.

ISBN: 979-8-9958036-7-6

Scripture quotations are taken from the King James Version (KJV) of the Bible, which is in the public domain.

This book is intended for educational and informational purposes only. The views expressed in this work are those of the author and are presented as part of a scriptural study.

Other Books by the Author:

The Great Rapture Debate

Examining the Biblical Case for the Timing of the Church's Departure

God is not Finished with Israel

A Scriptural Examination of the Covenants, the Church and the Error of Replacement Theology

The Great City Defined

Identifying the Woman on the Beast in Revelation 17

Prophecies of Christ in the Old Testament – Volumes 1-3

Table of Contents

Introduction

There is no greater subject than God Himself.

Every other question in theology eventually rests on this one. What is salvation, if we do not first know the God who saves? What is sin, if we do not understand the holiness of the One against whom sin is committed? What is grace, if we have no grasp of the justice from which grace rescues us? What is worship, if the God being worshiped has been thinned down, softened, or reshaped until He bears only partial resemblance to the One Scripture reveals?

The knowledge of God is not one doctrine among many. It is the ground beneath them all.

Yet it is possible to speak often about God and still know Him only in fragments. A person may speak much of His love while having little room for His wrath. Another may defend His sovereignty while failing to reflect the tenderness of His mercy. One may celebrate His patience while forgetting that patience is not the same as indifference. Another may affirm His justice but speak of it in ways that seem almost detached from His goodness. In each case, something true may be said. The problem is that the truth has been severed from the larger glory in which Scripture presents it.

God has not revealed Himself in pieces that compete with one another. He is not divided within Himself. His holiness does not restrain His love as though the two were rival impulses. His mercy does not overcome His justice as though compassion must persuade Him to set righteousness aside. His wrath is not a lapse in goodness. His sovereignty is not raw power detached from wisdom. His patience is not moral hesitation. He is, in all that He is, perfect and undivided.

The Bible does not ask us to choose between a loving God and a holy God, between a merciful God and a just God, between a God who forgives and a God who judges. It reveals the one true God who is all of these without contradiction. He is merciful and gracious, longsuffering, abundant in goodness and truth, forgiving iniquity and transgression and sin, and yet He will by no means clear the guilty. That is not an awkward tension in God's character. It is His own self-description.

Much confusion enters theology when we lose that fullness.

A diminished view of God will always leave its mark. It will shape the way the gospel is preached. It will alter the way judgment is understood. It will affect the way promises are read, the way prophecy is interpreted, the way suffering is explained, the way holiness is pursued, and the way assurance is grounded. False doctrine does not always begin with an open denial of Scripture. Sometimes it begins with an incomplete vision of God that quietly makes certain biblical truths harder to believe and others easier to distort.

This matters because the character of God is doctrinally revealing. Scripture never permits us to treat God's attributes as ornamental descriptions, beautiful but detached from the way we interpret His works and His Word. The God who speaks in Scripture is the same God who acts in Scripture. What He does will always be consistent with who He is. His promises arise from His faithfulness. His judgments proceed from His holiness and justice. His patience reflects His mercy. His salvation magnifies His grace without diminishing His righteousness.

For that reason, interpretations of Scripture should be examined not only for whether they can be argued from an isolated phrase, but also for whether they fit the full character of the God who has spoken. We must be careful here. God's character is not whatever our instincts tell us He ought to be. Human sentiment cannot sit in judgment over divine revelation. But once God has revealed Himself, we are not free to build doctrines that require Him to act against that revelation.

If Christ is the Bridegroom and the church is His bride, that truth matters when considering His relationship to His people in the day of wrath. If God cannot lie and does not break covenant, that truth matters when reading

His promises. If He is just as well as merciful, that truth matters when explaining the cross. If He is holy as well as loving, that truth matters when speaking about judgment, repentance, and eternal life. The character of God does not replace exegesis. It protects exegesis from becoming fragmented.

This book was written from the conviction that the church does not need a smaller God, a safer God, or a more culturally acceptable God. It needs to recover the God who has already made Himself known. The living God. The holy God. The gracious God. The God who forgives. The God who judges. The God whose love is purer than human affection, whose wrath is more righteous than human anger, whose mercy is deeper than human pity, and whose faithfulness cannot fail.

The purpose of this book is not merely to list divine attributes, though we will consider many of them carefully. Nor is it to flatten the mystery of God into a series of definitions, as though the infinite Lord could be mastered by arranging theological terms in the proper order. The goal is to look steadily at the biblical witness and recover the whole vision it gives us of who God is.

That recovery is needed because partial views of God are often persuasive. They usually appeal to something Scripture genuinely teaches. God is love. God is merciful. God is patient. God desires repentance. God welcomes sinners. All of that is gloriously true. But when such truths are removed from His holiness, truthfulness, justice, and righteous judgment, they begin to describe a god more agreeable to human preference than the God of the Bible.

The reverse error is also possible. A person may speak accurately of wrath, judgment, sovereignty, and holiness, yet do so in a way that seems to lose the warmth of God's compassion, the sincerity of His invitations, the tenderness of Christ toward the weak, or the astonishing generosity of grace. The full character of God corrects both distortions. It forbids sentimentalism, and it forbids severity detached from the heart of God as Scripture reveals Him.

To know God truly is to be drawn into both fear and comfort. His majesty forbids casualness. His goodness forbids despair. His holiness exposes us. His mercy invites us. His justice warns us. His faithfulness steadies us. His wisdom humbles us. His love gathers all who come to Him through Christ.

The chapters that follow will move slowly through this vision. We will begin with the importance of knowing God rightly, then consider how He has made Himself known in Scripture, in His own declarations, in the revelation of His names, in the mystery of the Trinity, and most fully in Jesus Christ. From there we will examine His character in its breadth: His holiness, glory, eternity, goodness, righteousness, justice, truth, faithfulness, love, mercy, grace, patience, kindness, knowledge, power, presence, wisdom, sovereignty, jealousy, and wrath. Then we will turn to the way His character guards doctrine, clarifies the gospel, and exposes interpretations that fracture truths God has joined together. Finally, we will ask what it means to worship, trust, fear, and obey the God who is all that Scripture declares Him to be.

This is not a study meant to leave God at a safe intellectual distance. It is meant to bring us nearer to the weight of His reality. The God of Scripture is not diminished by careful study. He grows greater in our sight. The more faithfully we behold Him, the more we discover that every simplified version of Him was too small.

The whole biblical vision of God is not less beautiful because it includes holiness, justice, and wrath. It is more beautiful. His mercy shines brighter because His justice is real. His grace becomes more astonishing because His holiness is uncompromised. His love becomes more secure because it is not sentimental or unstable, but rooted in the perfect character of the eternal God.

We do not need to rescue God from the parts of His character modern minds find difficult. We need to recover the fullness of the God who has spoken.

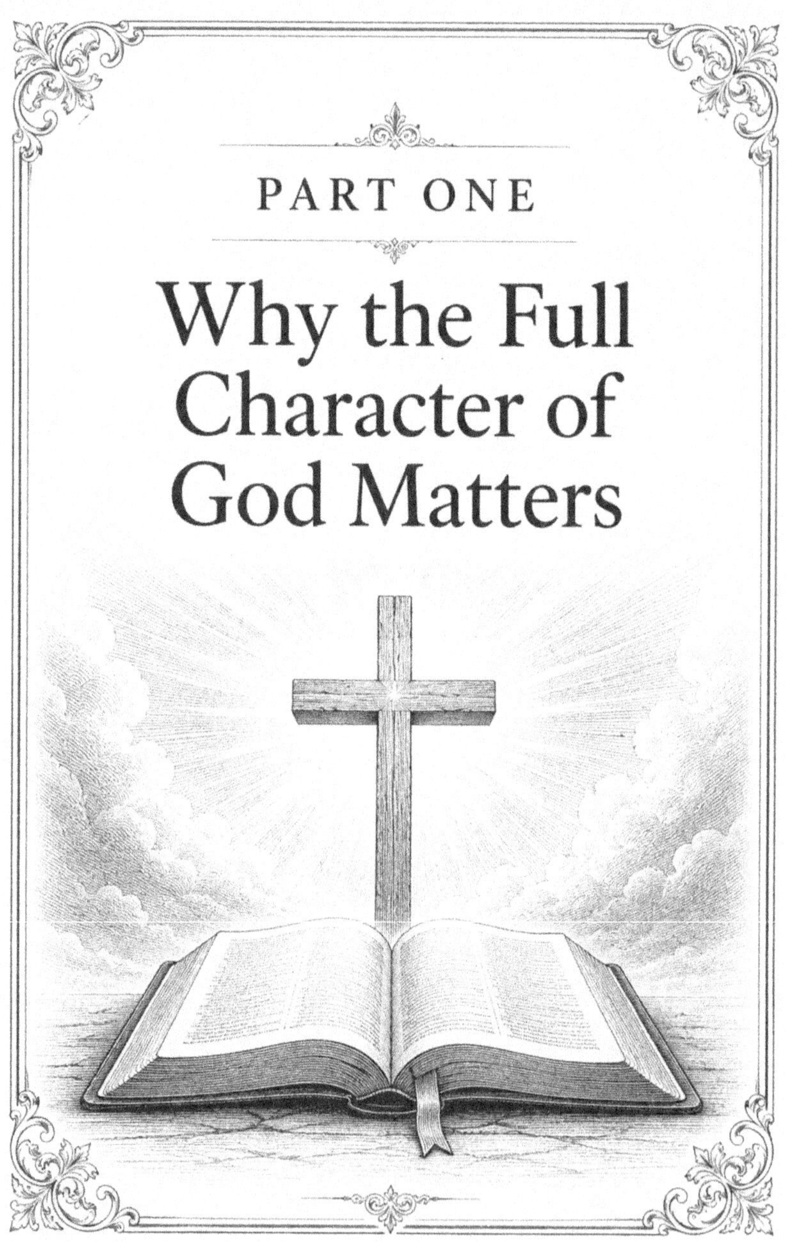

PART ONE

Why the Full Character of God Matters

Chapter 1 — The Most Important Thing We Can Know

The most important thing a person can know is not the future, though Scripture speaks of it. It is not the nature of salvation, though nothing matters more to the sinner than being reconciled to God. It is not the meaning of life, the purpose of suffering, the destiny of nations, or even the way of eternal life.

The most important thing we can know is **God Himself.**

Every other truth receives its weight from Him. Salvation matters because it is God who saves. Sin is terrible because it is rebellion against God. Heaven is glorious because it is the dwelling place of God. Judgment is fearful because it is the judgment of God. Scripture is authoritative because it is the Word of God. Worship is meaningful because God is worthy of it.

Remove God, and every doctrine loses its center. Distort God, and every doctrine begins to bend.

This is why theology cannot be reduced to collecting correct answers about individual subjects while leaving the character of God vague or underdeveloped. A man may memorize a doctrine of salvation, defend a position on prophecy, and speak confidently about the church, the kingdom, or the end of the age, while still carrying a thin and fragmented understanding of the One around whom all those doctrines revolve. That kind of theology may be technically busy, but it is unstable at the root.

The Bible does not treat the knowledge of God as an optional refinement for advanced believers. It presents it as the great dividing line between wisdom and folly, faithfulness and rebellion, life and death.

When Jeremiah confronted a people proud of their wisdom, strength, and riches, the Lord did not tell them to boast more carefully. He told them that the only proper ground of glory is knowing Him:

"Thus saith the LORD, Let not the wise man glory in his wisdom, neither let the mighty man glory in his might, let not the rich man glory in his riches: But let him that glorieth glory in this, that he understandeth and knoweth me, that I am the LORD which exercise lovingkindness, judgment, and righteousness, in the earth: for in these things I delight, saith the LORD." — **Jeremiah 9:23–24**

That passage does more than tell us that knowing God matters. It tells us **what kind of knowledge matters**. God is not asking to be acknowledged in a generic sense. He reveals Himself as the LORD who exercises **lovingkindness, judgment, and righteousness**. He names traits that many readers would be tempted to separate. Lovingkindness sounds warm. Judgment sounds severe. Righteousness sounds moral and exacting. Yet God brings them together and says, This is who I am. This is what I delight in.

To know God truly is to know Him as He reveals Himself, not as we would reduce Him.

That is where much confusion begins. People often say they want to know God, but what they really want is assurance that the God they already imagine is real. They want Him kind, but not holy in any way that disturbs them. They want Him forgiving, but not so righteous that forgiveness requires a cross. They want Him patient, but not a judge. They want Him sovereign when life feels uncertain, but not when His authority confronts human pride. They want a God who comforts, but not one before whom men fall on their faces.

Yet a god trimmed down to human preference cannot save, cannot rule, cannot reveal truth, and cannot be worshiped. He may be comforting as an idea, but he is not the God of Scripture.

The first responsibility of theology is not to make God acceptable to us. It is to receive what God has made known about Himself.

That truth matters because the human heart does not naturally preserve a clear vision of God. Left to itself, it darkens Him, reshapes Him, or trades Him for something easier to manage. Romans 1 describes humanity's downward movement into idolatry, and the first step is not atheism. It is the failure to honor God as God:

*"Because that, when they knew God, they glorified him not as God, neither were thankful; but became vain in their imaginations, and their foolish heart was darkened." — **Romans 1:21***

The tragedy is not merely that men reject facts about God. They refuse to glorify Him **as God**. Something about His true greatness becomes intolerable. The mind begins to dim. The heart turns inward. Before long, the Creator is exchanged for images more suited to the creature's desires.

Idolatry does not always wear the obvious form of carved stone. It can also appear as a theological portrait of God that keeps His name while altering His character. A God who never judges is not the God of Scripture. A God whose holiness is reduced to personal inspiration is not the God of Scripture. A God whose love has no moral shape, whose grace has no relation to truth, whose mercy never calls anyone to repentance, is not the God who has spoken.

The church is not immune from this danger. In some settings, God is spoken of with such sentimental softness that His majesty nearly disappears. In others, He is described with such cold severity that His goodness seems difficult to find. Some preach acceptance with almost no mention of holiness. Others defend judgment while sounding untouched by mercy. Some speak of God's sovereignty as though He were merely powerful, not wise and good. Others speak of His love as though it were the only attribute that finally matters.

All of those errors have something in common: they do not deny that God possesses certain attributes. They lose the **fullness** of His character.

That loss is never harmless.

A reduced view of God produces a reduced view of sin. If God is only vaguely good and mildly displeased by evil, then sin becomes a mistake, a wound, a dysfunction, or a failure to flourish—but not guilt before the Holy One. The sinner no longer needs reconciliation with God so much as reassurance about himself.

A reduced view of God produces a reduced view of salvation. If God's justice is pushed to the edge, the cross can be explained as a demonstration of love while its necessity becomes harder to account for. If wrath is considered beneath God, then substitutionary atonement begins to seem unnecessary or even offensive. But Scripture does not present the death of Christ as a dramatic gesture meant to move our emotions alone. It presents the cross as the place where God remains just while justifying the ungodly.

A reduced view of God produces a reduced view of worship. Worship becomes therapy, atmosphere, or emotional uplift. It may speak much about what God does for us while saying little about who He is in Himself. But biblical worship begins with revelation. The angels in Isaiah 6 do not sing of human need. They cry, "Holy, holy, holy, is the LORD of hosts: the whole earth is full of his glory." The response of Isaiah is not first self-expression. It is collapse before majesty.

A reduced view of God produces a reduced view of Scripture. If God is not firmly understood as truthful, wise, and faithful, then His Word can be handled with greater looseness than reverence permits. Clear statements become endlessly pliable. Promises become abstractions. Warnings become exaggerations. Prophecies become containers for meanings far removed from what was actually spoken. The character of God matters even for interpretation, because the One who speaks is not careless, deceptive, or confused.

A reduced view of God produces a reduced view of hope. The believer's confidence does not finally rest on optimism, circumstance, or emotional resilience. It rests on the character of God. He cannot lie. He does not forget His promises. He does not fail through weakness. He does not abandon His people through inconsistency. If God's faithfulness becomes a vague religious idea rather than a fixed perfection of His being, hope weakens with it.

The knowledge of God is therefore not one theological interest among many. It is the center from which every sound doctrine radiates.

This is why Scripture repeatedly speaks of knowing God as the great goal of His dealings with His people. He delivered Israel from Egypt so they would know that He is the LORD. He judged Egypt so Pharaoh would know that there is none like Him. He spoke through the prophets so His people would know His ways. He sent His Son so that the Father might be made known. And Jesus, on the night before the cross, defined eternal life in these words:

*"And this is life eternal, that they might know thee the only true God, and Jesus Christ, whom thou hast sent." — **John 17:3***

That sentence deserves careful attention. Eternal life is not presented merely as endless existence. It is life in relation to the true God through His Son. To be saved is to be brought into the knowledge of God, not merely delivered from consequences. Forgiveness opens the way to fellowship. Redemption restores what sin has estranged. The final blessedness of the redeemed is that "they shall see his face."

If knowing God is the essence of eternal life, then a shallow or distorted knowledge of Him cannot be treated casually.

The aim of this book is not to claim that God can be exhausted by human study. He cannot. The finite mind cannot contain the Infinite. Even the revelation He has given leaves us worshiping at depths we cannot sound. Paul, after tracing the wisdom of God in redemption, erupts into praise rather than concluding with mastery:

*"O the depth of the riches both of the wisdom and knowledge of God! how unsearchable are his judgments, and his ways past finding out!" — **Romans 11:33***

The incomprehensibility of God does not make true knowledge impossible. It means true knowledge should remain humble. We know Him because He has revealed Himself. We do not know Him exhaustively, but what He has made known is reliable, sufficient, and glorious.

That distinction matters. There is a false humility that treats confident statements about God as presumptuous. It says that because God is beyond us, we should avoid speaking too firmly about His character. Scripture does not reason that way. God is beyond us, yet He tells us He is holy. He tells us He is merciful. He tells us He is just. He tells us He is love. He tells us He is jealous. He tells us He is faithful. Reverence does not require silence where God has spoken. It requires that we say what He says, without shrinking it or enlarging it beyond His Word.

The church needs that kind of reverence again.

It needs a vision of God large enough to make sin dreadful and grace astonishing. Large enough to make worship weighty. Large enough to steady believers in suffering. Large enough to keep doctrine from drifting into whatever seems emotionally plausible in the moment. Large enough to expose the small gods we are always tempted to build in the image of our age.

There is no subject more important. There is no recovery more necessary.

Before we ask what God does, we must ask who God is. Before we explore how His character guards doctrine, we must look carefully at the character itself. Before we discuss the full biblical vision of God, we must feel the weight of why that vision matters.

The knowledge of God is not the beginning of theology only. It is its heart, its measure, and its end.

Chapter 2 — The Danger of a Partial God

Most distortions of God do not begin with an outright denial of Him. They begin with subtraction.

A person may affirm something true about God and yet produce a false picture of Him by refusing to hold that truth alongside everything else He has revealed. God is love. That is true. God is merciful. That is true. God is patient, gracious, and ready to forgive. All of that is true. But when those truths are detached from His holiness, righteousness, justice, and wrath against evil, they no longer give us the biblical God. They give us a partial god bearing the name of the true One.

The danger is especially subtle because partial views of God often sound more spiritual than open unbelief. They use biblical words. They quote familiar verses. They appeal to genuine Christian instincts. They may seem compassionate, hopeful, or reverent. Yet they quietly narrow the character of God until only the most emotionally acceptable features remain.

A false god does not always have to be invented from nothing. Sometimes he is made by taking the living God of Scripture and removing what we wish were not there.

This is why the first commandment matters so deeply:

*"Thou shalt have no other gods before me." — **Exodus 20:3***

The command is not limited to bowing before pagan statues. At its core, it forbids giving worship, trust, or obedience to any supposed deity other than the Lord as He truly is. Israel's history proves that idolatry can occur even when people use the language of devotion to the God who delivered them.

At Sinai, the people did not announce that they had rejected the LORD in favor of an entirely different religion. Aaron made a golden calf, and the people said:

"These be thy gods, O Israel, which brought thee up out of the land of Egypt."
— Exodus 32:4

Then Aaron built an altar before it and proclaimed:

"To morrow is a feast to the LORD." **— Exodus 32:5**

That last detail is arresting. The name of the LORD was still being spoken. Religious celebration was still taking place. The people were not claiming to abandon the God of the exodus. They were attempting to worship Him through a form He had forbidden and by means of an image that falsified who He is.

The calf was not merely a wrong object. It was a wrong portrayal.

The God who had thundered from the mountain, who had forbidden images, who had redeemed Israel by mighty judgment, was being made manageable. Visible. Familiar. Reduced to something that could stand in the center of the camp and be handled by human hands.

The same instinct remains. Human beings are always tempted to reduce God until He fits within the limits of what they find comfortable. Some make Him less holy. Some make Him less just. Some make Him less sovereign. Some make Him less merciful. The direction of the distortion may vary, but the impulse is the same: God must be made easier for us to live with.

Scripture gives no permission for that.

When the Lord speaks of Himself, He does not ask whether His character meets our expectations. He declares what is true. He is holy whether holiness comforts us or not. He is just whether judgment troubles us or not. He is merciful whether grace offends the proud or not. He is sovereign whether human independence resists that truth or not. He is who He is.

A partial vision of God often begins with one of two errors. The first is **selection**. We accept the attributes of God that appeal to us and neglect the rest. The second is **redefinition**. We keep the biblical word but fill it with a meaning drawn from human preference rather than Scripture.

Both are dangerous.

A person may say, "God is love," and mean by love that God affirms without judging, forgives without repentance, and comforts without confronting. The problem is not the confession that God is love. The problem is that love has been redefined until it no longer resembles the love of God revealed in Scripture.

Biblical love does not leave sinners undisturbed in rebellion. Christ loved the rich young ruler, yet He placed His finger directly upon the idol that held the man's heart. Christ wept over Jerusalem, yet He also announced judgment upon it. The Father so loved the world that He gave His only begotten Son, but that same verse stands within a chapter that warns of condemnation for the one who refuses to believe.

Love in Scripture is not moral indifference clothed in kindness. It is the holy, purposeful goodness of God directed toward what is truly good.

The same is true of mercy. Mercy is often treated as though it means God simply overlooks sin because He is gentle. But mercy is meaningful only where judgment is deserved. If no guilt exists, mercy is unnecessary. If God owes forgiveness, grace disappears. The wonder of mercy is not that God discovers sin was never very serious. The wonder is that the righteous God shows compassion to those who deserve judgment.

David understood this. After his sin, he did not appeal to the smallness of his offense. He appealed to the greatness of God's mercy:

*"Have mercy upon me, O God, according to thy lovingkindness: according unto the multitude of thy tender mercies blot out my transgressions." — **Psalm 51:1***

He asks for mercy because he knows he has sinned against God. He does not minimize guilt in order to feel forgiven. He confesses guilt in order to seek mercy.

A partial God reverses that order. He turns mercy into permission and forgiveness into assumption. Sin shrinks. Repentance thins out. The cross becomes less necessary. The holiness of God recedes into the background.

That is not harmless. It alters the gospel.

The gospel is good news precisely because the full character of God stands behind it. If God were loving but not just, the cross would be unnecessary. If He were just but not merciful, sinners would have no hope. If He were holy but not gracious, guilt would remain unanswered. If He were gracious but indifferent to righteousness, salvation would be sentimental rather than redemptive. The gospel shines because God is all that Scripture says He is.

Paul makes this clear when he explains the purpose of Christ's blood:

*"To declare, I say, at this time his righteousness: that he might be just, and the justifier of him which believeth in Jesus." — **Romans 3:26**God does not save by ceasing to be just. He saves in a way that displays His justice. The gospel does not resolve a conflict between divine mercy and divine righteousness by allowing one to defeat the other. It reveals that both are perfectly present in the work of Christ.*

Whenever one aspect of God's character is isolated from the rest, doctrine begins to deform.

- If God's love is separated from His holiness, sin becomes less offensive.
- If His grace is separated from His truth, repentance becomes optional.
- If His sovereignty is separated from His goodness, He begins to appear arbitrary.

- If His justice is separated from His mercy, He can be portrayed as cold severity.
- If His patience is separated from His wrath, delay begins to look like approval.
- If His faithfulness is separated from His truthfulness, promises become flexible impressions rather than binding words.

The problem is not that each of these attributes is insufficient in itself, as though God's love must be improved by His holiness or His justice completed by His mercy. God is not assembled out of parts. The problem lies in our perception. We misunderstand any one perfection of God when we attempt to consider it as though He were not also all that He has revealed Himself to be.

- God's love is the love of the Holy One.
- God's mercy is the mercy of the Just Judge.
- God's wrath is the wrath of the Good God.
- God's sovereignty is the sovereignty of infinite Wisdom.
- God's faithfulness is the faithfulness of the One who cannot lie.

These truths must remain together if we are to know Him rightly.

The danger of a partial God is not only theological. It is spiritual. The God we imagine shapes the life we live.

A soft, indulgent god produces shallow repentance. If God is assumed to be perpetually affirming and only mildly concerned with sin, holiness loses urgency. The believer no longer asks how to please the Lord, but how much compromise can coexist with a vague assurance of acceptance.

A harsh, distant god produces fear without communion. If God's justice is taught without His mercy, or His sovereignty without His fatherly tenderness, believers may obey outwardly while inwardly shrinking from Him. They may believe that God is powerful, yet struggle to trust that He is good.

A weak god produces anxiety. If God means well but cannot surely accomplish His purposes, prayer becomes uncertain, prophecy becomes fragile, and hope rests more on circumstances than on divine faithfulness.

A confused god produces confused interpretation. If God is not believed to speak truthfully and coherently, then Scripture may be treated as a field of hidden meanings detached from the plain force of its words. Clear promises can be emptied, direct warnings softened, and texts made to serve ideas they never expressed. A partial view of God eventually affects how His Word is handled.

This is why the recovery of God's full character matters so urgently. It is not a luxury for theologians. It is necessary for the church.

The Psalms repeatedly ground worship in the completeness of who God is. The Lord is praised for His mercy, but also for His righteousness. He is celebrated for forgiveness, but also for judgment. He is called good, but never morally pliable. Psalm 89 places mercy and truth together, righteousness and judgment together:

*"Justice and judgment are the habitation of thy throne: mercy and truth shall go before thy face." — **Psalm 89:14***

That verse is a picture of divine harmony. God's throne rests upon justice and judgment. Yet mercy and truth go before Him. Nothing in His character is out of place. Nothing embarrasses the rest. Nothing must be pushed into the shadows so another attribute can shine.

The same fullness appears in Nahum, a book often remembered for judgment. It opens with a declaration that modern readers may find severe:

*"God is jealous, and the LORD revengeth; the LORD revengeth, and is furious; the LORD will take vengeance on his adversaries, and he reserveth wrath for his enemies." — **Nahum 1:2***

But the prophet immediately continues:

*"The LORD is slow to anger, and great in power, and will not at all acquit the wicked." — **Nahum 1:3***

There it is again. Patience and judgment. Slowness to anger and refusal to clear wickedness. Power and restraint. The text does not apologize for this combination. It reveals God through it.

A partial God would force us to choose. Scripture does not.

We are not permitted to say that because God is slow to anger, He will never judge. Nor may we say that because He judges, He lacks patience. Both are true. Both are holy. Both belong to Him.

The habit of reducing God also damages our ability to read the life of Christ. Many prefer to remember Jesus welcoming children, touching lepers, forgiving sinners, and speaking peace to the weary. Those scenes are precious. They reveal the heart of God. But the same Jesus denounced hypocrisy with terrifying clarity. He pronounced woes upon the scribes and Pharisees. He warned of hell more vividly than anyone else in Scripture. He cleansed the temple. He spoke of coming judgment. Revelation presents men hiding from "the wrath of the Lamb."

The Lamb is wrathful. The Judge is the One who wept. The Savior who opens His arms to the repentant is the King who will tread the winepress of the fierceness and wrath of Almighty God. If our picture of Christ cannot hold all of that together, it is not yet full enough.

One of the chief purposes of this book is to resist that narrowing instinct. We do not need to protect God from His own revelation. We do not need to make Him more acceptable by diminishing whatever aspects of His character modern people find difficult. Nor should we exaggerate certain truths in ways that eclipse the warmth, compassion, and patience Scripture also assigns to Him.

We need the whole.

We need the God who told Moses He is merciful and gracious, and who in the same breath said He will by no means clear the guilty. We need the God whose throne is founded upon justice, yet before whose face mercy goes forth. We need the God whose holiness causes angels to cover their faces, and whose compassion moves Him to gather the undeserving. We need the God whose wrath makes evil tremble, and whose grace makes sinners sing.

Anything less is not merely incomplete. It is spiritually dangerous.

A partial god cannot bear the weight of Scripture. He cannot sustain the gospel. He cannot command worship. He cannot steady the believer. He cannot guide doctrine. He cannot be trusted with the soul.

The God of the Bible can.

And so the task before us is not to choose which aspects of God's character we find most compelling. It is to receive the full witness of Scripture with reverence. The true God does not become more beautiful when difficult truths are removed. He becomes less recognizable.

His fullness is His glory.

Chapter 3 — When God's Character Is Reduced, Doctrine Is Distorted

A distorted view of God rarely remains contained. It spreads.

At first, it may appear to touch only one subject. A person softens divine wrath because it seems difficult to reconcile with love. Another redefines mercy because judgment feels too severe. Another weakens God's faithfulness because certain promises do not fit a preferred theological system. Each adjustment may look isolated. Each may be defended as a small correction, a needed nuance, or a more mature way of understanding Scripture.

But the character of God is not a side issue. Once it is altered, other doctrines begin to shift with it.

This is why theology cannot be handled as though doctrines stand apart from one another in sealed compartments. The doctrine of God shapes the doctrine of sin. The doctrine of sin shapes the doctrine of salvation. The doctrine of salvation shapes the meaning of the cross. The meaning of the cross shapes preaching, worship, assurance, and hope. When the center is displaced, the outer circles do not remain untouched.

The first lie in Scripture attacked the character of God before it attacked the command of God.

The serpent did not begin by telling Eve to eat the fruit. He began by casting suspicion upon God's Word and God's goodness:

"Yea, hath God said, Ye shall not eat of every tree of the garden?" — **Genesis 3:1**

The question was not innocent. It framed God as restrictive. It suggested that His command was unreasonable, perhaps even unkind. Then the serpent denied the warning of judgment:

"Ye shall not surely die." — **Genesis 3:4**

And finally, he portrayed God as one who withholds what would truly benefit His creatures:

"For God doth know that in the day ye eat thereof, then your eyes shall be opened, and ye shall be as gods, knowing good and evil." — **Genesis 3:5**

Before Eve took the fruit, she was encouraged to doubt God's truthfulness, His goodness, and His motive. Sin entered through a theological distortion. God was made to appear less trustworthy than He is.

That pattern has not changed.

False doctrine often begins by making some part of God's character seem difficult to accept. His judgment is portrayed as excessive. His commands are treated as burdensome. His sovereignty is cast as unfair. His holiness is made to sound cruel. His patience is mistaken for indecision. His covenant faithfulness is reinterpreted until its concrete meaning disappears. In each case, the pressure falls first upon who God is. Once that pressure is accepted, the interpretation of His Word follows.

This matters because sound doctrine is not merely the accumulation of Bible verses arranged beneath theological headings. Sound doctrine is truth about God, His works, His ways, and His Word. If the God at the center of a doctrine has been subtly altered, the doctrine itself may preserve biblical vocabulary while losing biblical meaning.

Consider the gospel.

The gospel cannot be understood rightly if God's character has been reduced. If God is love but not holy, the cross becomes harder to explain. If He is merciful but not just, the necessity of atonement begins to fade. If He is patient but not wrathful against sin, final judgment seems out of place. If He is gracious but not truthful, His warnings lose their force. The gospel depends upon the full character of God.

Paul's argument in Romans 3 is not merely that Christ died so sinners could be forgiven. It is that the cross demonstrates the righteousness of God in forgiving sinners:

"Whom God hath set forth to be a propitiation through faith in his blood, to declare his righteousness for the remission of sins that are past, through the forbearance of God; To declare, I say, at this time his righteousness: that he might be just, and the justifier of him which believeth in Jesus." — **Romans 3:25–26**

The cross is necessary because God does not set aside His own righteousness in order to save. He justifies the believer without ceasing to be just. Mercy is not accomplished by ignoring justice. Grace is not shown by treating sin as harmless. Salvation is possible because God, in Christ, provides what His holiness requires.

A smaller god needs a smaller cross.

If sin is merely human brokenness rather than guilt before the Holy One, the cross may be reduced to a symbol of divine sympathy. If wrath is treated as primitive religious language, propitiation begins to seem unnecessary. If God's justice does not demand satisfaction, substitutionary atonement becomes one interpretation among many rather than the heart of the gospel's logic. What looks like a doctrinal adjustment is often the fruit of a prior reduction in the character of God.

The same is true of judgment.

The doctrine of final judgment becomes unstable when God's love is separated from His holiness. Some reason that because God is loving, He cannot finally condemn. Others argue that because He is merciful, judgment must eventually yield to universal restoration. These views do not arise merely from a different reading of one or two difficult passages. They often arise from a prior conviction about what love must mean, and then Scripture is asked to conform to that conviction.

But Scripture does not present judgment as a defect in God's character. It presents judgment as the rightful action of the God who loves righteousness and hates wickedness. Abraham appealed to God's justice when he said:

"Shall not the Judge of all the earth do right?" — **Genesis 18:25**

That question assumes something important. God's judgment is not morally suspect. It is the standard by which all true judgment is measured. The final judgment is fearful because God is holy, but it is also good because evil will not be allowed to reign forever without answer.

A theology that cannot account for God's judgment has not become more loving than Scripture. It has simply narrowed love until it no longer resembles God's.

The same reduction distorts repentance. If God is treated mainly as affirming and accepting, repentance may be presented as little more than the release of shame or the embrace of personal wholeness. Scripture speaks more seriously. Repentance is a turning from sin because sin is truly offensive to God. It is not self-hatred. It is not despair. It is the rightful response to the holiness and kindness of God.

Paul writes:

"Or despisest thou the riches of his goodness and forbearance and longsuffering; not knowing that the goodness of God leadeth thee to repentance?" — **Romans 2:4**

God's goodness does not tell the sinner to remain as he is. It leads him to repent. A partial view of goodness turns it into indulgence. The biblical view of goodness makes it a summons back to God.

Even grace can be distorted when God's character is reduced. Grace is one of the most beautiful words in Scripture, but it is not divine permission for unholiness. Paul anticipated that error and rejected it plainly:

"What shall we say then? Shall we continue in sin, that grace may abound? God forbid. How shall we, that are dead to sin, live any longer therein?" — **Romans 6:1–2**

Grace does not make holiness irrelevant because the God who gives grace is holy. He does not save men from the penalty of sin so they may settle comfortably into the power of sin. He saves them to bring them into the life of Christ. When grace is detached from God's holiness, it becomes something Paul would not recognize.

The doctrine of assurance is also weakened by a reduced view of God. Some believers struggle to rest in salvation because their confidence rests too heavily on the instability of their own emotions or performance. Scripture roots assurance in the character of God and the sufficiency of Christ. The believer's hope is secure because the One who promised is faithful.

Paul writes:

"For the which cause I also suffer these things: nevertheless I am not ashamed: for I know whom I have believed, and am persuaded that he is able to keep that which I have committed unto him against that day." — **2 Timothy 1:12**

The language is personal: "I know whom I have believed." Assurance does not rest merely on a remembered prayer, a past experience, or an inward feeling. It rests on the trustworthiness of the One believed. If God is faithful, if Christ is sufficient, if His promises are true, then Christian assurance has a foundation deeper than the fluctuating state of the believer's mind.

When God's faithfulness is made uncertain, assurance begins to tremble. When His saving purpose is made fragile, believers are pushed inward to search for certainty in themselves. The doctrine of God shapes the doctrine of assurance.

It also shapes the doctrine of Scripture.

If God is truthful, then His Word is truthful. If He is wise, His revelation is not careless. If He is orderly, His speech is not a chaos of contradictions. If He is faithful, His promises are not disposable. The nature of Scripture flows from the character of the God who breathed it out.

This has implications for interpretation. The Bible certainly contains symbols, parables, poetry, figures of speech, types, and apocalyptic imagery. A faithful reader must recognize those forms. But the existence of figurative language does not license a method that empties God's statements of their real force whenever the plain sense becomes difficult.

When God makes promises, the interpreter is not free to handle them as though clarity were a problem to overcome. When He warns, we should not dull the edge. When He describes future acts, we should not hastily dissolve them into abstractions. The question is not whether Scripture is ever symbolic. The question is whether our interpretation respects the character of the God who speaks.

A God of truth does not communicate in order to mislead. A God of order does not delight in confusion. A faithful God does not give promises whose actual fulfillment makes the original words functionally meaningless.

This is not a call to wooden literalism. It is a call to reverent interpretation.

Doctrine is distorted whenever interpretive methods quietly detach God's Word from God's character. If God can say one thing while intending something entirely unrelated, if His promises can be transformed so completely that the original hearers could never have understood them, if His covenants can be redirected without clear textual warrant, then the reader is left with a revelation whose plain meaning is increasingly unstable. That instability does not arise from Scripture itself. It arises from forgetting who the speaker is.

The character of God also matters for eschatology.

Prophecy is often treated as though it were the most speculative region of theology, somewhat detached from the more central doctrines of God and salvation. But eschatology concerns the promised future acts of God. It must therefore be interpreted in light of His faithfulness, justice, wrath, mercy, covenant love, and truthfulness.

- If God has promised to judge the wicked, He will judge.
- If He has promised to vindicate His people, He will vindicate.
- If He has promised a kingdom, His promise will not fail.
- If He has bound Himself by covenant, His integrity is at stake in the fulfillment.

The book will later consider a specific example involving Christ as Bridegroom, the church as His bride, and the wrath of the Lamb in Revelation 6. That question belongs to eschatology, but it is also a question about character. If Christ's relationship to the church is truly bridal and covenantal, then any view that places His bride under His own eschatological wrath deserves careful scrutiny. That conclusion cannot be established by character reasoning alone; it must be tested by Scripture. But neither may character be ignored, as though doctrine can be sound while requiring Christ to act in ways that strain against His own revealed relationship to His people.

The same principle applies to the promises of God. If God is faithful, then His covenant commitments must be taken seriously. If He cannot lie, His words cannot be treated as temporary scaffolding that later theology is free to dismantle. Interpretive systems must be measured not only by their internal elegance, but by their consistency with the truthfulness of the God who speaks.

This does not mean every doctrinal disagreement can be settled by asking what seems most fitting to us. Human intuition is too unreliable for that. Many truths about God exceed our expectations. The cross itself proves that divine wisdom may appear foolish to the world. The doctrine of God does not give us permission to revise Scripture according to preference.

But Scripture itself reveals God's character, and Scripture itself must not be interpreted in ways that contradict that revelation.

That principle is not a shortcut around exegesis. It is part of exegesis. The Bible is a unified revelation from a consistent God. A doctrine built from isolated texts while ignoring the character of the God who inspired them may be clever, but it is not complete.

Peter warns that unstable men can wrest the Scriptures "unto their own destruction." Paul tells Timothy to "rightly divide the word of truth." John commands believers to "try the spirits whether they are of God." Scripture assumes that doctrine can be corrupted, that texts can be misused, and that truth must be guarded. One of the most important safeguards is a full biblical vision of God.

Where God is reduced, doctrine becomes vulnerable.

- A God without wrath produces a gospel with no propitiation.
- A God without justice produces mercy without moral weight.
- A God without holiness produces grace without transformation.
- A God without faithfulness produces promises that cannot anchor hope.
- A God without truthfulness produces interpretation without stable meaning.
- A God without sovereign power produces a future that depends finally on uncertainty.
- A God without tenderness produces theology that may be correct in outline yet foreign to the heart of Christ.

The church needs more than doctrinal positions. It needs doctrines shaped by the full character of God.

That is why the recovery of God's character must come first. Before we discuss particular attributes in detail, before we trace the harmony of mercy and justice, before we examine how the cross reveals the whole glory of

God, we must understand the stakes. To lose sight of who God is will eventually change how we understand everything He has said and done.

Error often presents itself as compassion, sophistication, balance, or progress. It may promise a kinder gospel, a more inclusive salvation, a less troubling judgment, a more flexible handling of Scripture, or a theology better suited to modern instincts. But if the price of that refinement is a smaller God, the church has not gained wisdom. It has begun to drift.

The first task of faithful doctrine is to let God remain God.

Chapter 4 — God Must Be Known as He Is

There is a quiet arrogance in the human heart that does not always look like rebellion. Sometimes it looks like revision.

It does not openly say, "There is no God." It says, "Surely God is not like that." It does not deny revelation outright. It filters revelation through preference. It receives what is comforting, delays what is unsettling, and reinterprets what refuses to yield.

The result may still be called Christianity. It may use biblical language. It may speak of Jesus, grace, love, faith, and salvation. But if God is being reshaped to fit human approval, then the deepest error has already entered. The issue is no longer merely what we believe about one doctrine or another. The issue is whether we are willing to receive God on His own terms.

That question stands at the beginning of all true theology.

God must be known as He is, not as we would have Him be.

When Moses asked to know God's name, he was not given a title chosen to satisfy curiosity. He was given a declaration of divine self-existence:

*"And God said unto Moses, I AM THAT I AM: and he said, Thus shalt thou say unto the children of Israel, I AM hath sent me unto you." — **Exodus 3:14***

That name resists domestication. God does not define Himself by reference to anything outside Himself. He does not say, "I am what you need Me to be," or "I am what your age can accept," or "I am what your imagination can grasp." He simply is. Independent. Eternal. Unmeasured. The source of all being, yet dependent upon none.

That truth places every creature in the position of receiving rather than revising.

We do not discover God the way a scientist examines a specimen. We do not stand above Him, gather the evidence, and pronounce a judgment on whether His character is acceptable. God is not an object within creation available for human inspection. He is the Creator, the One from whom our reason, conscience, language, and life all come. We know Him because He has made Himself known.

Theology therefore begins with humility.

It begins by admitting that God is not answerable to our instincts. He does not become just because we approve of His judgments. He does not become loving because we find His mercy beautiful. He does not become true because His Word withstands our scrutiny. He is just, loving, and true in Himself. Our task is not to confer legitimacy upon His character. Our task is to bow before what He has revealed.

Job had to learn this.

The book that bears his name contains some of the most searching questions ever raised about suffering, justice, and the ways of God. Job is not treated as a shallow man. He is not a villain masquerading as a sufferer. Scripture calls him "perfect and upright." His agony is real. His questions are not dismissed as insincere. Yet when God finally answers, He does not submit Himself to Job's tribunal. He does not offer a detailed explanation of every hidden purpose behind the suffering. He reveals Himself.

*"Where wast thou when I laid the foundations of the earth? declare, if thou hast understanding." — **Job 38:4***

Again and again, the Lord presses Job with questions that expose the limits of creaturely vision. Who shut up the sea with doors? Who commanded the morning? Who entered the springs of the deep? Who sends the rain? Who guides the constellations? Who gives strength to the horse and understanding to the hawk?

The answer is not that Job's pain was imaginary or his questions irrelevant. The answer is that God remains God even when His purposes exceed human sight.

Job's response is not theological apathy. It is worshipful submission:

"I know that thou canst do every thing, and that no thought can be withholden from thee. Who is he that hideth counsel without knowledge? therefore have I uttered that I understood not; things too wonderful for me, which I knew not." — **Job 42:2–3**

That is one of the marks of genuine knowledge of God: it enlarges reverence. It does not make every mystery disappear, but it does make pride harder to sustain.

Modern thought often prefers a God who can be brought down to human scale. Such a god is easier to defend because he never says anything too difficult. He is easier to market because he rarely offends. He is easier to invoke because he can be made to support whatever moral assumptions are already in place. But a god who never rises above the preferences of his worshipers is not the God of Abraham, Isaac, and Jacob. He is a reflection of the age.

Scripture warns repeatedly against such exchange.

Paul writes of fallen humanity:

"Professing themselves to be wise, they became fools, And changed the glory of the uncorruptible God into an image made like to corruptible man, and to birds, and fourfooted beasts, and creeping things." — **Romans 1:22–23**

The ancient world expressed this exchange in visible idols. The modern world often makes the same exchange in less visible ways. God is not carved into wood or stone, but reduced in concept. He is reimagined in the likeness of contemporary moral instinct. His character is adjusted until it becomes difficult to distinguish divine revelation from cultural preference.

- A God who will not judge is easier to accept.

- A God who never commands repentance is easier to preach.

- A God who affirms every self-definition is easier to celebrate.

- A God who binds Himself to concrete promises and fulfills them exactly may be less convenient for certain systems of interpretation.

- A God who speaks clearly may be less useful to those who prefer endless ambiguity.

But convenience is not truth.

The God who speaks in Scripture is not always the God man would invent. That is part of the evidence that Scripture is revelation rather than projection. Human beings regularly fashion gods who flatter their desires or justify their ambitions. The God of the Bible does neither. He comforts the afflicted, but He also confronts the proud. He lifts the lowly, but He also humbles kings. He forgives sinners, but He does not call evil good. He promises rest, but He commands surrender. He is near to the brokenhearted, yet He remains "high and lifted up."

No human culture, left to itself, would invent Him whole.

Some would invent a god of power without mercy. Others a god of compassion without holiness. Some a god of tribal loyalty. Others a god of universal acceptance. Some would want a deity who rewards ritual. Others one who dismisses all moral demands. Scripture presents none of these partial constructions. It presents the living God, whose ways often cut across both ancient and modern instincts.

That is why revelation is necessary. If we are left merely to reason upward from creation, conscience, desire, and experience, we may arrive at certain truths about God's power and existence, but we will not discover the fullness of His character. Paul says that creation reveals God's eternal power and Godhead, leaving men without excuse. Yet the gospel, the Trinity, the incarnation, the cross, the covenantal faithfulness of God, the depth of His mercy, the holy meaning of His wrath—these are not truths man could construct unaided. God must tell us who He is.

And He has.

The tragedy is that even after God speaks, human beings may still resist the form His self-revelation takes. The Lord said through Isaiah:

"For my thoughts are not your thoughts, neither are your ways my ways, saith the LORD. For as the heavens are higher than the earth, so are my ways higher than your ways, and my thoughts than your thoughts." — **Isaiah 55:8–9**

These verses are often quoted to comfort believers when life is confusing, and rightly so. But in context, they are also a rebuke to human presumption. The wicked are called to forsake their way and the unrighteous man his thoughts because God's way of mercy exceeds human expectation:

"Let the wicked forsake his way, and the unrighteous man his thoughts: and let him return unto the LORD, and he will have mercy upon him; and to our God, for he will abundantly pardon." — **Isaiah 55:7**

God's thoughts are higher not only when His judgments confuse us, but also when His mercy astonishes us. He is beyond human invention in both directions. His holiness is higher than our moral leniency. His grace is higher than our instincts of measured forgiveness. His wisdom is higher than our systems. His purposes are higher than our immediate understanding.

To know God as He is, we must let Him correct us everywhere.

That includes the places where He appears more severe than we would prefer. It also includes the places where He appears more gracious than we feel comfortable allowing. Human beings can distort God in both directions. The self-righteous man may resist mercy as much as the worldly man resists judgment. Jonah is a striking example.

When God spared Nineveh after its repentance, Jonah was displeased. His anger reveals that he knew something true about God and did not like the way that truth had been applied:

"Therefore I fled before unto Tarshish: for I knew that thou art a gracious God, and merciful, slow to anger, and of great kindness, and repentest thee of the evil." — Jonah 4:2

Jonah's problem was not ignorance of God's mercy. It was resentment of it. He wanted judgment without mercy for Nineveh. God's character refused to fit that desire.

The elder brother in Christ's parable of the prodigal son has a similar spirit. He cannot rejoice when the father receives the repentant son. He sees mercy given to the unworthy and considers it an injustice against his own service. In both cases, the problem is not a denial of holiness but a refusal to embrace the generosity of God's compassion.

This matters because the command to receive God as He is must cut against every distortion, not merely the modern ones we find easiest to criticize. A sentimental age may need to hear that God is holy and wrathful against evil. A harsh religion may need to hear that God delights in mercy. A proud intellectual culture may need to hear that God's wisdom exceeds human reason. A fatalistic theology may need to hear that God is genuinely good. A shallow theology may need to hear that God is not simple in the sense of being easy.

The living God cannot be recruited to serve any one-sided agenda.

He reveals Himself, and we are responsible to believe Him.

This is one reason Scripture so often condemns unbelief. Unbelief is not merely the absence of certainty. It is frequently the refusal to receive God's testimony. John writes:

*"He that believeth on the Son of God hath the witness in himself: he that believeth not God hath made him a liar; because he believeth not the record that God gave of his Son." — **I John 5:10**

To disbelieve God's testimony is not a neutral intellectual posture. It implicates His character. It treats the truthful God as though His witness cannot be trusted.

That principle extends beyond the gospel message narrowly considered. Whenever God has spoken, His truthfulness is involved. To reinterpret His words carelessly, to suspend their force because they do not fit a preferred framework, or to treat His clearest statements as endlessly negotiable— these habits are not merely exegetical weaknesses. They betray a diminished sense of who the Speaker is.

The proper posture before Scripture is therefore not suspicion, embarrassment, or control. It is submission. Not mindless submission, as though faith requires us to avoid careful thought. Scripture commends examination, meditation, comparison, discernment. But all such study occurs under the authority of God, not above it.

The Bereans searched the Scriptures daily to test whether Paul's preaching was so. That was noble. Yet their nobility did not consist in standing as final judges over divine truth. It consisted in measuring claims by the Word God had already given. Their minds were active because their reverence was real.

The same must be true of us.

If God must be known as He is, then theology must proceed from revelation to conclusion, not from conclusion to revision. We do not begin with a doctrinal preference and then ask how far Scripture can be made to accommodate it. We begin with Scripture, attend to its words, observe its patterns, honor its claims, and allow the God who speaks to establish the boundaries of what we may say.

This is especially important where God's character presses against cherished assumptions.

Some reject divine wrath because they have first defined love in a way that leaves no room for it. Some reject eternal judgment because they have first defined goodness apart from holiness. Some dissolve covenant promises because their system has already determined what those promises must become. Some deny clear doctrinal distinctions because they prefer a simpler framework. In every case, the temptation is the same: permit theology to master revelation rather than allowing revelation to govern theology.

God must be known as He is.

That sentence sounds simple, but it demands everything. It means we do not sentimentalize Him. We do not harshen Him. We do not domesticate Him. We do not defend Him by denying what He has said. We do not praise one attribute in a way that places another under suspicion. We do not call Him loving while refusing His holiness, or faithful while loosening His promises, or wise while treating His Word as confused.

We receive the whole testimony.

At times that testimony will reassure us. At times it will unsettle us. Often it will do both. The same God who says, "Fear not," also says, "Be not highminded, but fear." The same Savior who invites the weary to come unto Him also warns men to fear Him who is able to destroy both soul and body in hell. The same Lord who says He will never leave His people nor forsake them also declares that judgment must begin at the house of God.

A selective theology chooses one voice and silences the others. Faith hears them all because they come from the same God.

This is not contradiction. It is fullness.

The child of God does not stand before a fragmented deity with competing moods. He stands before the unchanging Lord whose every word is pure, whose every act is righteous, whose mercy is real, whose holiness is real, whose judgments are true, and whose promises cannot fail.

That is the God this book seeks to behold.

Before we examine His character in detail, we must settle this first: God is not ours to edit. He is not clay in the hands of theology. He is not an idea to be updated until He aligns with the temper of the times. He is the eternal "I AM," and the beginning of wisdom is to receive Him as He has revealed Himself.

PART TWO

The God Who Reveals Himself

Chapter 5 — Scripture: The True Witness to God's Character

If God must be known as He is, then we must ask where that knowledge is found.

The answer cannot be human instinct. Instinct is unstable. It changes with personality, culture, suffering, upbringing, and desire. One person assumes God must be endlessly permissive because that seems loving. Another assumes He must be stern and distant because that seems holy. One imagines God chiefly as comfort. Another chiefly as threat. Neither instinct can safely carry the weight of theology.

Nor can experience serve as the final witness to God's character. Experience matters. God teaches His people through trials, providence, discipline, deliverance, and answered prayer. But experience must itself be interpreted. A delayed answer to prayer might tempt one man to think God is indifferent. A season of blessing might tempt another to think God approves of everything in his life. Suffering might be read as abandonment, prosperity as divine endorsement, silence as absence. Without revelation, experience is easily misunderstood.

Tradition cannot be the final authority either. The church should respect faithful teachers, creeds, confessions, and the accumulated wisdom of believers who have gone before us. We are not the first generation to read the Bible, and arrogance toward the past is no virtue. But tradition is valuable only insofar as it remains faithful to the Word of God. It may preserve truth. It may also preserve error. It can guide, but it cannot rule.

Culture is even less fit for the task. Every age imagines itself morally clearer than the generations before it. Every age has its favored virtues and its protected sins. Every age finds certain biblical truths inspiring and others embarrassing. A culture that applauds compassion may despise holiness. A culture that prizes autonomy may resent divine authority. A culture that celebrates self-definition may recoil at a God who names sin and commands repentance. If culture becomes the measure of God, revelation will always be pressured to change.

If we are to know God truly, we need a witness more reliable than ourselves.

We need Scripture.

The Bible is not merely a record of religious reflections about God. It is not a collection of human attempts to reach upward toward the divine. It is the written revelation of the God who has spoken. Through it, He makes known His acts, His commands, His promises, His judgments, His mercy, His purposes, and His character.

Paul writes:

*"All scripture is given by inspiration of God, and is profitable for doctrine, for reproof, for correction, for instruction in righteousness: That the man of God may be perfect, throughly furnished unto all good works." — **2 Timothy 3:16–17***

The phrase "given by inspiration of God" means that Scripture is breathed out by God. Its authority does not rest finally on the brilliance of its human writers, though many were profound. It does not rest on its literary power, though its beauty is incomparable. It does not rest on the church's recognition, though the church rightly receives it. Scripture is authoritative because God is its source.

That matters for this book. If Scripture is God-breathed, then the biblical revelation of His character is not a merely human portrait subject to correction by later preferences. When Scripture tells us that God is holy, that holiness is not an ancient religious impression. When it declares Him merciful, that mercy is not merely Israel's interpretation of providence. When it speaks of His wrath, judgment, jealousy, righteousness, patience, tenderness, or covenant faithfulness, we are not dealing with competing human viewpoints that we are free to rank according to modern taste. We are listening to God's own witness.

The Bible gives us the only trustworthy foundation for speaking about God because God alone knows God fully.

Paul makes this point when discussing the deep things of God:

"For what man knoweth the things of a man, save the spirit of man which is in him? even so the things of God knoweth no man, but the Spirit of God." — **1 Corinthians 2:11**

A human being may reveal his thoughts to another because he possesses inward knowledge of himself. In a far greater way, the Spirit of God knows the things of God and makes them known through divine revelation. We cannot climb into the mind of God by speculation. He must speak. Scripture is the appointed witness by which He has done so.

This is why Jesus treated Scripture as decisive. When tempted by Satan, He answered repeatedly, "It is written." When questioned about marriage, resurrection, the greatest commandment, the Messiah, and the meaning of the Law, He appealed to the written Word. He rebuked error not by suggesting that Scripture was obscure beyond use, but by asking, "Have ye not read?" He expected the Word of God to be heard, understood, and obeyed.

In His prayer to the Father, Jesus said:

"Sanctify them through thy truth: thy word is truth." — **John 17:17**

He did not merely say that God's Word contains truth, though it certainly does. He said, "thy word is truth." Scripture is not judged by an external standard of truth. It bears the character of the God who speaks. Because God is true, His Word is true.

That connection cannot be overstated.

A false view of Scripture will eventually produce a false view of God. If the Bible is treated as a flawed human record whose teachings must be sifted through modern moral judgment, then any aspect of God's character that offends the age can be set aside as primitive or culturally conditioned. His wrath may be dismissed. His judgments may be softened. His claims to exclusive worship may be regarded as ancient tribalism. His commands may be reclassified as temporary limitations. Once Scripture's authority is weakened, God is increasingly remade according to human preference.

But the reverse is also true. A diminished view of God will eventually produce a diminished view of Scripture. If God is thought to be imprecise, then His words can be handled loosely. If He is treated as emotionally affirming above all else, then severe texts will be explained away. If His faithfulness is not taken seriously, then promises can be stretched beyond recognition. The doctrine of Scripture and the doctrine of God stand close together because the character of the Speaker shapes our view of the speech.

The psalmist understood this. He did not speak of God's Word as a burden upon the soul, but as something pure, stable, and worthy of trust:

*"The words of the LORD are pure words: as silver tried in a furnace of earth, purified seven times." — **Psalm 12:6***

And again:

*"Thy word is true from the beginning: and every one of thy righteous judgments endureth for ever." — **Psalm 119:160***

The Word is pure because the Lord is pure. It is true because He is true. His judgments endure because His righteousness does not decay.

Scripture reveals God through direct declaration. It tells us plainly that He is holy, righteous, merciful, gracious, faithful, good, true, wise, and just. These statements form the foundation of theology. We do not infer God's holiness merely from observing judgment in the biblical narrative. Scripture says directly, "Holy, holy, holy, is the LORD of hosts." We do not infer His love only from His acts of kindness. Scripture says, "God is love." We do not guess at His immutability. He declares, "I am the LORD, I change not."

But Scripture also reveals God through His actions.

We see His holiness at Sinai, where the mountain quakes beneath His descent. We see His justice in the flood, in the judgment of Sodom, in the exile of Israel, and finally in the cross where sin is not overlooked but answered. We see His mercy in the covering of Adam and Eve, the preservation of Noah, the deliverance of Israel, the forgiveness of David, and the compassion of Christ toward sinners. We see His patience throughout the long history of human rebellion. We see His faithfulness in covenant promise and fulfillment. We see His sovereignty in empires raised and cast down, kings humbled, enemies restrained, and salvation accomplished through what appeared to be defeat.

The Bible does not present God in abstractions only. It gives us the history of His dealings. The doctrines of God's character are rooted in the acts of God across redemptive history.

That matters because an attribute disconnected from Scripture's story can become vague. We may say "God is good," but the Bible shows us what His goodness looks like. It is good when He creates. It is good when He gives rain to the undeserving. It is good when He feeds the hungry. It is good when He disciplines His people rather than abandoning them. It is good when He judges evil. It is good when He sends His Son to die for sinners. Biblical goodness is not merely pleasantness. It is God always acting in perfect accord with His own holy excellence.

The same is true of love. Scripture does not leave us to define love according to sentimental instinct. It points to Christ:

"Hereby perceive we the love of God, because he laid down his life for us." **— I John 3:16**

And again:

"In this was manifested the love of God toward us, because that God sent his only begotten Son into the world, that we might live through him." **— I John 4:9**

God's love is not established by human imagination. It is revealed in the incarnation and the cross. The Word tells us what love means by showing us what God has done.

Scripture also guards us from isolating certain truths about God from others. Human preference tends to select. Scripture compels us to receive the whole. It will not allow us to praise divine mercy while ignoring judgment, nor to proclaim judgment while suppressing compassion. It gives both.

Consider Psalm 103, one of the richest celebrations of God's mercy:

"The LORD is merciful and gracious, slow to anger, and plenteous in mercy. He will not always chide: neither will he keep his anger for ever." — **Psalm 103:8–9**

That passage is tender. It has comforted believers for generations. Yet the same psalm says:

"But the mercy of the LORD is from everlasting to everlasting upon them that fear him, and his righteousness unto children's children; To such as keep his covenant, and to those that remember his commandments to do them." — **Psalm 103:17–18**

Mercy is real. Fear of the Lord is real. Covenant obedience is real. Scripture gives no permission to preserve one portion of the passage while neglecting the other.

Or consider the book of Romans. It speaks magnificently of grace, justification, peace with God, freedom from condemnation, and the certainty that nothing can separate believers from the love of God in Christ Jesus. Yet the same epistle begins by announcing that "the wrath of God is revealed from heaven against all ungodliness and unrighteousness of men." Grace does not appear in Romans because wrath was never a serious reality. Grace appears precisely because wrath is real and the righteousness of God must be revealed.

The Bible protects us from building a theology of God out of favored verses while neglecting the rest of His testimony.

That means we must read widely, not selectively. A person who reads only passages about tenderness may struggle to receive divine severity. A person who reads only judgment texts may speak of God in a way Scripture itself would not. A mature knowledge of God requires patience with the whole counsel of His Word.

Paul told the Ephesian elders:

*"For I have not shunned to declare unto you all the counsel of God." — **Acts 20:27***

That phrase matters. The whole counsel of God includes every part of divine truth He has chosen to give. A church is not faithfully taught when only the easiest truths are preached. Nor is it faithfully taught when certain doctrines are pressed in ways that crowd out others equally revealed. If we want a full vision of God, we must refuse a partial Bible.

Scripture also teaches us that God's revelation has a center: Jesus Christ.

The written Word prepares for Him, bears witness to Him, and explains Him. Christ does not replace Scripture. He fulfills it. He does not correct the Old Testament's portrayal of God. He reveals the same God more fully. The Law, the Prophets, the Psalms, the Gospels, the Epistles, and Revelation speak with one divine voice because the God who authored them is one.

After His resurrection, Jesus rebuked the two on the road to Emmaus for failing to believe the prophetic Scriptures:

*"O fools, and slow of heart to believe all that the prophets have spoken: Ought not Christ to have suffered these things, and to enter into his glory?" — **Luke 24:25–26***

Then Luke tells us:

"And beginning at Moses and all the prophets, he expounded unto them in all the scriptures the things concerning himself." — **Luke 24:27**

Christ is not a late theological improvement upon the Bible. He is the promised center toward which the Scriptures move. To know God rightly, we must know Him as revealed in Christ. Yet to know Christ rightly, we must receive the Scriptures that testify of Him.

This will matter later when we consider the character of God in the person of Jesus. The Lord who touches lepers and receives repentant sinners is the same Lord who speaks of Gehenna, pronounces woe upon hypocrites, and will return as Judge. The Jesus of Scripture cannot be reduced to one favored set of scenes. He must be received in the fullness of the biblical witness.

A trustworthy revelation also gives us a trustworthy standard by which to reject false portrayals of God.

Not every statement made in the name of God should be believed. The world is filled with spiritual claims. Some come from false religions. Some arise from human imagination. Some appear within Christian circles but distort the Lord's character under the banner of relevance, compassion, or prophetic insight. Scripture is the test.

Isaiah says:

"To the law and to the testimony: if they speak not according to this word, it is because there is no light in them." — **Isaiah 8:20**

That standard remains essential. Any teaching about God that contradicts His written revelation must be refused, however appealing it sounds. If it makes God less holy than Scripture does, it is false. If it makes Him less merciful than Scripture does, it is false. If it strips His promises of meaning, it is false. If it turns His wrath into cruelty, it is false. If it turns His love into moral indifference, it is false.

Scripture is not merely a source we consult when forming our doctrine of God. It is the authority that governs it.

This authority should produce confidence, but not carelessness. The Bible is clear enough to reveal God truly, but it is not shallow. Its truths require meditation. Its passages must be read in context. Its genres must be respected. Its symbols must be interpreted from the text rather than from imagination. Its statements must be allowed to stand with their proper force. Reverence for Scripture does not eliminate study. It demands better study.

The psalmist describes the man whose delight is in the law of the LORD:

*"But his delight is in the law of the LORD; and in his law doth he meditate day and night." — **Psalm 1:2***

Meditation assumes depth. The Word of God rewards sustained attention. A hurried reader may miss connections that a patient reader begins to see. A careless interpreter may flatten what the text distinguishes or separate what the text joins. Because Scripture is divine revelation, we should approach it neither casually nor suspiciously, but humbly and carefully.

The study of God's character demands that care.

We will not discover the fullness of God by collecting isolated quotations without regard for context. Nor will we recover it by allowing one doctrine to silence another. We must read the Bible as a whole. We must listen where it speaks directly. We must watch how God acts in history. We must see the way His character is unveiled in Christ. We must let clear passages govern our understanding of difficult ones. We must refuse interpretive methods that strain Scripture against the character of its Author.

Only then can we begin to speak responsibly about who God is.

The church does not need a God drawn from instinct, experience, tradition, or culture, however persuasive those sources may sometimes seem. It needs the God of Scripture. The God who speaks. The God whose Word is truth.

The God who has not left His people to grope through religious uncertainty, but has revealed Himself with sufficient clarity for faith, worship, obedience, and hope.

If we want to recover the whole biblical vision of God, we must begin where that vision is given.

We must return to His Word.

Chapter 6 — "The LORD, the LORD God": God's Own Description of Himself

There are many places in Scripture where God reveals His character. Some display it through action. Some declare it through direct statement. Some unfold it across centuries of covenant faithfulness, judgment, patience, and mercy. But few passages are as important for this book as Exodus 34:6–7.

Here, God does not merely act in a way that allows us to draw conclusions about Him. He speaks His own name and announces His own character.

*"And the LORD passed by before him, and proclaimed, The LORD, The LORD God, merciful and gracious, longsuffering, and abundant in goodness and truth, Keeping mercy for thousands, forgiving iniquity and transgression and sin, and that will by no means clear the guilty; visiting the iniquity of the fathers upon the children, and upon the children's children, unto the third and to the fourth generation." — **Exodus 34:6–7**

This is not a casual description. It comes at a moment of crisis in Israel's history.

The nation has scarcely entered covenant with God before it violates the covenant in open idolatry. While Moses is on Sinai receiving the tablets of the law, the people make the golden calf. They worship before it. They call for a feast to the LORD, while standing before an image God had forbidden. Their sin is not hidden, accidental, or minor. It is covenant betrayal at the very beginning of covenant life.

The judgment that follows is severe. Moses descends from the mountain, breaks the tablets, destroys the calf, confronts Aaron, calls the faithful to the LORD's side, and roughly three thousand men fall that day. The people have learned that the God who redeemed them from Egypt is not to be treated lightly.

Yet Moses intercedes. He pleads for the presence of God to continue with Israel. He asks that the Lord not abandon His people. Then, in one of the boldest prayers in Scripture, he says:

"I beseech thee, shew me thy glory." — **Exodus 33:18**

God's answer is striking. He says:

"I will make all my goodness pass before thee, and I will proclaim the name of the LORD before thee; and will be gracious to whom I will be gracious, and will shew mercy on whom I will shew mercy." — **Exodus 33:19**

Moses asks to see God's glory. God answers by promising to proclaim His name, display His goodness, and reveal His mercy and grace. Then, in the next chapter, He does exactly that.

This matters. The glory of God is not detached from the character of God. His glory is not raw brightness, power, or majesty conceived in isolation. His glory is the radiant excellence of who He is. When God reveals His glory to Moses in this scene, He reveals His character.

And the character He declares is not one-sided.

He does not say only that He is merciful. He does not say only that He judges. He does not present compassion as His real nature and justice as an unfortunate necessity. Nor does He present judgment as His central identity with mercy appearing only at the margins.

He proclaims Himself in fullness.

The LORD, the LORD God

The declaration begins:

"The LORD, The LORD God…"

The repetition is weighty. The covenant name of God is placed first and repeated: **Jehovah**, the LORD, the self-existent, covenant-keeping God who revealed Himself to Moses at the burning bush and acted in power to redeem Israel from Egypt. He is not introducing a new identity in Exodus 34. He is unfolding the character of the same LORD who has already made Himself known.

This is important because some readers are tempted to divide the God of Scripture into opposing portraits. They imagine a severe God in one place and a merciful God in another, as though the Bible presents a tension that later theology must somehow reconcile. Exodus 34 will not allow that. The God who sent plagues upon Egypt, drowned Pharaoh's army, thundered from Sinai, and judged the calf worshipers is the same God who declares Himself merciful, gracious, longsuffering, and abundant in goodness and truth.

His severity did not contradict His mercy. His mercy does not erase His severity. Both belong to the one LORD.

The phrase "The LORD God" also reminds us that the God who enters covenant with His people is still God. Covenant nearness does not domesticate Him. His mercy does not reduce His majesty. The God who bends toward His people in compassion remains the absolute Lord over all things.

When we study the character of God, we must never mistake intimacy for equality. The LORD may speak with Moses "face to face, as a man speaketh unto his friend," yet Moses still must be hidden in the cleft of the rock because no man can see God's face and live. The nearness of God is never casual. It is holy nearness.

Merciful and Gracious

The first qualities named are mercy and grace:

"merciful and gracious…"

This order should not be overlooked. God has just judged grievous sin, yet when He reveals His name, He begins with compassion.

The word translated **merciful** carries the idea of deep pity and tender compassion. God is not indifferent to misery. He is not emotionally barren. He is not reluctant to care. Scripture reveals Him as one who sees affliction, hears cries, remembers covenant, and moves toward the helpless.

When Israel groaned under Egyptian bondage, God said:

"I have surely seen the affliction of my people which are in Egypt, and have heard their cry by reason of their taskmasters; for I know their sorrows." — **Exodus 3:7**

That is mercy in action. God is not detached from suffering. He sees. He hears. He knows.

The word **gracious** speaks of favor shown to the undeserving. Grace is not merely kindness. It is kindness where no claim exists. It is divine favor flowing freely from God rather than rising in response to human merit.

This matters deeply in Exodus 34. Israel has not earned renewed favor. The nation has shattered the covenant almost as soon as it received it. If God were to deal with them strictly according to their worthiness, the story could end at Sinai. Yet He reveals Himself as gracious.

Grace does not deny sin. The calf was real. The judgment was real. The breach was real. But grace means that guilt does not force God's hand into immediate and total destruction where He has purposed to show mercy.

This same pairing of mercy and grace appears repeatedly through the Old Testament. Psalm 103 says:

"The LORD is merciful and gracious, slow to anger, and plenteous in mercy." **— Psalm 103:8**

Joel urges the people to return to God on the same basis:

"for he is gracious and merciful, slow to anger, and of great kindness, and repenteth him of the evil." — **Joel 2:13**

Jonah, as we saw earlier, knows this about God and is angered when that mercy is extended to Nineveh:

*"for I knew that thou art a gracious God, and merciful, slow to anger, and of great kindness, and repentest thee of the evil." — **Jonah 4:2***

Exodus 34 becomes a repeated theological confession throughout Scripture because it is a foundational revelation of God's character. The prophets, psalmists, and later biblical writers return to it because they recognize that when God proclaimed His name to Moses, He gave His people a pattern for understanding Him.

Longsuffering

God next declares Himself:

"longsuffering…"

This is one of the most misread attributes of God. Divine patience is often treated as though it means divine softness, indecision, or unwillingness to confront evil. Scripture presents it differently. God is longsuffering because He is slow to anger, not because sin does not matter.

The same God who delays judgment may eventually judge with terrifying certainty. His patience should never be mistaken for permission.

Peter makes this clear when explaining the apparent delay of Christ's return:

*"The Lord is not slack concerning his promise, as some men count slackness; but is longsuffering to us-ward, not willing that any should perish, but that all should come to repentance." — **2 Peter 3:9***

Then, in the very next verse, he says:

*"But the day of the Lord will come as a thief in the night…" — **2 Peter 3:10***

Patience does not cancel judgment. It delays it for a purpose. God's longsuffering gives space for repentance. It reveals the richness of His mercy. It magnifies the justice of His final judgment because no one can say He acted hastily or without warning.

We see this pattern throughout Scripture. Before the flood, God bears with human wickedness for generations. In Genesis 15, He tells Abraham that his descendants will not yet possess the promised land because "the iniquity of the Amorites is not yet full." God endures rebellion patiently, but His patience has a moral purpose and a righteous end.

Israel's own history is a testimony to divine longsuffering. Again and again the nation rebels. Again and again the Lord sends prophets. Again and again He calls them back. The exile does not come suddenly or without warning. It comes after centuries of patience abused.

Nehemiah summarizes this history:

"Yet many years didst thou forbear them, and testifiedst against them by thy spirit in thy prophets: yet would they not give ear: therefore gavest thou them into the hand of the people of the lands." — **Nehemiah 9:30**

God's longsuffering is not weakness. It is restrained power. It is holiness that does not rush blindly into wrath, mercy that gives opportunity to repent, and justice that remains certain even while delayed.

When Exodus 34 declares God longsuffering, it gives Israel hope. The covenant has been violated, but God is not quick to destroy. Yet it also gives warning. Longsuffering must not be presumed upon. The God who delays judgment is still the God who judges.

Abundant in Goodness and Truth

The proclamation continues:

"and abundant in goodness and truth…"

The word rendered **goodness** is often associated with covenant love, steadfast kindness, or loyal mercy. It speaks of God's generous, faithful benevolence toward those upon whom He sets His love. He is not merely good in the abstract. He acts in goodness. He gives. He preserves. He restores. He does good because He is good.

The psalmist repeatedly joins goodness and mercy in praise:

"Surely goodness and mercy shall follow me all the days of my life: and I will dwell in the house of the LORD for ever." — **Psalm 23:6**

And again:

"O give thanks unto the LORD; for he is good: because his mercy endureth for ever." — **Psalm 118:1**

God's goodness is not fragile sentiment. It is enduring, active, faithful benevolence. His goodness undergirds creation, providence, covenant, redemption, and the hope of eternal life.

But Exodus 34 does not say only that He is abundant in goodness. It says He is abundant in **goodness and truth**.

That pairing matters enormously.

God's kindness is never dishonest. His mercy is never deceptive. His compassion does not require Him to obscure reality, deny guilt, or speak falsely. He is good and true together.

Truth means reliability, firmness, faithfulness, trustworthiness. God is never unstable in His speech. He does not deceive. He does not promise carelessly. He does not make declarations that evaporate under pressure. What He says stands because He stands.

Moses later declares:

"He is the Rock, his work is perfect: for all his ways are judgment: a God of truth and without iniquity, just and right is he." — **Deuteronomy 32:4**

God's truth is inseparable from His righteousness. He does not lie because falsehood would contradict His perfect nature. He does not break promises because covenant failure would contradict His faithfulness. He does not speak in confusion because His wisdom and truth are whole.

This becomes a critical principle for doctrine and interpretation. If God is abundant in truth, then His Word is not a disposable set of religious impressions. It is not designed to mislead His people. He may speak in poetry, symbol, type, parable, or prophecy. But whatever form His speech takes, He remains true. Figurative language is still truthful language. Symbol does not mean dishonesty. Mystery does not mean incoherence.

The God who is abundant in truth does not say what He does not mean.

That does not remove the need for careful interpretation. It deepens it. We must ask what God has actually said, in the form He chose to say it, and we must receive it as meaningful because the Speaker is true.

Keeping Mercy for Thousands

God then says He is:

"Keeping mercy for thousands…"

The mercy of God is not brief or easily exhausted. He stores it, preserves it, extends it. The language suggests abundance beyond immediate measure. His mercy does not appear in one isolated generation and disappear in the next. It reaches onward.

This should be read in light of the contrast later in the verse. God speaks of visiting iniquity "unto the third and to the fourth generation," but mercy is kept "for thousands." The contrast is not merely numerical; it reveals the largeness of divine compassion. Judgment is real, but God delights in mercy. His desire to show mercy is not narrow or grudging.

This does not mean He overlooks sin. The same verse forbids that conclusion. But it does mean Scripture will not permit us to imagine God as more eager to condemn than to show compassion. Ezekiel records His own declaration:

"As I live, saith the Lord GOD, I have no pleasure in the death of the wicked; but that the wicked turn from his way and live." — **Ezekiel 33:11**

God's mercy is not forced from Him against His nature. He delights in it. Micah says:

"he retaineth not his anger for ever, because he delighteth in mercy." — **Micah 7:18**

That phrase should be allowed to stand with full force. God delights in mercy. Yet again, it must stand alongside Exodus 34's declaration that He will by no means clear the guilty. His mercy is abundant, but not lawless. His compassion is deep, but not morally careless.

The gospel will ultimately reveal how mercy can be kept without guilt being ignored. At Sinai, God announces the truth. At Calvary, He displays its redemptive fulfillment.

Forgiving Iniquity and Transgression and Sin

God continues:

"forgiving iniquity and transgression and sin…"

The piling up of terms is deliberate. Scripture uses multiple words for human wrongdoing because sin is not a shallow reality. **Iniquity** speaks of crookedness or perversity. **Transgression** points to rebellion, the crossing of a boundary God has set. **Sin** speaks broadly of failing to meet God's righteous standard.

God's forgiveness is large enough to address all of it.

This is one of the most astonishing features of Exodus 34. God reveals Himself as forgiving immediately after Israel's grave covenant transgression. He does not deny the offense. He does not call the calf incident a misunderstanding. He does not minimize the rebellion. Yet He declares that forgiveness belongs to His character.

Forgiveness is not something God occasionally agrees to do against His deeper instincts. It flows from who He is.

David relied upon this after his own terrible sin:

"For thou, Lord, art good, and ready to forgive; and plenteous in mercy unto all them that call upon thee." — **Psalm 86:5**

Isaiah appeals to the same character of God when he calls the wicked to return:

"let him return unto the LORD, and he will have mercy upon him; and to our God, for he will abundantly pardon." — **Isaiah 55:7**

This readiness to forgive should not be flattened into easy acceptance. Forgiveness in Scripture is precious because sin is grievous. The God who forgives is the God who sees sin truly. That is why confession matters. That is why repentance matters. That is why atonement matters.

Without the cross, Exodus 34 would leave an unresolved question: How can the God who forgives also refuse to clear the guilty? How can mercy and justice both be perfectly maintained? The answer unfolds through the sacrificial system, the Day of Atonement, the suffering servant of Isaiah 53, and finally the death of Christ.

Paul states the answer with precision:

"Whom God hath set forth to be a propitiation through faith in his blood, to declare his righteousness for the remission of sins that are past, through the forbearance of God; To declare, I say, at this time his righteousness: that he might be just, and the justifier of him which believeth in Jesus." — **Romans 3:25–26**

God's forgiveness does not contradict His refusal to clear guilt. In Christ, guilt is truly dealt with. The sinner is forgiven because judgment has not been ignored, but borne.

Exodus 34 therefore points beyond itself. It gives us a revelation of God's forgiving character that will one day be displayed in its fullest glory at the cross.

By No Means Clearing the Guilty

Then comes the phrase modern readers are often tempted to soften:

"and that will by no means clear the guilty…"

This is not an unfortunate qualification added to an otherwise beautiful revelation. It is part of the beauty.

A God who forgives but does not care about guilt would not be morally excellent. A God who shows mercy by pretending evil is not evil would not be good. A God who absolves without righteousness would not be holy. The refusal to clear the guilty is not a defect in God's character. It is one of the reasons His mercy is meaningful.

The Hebrew construction behind the phrase is emphatic. God will certainly not leave guilt unaddressed. Sin cannot simply disappear into divine neglect. It must be judged, forgiven through atonement, or carried by the guilty one.

This truth guards us from sentimental theology. God's compassion is real. His willingness to forgive is real. His delight in mercy is real. But none of these truths means He is indifferent to wickedness.

Abraham understood this when he asked:

"Shall not the Judge of all the earth do right?" — **Genesis 18:25**

The answer is not uncertain. The Judge of all the earth will do right. Always.

That is good news for the oppressed. It means cruelty will not be forgotten. It means injustice will not be eternally overlooked. It means tyrants, abusers, deceivers, murderers, and the unrepentant wicked do not finally escape moral reality. A world with no judgment would not be more compassionate. It would be abandoned to evil without final answer.

It is also a warning to every sinner. God does not clear guilt by denial. Sin must be dealt with. The wonder of the gospel is that He has provided a righteous way for sinners to be forgiven without His justice being compromised.

Exodus 34 keeps us from treating mercy and justice as enemies. God does not move from one to the other as though His character shifts. He reveals both in the same breath because both are eternally true of Him.

Visiting Iniquity

The final portion of the declaration is often difficult for readers:

"visiting the iniquity of the fathers upon the children, and upon the children's children, unto the third and to the fourth generation."

This must be read carefully and in harmony with the rest of Scripture. God does not punish innocent children for sins in which they bear no moral share. Deuteronomy 24:16 says:

*"The fathers shall not be put to death for the children, neither shall the children be put to death for the fathers: every man shall be put to death for his own sin." — **Deuteronomy 24:16***

Ezekiel 18 likewise insists that the soul that sinneth shall die and that a righteous son will not bear the guilt of a wicked father merely because of family descent.

So what does Exodus 34 mean?

It speaks to the generational consequences and covenantal patterns of iniquity. Sin rarely remains private. Idolatry, rebellion, violence, and moral corruption travel through families, households, and cultures. Children often inherit not guilt apart from their own sin, but patterns of life, environments of rebellion, and consequences created by prior generations. When later generations continue in the sins of their fathers, they experience the visitation of judgment upon a deepening line of iniquity.

This fits the wording of Exodus 20:5, where God speaks of visiting "the iniquity of the fathers upon the children unto the third and fourth generation of them that hate me." The judgment is not arbitrary. It falls where hatred of God persists.

The point in Exodus 34 is not to weaken the mercy of God. It is to show that His justice extends beyond superficial accounting. He sees the full moral reach of sin. He sees what rebellion becomes when it is normalized, taught, defended, and handed forward. His judgment is not impulsive. It is exact.

Again, His mercy remains the dominant contrast. Judgment reaches to the third and fourth generation. Mercy is kept for thousands. The text does not present God as balanced on a knife's edge between equal impulses to bless and destroy. It presents Him as abundantly merciful, truly forgiving, deeply patient, and uncompromisingly just.

The Whole Character in One Revelation

Exodus 34:6–7 is one of the clearest proofs that the biblical God cannot be reduced to a single favorite attribute. He declares Himself:

- merciful
- gracious
- longsuffering
- abundant in goodness
- abundant in truth
- keeping mercy
- forgiving iniquity, transgression, and sin
- refusing to clear the guilty

These are not separate gods. They are not competing parts of God waiting to prevail over one another. They are the self-declared perfections of the one LORD.

This revelation should guide everything that follows in this book.

When we speak of God's love, we must remember that He is also holy and true.

When we speak of His justice, we must remember that He is merciful and gracious.

When we speak of His patience, we must remember that He will by no means clear the guilty.

When we speak of His forgiveness, we must remember that forgiveness is not denial of guilt but the gracious answer to real guilt.

When we speak of doctrine, we must remember that theology is safe only when it remains consistent with the God who has declared Himself here.

Exodus 34 is not merely an Old Testament text to be admired. It is a theological anchor. The rest of Scripture repeatedly returns to it because the God who spoke to Moses did not change. The prophets appeal to it. The psalmists praise Him with its language. Jonah resents its mercy. Nehemiah confesses it. Joel uses it to summon repentance. The New Testament reveals its deepest fulfillment in Christ.

At Sinai, God proclaimed His name. At Calvary, He displayed its fullness.

The cross tells us that the merciful God truly forgives, and the just God truly does not clear guilt without satisfaction. The empty tomb tells us that His goodness, truth, power, and faithfulness cannot fail. The promise of Christ's return tells us that His patience will not last forever and His judgment will be righteous.

If we want to recover the whole biblical vision of God, we must return again and again to the place where He proclaimed who He is.

"The LORD, The LORD God, merciful and gracious, longsuffering, and abundant in goodness and truth…"
70

Chapter 7 — The Names of God and the Revelation of His Nature

Names matter in Scripture.

They often reveal something about a person's calling, character, history, or place in God's purpose. Abram becomes Abraham. Jacob becomes Israel. Simon becomes Peter. Names are not always explanatory in the same way, but Scripture repeatedly treats them as more than convenient labels.

That is especially true of the names of God.

God's names do not merely give His people different ways to address Him in prayer. They reveal who He is. They disclose something of His nature, His authority, His covenant faithfulness, His sufficiency, His care, and His saving purpose. Because God is infinite, no single name exhausts Him. Each name opens a window into the character of the One who cannot be fully contained by human speech.

This chapter is not intended to catalog every title of God found in Scripture. That would require a book of its own. The goal here is narrower: to show that God's names form part of His self-revelation. He does not leave His people with an undefined deity. He makes Himself known. His names are one of the ways He does so.

The first verse of Scripture introduces Him with majestic simplicity:

"In the beginning God created the heaven and the earth." — **Genesis 1:1**

The Hebrew term behind "God" here is **Elohim**. It is the name used throughout the creation account. Before Scripture tells us about man, sin, Israel, covenant, sacrifice, or redemption, it begins with God as Creator. He speaks, and worlds exist. Light appears because He commands it. Seas gather where He appoints them. The heavens declare His wisdom before any human eye has seen them.

The Bible does not argue God into existence. It begins with Him.

That opening matters. The God whose character we study is not one being among others. He is the Maker of all things. Nothing precedes Him. Nothing rivals Him. Nothing gives Him permission to act. Creation is not merely an event He performed; it reveals His power, wisdom, order, generosity, and absolute distinction from the world He made.

The psalmist writes:

"Know ye that the LORD he is God: it is he that hath made us, and not we ourselves; we are his people, and the sheep of his pasture." — **Psalm 100:3**

God's creatorship grounds His authority. He made us. We belong to Him. We do not define reality for ourselves and then ask God to bless our definitions. The One who made all things has the right to name what is true, what is good, what is evil, what man is, and what man owes Him.

That is already a corrective to much modern confusion. The denial of God's authority rarely begins with a direct rejection of His existence. More often, it begins with a practical refusal to receive creation as revelation of His right to rule. Man wants life without a Maker, identity without design, morality without a Lawgiver, and blessing without obedience. The name by which God first appears in Scripture quietly dismantles all of that. He is God because He is Creator, and we are creatures because He made us.

Yet the God of Genesis 1 is not distant force. As Scripture unfolds, He reveals Himself personally, relationally, and covenantally.

El Shaddai — God Almighty

In Genesis 17, the Lord appears to Abram and says:

"I am the Almighty God; walk before me, and be thou perfect." — **Genesis 17:1**

The title translated "Almighty God" is traditionally rendered **El Shaddai.**

This revelation comes at a significant point. Abram is ninety-nine years old. The promised son has not yet come. Human strength has failed. Natural expectation has collapsed. Into that setting, God does not first explain the delay. He declares who He is: **"I am the Almighty God."**

The promise rests not upon Abram's vitality, Sarah's womb, or the plausibility of circumstances. It rests upon the sufficiency of God.

That is the force of the name in context. God is able to do what He has promised. He is not limited by the weakness that limits His creatures. His covenant word does not become fragile when circumstances turn impossible. The promise of Isaac is grounded in the character of El Shaddai.

This same title appears again when Isaac blesses Jacob:

"And God Almighty bless thee, and make thee fruitful, and multiply thee, that thou mayest be a multitude of people." — **Genesis 28:3**

And when God appears to Jacob after his return to Bethel:

"And God said unto him, I am God Almighty: be fruitful and multiply; a nation and a company of nations shall be of thee, and kings shall come out of thy loins." — **Genesis 35:11**

In each case, the name is connected to God's power to fulfill covenant promises. He is not merely mighty in an abstract sense. He is mighty to accomplish what He has spoken.

That distinction matters. Christians sometimes speak of God's omnipotence as though it means only that He can perform spectacular acts. Scripture gives us something richer. His power serves His purpose. His might stands behind His faithfulness. When God binds Himself by promise, His power guarantees that no obstacle can finally overturn His word.

This becomes important throughout biblical doctrine. The resurrection of Christ, the preservation of Israel, the salvation of sinners, the resurrection of the dead, and the coming kingdom all depend upon the fact that the God who promises is Almighty. A weak god may mean well and still fail. El Shaddai cannot.

Adonai — Lord and Master

Another important title is **Adonai**, commonly translated "Lord." It emphasizes God's lordship, mastery, and sovereign authority.

Abraham uses it when he speaks with God in Genesis 15:

"And Abram said, Lord GOD, what wilt thou give me, seeing I go childless..." **— Genesis 15:2**

The title reflects reverence. Abram is in covenant relationship with God, yet he does not approach Him casually. He speaks to the One who has authority over his life and future.

David uses similar language in Psalm 8:"O LORD our Lord, how excellent is thy name in all the earth!" — **Psalm 8:1**

The verse joins the covenant name **LORD** with the title **Lord**. The God who binds Himself graciously to His people remains their sovereign Master. His nearness never cancels His authority.

This point deserves more attention than it often receives. Modern Christian language sometimes emphasizes relationship with God in ways that unintentionally weaken reverence. Believers are indeed brought near. Christ teaches His disciples to pray, "Our Father." The Spirit bears witness that we are children of God. Yet the God who is Father remains Lord. Grace does not convert obedience into a negotiable preference. Intimacy with God deepens reverence; it does not dissolve it.

Jesus Himself pressed this issue:

"And why call ye me, Lord, Lord, and do not the things which I say?" **— Luke 6:46**

To call Him Lord while refusing His authority is contradiction. The title carries a claim upon the life of the one who uses it.

A study of God's character that emphasizes His love, mercy, and nearness while neglecting His lordship will produce an imbalanced spirituality. We will begin to think of God chiefly as the One who comforts us, helps us, and supports us, rather than as the One who commands us, owns us, and has every right to direct our lives. Scripture will not permit such reduction. The God who loves His people is their Lord.

The LORD — The Covenant God Who Is

The most significant name of God in the Old Testament is represented in the King James Bible by **LORD** in capital letters. It is the covenant name revealed with special clarity to Moses.

At the burning bush, Moses asks God what name he should give to the children of Israel when they ask who has sent him. God answers:

*"I AM THAT I AM: and he said, Thus shalt thou say unto the children of Israel, I AM hath sent me unto you." — **Exodus 3:14***

He continues:

*"Thus shalt thou say unto the children of Israel, The LORD God of your fathers, the God of Abraham, the God of Isaac, and the God of Jacob, hath sent me unto you: this is my name for ever, and this is my memorial unto all generations." — **Exodus 3:15***

The name is bound to God's self-existence. He is not derived. He is not dependent. He does not become. He simply is. All creatures receive being; God possesses it in Himself. Every created thing can say, in some sense, "I became." God alone says, "I AM."

Yet in Exodus 3, this name is not revealed as a detached metaphysical concept. It appears in the context of covenant remembrance and coming deliverance. God has heard the cries of Israel. He remembers His covenant with Abraham, Isaac, and Jacob. He is about to redeem His people from bondage. The One who simply is is also the One who keeps His word.

That connection appears again in Exodus 6. God says to Moses:

"And I appeared unto Abraham, unto Isaac, and unto Jacob, by the name of God Almighty, but by my name JEHOVAH was I not known to them." — **Exodus 6:3**

The patriarchs had encountered the name of the LORD in some form, so the point cannot be that the word itself had never been heard. Rather, God is about to make the full significance of that name known in a new historical way. He will show Himself as the covenant-keeping Redeemer who acts in power to accomplish what He has promised.

He continues:

"Wherefore say unto the children of Israel, I am the LORD, and I will bring you out from under the burdens of the Egyptians, and I will rid you out of their bondage, and I will redeem you with a stretched out arm, and with great judgments." — **Exodus 6:6**

The phrase "I am the LORD" becomes a repeated anchor throughout the passage. God's acts of deliverance are grounded in His name. He will redeem because He is the LORD. He will keep covenant because He is the LORD. He will take Israel to Himself because He is the LORD. His name guarantees His action.

This is one reason the name of the LORD occupies such a central place in Israel's worship. To call upon the LORD is to call upon the self-existent, faithful, covenant-keeping God who reveals Himself truly and keeps every word He speaks.

The psalmist says:

"The name of the LORD is a strong tower: the righteous runneth into it, and is safe." — **Proverbs 18:10**

The safety is not in the syllables of the name as though it were a charm. It is in the God the name reveals. His name stands for His character. Because He is what He has revealed Himself to be, His people may trust Him.

That truth carries directly into the New Testament. When Jesus says in John 8:

*"Before Abraham was, I am." — **John 8:58***

He is not merely claiming prior existence. He is speaking in language that reaches back to the divine self-revelation of Exodus. His hearers understood the weight of it, which is why they took up stones to cast at Him. The One standing before them is not simply a teacher claiming antiquity. He is identifying Himself with the eternal "I AM."

This matters for the doctrine of Christ and for the character of God. Jesus does not merely reveal God by teaching accurately about Him. He reveals God because He is God the Son in the flesh. The covenant LORD who delivered Israel is not absent from the Gospels. He is present in the person of Christ.

The LORD Will Provide

Genesis 22 gives us another profound name.

God commands Abraham to take Isaac, the son of promise, and offer him upon one of the mountains He will show him. The narrative is deeply solemn. Isaac is not merely beloved; he is the child through whom God has promised that Abraham's seed will be called. The command appears to place promise and obedience in severe tension.

Abraham obeys. At the decisive moment, the angel of the LORD stops him, and Abraham sees a ram caught in a thicket. He offers the ram instead of his son. Then Scripture says:

*"And Abraham called the name of that place Jehovah-jireh: as it is said to this day, In the mount of the LORD it shall be seen." — **Genesis 22:14***

Jehovah-jireh is often rendered, "The LORD will provide." The King James phrase, "In the mount of the LORD it shall be seen," preserves the connection between God's seeing and God's provision. The God who sees the need provides what is required.

In the immediate context, He provides a substitute sacrifice. Isaac does not die; the ram dies in his place. The theological significance reaches far beyond the mountain. The scene anticipates the greater provision of God in Christ. The Father will give His only begotten Son. A true substitute will bear what sinners deserve. Salvation will not arise from human ingenuity, but from divine provision.

This name reveals God as the One who provides according to His own promise and purpose. He sees what His people cannot supply. He gives what they could never produce.

That has implications for the whole gospel. The deepest human need is not improved circumstances, emotional reassurance, or earthly success. It is reconciliation with God. And where man had no sacrifice sufficient to remove sin, God provided the Lamb.

John the Baptist announces:

*"Behold the Lamb of God, which taketh away the sin of the world." — **John 1:29***

The God who provides does not merely assist human effort. He gives the very salvation we need.

The LORD That Healeth Thee

After the exodus, Israel comes to Marah and finds bitter waters. The people murmur. Moses cries unto the LORD, and the Lord shows him a tree, which he casts into the waters, and they are made sweet. Then God says:

"If thou wilt diligently hearken to the voice of the LORD thy God, and wilt do that which is right in his sight, and wilt give ear to his commandments, and

keep all his statutes, I will put none of these diseases upon thee, which I have brought upon the Egyptians: for I am the LORD that healeth thee." — **Exodus 15:26**

The phrase "the LORD that healeth thee" is often associated with the title **Jehovah-rapha**.

The context matters. God's healing here is connected to His covenant dealings with Israel, His authority, and the people's obligation to listen. It should not be detached from its setting and made into a simplistic guarantee that every faithful person will experience immediate bodily healing in this age. Scripture itself does not sustain that conclusion. Faithful servants of God suffer sickness. Paul leaves Trophimus at Miletum sick. Timothy has frequent infirmities. Epaphroditus nearly dies.

Yet neither should this name be emptied of meaning. God is healer. He restores. He rescues. He can heal the body, and He alone heals the deeper disease of sin. The prophets speak of healing in relation to the nation's spiritual restoration. The Messiah's wounds are connected to our peace and healing. Christ's earthly ministry displays divine compassion in His healing of the blind, lame, leprous, and oppressed.

The name reveals something true about God's character: He is not indifferent to ruin. He moves toward what is broken according to His righteous purpose. Sometimes He heals immediately. Sometimes He sustains through suffering. Ultimately, in the resurrection, He will remove all corruption from His people forever. The final healing is certain because the Lord who heals will complete His work.

The LORD Our Banner

In Exodus 17, Amalek attacks Israel. Moses stands on the hill with the rod of God in his hand. When his hands are raised, Israel prevails; when they fall, Amalek prevails. Aaron and Hur support his hands until the going down of the sun, and Joshua defeats Amalek. Afterward:

*"Moses built an altar, and called the name of it Jehovah-nissi." — **Exodus 17:15***

The LORD is our banner.

A banner in battle identifies the people and gathers them beneath a common cause. The name reveals that Israel's victory does not ultimately rest in Joshua's sword, Moses' endurance, or the strength of the army. Their hope is the LORD Himself. He is the rallying point, the defender, and the One under whose authority His people stand.

This again teaches us to resist reduction. God's people are not merely comforted by Him; they are enlisted under Him. He gives peace, but He also calls for loyalty. He protects, but He also claims allegiance. The Christian life is not passive self-soothing. It is faithful endurance under the banner of the Lord.

The New Testament develops this pattern in the warfare of faith. Believers wrestle not against flesh and blood, but against spiritual wickedness. They take up the whole armor of God. They overcome by the blood of the Lamb and the word of their testimony. Their victory is never self-generated. It belongs to the Lord.

The LORD Is Peace

In Judges 6, Gideon encounters the angel of the LORD. The scene leaves him shaken, for he realizes he has seen the angel of the LORD face to face. The LORD says to him:

*"Peace be unto thee; fear not: thou shalt not die." — **Judges 6:23***

Then Scripture says:

*"Then Gideon built an altar there unto the LORD, and called it Jehovah-shalom." — **Judges 6:24***

The LORD is peace.

This name emerges in a moment of fear before divine presence. Gideon does not manufacture peace through denial. Peace comes because God speaks it. The Holy One who could justly be feared grants assurance.

Biblical peace is never mere calmness of mood. It is wholeness, safety, and well-being rooted in right relation to God. A conscience at war with God cannot be brought into true peace by distraction. It must be reconciled. That is why the New Testament says:

"Therefore being justified by faith, we have peace with God through our Lord Jesus Christ." — **Romans 5:1**

Peace is not primarily the absence of uncomfortable feelings. It is the end of enmity through Christ. The God who is peace does not give peace by pretending sin is irrelevant. He gives it through righteousness accomplished at the cross.

The LORD Our Righteousness

One of the most theologically rich names appears in Jeremiah's prophecy of the coming Branch from David's line:

"Behold, the days come, saith the LORD, that I will raise unto David a righteous Branch, and a King shall reign and prosper, and shall execute judgment and justice in the earth. In his days Judah shall be saved, and Israel shall dwell safely: and this is his name whereby he shall be called, THE LORD OUR RIGHTEOUSNESS." — **Jeremiah 23:5–6**

The promised King bears the name **The LORD Our Righteousness**.

This title is astonishing. Israel does not ultimately secure righteousness by its own covenant performance. The coming Davidic King Himself is identified as the righteousness of His people. The passage is messianic, royal, and deeply tied to salvation.

The name reveals both a need and a provision. God's people need righteousness. They cannot stand before the Holy One by their own merit. God provides what He requires in the person of the Messiah.

Paul's language in the New Testament resonates strongly with this truth:

*"But of him are ye in Christ Jesus, who of God is made unto us wisdom, and righteousness, and sanctification, and redemption." — **I Corinthians 1:30***

The God who is righteous does not lower His standard in order to save. He provides righteousness in Christ. Again, God's character shapes doctrine. If His righteousness were negotiable, the gospel could be sentimental. Because His righteousness is perfect, salvation must be far greater. It must be a salvation in which sinners are made acceptable through the righteousness God Himself provides.

The LORD Is My Shepherd

Psalm 23 opens with perhaps the most beloved declaration of divine care in all of Scripture:

*"The LORD is my shepherd; I shall not want." — **Psalm 23:1***

This is not usually listed among the compound names in the same way as Jehovah-jireh or Jehovah-shalom, but it functions similarly as a revelation of God's character. The LORD is not only Creator, Almighty, Judge, and King. He is Shepherd.

He feeds. He leads. He restores. He guides. He protects. He prepares a table in the presence of enemies. He causes goodness and mercy to follow His people all the days of their lives.

The tenderness of this psalm should be received without embarrassment. God's majesty is not threatened by His gentleness. His authority does not make Him remote. The One whose voice creates stars also leads His people beside still waters.

Yet the Shepherd is not weak. David says:

"Yea, though I walk through the valley of the shadow of death, I will fear no evil: for thou art with me; thy rod and thy staff they comfort me." — **Psalm 23:4**

The rod is not sentimental. It speaks of defense and rule. The staff guides. The Shepherd comforts because He is present, powerful, and faithful.

Jesus claims this identity in John 10:

"I am the good shepherd: the good shepherd giveth his life for the sheep." — **John 10:11**

The Shepherd of Psalm 23 is revealed in the incarnate Christ. He knows His sheep, calls them by name, lays down His life for them, and keeps them. Later in this book, when we consider the doctrinal significance of God's character for assurance, this revelation will matter. The Shepherd does not treat His sheep as disposable. His care reflects who He is.

The Meaning of God's Name

These names and titles could be multiplied. Scripture speaks of God as **the Most High, the Everlasting God, the Holy One of Israel, the God of Hosts, the Rock, the Father of mercies**, and many more. Each name gives us a truthful angle on His character. None exhausts Him. Together, they help form a richer biblical vision of who He is.

They also remind us that theology must be personal. We are not studying a collection of abstract properties. We are learning the name of the living God.

When Scripture speaks of God's name, it often means more than a verbal designation. His name represents His revealed character, reputation, and glory. He acts for His name's sake. He warns against profaning His name. He gathers His people in His name. He promises that the earth will be filled with the knowledge of His glory.

The third commandment says:

"Thou shalt not take the name of the LORD thy God in vain; for the LORD will not hold him guiltless that taketh his name in vain." — **Exodus 20:7**

This certainly forbids careless or irreverent use of God's name in speech. But the command reaches beyond verbal profanity. To bear God's name falsely, to invoke Him lightly, to attach His name to what contradicts His character, is a serious offense. His name is holy because He is holy.

That gives weight to Christian confession. To say we belong to God is to bear His name before the world. To speak of His character falsely is not a minor error. To present Him as less holy, less truthful, less merciful, less just, or less faithful than He has revealed Himself to be is to misrepresent His name.

The names of God therefore call us to reverence. They call us to trust. They call us to obedience. They call us to interpret Scripture in keeping with the character of the One whose name is upon it.

God does not remain anonymous in His Word. He reveals Himself. He names Himself. He lets His people know that the One who creates is Almighty, that the One who rules is Lord, that the One who redeems is the eternal LORD, that the One who tests provides, that the One who wounds heals, that the One who calls to battle is the banner of His people, that the One whose presence causes fear gives peace, that the One who demands righteousness becomes the righteousness of His own, and that the Lord of glory is also the Shepherd who leads His flock home.

The names of God are not decorative language. They are revelation.

To know His name is to begin to know His character.

Chapter 8 — The Triune God: Perfect Fullness Before Creation

Before there was a world, before there were angels, before there was light, time, matter, or space, God was.

That truth is familiar enough to be stated easily, but its implications are immense. God did not begin when creation began. He did not become glorious when heavenly hosts first praised Him. He did not become loving when He made creatures capable of receiving His love. He did not become Father only after human families existed. He did not discover fellowship when man was formed from the dust of the ground.

God was eternally complete in Himself.

This matters because one of the most common misunderstandings about God is the idea that He created out of need. People sometimes imagine that God made humanity because He was lonely, because He wanted someone to love, or because He lacked relationship before creation. That idea may sound warm, but it quietly diminishes Him. It turns creation into a remedy for divine deficiency.

Scripture reveals something far greater.

The God who created all things is the **Triune God**: Father, Son, and Holy Spirit. He did not create because He lacked love. He created from the fullness of love already perfect within His own eternal being. He did not make creatures because He was incomplete. He made them because goodness delights to give, wisdom delights to order, and glory delights to be displayed.

The doctrine of the Trinity is not a distant theological puzzle to be tolerated because Christian orthodoxy requires it. It is central to knowing the character of God. Without it, we misunderstand divine love, divine self-sufficiency, divine revelation, salvation, prayer, worship, and the gospel itself.

The Bible teaches with unwavering clarity that there is one God.

"Hear, O Israel: The LORD our God is one LORD." — **Deuteronomy 6:4**

Isaiah records the Lord's own declaration:

"I am the LORD, and there is none else, there is no God beside me." — **Isaiah 45:5**

The New Testament does not weaken this confession. Paul writes:

"But to us there is but one God, the Father, of whom are all things, and we in him; and one Lord Jesus Christ, by whom are all things, and we by him." — **I Corinthians 8:6**

Christianity is not tritheism. It does not teach three gods cooperating with one another. There is one God.

Yet Scripture also reveals the Father as God, the Son as God, and the Holy Spirit as God. The Father is not the Son. The Son is not the Spirit. The Spirit is not the Father. They are personally distinct, yet not divided in essence. The one true God eternally exists as Father, Son, and Holy Spirit.

We do not arrive at that confession by imposing a philosophical scheme upon the Bible. We arrive there because Scripture requires it.

The Father is plainly called God. Jesus prays:

"And this is life eternal, that they might know thee the only true God, and Jesus Christ, whom thou hast sent." — **John 17:3**

The Son is also plainly revealed as God. John opens his Gospel with words that refuse reduction:

"In the beginning was the Word, and the Word was with God, and the Word was God." — **John 1:1**

He continues:

"All things were made by him; and without him was not any thing made that was made." — **John 1:3**

The Word is distinct from God the Father, for He was "with God," yet He is fully divine, for "the Word was God." He is not a created agent through whom God later works. He is the eternal Creator of all created things.

Thomas, after seeing the risen Christ, addresses Him:

"My Lord and my God." — **John 20:28**

Jesus does not rebuke him for blasphemy. He receives the confession.

The writer of Hebrews applies the language of divine kingship directly to the Son:

"But unto the Son he saith, Thy throne, O God, is for ever and ever: a sceptre of righteousness is the sceptre of thy kingdom." — **Hebrews 1:8**

The Son is not less than God. He is God the Son.

The Holy Spirit is likewise revealed as divine. In Acts 5, Peter confronts Ananias for lying about the proceeds of a sale:

"Ananias, why hath Satan filled thine heart to lie to the Holy Ghost…" — **Acts 5:3**

Then Peter says:

"thou hast not lied unto men, but unto God." — **Acts 5:4**

To lie to the Holy Ghost is to lie to God. The Spirit is not an impersonal force, a mere influence, or simply the activity of God described poetically. He speaks, teaches, grieves, intercedes, distributes gifts according to His will, and is fully divine.

At the baptism of Jesus, the three persons appear together:

"And Jesus, when he was baptized, went up straightway out of the water: and, lo, the heavens were opened unto him, and he saw the Spirit of God

*descending like a dove, and lighting upon him: And lo a voice from heaven, saying, This is my beloved Son, in whom I am well pleased." — **Matthew 3:16–17***

The Son stands in the water. The Spirit descends. The Father speaks from heaven. The passage cannot be reduced to one person appearing in three modes. The distinctions are real.

The Great Commission gives the same triune pattern:

*"Go ye therefore, and teach all nations, baptizing them in the name of the Father, and of the Son, and of the Holy Ghost." — **Matthew 28:19***

Notice that Jesus does not say "in the names," as though three gods were being listed. He says "in the name" singular, followed by Father, Son, and Holy Ghost. The unity and distinction are both present.

The apostolic blessing in 2 Corinthians 13:14 does the same:

*"The grace of the Lord Jesus Christ, and the love of God, and the communion of the Holy Ghost, be with you all. Amen." — **2 Corinthians 13:14***

The Trinity is woven into Christian worship, Christian baptism, Christian salvation, and Christian life because the God who saves us is triune.

God Was Never Lonely

This doctrine matters immediately for the character of God.

If God were a solitary person who existed alone before creation, then one might ask in what sense God could eternally be love. Love, as we know it, moves toward another. It gives. It delights. It knows and is known. If no other existed until creation, then one might be tempted to say that love became active only after God made creatures.

But Scripture reveals something richer. The Father loved the Son before the foundation of the world.

Jesus prays:

*"Father, I will that they also, whom thou hast given me, be with me where I am; that they may behold my glory, which thou hast given me: for thou lovedst me before the foundation of the world." — **John 17:24***

Before there was a world, the Father loved the Son. Before there were redeemed saints to behold Christ's glory, that glory was already His. Before creation existed, divine love was not waiting for an object. It was eternally full within God Himself.

The Son also speaks of His love for the Father:

*"But that the world may know that I love the Father; and as the Father gave me commandment, even so I do." — **John 14:31***

The relationship between Father and Son is not an arrangement that begins in time. The incarnation reveals in history what belongs eternally to the life of God. The Son's obedience in His earthly mission is not proof that He is less divine; it is the incarnate outworking of His perfect love toward the Father within the redemptive plan of God.

The Holy Spirit is not absent from this divine fullness. Scripture speaks of "the love of the Spirit" in Romans 15:30, and the Spirit searches "the deep things of God" in 1 Corinthians 2:10. He is not a detached energy operating at the margins of divine life. He is fully personal, fully divine, and perfectly united with the Father and the Son.

The triune God did not need creation in order to become relational. He did not need humanity in order to exercise love. He did not need angels in order to receive glory. Within Father, Son, and Holy Spirit there is eternal life, eternal communion, eternal delight, eternal perfection.

Creation is therefore not the solution to God's loneliness. It is the free overflow of His goodness and glory.

That changes the way we think about everything.

If God created from need, then creatures supply something lacking in Him. Worship begins to look like flattery He requires. Prayer begins to look like attention He craves. Redemption begins to look like an act of self-completion. But if God created from fullness, then all His works toward us are grace. He gives because He is good, not because He is needy. He invites fellowship because He is generous, not because He is incomplete. He saves sinners because His mercy abounds, not because heaven would be deficient without them.

Paul speaks directly to this in Athens:

"God that made the world and all things therein, seeing that he is Lord of heaven and earth, dwelleth not in temples made with hands; Neither is worshipped with men's hands, as though he needed any thing, seeing he giveth to all life, and breath, and all things." — **Acts 17:24–25**

God does not need anything from us. We need everything from Him.

That is not a cold doctrine. It is freeing. If God's love rested upon our ability to complete Him, it would be unstable. If His joy depended upon our performance, it would rise and fall with us. But because He is eternally blessed in Himself, His grace toward His people is not fragile. He loves from fullness. He gives from abundance. He remains who He is whether men worship Him or refuse Him.

The Trinity and the Meaning of Love

The doctrine of the Trinity protects the biblical meaning of love.

Modern culture often speaks of love as affirmation, emotional warmth, or unconditional approval. Scripture gives us a deeper and more demanding vision. Divine love is personal, holy, self-giving, truthful, and ordered. The Father loves the Son. The Son loves the Father. The Spirit glorifies the Son and applies the work of redemption to God's people. There is no selfishness, no rivalry, no insecurity, no competition within God.

Jesus says of the Spirit:

"He shall glorify me: for he shall receive of mine, and shall shew it unto you."
*— **John 16:14***

The Spirit does not draw attention away from Christ in order to establish His own independent prominence. He glorifies the Son. The Son glorifies the Father. The Father glorifies the Son. Within the triune life of God, glory is not hoarded in pride. It is perfectly shared in the unity of divine being and the distinction of divine persons.

Jesus prays:

*"Father, glorify thy name. Then came there a voice from heaven, saying, I have both glorified it, and will glorify it again." — **John 12:28***

And again:

*"Father, glorify thy Son, that thy Son also may glorify thee." — **John 17:1***

The love of God is inseparable from the glory of God. The Father loves the Son and gives Him glory. The Son loves the Father and seeks His glory. This is why divine love can never be reduced to mere indulgence. Love, in its highest form, delights in what is truly glorious. God's love does not deny holiness, because holiness is beautiful. It does not ignore truth, because truth is glorious. It does not excuse sin as though evil were harmless, because sin opposes what God perfectly loves.

The Trinity helps us see that God's love is not sentimental. It is bound up with truth, holiness, glory, and self-giving delight in the good.

That matters for doctrine and for Christian life. When Scripture commands believers to love one another, it does not call them merely to be pleasant. It calls them into a love patterned after God's own life and displayed in Christ's sacrifice.

Jesus says:

"As the Father hath loved me, so have I loved you: continue ye in my love."
*— **John 15:9***

Then He adds:

"This is my commandment, That ye love one another, as I have loved you."
— **John 15:12**

The love believers are called to show is rooted in the Father's love for the Son and the Son's love for His people. It is not self-centered affection. It is costly, obedient, truth-shaped love.

The Trinity and Revelation

The triune nature of God also matters because revelation itself is triune.

The Father sends the Son. The Son makes the Father known. The Spirit bears witness to the Son and illuminates the truth of God to His people.

John writes:

"No man hath seen God at any time; the only begotten Son, which is in the bosom of the Father, he hath declared him." — **John 1:18**

The Son declares the Father because He eternally knows the Father. He is not an outsider reporting limited observations. He comes from the bosom of the Father. His revelation is perfect because His communion is eternal.

Jesus says:

"All things are delivered unto me of my Father: and no man knoweth the Son, but the Father; neither knoweth any man the Father, save the Son, and he to whomsoever the Son will reveal him." — **Matthew 11:27**

The Father and Son know one another uniquely. The Son reveals the Father to whom He will. True knowledge of God is not seized by human effort; it is granted through Christ.

The Spirit continues this work of revelation. Jesus tells His disciples:

"Howbeit when he, the Spirit of truth, is come, he will guide you into all truth: for he shall not speak of himself; but whatsoever he shall hear, that shall he

*speak: and he will shew you things to come. He shall glorify me: for he shall receive of mine, and shall shew it unto you." — **John 16:13–14**

The Spirit does not create a competing revelation detached from the Son. He glorifies Christ by making known what belongs to Christ. The knowledge of God comes from the Father, through the Son, by the Spirit.

This protects Christian theology from two opposite errors. On one side, it protects us from thinking we can know God apart from Christ. A vague belief in deity is not the same as knowing the Father. Jesus said plainly:

*"I am the way, the truth, and the life: no man cometh unto the Father, but by me." — **John 14:6**

On the other side, it protects us from claiming spiritual revelation that contradicts the written witness to Christ. The Spirit who inspired Scripture does not now lead believers away from Scripture. The Spirit of truth glorifies the Son whom Scripture reveals. Claims of divine insight that distort Christ, deny His Word, or loosen the authority of Scripture do not arise from the Holy Ghost.

The Trinity gives us a solid framework for revelation. God is not silent. The Father has spoken in the Son. The Spirit has borne witness. Scripture records that revelation faithfully. Christian knowledge of God is not guesswork.

The Trinity and Salvation

The gospel itself is unmistakably triune.

The Father plans salvation and sends the Son. The Son accomplishes salvation through His incarnation, obedience, death, and resurrection. The Spirit applies salvation by convicting, regenerating, indwelling, sanctifying, and sealing believers.

Paul describes this pattern in Ephesians 1. The Father chooses in Christ before the foundation of the world:

"According as he hath chosen us in him before the foundation of the world, that we should be holy and without blame before him in love." — **Ephesians 1:4**

The Son redeems through His blood:

"In whom we have redemption through his blood, the forgiveness of sins, according to the riches of his grace." — **Ephesians 1:7**

The Spirit seals those who believe:

"In whom ye also trusted, after that ye heard the word of truth, the gospel of your salvation: in whom also after that ye believed, ye were sealed with that holy Spirit of promise." — **Ephesians 1:13**

Salvation is not the work of one divine person persuading another reluctant divine person to show mercy. That caricature sometimes appears in crude presentations of the cross, as though the Son loves sinners while the Father only needs to be appeased. Scripture will not allow it. The Father sends the Son in love. The Son gives Himself willingly. The Spirit brings the benefits of that redemption to the believer.

Jesus says:

"For God so loved the world, that he gave his only begotten Son, that whosoever believeth in him should not perish, but have everlasting life." — **John 3:16**

Paul says of Christ:

"who loved me, and gave himself for me." — **Galatians 2:20**

And the writer of Hebrews says Christ offered Himself "through the eternal Spirit":

"How much more shall the blood of Christ, who through the eternal Spirit offered himself without spot to God, purge your conscience from dead works to serve the living God?" — **Hebrews 9:14**

The one work of salvation is the harmonious work of the triune God.

This matters for the character of God because it reveals no division within Him. The Father is not less merciful than the Son. The Son is not more willing to save than the Father. The Spirit is not an afterthought. Redemption arises from the united purpose of God. The whole God saves.

That same unity appears in the believer's access to God:

"For through him we both have access by one Spirit unto the Father." — **Ephesians 2:18**

Through the Son, by the Spirit, unto the Father. Christian prayer, worship, and communion with God are triune realities.

The Trinity and the Cross

The cross cannot be understood rightly apart from the Trinity.

The Son becomes incarnate. The Son suffers. The Son dies. But He is sent by the Father, sustained in perfect obedience to the Father's will, and offers Himself through the eternal Spirit. The cross is not an act of divine disagreement. It is not the compassionate Son rescuing sinners from an unwilling Father. It is the love, justice, wisdom, and mercy of the one triune God displayed in redemption.

Isaiah says:

"Yet it pleased the LORD to bruise him; he hath put him to grief: when thou shalt make his soul an offering for sin..." — **Isaiah 53:10**

This verse must not be misread as though the Father delights cruelly in the suffering of the Son. The pleasure of the LORD is the righteous purpose of redemption being accomplished. The cross satisfies divine justice, fulfills divine promise, and secures the salvation of God's people. The Son is not an unwilling victim of the Father. He says:

"Therefore doth my Father love me, because I lay down my life, that I might take it again. No man taketh it from me, but I lay it down of myself. I have power to lay it down, and I have power to take it again. This commandment have I received of my Father." — **John 10:17–18**

The Father loves the Son in His voluntary obedience. The Son lays down His life willingly. The cross reveals divine harmony, not divine conflict.

This point will become even more important later in the book when we examine how the cross displays the full character of God. For now, we should see that the triune nature of God prevents us from imagining salvation as though one divine person must soften another. The Father, Son, and Spirit are perfectly united in the redemption of sinners.

The Trinity and God's Self-Sufficiency

The fullness of the triune God also guards the doctrine of divine self-sufficiency.

God is not improved by creation. He is not completed by worship. He is not emotionally dependent upon creatures. He did not make angels because He needed praise or humanity because He needed affection. Before creation, the Father was glorified in the Son, the Son rejoiced in the Father, and the Spirit existed in perfect divine communion. Nothing was lacking.

Jesus speaks of the glory He had with the Father before the world was:

"And now, O Father, glorify thou me with thine own self with the glory which I had with thee before the world was." — **John 17:5**

That is staggering. Before Bethlehem, before Eden, before Genesis 1:1, the Son possessed glory with the Father. The incarnation does not begin His existence. It marks His entrance into human nature for our salvation.

The glory of God is therefore not dependent on creation. Creation displays it, but does not create it. Worship acknowledges it, but does not supply it. Salvation magnifies it, but does not complete it.

This makes grace genuinely gracious. God gains nothing He lacked by saving us. He is not made whole by our redemption. He saves because He is merciful. He adopts because He is loving. He brings sinners into fellowship with Himself not to fill a void in His being, but to share the riches of His own fullness.

Paul says:

*"For of him, and through him, and to him, are all things: to whom be glory for ever. Amen." — **Romans 11:36***

Everything begins with God, is sustained through God, and reaches its proper end in God. He is not one participant in reality. He is its source and goal.

The Trinity and the Full Character of God

The doctrine of the Trinity does not explain away the mystery of God. It deepens it. We are speaking about the eternal being of the infinite Lord. Human language reaches its limit quickly. The church has had to speak carefully here because error arises when men attempt either to simplify what Scripture maintains or to speculate beyond what God has revealed.

We must not deny the unity of God in order to preserve the distinction of persons. We must not deny the distinction of persons in order to preserve the unity of God. We must not imagine the Father, Son, and Spirit as three parts of God, for each is fully God. We must not imagine one person merely wearing three masks, for Scripture reveals real personal distinction.

The truth stands because Scripture teaches it, whether or not our minds can compress it into something easy.

Yet this doctrine is not an abstract burden placed upon faith. It is one of the glories of the Christian revelation. It tells us that God is eternally living, eternally personal, eternally loving, eternally full. It tells us that revelation, redemption, and communion with God are rooted in His own triune life.

It tells us that the love poured out upon believers is not a temporary mood in God, but flows from the eternal love that belongs to His very being.

Jesus says to the Father:

*"And hast loved them, as thou hast loved me." — **John 17:23***

That sentence deserves careful thought. The Father's love for believers in Christ is spoken of in relation to His love for the Son. The redeemed are not loved casually. They are loved in the Son, received in the Beloved, drawn into fellowship with the triune God.

No lesser vision of God can sustain the gospel.

A solitary deity created from lack. The triune God creates from fullness.

A solitary deity might seek worship to meet need. The triune God receives worship because He is infinitely worthy.

A solitary deity might begin to love after creatures appear. The triune God is eternally love.

A diminished theology of God makes redemption seem like divine response to something absent in Himself. The Trinity reveals redemption as the gracious overflow of a God who was already perfectly blessed, perfectly glorious, and perfectly complete before the world began.

- This is the God Scripture reveals.
- This is the God who made us.
- This is the God who saves.

And if we are to recover the full biblical vision of who He is, we cannot leave the Trinity at the margins. The Father, the Son, and the Holy Ghost are not an appendix to the doctrine of God. They are the living God Himself.

Chapter 9 — The Son Who Makes the Father Known

The character of God is not revealed most fully in an abstract definition, a philosophical argument, or even a single thunderous declaration from heaven.

It is revealed in a Person.

Jesus Christ does not merely speak truth about God. He makes God known. He is not one witness among many, standing at a distance and reporting what He has learned. He comes from the Father, shares the Father's nature, bears the Father's image, speaks the Father's words, performs the Father's works, and reveals the Father without distortion.

John writes:

*"No man hath seen God at any time; the only begotten Son, which is in the bosom of the Father, he hath declared him." — **John 1:18***

That verse belongs near the center of any serious study of God's character.

The invisible God has not left Himself unknown. The Son has declared Him. The word translated "declared" carries the idea of making known, unfolding, or explaining. The Son interprets the Father to us, not because the Father was previously contrary to Him, but because the Son alone knows the Father perfectly and reveals Him truly.

Jesus says:

*"All things are delivered unto me of my Father: and no man knoweth the Son, but the Father; neither knoweth any man the Father, save the Son, and he to whomsoever the Son will reveal him." — **Matthew 11:27***

No creature knows the Father as the Son knows Him. No prophet, priest, angel, or apostle speaks from the same eternal intimacy. Others receive revelation. The Son reveals from within the very life of God.

That is why any attempt to understand God while marginalizing Christ is doomed from the beginning. The God of Scripture cannot be known truly while the Son who reveals Him is treated as optional, secondary, or merely illustrative. To see Christ rightly is to behold the character of God in its clearest historical manifestation.

Yet this truth is often mishandled in two opposite directions.

Some treat Jesus as though He corrects the God of the Old Testament. In this telling, the earlier Scriptures present a severe, wrathful, demanding deity, while Jesus arrives to reveal a gentler and more merciful God. Others, rightly rejecting that error, sometimes speak of Christ's deity in such a way that the human life of Jesus becomes little more than a doctrinal proof rather than the living revelation of God's heart, holiness, compassion, and authority.

Both errors must be resisted.

Jesus does not revise the Old Testament portrait of God. He confirms it, embodies it, and brings it into its fullest light. At the same time, His earthly life is not incidental to the doctrine of God. The words He speaks, the sinners He receives, the hypocrites He rebukes, the tears He sheds, the authority He exercises, the cross He embraces, and the judgment He promises all reveal who God is.

The Son makes the Father known.

The Image of the Invisible God

Paul writes of Christ:

"Who is the image of the invisible God, the firstborn of every creature: For by him were all things created, that are in heaven, and that are in earth, visible and invisible, whether they be thrones, or dominions, or principalities, or powers: all things were created by him, and for him: And he is before all things, and by him all things consist." — **Colossians 1:15–17**

Christ is "the image of the invisible God." This does not mean He is a lesser copy of God, as though He only resembles the Father from a distance. The surrounding verses forbid such a reading. He creates all things. He precedes all things. He sustains all things. He is not a creature standing near God. He is the eternal Son through whom creation exists.

The writer of Hebrews says He is:

"the brightness of his glory, and the express image of his person." — **Hebrews 1:3**

The Son is the radiance of divine glory and the exact imprint of divine being. He does not approximate the Father. He reveals Him perfectly.

This is why Jesus can say to Philip:

"Have I been so long time with you, and yet hast thou not known me, Philip? he that hath seen me hath seen the Father; and how sayest thou then, Shew us the Father?" — **John 14:9**

Jesus is not saying that He is the same Person as the Father. He has already spoken repeatedly of going to the Father, praying to the Father, and being sent by the Father. He is saying that the Father is perfectly revealed in Him. There is no hidden divine character behind Jesus that contradicts what Jesus displays. To know the Son is to know the Father's heart, holiness, truth, and glory.

This should transform the way we read the Gospels. The compassion of Christ is the compassion of God. The authority of Christ is the authority of God. The purity of Christ is the holiness of God. The patience of Christ is the patience of God. The wrath of Christ against hypocrisy is the wrath of God. The tears of Christ at Lazarus's tomb and over Jerusalem reveal no weakness in divinity; they reveal the heart of the incarnate Son, and through Him, the heart of God.

Jesus and the Mercy of God

The mercy of God is vividly displayed in the earthly ministry of Christ.

Again and again, the Gospels show Him moved with compassion. He does not merely perform miracles as public demonstrations of power. He sees distress. He responds to human ruin. He touches the untouchable. He receives those whom respectable religion has pushed aside.

When a leper comes to Him saying, "Lord, if thou wilt, thou canst make me clean," Mark records:

*"And Jesus, moved with compassion, put forth his hand, and touched him, and saith unto him, I will; be thou clean." — **Mark 1:41***

The detail matters. Jesus could have healed him with a word from a distance, as He did on other occasions. Instead, He touched him. The one who had lived separated from ordinary human contact feels the hand of the Holy One upon his uncleanness, and the uncleanness does not spread to Christ. Cleanness flows from Christ to him.

That is mercy.

When Jesus sees the crowds wandering without faithful shepherds, Matthew says:

*"But when he saw the multitudes, he was moved with compassion on them, because they fainted, and were scattered abroad, as sheep having no shepherd." — **Matthew 9:36***

His compassion is not vague sentiment. It sees spiritual need. The people do not merely lack food, health, or political stability. They are like sheep without a shepherd. They need truth. They need guidance. They need the kingdom of God proclaimed.

When Jesus encounters the widow of Nain walking beside the bier of her only son, Luke writes:

*"And when the Lord saw her, he had compassion on her, and said unto her, Weep not." — **Luke 7:13***

Then He raises the young man from the dead. His compassion does not remain inward. It acts.

These scenes reveal God's character. The Son does not arrive on earth with a tenderness absent from the Father. He reveals the Father's tenderness. The compassion of Christ is not a softening of divinity. It is divinity expressed in incarnate mercy.

This matters because some theological portraits of God retain His sovereignty, wrath, and authority while speaking too little of His tenderness. They can affirm that God is merciful in principle yet leave the reader with a sense that mercy is something reluctantly granted after justice has had its say. The Gospels will not support that impression. Christ does not receive the broken grudgingly. He invites them.

*"Come unto me, all ye that labour and are heavy laden, and I will give you rest." — **Matthew 11:28***

The invitation comes from the same Son who will later speak of judgment. His tenderness is not weak. His authority is not harsh. In Him, mercy and majesty meet without strain.

Jesus and the Holiness of God

The same Christ who welcomes the weary also exposes sin with unsparing clarity.

A partial view of Jesus tends to remember only the scenes that fit modern sentiment. He eats with publicans and sinners. He rescues the adulterous woman from mob violence. He blesses children. He heals the sick. All of this is true and precious. But the Jesus of the Gospels is also the One who declares:

*"Except ye repent, ye shall all likewise perish." — **Luke 13:3***

He tells men to cut off the hand or pluck out the eye rather than be cast into hell. He warns that many will say to Him, "Lord, Lord," and yet hear,

"I never knew you." He says that broad is the way that leadeth to destruction. He speaks of weeping and gnashing of teeth. No one in Scripture gives more vivid warnings of final judgment than Jesus Christ.

This does not contradict His mercy. It reveals His holiness.

The Son who makes the Father known does not treat sin lightly. He does not speak of rebellion as a harmless mistake. He does not flatter self-righteous religion or soothe unrepentant hypocrisy. His words to the scribes and Pharisees in Matthew 23 are among the fiercest in the Bible:

"Woe unto you, scribes and Pharisees, hypocrites!" — **Matthew 23:13**

Again and again, He pronounces woe. He exposes their outward religion, their inward corruption, their pride, their manipulation of others, their blindness to justice, mercy, and faith. He calls them "serpents" and a "generation of vipers," and asks:

"how can ye escape the damnation of hell?" — **Matthew 23:33**

This is not a different Jesus from the One who says, "Come unto me." It is the same Jesus. His compassion toward the humble and His severity toward hardened hypocrisy flow from the same holy character.

The modern world often imagines love and moral confrontation as opposites. Christ shows that they are not. Because He loves what is good, He hates what destroys. Because He is true, He exposes lies. Because He is merciful, He calls sinners to repentance rather than confirming them in death. Because He is holy, He will not baptize rebellion with religious language.

No one who studies the Gospels carefully can sustain the idea that Jesus reveals a God who is loving but not holy, accepting but not judging, merciful but uninterested in righteousness.

The Son reveals the Father, and the Father is holy.

Jesus and Divine Authority

Christ's authority also reveals the character of God.

He teaches not as one merely repeating received tradition, but as one whose words carry inherent authority. At the end of the Sermon on the Mount, Matthew says:

*"And it came to pass, when Jesus had ended these sayings, the people were astonished at his doctrine: For he taught them as one having authority, and not as the scribes." — **Matthew 7:28–29***

He speaks with the authority of one who knows God, knows man, and knows the true meaning of the law. Again and again in Matthew 5, He says, "But I say unto you." He is not abolishing Moses. He is exposing the shallow interpretations that had reduced God's commands to external compliance while leaving the heart untouched.

He forgives sins. When the paralytic is brought before Him, Jesus says:

*"Son, thy sins be forgiven thee." — **Mark 2:5***

The scribes reason correctly that only God can forgive sins. Their error is not in the principle. Their error is in failing to recognize who stands before them. Jesus then heals the man to demonstrate that the Son of man has power on earth to forgive sins.

He commands demons, and they obey. He rebukes the wind and sea, and there is a great calm. His disciples ask:

*"What manner of man is this, that even the winds and the sea obey him!" — **Matthew 8:27***

The question is answered by the identity of the One in the boat. The sea obeys because the Creator is present. The demons flee because the Holy One has come. Death yields because life stands beside the tomb.

When Jesus cries, "Lazarus, come forth," the dead man comes. The Lord does not pray as one uncertain whether help will arrive. He thanks the Father aloud for the sake of those standing by, and then He calls death backward. The sign reveals that resurrection power belongs to Him because life belongs to Him.

He says:

*"I am the resurrection, and the life: he that believeth in me, though he were dead, yet shall he live." — **John 11:25***

This is not merely power. It is authority rooted in divine identity. Christ does not merely receive life from God as a prophet who raises the dead by request. He is life. The Son reveals the Father as the living God, the One over whom death has no claim.

Jesus and the Truthfulness of God

The character of God is also revealed in Christ's relation to truth.

Jesus does not merely tell the truth. He identifies Himself with it:

*"I am the way, the truth, and the life: no man cometh unto the Father, but by me." — **John 14:6***

Truth is not a concept external to Christ that He happens to understand well. He is the truth in person. In Him, God's self-revelation is perfectly reliable.

This matters in an age that prefers spiritual flexibility. Jesus does not leave the path to God open-ended. He does not say that He is one way among many, or that sincerity will finally substitute for truth. He says no man comes unto the Father but by Him. The exclusivity of Christ is not human arrogance; it is divine revelation.

The Father is known through the Son because the Son alone reveals Him perfectly. Any supposed knowledge of God that rejects Christ is not fuller than Christian faith. It is deficient at the center.

Jesus also speaks of Scripture with absolute confidence. He says:

*"the scripture cannot be broken." — **John 10:35***

He declares:

"Till heaven and earth pass, one jot or one tittle shall in no wise pass from the law, till all be fulfilled." — **Matthew 5:18**

The Son who reveals the Father does not treat God's written Word as unstable, disposable, or loosely authoritative. He fulfills it, appeals to it, and expects it to stand. His view of Scripture should govern ours.

This becomes especially important for a book concerned with God's character and doctrine. If Christ reveals the Father, and Christ treats the Word of God as inviolable, then any theology that claims to honor Jesus while loosening confidence in Scripture has already divided what He joined together. The truthful Son bears witness to the truthful Word of the truthful God.

Jesus and the Father's Love

The love of the Father becomes visible in the sending of the Son.

John 3:16 is familiar, but familiarity must not be allowed to drain its force:

"For God so loved the world, that he gave his only begotten Son, that whosoever believeth in him should not perish, but have everlasting life." — **John 3:16**

The cross is not evidence that Jesus loves us while the Father remains distant. The giving of the Son begins in the love of God. The Father does not stand behind redemption reluctantly. He gives what is most precious.

Paul writes:

"He that spared not his own Son, but delivered him up for us all, how shall he not with him also freely give us all things?" — **Romans 8:32**

The argument depends upon the Father's generosity. If He gave the Son, He will not fail to complete the saving purpose bound up with that gift.

Jesus Himself says:

*"For the Father himself loveth you, because ye have loved me, and have believed that I came out from God." — **John 16:27***

This statement is important because believers may sometimes imagine the Son as their compassionate advocate before a less willing Father. Scripture does teach that Christ intercedes for His people. But that intercession does not overcome reluctance in the Father. The Father Himself loves those who belong to the Son.

The Son reveals the Father's love not only by dying, but by telling us plainly that the Father loves His people.

That love is not sentimental. The Father disciplines His children. He sanctifies them. He conforms them to the image of His Son. Yet all of that arises from real fatherly love, not from cold distance.

Jesus teaches His disciples to pray:

*"Our Father which art in heaven, Hallowed be thy name." — **Matthew 6:9***

The first word grants astonishing nearness: "Our Father." The second clause preserves reverence: "Hallowed be thy name." Christ does not set intimacy against holiness. He teaches us to approach the holy God as Father because, through the Son, that is what He truly is to His redeemed people.

Jesus and the Wrath of God

If Christ reveals the Father, then we must also receive what Christ reveals about divine wrath.

The same Gospel that gives us John 3:16 says:

"He that believeth on the Son hath everlasting life: and he that believeth not the Son shall not see life; but the wrath of God abideth on him." — **John 3:36**

The wrath of God is not a later theological embarrassment imposed upon the gentler message of Jesus. It stands in the Gospel that most majestically declares divine love.

Jesus speaks repeatedly of judgment. He describes the Son of man coming in glory and separating the nations as a shepherd divides sheep from goats. He says to the wicked:

"Depart from me, ye cursed, into everlasting fire, prepared for the devil and his angels." — **Matthew 25:41**

The book of Revelation brings this into its final eschatological form. Men cry to the mountains and rocks:

"Fall on us, and hide us from the face of him that sitteth on the throne, and from the wrath of the Lamb: For the great day of his wrath is come; and who shall be able to stand?" — **Revelation 6:16–17**

The phrase "wrath of the Lamb" is startling precisely because it joins what many minds would separate. A lamb suggests meekness, sacrifice, gentleness. Wrath suggests judgment. Scripture does not choose one image and discard the other. The Lamb who was slain is the Lamb whose wrath terrifies the unrepentant world.

This will matter later when we consider the Bridegroom, His bride, and the day of wrath. For now, the point is broader: if Jesus reveals God, then the wrath of Christ must be included in our understanding of God's character. A theology that keeps the compassion of Jesus but removes His judgment has not preserved Christ. It has edited Him.

Jesus and the Unity of God's Character

The Gospels give us no divided Christ.

- He receives sinners and overturns tables in the temple.
- He blesses children and calls religious leaders blind guides.
- He weeps at a grave and commands the dead to rise.
- He tells the weary to come and tells the unrepentant to fear hell.
- He washes His disciples' feet and declares that all judgment has been committed unto Him.
- He is the Lamb of God and the King who will return in glory.

Every one of these scenes matters.

Christ does not reveal one portion of God's character while leaving the rest to other parts of Scripture. He reveals the fullness of the divine character in human life. Not exhaustively, for the infinite God cannot be exhausted by finite observation, but perfectly, without falsehood or omission.

Paul writes:

*"For in him dwelleth all the fulness of the Godhead bodily." — **Colossians 2:9***

That verse should govern how we think about Christ. The fullness of deity dwells bodily in Him. He is not one slice of God's character made visible while other, sterner truths remain elsewhere. In Him dwells all the fullness.

This also means that the more clearly we behold Christ, the more accurately we know God. The compassion of Christ corrects harsh theology. The holiness of Christ corrects permissive theology. The authority of Christ corrects self-directed spirituality. The truthfulness of Christ corrects religious relativism. The wrath of Christ corrects sentimental reduction. The obedience of Christ corrects careless ideas of love. The cross of Christ corrects every attempt to imagine mercy apart from justice.

The Son makes the Father known, and the Father He reveals is the God of Scripture in all His fullness.

No Knowledge of God Apart from the Son

The final implication is unavoidable: there is no true knowledge of God apart from Jesus Christ.

This does not mean that unbelievers know nothing about God in any sense. Romans 1 teaches that creation reveals His eternal power and Godhead. Conscience bears witness to moral reality. The heavens declare the glory of God. But saving, reconciled, personal knowledge of the Father comes only through the Son.

Jesus says:

"I am the door: by me if any man enter in, he shall be saved, and shall go in and out, and find pasture." — **John 10:9**

He says:

"Neither knoweth any man the Father, save the Son, and he to whomsoever the Son will reveal him." — **Matthew 11:27**

John writes:

"Whosoever denieth the Son, the same hath not the Father: but he that acknowledgeth the Son hath the Father also." — **1 John 2:23**

There is no honoring the Father while rejecting the Son. There is no reaching God by a path Christ has denied. There is no fuller spiritual knowledge that leaves Jesus behind.

This is not narrowness invented by Christians. It is the testimony of the Son who came from the Father to make Him known.

And this exclusivity is good news. We are not left searching through the fog of competing spiritual claims, hoping one of them may lead upward. God has come down. The Word was made flesh. The only begotten Son has declared the Father. The way to God is not hidden from those willing to receive Him. It has a name.

Jesus Christ.

To know Him is to know the Father. To reject Him is to refuse the clearest revelation God has given of Himself. To study the character of God while neglecting Christ would be to study light while closing our eyes to the sun.

The Son makes the Father known.

Therefore, as we continue seeking the full biblical vision of God, we must never move away from Christ as though He were merely one chapter in the subject. Every attribute we examine belongs to the God revealed in Him. The holiness of God is seen in Christ. The mercy of God is seen in Christ. The justice of God is seen in Christ. The truth of God is seen in Christ. The wrath of God is seen in Christ. The love of God is seen in Christ. The faithfulness of God is seen in Christ.

He is not only the Savior we need.

He is the revelation of the God we must know.

Chapter 10 — God Is Not the Author of Confusion

God speaks because He intends to be understood.

That does not mean every passage of Scripture is equally simple. It does not mean every prophecy is immediately transparent, every doctrine free of mystery, or every difficult text answerable in a sentence. Peter acknowledged that some things in Paul's letters were "hard to be understood." The disciples often failed to grasp what Jesus plainly told them until after His resurrection. Daniel received visions that left him troubled and searching. Scripture has depth because God is infinite and His works reach beyond the limits of human sight.

But depth is not disorder. Mystery is not confusion. Difficulty is not deception.

The God who reveals Himself in Scripture is the God of truth, wisdom, order, and faithfulness. He does not speak carelessly. He does not make promises with one meaning in the ears of the hearers and an entirely unrelated meaning in fulfillment. He does not use revelation to obscure Himself while pretending to make Himself known. He may require patience, humility, and careful study from the reader, but He is not the author of confusion.

Paul writes:

*"For God is not the author of confusion, but of peace, as in all churches of the saints." — **I Corinthians 14:33***

In its immediate context, Paul is correcting disorder in the Corinthian assembly. Spiritual gifts were being exercised in a way that produced noise, interruption, and lack of edification. Prophets were not to speak over one another. Tongues were not to be used without interpretation. Worship was to proceed in a way that benefited the church rather than displaying private excitement.

Paul's argument rests on the character of God. The churches are not to embrace chaos in worship because God Himself is not the author of confusion. His nature should shape the conduct of His people.

That principle should not be wrenched from its context and made to say whatever we wish. Yet neither should we act as though it has no wider significance. Paul appeals to God's character to correct disorder because God's character is orderly. Confusion is inconsistent with Him. Disorder does not reflect Him. That truth matters not only for church gatherings, but also for how we understand His creation, His revelation, and His speech.

The Bible opens with order brought forth by the word of God.

"In the beginning God created the heaven and the earth." — **Genesis 1:1**

The earth is described as "without form, and void," with darkness upon the face of the deep. Then God speaks. Light appears. Light is divided from darkness. Waters are separated. Dry land appears. The heavens are ordered. The sun, moon, and stars are appointed "for signs, and for seasons, and for days, and years." Living creatures are made according to their kinds. Man is created in the image of God and given dominion.

Creation is not presented as a divine struggle against rival powers. God speaks, and reality takes form. His Word establishes distinctions. Light and darkness are not confused. Sea and land are not blurred. Male and female are not interchangeable inventions. Days, seasons, kinds, and purposes exist because God's wisdom orders what He makes.

The created world bears witness to a God of intelligibility.

The psalmist says:

"The heavens declare the glory of God; and the firmament sheweth his handywork. Day unto day uttereth speech, and night unto night sheweth knowledge." — **Psalm 19:1–2**

Creation does not speak with audible syllables, yet it communicates. It testifies to wisdom, power, proportion, and design. The universe is not divine, but it is meaningful because it comes from the God of meaning. The very possibility of knowledge rests upon the fact that reality has order and that the human mind, made by God, is capable of receiving truth about it.

The same Psalm then turns from creation to Scripture:

*"The law of the LORD is perfect, converting the soul: the testimony of the LORD is sure, making wise the simple. The statutes of the LORD are right, rejoicing the heart: the commandment of the LORD is pure, enlightening the eyes." — **Psalm 19:7–8***

The God whose creation declares His glory has also spoken in words. His law is not unstable. His testimony is "sure." His commandments enlighten. Revelation is given to make wise, not to render truth unknowable.

This matters greatly. If God is a God of order, then His Word should not be approached as though it were a maze of meanings detached from the language He chose. If He is a God of truth, then we should not presume that His clearest statements conceal realities opposite to their ordinary sense. If He is faithful, then the meaning of His promises cannot be treated as elastic whenever a theological system requires it.

The Bible contains symbols. It contains poetry. It contains parables, visions, figures, metaphors, types, and prophetic imagery. A reverent reader must honor those forms. When Jesus says, "I am the door," we do not imagine Him made of wood and hinges. When the Psalms say the mountains skipped like rams, we do not read them as a geological report. When Revelation describes beasts, horns, lampstands, and stars, we recognize symbolic features because the text itself signals them and often interprets them.

The issue is not whether figurative language exists. It clearly does.

The issue is whether figurative language gives interpreters permission to abandon stable meaning.

It does not.

A metaphor means something. A symbol points to something. A parable teaches something. A type anticipates something. Apocalyptic imagery communicates truth, even when that truth is conveyed through vision and symbol. The proper response to figurative language is not imaginative freedom, but careful interpretation. We ask what the image means from the text, from its context, and from the patterns Scripture itself establishes.

God's use of symbols does not make His speech less truthful. It means truth is sometimes communicated through symbol.

That distinction must be guarded.

Too often, "symbolic" becomes a convenient word for "not binding in its ordinary force." A promise becomes symbolic when its concrete fulfillment is inconvenient. A prophecy becomes spiritualized when its details resist a favored system. A passage becomes allegorical not because the text warrants it, but because its plain sense is theologically disruptive. The result is not a richer handling of Scripture. It is a loosening of Scripture from the character of the God who speaks.

God is not honored when we treat His words as though precision were beneath Him.

The prophets repeatedly ground their authority in the fact that the Lord has spoken. Isaiah begins oracles with "Thus saith the LORD." Jeremiah declares the words God puts in his mouth. Ezekiel repeatedly hears, "Son of man, say unto them." The prophets do not present themselves as poets offering suggestive religious possibilities. They deliver the Word of God.

That is why the failure of prophecy would implicate God's character. Moses gives Israel a test:

"When a prophet speaketh in the name of the LORD, if the thing follow not, nor come to pass, that is the thing which the LORD hath not spoken, but the

prophet hath spoken it presumptuously: thou shalt not be afraid of him.” — **Deuteronomy 18:22**

The standard assumes that when God makes a predictive declaration, fulfillment matters. Prophecy is not protected from testing by making its terms endlessly malleable. If the word does not come to pass, the prophet has not spoken for God.

The same principle is visible in the repeated refrain, "that ye may know that I am the LORD." God foretells, acts, and then declares the result a revelation of His identity. His words and His works correspond because He is true.

Through Isaiah, the Lord says:

"Remember the former things of old: for I am God, and there is none else; I am God, and there is none like me, Declaring the end from the beginning, and from ancient times the things that are not yet done, saying, My counsel shall stand, and I will do all my pleasure." — **Isaiah 46:9–10**

God's uniqueness is displayed in His ability to declare and accomplish. He announces the end from the beginning because His counsel stands. His word does not drift. His purpose does not fail. His foretelling and His fulfillment agree.

This gives prophecy theological weight. It is not merely information about the future. It is revelation of God's character. Fulfilled prophecy demonstrates that He knows, speaks, governs, and keeps His Word. Future prophecy rests upon the same character. The certainty of Christ's return, resurrection, judgment, kingdom, and restoration does not depend on human calculation. It rests upon the God who cannot lie.

Paul begins Titus with that very foundation:

"In hope of eternal life, which God, that cannot lie, promised before the world began." — **Titus 1:2**

Hope exists because God cannot lie. Promise has force because God's character gives it force.

This is why the way we interpret promises matters. A promise from God is not merely a religious impression that later interpreters may reshape at will. It is speech from the truthful God. The form of fulfillment may sometimes be greater than the original hearers understood. Scripture itself shows that. The promise of a seed to Abraham unfolds across Isaac, Israel, Christ, and all who are in Christ. The Davidic covenant reaches its ultimate glory in the Messiah. The sacrificial system contains patterns fulfilled in the cross. But greater fulfillment does not mean unrelated fulfillment. Fulfillment may expand, deepen, and glorify the promise. It does not make God's original words misleading.

When God promises David a son who will sit upon his throne, the fulfillment in Christ does not erase Davidic kingship. It secures it in its highest form. When God promises a new covenant with the house of Israel and the house of Judah, the participation of Gentile believers in new covenant blessings does not require that the stated covenant people disappear from the promise. When God speaks of resurrection, the spiritual life believers receive now does not cancel the bodily resurrection still to come.

God's revelation has coherence. Later Scripture sheds light on earlier Scripture, but it does not turn truth into its opposite. Development is not contradiction. Fulfillment is not cancellation disguised in theological language.

This is where a doctrine of God becomes a guardrail for interpretation.

If God is faithful, He keeps His promises. If God is truthful, He does not mislead. If God is wise, His revelation is purposeful. If God is orderly, His Word has coherence rather than chaos. If God is not the author of confusion, then our theology should not depend upon turning plain declarations into meanings no ordinary reader could have reasonably drawn from the text.

That final sentence must be handled carefully. Scripture contains truths that were not fully understood by the first hearers. The prophets themselves searched what the Spirit of Christ in them signified when He testified beforehand of Christ's sufferings and the glory that should follow. The disciples heard Jesus predict His death and resurrection and still did not understand. Progressive revelation is real. God often says more than His people initially grasp.

But saying **more** is not the same as meaning **the reverse**.

A promise may contain depths not yet seen. A prophecy may be fulfilled in stages. A type may carry significance beyond what the historical participants understood. Yet if later interpretation makes the original statement functionally untrue, the interpreter should pause. The God who speaks may exceed initial understanding. He does not betray it.

Jesus' use of Scripture confirms this.

When the Sadducees denied the resurrection, Jesus did not correct them by claiming that the Old Testament was too fluid to support doctrinal certainty. He took them to God's words at the burning bush:

*"But as touching the resurrection of the dead, have ye not read that which was spoken unto you by God, saying, I am the God of Abraham, and the God of Isaac, and the God of Jacob? God is not the God of the dead, but of the living." — **Matthew 22:31–32***

His argument depends on the exact force of the present tense: "I am." Abraham, Isaac, and Jacob are not annihilated. God remains their God. Christ expects Scripture's wording to sustain close reasoning because Scripture is the Word of God.

When tempted by Satan, Jesus answers with specific texts from Deuteronomy. He does not treat them as vague spiritual suggestions. They have fixed meaning and governing authority:

"It is written, Man shall not live by bread alone, but by every word that proceedeth out of the mouth of God." — **Matthew 4:4**

Every word matters because it comes from God.

When the Pharisees sought to weaken the permanence of marriage, Jesus returned to the creation account:

"Have ye not read, that he which made them at the beginning made them male and female, And said, For this cause shall a man leave father and mother, and shall cleave to his wife: and they twain shall be one flesh?" — *Matthew 19:4–5*

He treats Genesis as authoritative, meaningful, and determinative. The words given at creation still govern the doctrine of marriage. Jesus does not approach Scripture as a collection of elastic symbols awaiting reinterpretation by religious experts. He receives it as the speech of God.

This should shape us.

There is a kind of interpretation that prides itself on sophistication because it refuses to be bound by the most natural sense of the text. It sees hidden layers everywhere, even where Scripture gives no warrant for them. It mistrusts straightforward readings as though clarity were spiritually inferior. It can turn any historical event into an allegory, any prophecy into an abstraction, any promise into a metaphor. In doing so, it often claims to reach "deeper" meaning. But depth that abandons the text is not depth. It is displacement.

The early church fathers sometimes read Scripture with rich typological instincts, and genuine typology absolutely belongs in Christian interpretation because the New Testament itself teaches it. Adam is a figure of Christ. The Passover lamb points to Christ. The bronze serpent is taken up by Jesus as a picture of His lifting up. The tabernacle and sacrifices bear witness to greater realities fulfilled in Him. Scripture is filled with patterns designed by God.

But biblical typology differs from uncontrolled allegory.

Typology grows from real historical persons, events, and institutions that God sovereignly shaped to anticipate later fulfillment. It does not deny their historical meaning. It builds upon it. Adam must be a real man in a real history for his relationship to Christ in Romans 5 to matter. The exodus must be a real deliverance for Paul's use of Israel's wilderness history in 1 Corinthians 10 to carry moral force. The sacrificial system must have meant what Leviticus says it meant before it can anticipate Christ.

Allegorization becomes dangerous when it treats the surface meaning as expendable and replaces it with a spiritual meaning disconnected from textual controls. At that point, the interpreter's imagination begins to govern the Bible rather than the Bible governing the interpreter.

God's character should make us wary of that.

A God of truth is not honored by interpretations that make His words say whatever the reader needs them to say. A God of order is not glorified by doctrinal chaos presented as profundity. A God who speaks meaningfully should not be handled as though His revelation were a puzzle box meant to conceal rather than communicate.

The Lord rebuked Israel for refusing to hear what He had plainly said. Through Jeremiah, He said:

"But this thing commanded I them, saying, Obey my voice, and I will be your God, and ye shall be my people: and walk ye in all the ways that I have commanded you, that it may be well unto you. But they hearkened not, nor inclined their ear, but walked in the counsels and in the imagination of their evil heart, and went backward, and not forward." — **Jeremiah 7:23–24**

The problem was not that God's command had been impossible to decipher. The problem was that the people would not listen. Often, what we call interpretive complexity is actually moral resistance. A command becomes "unclear" when obedience is costly. A promise becomes "symbolic" when its fulfillment is unwelcome. A warning becomes "culturally conditioned" when its force confronts the age.

That does not mean every disagreement arises from rebellion. Serious and faithful interpreters differ on many difficult matters. Charity is necessary. Humility is necessary. But the existence of legitimate complexity should not be used to deny the clarity of what God has made clear.

Moses told Israel:

"The secret things belong unto the LORD our God: but those things which are revealed belong unto us and to our children for ever, that we may do all the words of this law." — **Deuteronomy 29:29**

There are secret things. We should not pretend otherwise. God has not answered every question curiosity may ask. There are dimensions of His counsel we cannot enter. Yet the things revealed are truly revealed, and they are given for faithfulness. Revelation creates responsibility.

The proper response to difficult passages is not to flatten them into our assumptions. It is to study more carefully. The proper response to clear passages is not to complicate them until they lose authority. It is to obey.

This chapter has a special place in a book about the full character of God because interpretation is never detached from theology. Our view of God influences the way we read His Word. If He is mostly a projection of human religious aspiration, then Scripture can be revised. If He is true but not especially precise, then promises may be handled loosely. If He is gracious but not holy, then warnings may be softened. If He is faithful but His speech is indefinitely symbolic, then fulfillment becomes difficult to evaluate.

But if He is the God Scripture reveals—truthful, wise, faithful, orderly, and not the author of confusion—then His Word must be approached with reverence. We do not make it simpler than it is. We do not make it more obscure than it is. We do not deny figures of speech. We do not impose them where the text does not invite them. We do not reject mystery. We do not use mystery as cover for interpretive lawlessness.

God says what He means. And because He is God, what He means matters.

The clarity of Scripture is not the claim that every reader instantly understands every passage. It is the confidence that God has spoken adequately, truly, and purposefully. His Word is sufficient to make wise the simple, to give light to the eyes, to teach doctrine, to expose error, to correct the wandering, and to furnish the man of God for every good work. It can accomplish that because it is not confusion from man. It is revelation from God.

The church needs this conviction. Without it, doctrine becomes untethered. Preaching becomes impressionistic. Prophecy becomes endlessly elastic. Promises become difficult to trust. The average believer begins to assume that Scripture's meaning is locked away behind technical systems only experts can access. In time, reverence gives way either to dependence on authorities who claim secret insight or to fatigue that stops expecting clarity at all.

Neither outcome reflects the God who speaks.

He gave His Word to be read, preached, believed, obeyed, and treasured. He speaks through law, history, wisdom, prophecy, Gospel, epistle, and apocalypse. Each form must be honored according to its nature. Yet beneath all those forms is one truthful God, one coherent revelation, and one divine purpose moving through Scripture toward Christ, judgment, redemption, and glory.

- The God of Scripture is not confused.
- His revelation is not careless.
- His promises are not empty.
- His words are not disposable.

Those truths will matter repeatedly in the chapters ahead. They will matter when we speak of His truthfulness. They will matter when we consider His faithfulness to covenant promises. They will matter when we examine how divine character protects doctrine from distortion. And they matter now, at the foundation, because we cannot recover the whole biblical vision of God while treating His own self-revelation as though its meaning were endlessly negotiable.

The God who made a world of order has given a Word of truth.

We honor Him by listening carefully.

PART THREE

The Full
Character of God

Chapter 11 — One God, Perfect in All His Ways

God is not divided within Himself.

That truth must stand before us before we begin examining His attributes one by one. A book on the character of God can easily create the wrong impression if we are not careful. When we speak of His holiness, justice, mercy, love, faithfulness, wisdom, wrath, and goodness in separate chapters, we do so because human minds need order in study. We consider one perfection at a time so that we may see it more clearly. But God does not possess His attributes the way a man possesses traits that can rise and fall, compete for prominence, or appear unevenly from one moment to the next.

God is always fully Himself.

He is not loving in one act and just in another as though love and justice take turns governing Him. He is not merciful until His patience runs out and then, for a time, becomes wrathful instead. He is not sovereign when displaying power and gentle when stooping in compassion, as though different portions of His character emerge depending on the circumstance.

Every act of God is the act of the whole God.

- His mercy is holy mercy.
- His justice is good justice.
- His wrath is righteous wrath.
- His patience is sovereign patience.
- His love is truthful love.
- His judgment is wise judgment.

The distinctions we make are real. God's mercy is not identical in meaning to His justice. His omniscience is not the same concept as His omnipotence. His holiness and His goodness are not merely interchangeable terms.

Scripture uses different words because there are different truths to receive. Yet those truths never exist in isolation from one another within God. They are not parts assembled into a whole. They are the many perfections of the one undivided God.

Moses says:

"He is the Rock, his work is perfect: for all his ways are judgment: a God of truth and without iniquity, just and right is he." — **Deuteronomy 32:4**

The verse moves from God's perfection to His works, His ways, His truth, His freedom from iniquity, and His justice. It does not present these as separate realities struggling to coexist. Because God is perfect, His work is perfect. Because He is true and without iniquity, His ways are just and right. What He does accords with who He is.

The same conviction appears in the psalms:

"The LORD is righteous in all his ways, and holy in all his works." — **Psalm 145:17**

All His ways. All His works.

There is no corner of divine action that falls outside His righteousness. There is no hidden activity in which His holiness disappears. Creation, providence, judgment, deliverance, discipline, covenant, incarnation, cross, resurrection, and final restoration all proceed from the same perfect God. He does nothing unworthy of Himself.

This matters because many errors arise from imagining tension inside God that Scripture does not place there.

Some speak as though God's love inclines Him to save, while His justice resists that desire. In that telling, the cross becomes a kind of internal settlement between opposing divine impulses. Mercy wants one thing. Justice demands another. Christ's death allows mercy to prevail without completely offending justice.

But Scripture does not describe God that way.

The Father's love sends the Son. The Son's obedience fulfills the Father's will. The Spirit participates in the offering of Christ. The cross is not the resolution of a conflict within God. It is the unified display of His character. Love does not defeat justice there. Justice does not reluctantly make room for mercy. God is just and the justifier because the cross manifests both without division.

Paul says:

"But God commendeth his love toward us, in that, while we were yet sinners, Christ died for us." — **Romans 5:8**

And he says:

"Whom God hath set forth to be a propitiation through faith in his blood, to declare his righteousness for the remission of sins that are past, through the forbearance of God; To declare, I say, at this time his righteousness: that he might be just, and the justifier of him which believeth in Jesus." — **Romans 3:25–26**

The same cross commends God's love and declares God's righteousness. It does not show two attributes negotiating with one another. It shows one God acting in perfect harmony with Himself.

The problem lies not in God, but in us. We understand truth in sequence. We emphasize one point and then another. We isolate an attribute for study, then attempt to relate it to the others. We are finite. We reason through distinctions. God is not finite. He does not move from partial awareness to fuller awareness. He does not deliberate because one perfection might undermine another. He does not discover the balance between mercy and justice. He is eternally, perfectly, infinitely all that He is.

This is one reason human analogies can mislead when applied to God without care. A man may be loving but unjust, patient but cowardly, strong but cruel, principled but unmerciful. Human traits often exist in tension because human beings are morally inconsistent. A judge may struggle between compassion for an offender and obligation to uphold the law. A parent may discipline too harshly in anger or fail to discipline at all from misplaced softness. A ruler may exercise power without wisdom or show kindness without courage.

God is not like that.

His perfections do not correct deficiencies in one another because there are no deficiencies to correct. His mercy does not soften an otherwise excessive justice. His justice does not restrain a mercy that would otherwise become lawless. His wisdom does not keep His power from becoming reckless, as though omnipotence needed supervision. The language of correction belongs to us, not to Him. God is always wholly perfect in every perfection.

James writes:

"Every good gift and every perfect gift is from above, and cometh down from the Father of lights, with whom is no variableness, neither shadow of turning." — **James 1:17**

There is no instability in God. No shifting light. No moral fluctuation. No shadowed region of character where He becomes less than what He has declared Himself to be. His gifts are good because He is good, and His goodness does not vary.

That truth gives firmness to worship. We do not praise a God whose character must be watched nervously lest one side overwhelm another. We praise the God whose whole being is worthy of trust. His tenderness will never become indulgence. His wrath will never become injustice. His sovereignty will never become tyranny. His patience will never become moral apathy. His faithfulness will never become rigidity detached from goodness. Everything in Him is perfect because He is perfect.

When Scripture says:

"As for God, his way is perfect: the word of the LORD is tried: he is a buckler to all those that trust in him." — **Psalm 18:30**

It places His perfect way, His tested Word, and the safety of trusting Him together. Because God's way is perfect, His Word can be trusted. Because His Word can be trusted, His people may flee to Him for refuge. The integrity of God's character is the foundation of confidence.

It is also the foundation of doctrine.

A doctrinal system that requires God to act inconsistently with Himself should be examined carefully. If an interpretation makes His faithfulness unstable, His truthfulness elusive, His justice careless, or His covenant love self-contradictory, something is wrong. That does not mean every difficult doctrine can be dismissed because it initially strains our instincts. Scripture frequently confronts instinct. But it does mean that theology must remain coherent with the character of the God Scripture reveals.

God's perfection is not an abstract premise floating above the Bible. It is repeatedly declared within the Bible and displayed through His works. Abraham appealed to it when he asked:

"Shall not the Judge of all the earth do right?" — **Genesis 18:25**

He did not understand every dimension of God's impending judgment upon Sodom, but he knew the character of the Judge. God would not destroy the righteous with the wicked as though moral distinctions were irrelevant. His justice would be righteous justice.

Moses appealed to God's character when Israel sinned with the golden calf. He pleaded that the Lord's name not be dishonored among the Egyptians and that His covenant promises to Abraham, Isaac, and Israel be remembered. Moses did not appeal to a sentimental mercy detached from holiness. He appealed to the Lord as the God whose name, promise, and glory were bound up with His treatment of His people.

The prophets appealed to God's character when calling Israel to repentance. Joel does not say that God may perhaps become merciful if the people persuade Him. He says:

*"turn unto the LORD your God: for he is gracious and merciful, slow to anger, and of great kindness, and repenteth him of the evil." — **Joel 2:13***

Repentance is encouraged by the known character of God. The sinner is not invited to guess what kind of God he may find. He is called to return because the Lord has made Himself known.

The apostles reason the same way. John writes:

*"If we confess our sins, he is faithful and just to forgive us our sins, and to cleanse us from all unrighteousness." — **1 John 1:9***

Many readers expect John to say that God is merciful and gracious to forgive, and He is. But John says He is **faithful and just** to forgive. Forgiveness is not a violation of God's justice because Christ's work has dealt with sin. Nor is it uncertain, because God is faithful to His promise. The gospel rests upon the wholeness of His character.

This also guards us from a shallow reading of divine wrath. If wrath is considered apart from goodness, it can be misunderstood as divine volatility. Human anger often erupts from wounded pride, impatience, envy, or selfishness. God's wrath is nothing like that. His wrath is the holy revulsion of His righteous nature against evil. It is not less good than His mercy. It is one expression of His goodness toward what is morally real.

A God who never hated evil would not be good.

A God who never judged evil would not be just.

A God who never opposed evil would not be loving in any biblical sense.

When Scripture celebrates the Lord's coming to judge the earth, it does not treat judgment as a blemish upon divine glory. Psalm 98 calls the seas, floods, and hills to rejoice:

*"Before the LORD; for he cometh to judge the earth: with righteousness shall he judge the world, and the people with equity." — **Psalm 98:9***

Judgment is cause for rejoicing because the Judge is righteous. The world is not finally abandoned to oppression, deceit, violence, and death. God will set things right. His judgment belongs to His perfection.

The same fullness must shape how we understand His mercy. Mercy is not emotional softness. It is not God pretending that sin is harmless because He prefers reconciliation. Mercy is compassion extended by the holy God toward the guilty and miserable. Because He is just, mercy is astonishing. Because He is holy, forgiveness is weighty. Because He is truthful, His pardon can be trusted. Because He is sovereign, none can prevent Him from saving those upon whom He sets His grace.

The beauty of mercy is not that it suspends God's other perfections. It is that it flows from the God who is perfect in all of them.

This gives the full character of God a different feel from the way many people imagine theology. Theology is not the attempt to keep competing divine attributes in balance, as though God Himself were an unstable equation. It is the attempt to understand, as far as revelation permits, the harmony that already exists eternally in Him.

We do not make God coherent. He is coherent. We do not reconcile His perfections. They are reconciled because they were never divided. We do not solve a tension within His being. We learn to abandon tensions created by our incomplete perceptions.

This is not to deny that Scripture presents truths that stretch the mind. God is sovereign, and man is responsible. Christ is fully God and fully man. God is one, and God is Father, Son, and Holy Ghost. His kingdom is present in one sense and future in another. Believers are already sanctified and still being sanctified. These truths are not shallow. They require care. But difficulty in our understanding does not mean contradiction in God.

The Lord says through Isaiah:

*"For my thoughts are not your thoughts, neither are your ways my ways, saith the LORD. For as the heavens are higher than the earth, so are my ways higher than your ways, and my thoughts than your thoughts." — **Isaiah 55:8–9***

God's ways exceed ours, but they do not violate His character. They are higher, not incoherent. His wisdom surpasses us, but it is still wisdom. His judgments are unsearchable, but they are still righteous. His purposes may be hidden from us, but they are never morally disordered.

Paul reaches this point in Romans 11. After tracing God's dealings with Israel, the Gentiles, unbelief, mercy, hardening, and future restoration, he does not conclude that God's ways are contradictory. He worships:

*"O the depth of the riches both of the wisdom and knowledge of God! how unsearchable are his judgments, and his ways past finding out!" — **Romans 11:33***

The depths of God do not produce despair in Paul. They produce praise. He is not troubled that God is greater than his comprehension. He is amazed.

A full doctrine of God should do the same to us.

It should humble our confidence where Scripture has not spoken. It should strengthen our confidence where Scripture has spoken clearly. It should prevent us from reducing God to a set of manageable slogans. It should warn us against emphasizing one truth about Him until another revealed truth becomes difficult to maintain. It should rescue us from sentimentalism on one side and severity on the other. It should give us a God large enough to trust when His ways exceed our sight.

The unity of God's character also explains why the Christian life cannot be built around a selective pursuit of resemblance to Him. Believers are called to be holy because He is holy. They are called to be merciful because He is merciful. They are called to forgive because He forgives. They are called to walk in love because Christ loved them. They are called to speak truth because God is true. They are called to pursue justice, patience, kindness, and faithfulness because these reflect the character of the God whose children they are.

The imitation of God is never one-dimensional. A Christian who prizes truth while neglecting mercy does not resemble God as he should. A Christian who speaks constantly of love while disregarding holiness does not resemble God as he should. A church that emphasizes doctrinal precision but lacks compassion is malformed. A church that celebrates compassion while refusing doctrinal precision is also malformed. The full character of God becomes the measure of spiritual maturity.

Paul writes:

*"Be ye therefore followers of God, as dear children; And walk in love, as Christ also hath loved us, and hath given himself for us an offering and a sacrifice to God for a sweetsmelling savour." — **Ephesians 5:1–2***

The call to imitate God is immediately grounded in the love of Christ expressed through sacrifice. Yet the surrounding chapter also calls believers to flee fornication, uncleanness, covetousness, foolish talking, and fellowship with darkness. Love and holiness are not separated. God's children are to reflect both because God is both.

This book will now turn to examine His character in greater detail. We will speak of His holiness, glory, eternity, immutability, goodness, righteousness, justice, truth, faithfulness, love, mercy, grace, patience, kindness, knowledge, power, presence, wisdom, sovereignty, jealousy, and wrath. Each deserves careful attention. Each is revealed in Scripture. Each matters for worship, doctrine, and life.

But as we proceed, this chapter must remain in the background.

We are not moving through disconnected topics. We are beholding one God.

The God who is holy is the God who is merciful. The God who is wrathful against evil is the God who delights in mercy. The God who judges the world in righteousness is the God who sent His Son to save sinners. The God who cannot lie is the God who cannot fail. The God whose ways are past finding out is the God whose works are perfect.

He is one God, perfect in all His ways.

And everything that follows must be read in light of that.

Part Three — The Full Character of God

Chapter 12 — God Is Holy

Among all the words Scripture uses to describe God, few carry more weight than **holy**.

The Bible says that God is good. It says He is merciful. It says He is righteous, faithful, gracious, wise, and true. But when heavenly beings cry out before His throne, they do not say, "Merciful, merciful, merciful," or "Love, love, love," though He is perfectly merciful and He is love. They cry:

"Holy, holy, holy, is the LORD of hosts: the whole earth is full of his glory." — ***Isaiah 6:3***

The threefold repetition is not casual. In the Hebrew way of speaking, repetition intensifies. To say something twice adds emphasis. To say it three times lifts it to the highest expression. God is not merely holy. He is **holy, holy, holy**.

Yet the triple cry may invite another reflection as well. Read within Isaiah 6 itself, the emphasis falls upon the surpassing holiness of God. But read in light of the fuller revelation of Scripture, where the one true God is made known as Father, Son, and Holy Ghost, many Christian readers have also heard in this thrice-repeated praise a fitting echo of the Trinity. Isaiah 6:3 should not be made to carry the doctrine of the Trinity by itself. Still, it is not difficult to see why the worship of heaven—**"Holy, holy, holy"**—has so naturally been heard as praise suited to the triune God. The Father is holy. The Son is holy. The Spirit is holy. The one LORD is holy beyond measure.

This connection becomes even more striking when the New Testament refers back to Isaiah's vision. John, after quoting from Isaiah 6, says:

"These things said Esaias, when he saw his glory, and spake of him." — ***John 12:41***

In context, John is speaking of Christ. The Lord whom Isaiah saw high and lifted up is not a being other than the Son revealed in the Gospel. Isaiah's vision of divine glory belongs within the full biblical revelation of the triune God. The holy LORD of hosts is the God made known as Father, Son, and Holy Ghost.

The holiness of God is not a narrow doctrine tucked among His other attributes. It is one of the great governing truths of Scripture. It stands behind His glory, His moral perfection, His separation from sin, His judgments, His commands, His worship, His redemptive work, and the transformation He demands of His people.

Without holiness, God's love becomes sentiment. His grace becomes indulgence. His mercy becomes moral carelessness. His wrath becomes difficult to understand. His commands appear arbitrary. His judgment seems excessive. His worship grows casual. His presence becomes ordinary.

But Scripture never presents God as ordinary.

He is holy.

The Meaning of Holiness

The basic idea of holiness is **separation**. That definition is often stated, and rightly so, but it must not be left thin. God's holiness does not mean merely that He is "set apart" in a vague or spatial sense. He is set apart because He is utterly unlike all that is created, all that is finite, all that is morally corrupt, and all that is common.

- He is unique in being.
- He is incomparable in majesty.
- He is perfect in purity.
- He is untouched by evil.
- He belongs to a category occupied by Himself alone.

When Hannah prayed after the Lord gave her Samuel, she said: "There is none holy as the LORD: for there is none beside thee: neither is there any rock like our God." — **1 Samuel 2:2**

Notice how holiness is connected to God's incomparability: **"there is none beside thee."** His holiness is not merely moral cleanness, though it certainly includes that. It is His absolute uniqueness. No creature shares His mode of existence. No being rivals His glory. No one stands beside Him as equal.

Moses asked:

"Who is like unto thee, O LORD, among the gods? who is like thee, glorious in holiness, fearful in praises, doing wonders?" — ***Exodus 15:11***

God is **glorious in holiness**. His holiness is not cold sterility. It is radiant majesty. It is beauty so pure, so immense, so unlike the world, that it produces both praise and fear.

This distinction matters. People sometimes hear that God is holy and think only of moral restriction. Holiness becomes a list of prohibited behaviors, or a spiritual atmosphere drained of warmth and joy. Scripture gives us something far greater. God's holiness is the blazing perfection of His entire being. It is the beauty of His otherness. It is the moral splendor of who He is.

When we later speak of His love, mercy, justice, truth, wrath, and faithfulness, we must remember that each is holy. He does not merely possess holiness alongside other attributes. Everything in Him bears the quality of His holiness.

- His name is holy.
- His arm is holy.
- His habitation is holy.
- His way is holy.
- His Word is holy.

- His covenant is holy.
- His Spirit is holy.

Holiness belongs to God in a way it belongs to nothing else.

The Holy One of Israel

One of the most striking titles for God in the Old Testament is **"the Holy One of Israel."** It appears repeatedly, especially in Isaiah. The title joins God's utter transcendence with His covenant relationship to a particular people. He is not merely "the Holy One," distant and unreachable. He is **"the Holy One of Israel,"** the God who has set His love upon a people while remaining entirely unlike them.

Isaiah says:

*"Thus saith the LORD, thy Redeemer, the Holy One of Israel; I am the LORD thy God which teacheth thee to profit, which leadeth thee by the way that thou shouldest go." — **Isaiah 48:17***

The Holy One is also Redeemer. His holiness does not make redemption impossible. It makes redemption necessary and glorious. Israel's sin is not ignored because God is holy. Israel's salvation is not abandoned because God is holy. His holiness demands judgment upon sin, but His covenant faithfulness provides redemption according to His promise.

The title **"Holy One of Israel"** also exposes the ugliness of rebellion. Israel's sin is repeatedly described as provoking, despising, or turning away from the Holy One.

*"Ah sinful nation, a people laden with iniquity, a seed of evildoers, children that are corrupters: they have forsaken the LORD, they have provoked the Holy One of Israel unto anger, they are gone away backward." — **Isaiah 1:4***

Sin is not merely a bad choice in the abstract. It is revolt against the Holy One. The more clearly we see God's holiness, the more clearly we see the horror of sin. What appears small to us becomes grievous when placed against His purity.

This is one reason modern thought so easily trivializes sin. It has lost the holiness of God. Where God is reduced to vague benevolence, sin becomes chiefly harmful behavior, psychological woundedness, or social dysfunction. Those categories may describe some effects of sin, but they do not reach its heart. Sin is offensive because God is holy.

David understood this after his grievous fall. He had sinned against Bathsheba, against Uriah, against his own household, and against Israel. Yet in Psalm 51 he says to God:

*"Against thee, thee only, have I sinned, and done this evil in thy sight: that thou mightest be justified when thou speakest, and be clear when thou judgest." — **Psalm 51:4***

David is not denying the real damage done to others. He is locating sin at its deepest level. Every sin is ultimately against God because His holiness is the standard violated.

Isaiah Before the Holy God

No passage reveals the effect of divine holiness upon a human being more powerfully than Isaiah 6.

Isaiah writes:

*"In the year that king Uzziah died I saw also the Lord sitting upon a throne, high and lifted up, and his train filled the temple." — **Isaiah 6:1***

The earthly king is dead. The throne of Judah is shaken. Political uncertainty hangs in the background. But Isaiah is given a vision of a throne that is not empty, unstable, or threatened. The Lord sits above all earthly upheaval, high and lifted up.

Seraphim stand above Him:

"Above it stood the seraphims: each one had six wings; with twain he covered his face, and with twain he covered his feet, and with twain he did fly." — **Isaiah 6:2**

Even these sinless heavenly beings cover themselves before the Lord. They do not glance casually upon His majesty. Their posture conveys reverence. Then they cry:

"Holy, holy, holy, is the LORD of hosts: the whole earth is full of his glory." — **Isaiah 6:3**

The doorposts move. The house fills with smoke. The vision is overwhelming.

Isaiah's response is not curiosity. It is collapse.

"Then said I, Woe is me! for I am undone; because I am a man of unclean lips, and I dwell in the midst of a people of unclean lips: for mine eyes have seen the King, the LORD of hosts." — **Isaiah 6:5**

He does not compare himself favorably with other men. He does not note that he is a prophet, a servant of God, perhaps more righteous than many in Judah. The vision of holiness destroys all self-protective comparison. Standing before the Holy One, Isaiah sees himself truly.

This is what the holiness of God does. It strips away illusion.

The world trains us to measure ourselves horizontally. We compare sin with worse sin, pride with uglier pride, selfishness with more obvious selfishness. In that scale, many people imagine themselves decent. The holiness of God removes the false scale. It places man before the One who is pure in every thought, righteous in every judgment, and radiant in every perfection. Then the soul begins to understand.

Isaiah says, **"I am undone."** That is more than embarrassment. It is disintegration before majesty. He sees his uncleanness, and the particular point of conviction is his lips. The prophet's mouth, the instrument of his calling, is unclean. What appears strongest in him is still defiled when measured against God's holiness.

Yet the vision does not end with ruin.

*"Then flew one of the seraphims unto me, having a live coal in his hand, which he had taken with the tongs from off the altar: And he laid it upon my mouth, and said, Lo, this hath touched thy lips; and thine iniquity is taken away, and thy sin purged." — **Isaiah 6:6–7***

The Holy God who exposes sin also provides cleansing. He does not lower His holiness to make room for Isaiah. He purges Isaiah so that Isaiah may stand and serve. Grace does not bypass holiness. It answers the need holiness reveals.

Only after this cleansing does the call come:

*"Also I heard the voice of the Lord, saying, Whom shall I send, and who will go for us? Then said I, Here am I; send me." — **Isaiah 6:8***

Service follows purification. Commission follows cleansing. The sequence matters. No one truly serves the Holy One while remaining casual about sin. The God who sends His servants first teaches them to tremble before His glory and receive His cleansing.

Holiness and Moral Purity

God's holiness includes His absolute separation from sin. He is not morally mixed. He is not capable of evil. He is not tempted by sin, drawn toward corruption, or vulnerable to compromise.

James writes:

*"Let no man say when he is tempted, I am tempted of God: for God cannot be tempted with evil, neither tempteth he any man." — **James 1:13***

This verse protects the moral purity of God. He may test His people. Scripture clearly shows that He does. He tested Abraham. He proved Israel in the wilderness. Trials refine faith. But He never entices anyone into evil as though evil had any place in Himself. Sin does not originate in God. It arises from the creature's own lust and rebellion.

Habakkuk says:

"Thou art of purer eyes than to behold evil, and canst not look on iniquity…" **— Habakkuk 1:13**

The prophet's language does not mean God lacks awareness of evil. The entire book assumes that He sees it. The point is that God cannot look upon wickedness with approval. Evil is abhorrent to Him. He does not accommodate Himself morally to corruption. He does not become comfortable with what He condemns.

This truth should unsettle an age that treats moral categories as flexible. God does not revise holiness according to cultural preference. What He calls evil does not become good because a generation normalizes it. What He calls good does not become oppressive because a generation resents it. His holiness is fixed because He is fixed.

The Lord says:

"For I am the LORD, I change not…" **— Malachi 3:6**

That immutability applies to His moral character. God does not grow more tolerant of sin with time. He does not mature beyond former holiness. He does not look back upon His own commandments as relics of a less enlightened stage. The moral perfection revealed in Scripture reflects His unchanging nature.

This has enormous importance for doctrine and ethics. If God is holy, then holiness is not a social construct. Purity is not arbitrary. Righteousness is not merely preference. His commands arise from His character. He forbids adultery because covenant faithfulness reflects Him. He condemns falsehood because He is truth. He opposes idolatry because He alone is

God. He commands justice because He is just. He calls His people to mercy because He is merciful.

Morality is not external to God, as though He submits to a standard above Himself. Nor is morality arbitrary, as though good simply means whatever God might decide at any moment. Goodness, righteousness, and holiness are rooted in His own eternal character. He commands in keeping with who He is.

Holiness and Worship

The holiness of God demands reverent worship.

The psalmist says:

"Exalt ye the LORD our God, and worship at his footstool; for he is holy." — **Psalm 99:5**

And again:

"Exalt the LORD our God, and worship at his holy hill; for the LORD our God is holy." — **Psalm 99:9**

The reason for worship is not merely that God blesses us, rescues us, or gives us joy. We worship because He is holy. His being is worthy. His name deserves honor. His presence calls for reverence.

This is why Scripture so often ties worship to fear. The fear of the Lord is not a contradiction of love. It is the proper response of creatures before the Holy One. The redeemed do not fear condemnation, for there is no condemnation to them which are in Christ Jesus. But they do not outgrow reverence. Grace does not make God less holy. It brings us near to holiness through the blood of Christ.

Hebrews says:

"Wherefore we receiving a kingdom which cannot be moved, let us have grace, whereby we may serve God acceptably with reverence and godly fear: For our God is a consuming fire." — **Hebrews 12:28–29**

That passage is addressed to believers. The New Covenant does not dismiss reverence as an Old Testament emotion. It deepens it. Those who receive an unshakable kingdom should serve God with reverence and godly fear because the God they serve remains a consuming fire.

This should challenge the casualness that can creep into worship. God's people may come boldly to the throne of grace because Christ has opened the way. But boldness is not flippancy. Familiar access is not irreverence. The throne remains a throne. Grace remains grace precisely because the One who grants access is holy beyond comprehension.

The earthly worship of Israel was structured around this truth. The tabernacle and temple were not designed to create unnecessary distance for its own sake. They taught the holiness of God. There was a courtyard, a holy place, and a most holy place. Sacrifices were required. Priests were consecrated. Incense, washings, garments, altars, and restrictions all reinforced a single reality: sinful man does not stroll casually into the presence of the Holy One.

When Nadab and Abihu offered strange fire before the LORD, they were consumed:

"And Nadab and Abihu, the sons of Aaron, took either of them his censer, and put fire therein, and put incense thereon, and offered strange fire before the LORD, which he commanded them not. And there went out fire from the LORD, and devoured them, and they died before the LORD." — **Leviticus 10:1–2**

Then Moses said to Aaron:

"This is it that the LORD spake, saying, I will be sanctified in them that come nigh me, and before all the people I will be glorified." — **Leviticus 10:3**

The event is severe. It is meant to be. Those who draw near to God must regard Him as holy. Worship cannot be shaped by human creativity alone, as though sincerity were sufficient regardless of what God has commanded. He determines how He is to be approached.

The New Testament does not lessen this truth. Ananias and Sapphira lie to the Holy Ghost and fall dead in the early church. Paul warns the Corinthians that some among them are weak, sickly, and sleep because they partake of the Lord's Supper unworthily. God's grace in Christ does not make irreverence safe.

The holiness of God should make worship more joyful, not less. A God who is casual, changeable, and morally blurred cannot command awe. The Holy One can. His holiness gives worship its weight. His mercy gives worship its sweetness. We need both.

Holiness and the Law

God's holiness is also reflected in His law.

When the Lord gave commandments to Israel, He did not present obedience as an arbitrary test detached from His character. Again and again, He grounded their calling in who He is:

"For I am the LORD your God: ye shall therefore sanctify yourselves, and ye shall be holy; for I am holy…" — **Leviticus 11:44**

And again:

"Ye shall be holy: for I the LORD your God am holy." — **Leviticus 19:2**

The people of God are called to holiness because they belong to the Holy God. Their conduct is meant to reflect His character in creaturely form. They cannot share His infinite holiness, but they are to be set apart from corruption, devoted to Him, and obedient to His Word.

Peter applies this directly to Christians:

"But as he which hath called you is holy, so be ye holy in all manner of conversation; Because it is written, Be ye holy; for I am holy." — **I Peter 1:15–16**

The call to holiness does not disappear under grace. It becomes more urgent, because believers have been redeemed at the cost of Christ's precious blood. Peter continues:

"Forasmuch as ye know that ye were not redeemed with corruptible things, as silver and gold, from your vain conversation received by tradition from your fathers; But with the precious blood of Christ, as of a lamb without blemish and without spot." — **I Peter 1:18–19**

Redemption does not free us from holiness. It frees us for holiness.

This must be stated clearly because grace is often misunderstood. Grace is not God's agreement to ignore the moral transformation of His people. Grace pardons, cleanses, teaches, disciplines, and trains. Paul writes:

"For the grace of God that bringeth salvation hath appeared to all men, Teaching us that, denying ungodliness and worldly lusts, we should live soberly, righteously, and godly, in this present world." — **Titus 2:11–12**

Grace teaches holiness because grace comes from the Holy God.

Any version of Christianity that treats holiness as optional has misunderstood the God of the gospel. Any gospel that says Christ saves from hell while leaving the sinner unaltered in love for sin is not the apostolic gospel. The God who justifies also sanctifies. The Christ who forgives also says, **"Go, and sin no more."** The Spirit who comforts is the **Holy** Spirit.

Holiness and the Atonement

The holiness of God explains why the atonement was necessary.

If God were merely benevolent in a sentimental sense, sin could perhaps be dismissed by divine generosity. He could simply declare forgiveness with no sacrifice, no cross, no blood, no judgment upon sin. But God is holy. His forgiveness cannot be the denial of His own moral perfection.

The sacrificial system in the Old Testament trained Israel to understand that sin brings defilement, separation, and death. The altar was not theater. Blood mattered because life had been forfeited. The book of Hebrews says:

"And almost all things are by the law purged with blood; and without shedding of blood is no remission." — **Hebrews 9:22**

This does not mean animal blood could finally take away sins. Hebrews explicitly says it could not. Those sacrifices pointed forward. They taught the seriousness of sin and prepared for the once-for-all offering of Christ.

The cross reveals holiness more fully than Sinai.

At Calvary, God does not relax His righteousness. He pours judgment upon sin in the person of the willing substitute. Isaiah foretold:

"But he was wounded for our transgressions, he was bruised for our iniquities: the chastisement of our peace was upon him; and with his stripes we are healed." — **Isaiah 53:5**

And again:

"Yet it pleased the LORD to bruise him; he hath put him to grief: when thou shalt make his soul an offering for sin…" — **Isaiah 53:10**

Paul says God set Christ forth:

"to declare his righteousness for the remission of sins that are past, through the forbearance of God; To declare, I say, at this time his righteousness: that he might be just, and the justifier of him which believeth in Jesus." — **Romans 3:25–26**

The cross declares God's righteousness because forgiveness is not granted by ignoring sin. Sin is judged. Justice is satisfied. The Holy God saves sinners without ceasing to be holy.

This is why the love of God at the cross is so glorious. He does not love by becoming less holy. He loves at immeasurable cost while remaining perfectly holy. The blood of Christ does not persuade an otherwise unwilling God to become merciful. It is the very provision of the merciful God whose holiness required a righteous salvation.

Those who remove holiness from the gospel inevitably weaken the cross. If sin is not truly defiling, the cleansing blood of Christ seems excessive. If guilt is not real, substitution becomes difficult to defend. If God's holiness is muted, atonement loses its necessity. The cross can then be recast as example, solidarity, or public demonstration alone. Scripture gives us more. The cross is where divine holiness, justice, mercy, love, wisdom, and grace meet in the salvation of sinners.

Holiness and Judgment

The holiness of God also guarantees judgment.

The biblical God does not tolerate evil forever. His patience is vast, but it is not moral indifference. His mercy is real, but it does not abolish His opposition to sin. Because He is holy, wickedness cannot stand eternally unaddressed.

The seraphim of Isaiah 6 cry that the whole earth is full of God's glory. Yet Isaiah's commission immediately involves preaching to a hard-hearted people who will refuse to hear until judgment comes. The vision of holiness leads into a ministry of warning. God's glory does not render sin irrelevant. It makes sin intolerable.

Throughout Scripture, divine judgment arises from divine holiness. The flood, Babel, Sodom, the plagues of Egypt, the conquest judgments, the exile, the destruction of Jerusalem, and the final judgment all reveal that God is not morally neutral toward evil. Each judgment must be studied in context, but taken together they form an unmistakable witness: the Holy One judges.

Revelation gives the worship of heaven as God's judgments unfold:

*"And I heard another out of the altar say, Even so, Lord God Almighty, true and righteous are thy judgments." — **Revelation 16:7***

Heaven does not apologize for God's judgments. It declares them true and righteous.

This is difficult for modern ears because many have been taught to think that judgment is the opposite of goodness. Scripture teaches otherwise. A judge who refuses to condemn evil is not good. A ruler who allows violence, deception, exploitation, and rebellion to continue forever without answer is not loving. God's holiness ensures that evil has an end.

Final judgment is not a stain on divine character. It is the vindication of divine character before all creation.

That truth should produce fear in the unrepentant and comfort in the oppressed. The world's evils are not eternal. God sees. God remembers. God will judge. Every wrong not answered in history will be answered by the Judge of all the earth.

Holiness and the Fear of the Lord

The holiness of God gives depth to the fear of the Lord.

Scripture speaks constantly of this fear. It is the beginning of wisdom. It is clean, enduring forever. It leads men to depart from evil. It is associated with reverence, obedience, humility, and worship.

*"The fear of the LORD is the beginning of knowledge: but fools despise wisdom and instruction." — **Proverbs 1:7***

*"By the fear of the LORD men depart from evil." — **Proverbs 16:6***

*"Let all the earth fear the LORD: let all the inhabitants of the world stand in awe of him." — **Psalm 33:8***

The fear of the Lord is not irrational terror before a capricious deity. It is the proper response of creatures before the Holy One. It includes awe, humility, trembling, reverence, and the recognition that God is not to be handled lightly.

For the believer, this fear does not compete with love. In fact, love for God without reverence becomes sentimental familiarity. Reverence without love becomes distance. Scripture joins the two. The redeemed child of God loves the Father and fears His name. He draws near with confidence because of Christ, yet he does not forget who has granted the access.

The Lord says through Isaiah:

"But to this man will I look, even to him that is poor and of a contrite spirit, and trembleth at my word." — **Isaiah 66:2**

Trembling at God's Word is not spiritual immaturity. It is humility. The person who truly sees God's holiness does not treat revelation casually, does not play games with obedience, and does not approach Scripture as material to be manipulated.

This connects holiness to interpretation. If God is holy, His Word is holy. If His Word is holy, it should be handled with reverence. Careless allegorizing, doctrinal novelty pursued for its own sake, and selective obedience all become harder to justify when we remember whose words we are handling.

Holiness and Christ

The holiness of God is perfectly revealed in Jesus Christ.

The angel told Mary:

"The Holy Ghost shall come upon thee, and the power of the Highest shall overshadow thee: therefore also that holy thing which shall be born of thee shall be called the Son of God." — **Luke 1:35**

Jesus is holy from conception. He is not made holy by later obedience. He enters the world unstained. Demons recognize Him and cry:

"Let us alone; what have we to do with thee, thou Jesus of Nazareth? art thou come to destroy us? I know thee who thou art, the Holy One of God." — **Mark 1:24**

Peter later says to the people of Israel:

"But ye denied the Holy One and the Just, and desired a murderer to be granted unto you." — **Acts 3:14**

The title belongs to Christ because He shares the holiness of God.

His life displays it. He touches lepers without becoming unclean. He eats with sinners without participating in sin. He moves through a corrupt world without inward contamination. He is tempted in all points like as we are, yet without sin. He speaks truth without deceit. He loves without selfishness. He obeys the Father without hesitation. His righteousness is not merely outward conformity. It is perfect holiness in thought, desire, word, and act.

At the cross, His holiness is not compromised. He bears sin, yet He is not sinful. Peter writes:

"Who did no sin, neither was guile found in his mouth." — **1 Peter 2:22**

He is the spotless Lamb. Only a holy substitute could bear the sins of others. If Christ were guilty, His death would answer only for Himself. Because He is holy, His sacrifice is sufficient for sinners.

His resurrection also declares His holiness. Paul says He was:

"declared to be the Son of God with power, according to the spirit of holiness, by the resurrection from the dead." — **Romans 1:4**

Death could not hold the Holy One. Peter, preaching from Psalm 16, says:

"Because thou wilt not leave my soul in hell, neither wilt thou suffer thine Holy One to see corruption." — **Acts 2:27**

Christ's holiness is central to His person and work. He reveals the Holy God not only by what He says, but by who He is.

The Holiness of God and the Hope of His People

For sinners, the holiness of God is terrifying apart from grace. Isaiah is undone. Israel trembles at Sinai. The men of Beth-shemesh ask, **"Who is able to stand before this holy LORD God?"** Peter falls at Jesus' knees and says, **"Depart from me; for I am a sinful man, O Lord."**

But for the redeemed, holiness becomes part of their hope.

God does not merely forgive His people and leave them forever entangled in corruption. He intends to make them holy. Paul says Christ loved the church and gave Himself for it:

"That he might sanctify and cleanse it with the washing of water by the word, That he might present it to himself a glorious church, not having spot, or wrinkle, or any such thing; but that it should be holy and without blemish." — **Ephesians 5:26–27**

The holiness of God, which exposes sin, also defines the destiny of the saints. They will be made fit for His presence. They will be purified. They will see His face without shrinking back in guilt. Revelation says of the New Jerusalem:

"And there shall in no wise enter into it any thing that defileth, neither whatsoever worketh abomination, or maketh a lie: but they which are written in the Lamb's book of life." — **Revelation 21:27**

That exclusion is not grim. It is glorious. A world free from defilement is the world our hearts long for even when we do not know how to name it. No lie. No exploitation. No hidden cruelty. No corruption. No betrayal. No uncleanness. Nothing that wounds love or profanes goodness. The final dwelling of God with man is holy because God is holy.

The believer's sanctification now is preparation for that world. Holiness is not merely a command laid upon us; it is the shape of our coming joy. Sin promises freedom but produces ruin. Holiness appears costly in the present but belongs to life, peace, clarity, and communion with God. The command to be holy is not God withholding happiness. It is God calling His people toward the only kind of life that can flourish in His presence.

The God We Must Not Diminish

The holiness of God is often the first attribute lost when people try to make Him easier to accept. It is not always denied outright. More often, it is softened. God is said to be loving, but the love being described no longer hates evil. He is said to forgive, but forgiveness no longer requires repentance or atonement. He is said to welcome, but welcome is detached from transformation. He is said to be near, but nearness is emptied of reverence.

Once holiness recedes, the whole doctrine of God begins to blur.

- Sin becomes smaller.
- Grace becomes cheaper.
- The cross becomes less necessary.
- Worship becomes less weighty.
- Scripture becomes easier to negotiate.
- Judgment becomes embarrassing.
- Sanctification becomes optional.

The church cannot recover the full character of God without recovering His holiness.

We must hear the seraphim again. We must stand with Isaiah in the temple. We must let the smoke fill the room, the thresholds shake, and the cry of heaven silence every casual thought about God. We must see that His holiness does not diminish His mercy. It gives mercy its brilliance. It does not make grace less beautiful. It makes grace astonishing. It does not turn judgment into cruelty. It proves that evil will not have the final word.

- God is holy.
- There is none like Him.
- There is no impurity in Him.

There is no shadow of corruption in His thoughts, no flaw in His judgments, no blemish in His works.

- His love is holy.
- His mercy is holy.
- His wrath is holy.
- His promises are holy.
- His name is holy.

And because He is holy, everything else we say about Him must be spoken with reverence.

Chapter 13 — God Is Glorious

God is not merely good. He is glorious.

That word can become familiar enough to lose its force. Christians speak of the glory of God in songs, prayers, sermons, and casual expressions of praise. Yet Scripture uses the term with immense weight. God's glory is not a decorative quality attached to His being. It is the splendor of who He is made known. It is the visible, knowable, worship-commanding display of His infinite worth, majesty, holiness, beauty, and excellence.

God's glory is what His holiness looks like when it shines.

When Moses asked to see God's glory, the Lord answered by proclaiming His name and declaring His character:

*"And he said, I beseech thee, shew me thy glory. And he said, I will make all my goodness pass before thee, and I will proclaim the name of the LORD before thee; and will be gracious to whom I will be gracious, and will shew mercy on whom I will shew mercy." — **Exodus 33:18–19***

That answer is revealing. Moses asks for glory. God speaks of His goodness, His name, His grace, and His mercy. Then in Exodus 34, as we have already seen, He proclaims Himself merciful, gracious, longsuffering, abundant in goodness and truth, forgiving sin, and yet by no means clearing the guilty.

The glory of God is not empty radiance. It is the splendor of His character.

That does not mean His glory is merely an idea. Scripture often presents it with visible majesty: fire, cloud, brightness, smoke, a throne high and lifted up, light that overwhelms human sight. But these manifestations are glorious because they belong to the God whose being is infinitely excellent. The outward display corresponds to the inward perfection.

A lesser being clothed in brightness would not become glorious in the biblical sense. God's glory is not costume. It is the proper revelation of who He already is.

The Weight of Glory

In the Old Testament, the word commonly translated **glory** carries the sense of weight, heaviness, or worth. To speak of God's glory is to speak of His incomparable significance. He is not light, trivial, or common. He is not one concern among many. He is the One before whom all other concerns find their true size.

When Eli's daughter-in-law heard that the ark of God had been taken by the Philistines, she named her newborn son Ichabod, saying:

"The glory is departed from Israel: because the ark of God was taken." — I Samuel 4:22

The ark itself was not God, but it represented His covenant presence among His people. Its capture signaled something catastrophic. Israel had treated God lightly, and now the sign of His presence was gone from the camp. The tragedy was not merely military defeat. It was the departure of glory.

That story exposes a danger that remains. Men often measure loss by visible circumstances—money, influence, stability, comfort, victory. Scripture teaches us to ask a deeper question: **Has the glory of God become small in our eyes?**

A church may retain activity, budgets, programs, and public recognition while losing its sense of divine weight. A believer may remain outwardly religious while God's majesty no longer governs his choices. A theological system may become intricate and impressive while the glory of God quietly fades from the center.

Once God is treated as light, everything else becomes disordered.

Sin seems manageable. Worship becomes casual. Doctrine becomes negotiable. Human approval becomes more pressing than divine honor. The fear of the Lord gives way to the fear of man. That is why the glory of

God is not a secondary subject. To recover the full character of God, we must recover His weight.

The Heavens Declare His Glory

Scripture first directs our eyes outward.

"The heavens declare the glory of God; and the firmament sheweth his handywork." — **Psalm 19:1**

Creation is not divine, but it is revelatory. The heavens do not explain the gospel. They do not declare the incarnation, the cross, or the resurrection. But they do proclaim that the God who made them is powerful, wise, beautiful, and worthy of awe.

The sheer scale of the universe humbles man. The constellations stretch beyond his reach. The sun rises without consulting him. Seasons continue whether kings reign or kingdoms fall. The world bears marks of order, abundance, and design. Creation says something about its Maker. It is not self-explanatory. It points beyond itself.

Paul writes:

"For the invisible things of him from the creation of the world are clearly seen, being understood by the things that are made, even his eternal power and Godhead; so that they are without excuse." — **Romans 1:20**

The created order reveals enough of God's glory to render human suppression of truth inexcusable. Men may refuse to worship, but they do not refuse in darkness untouched by revelation. The world they inhabit testifies against them.

This is why idolatry is so offensive. It exchanges the glory of the incorruptible God for images of corruptible creatures:

"And changed the glory of the uncorruptible God into an image made like to corruptible man, and to birds, and fourfooted beasts, and creeping things." — **Romans 1:23**

The problem with idolatry is not only that it worships the wrong object. It lowers God. It trades infinite glory for something made. It takes the One whose glory fills heaven and earth and represents Him through what depends entirely upon Him for existence.

All false worship diminishes God.

Modern idolatry may not bow before carved animals, but it still exchanges glory. It places human desire, political power, self-expression, wealth, sexuality, national identity, or even religious tradition where God alone belongs. Whatever becomes ultimate in the heart functions as an idol. It receives weight that belongs to God.

The cure is not merely better moral discipline. It is a renewed sight of glory. Lesser things lose their false greatness when God is seen as He is.

The Glory That Fills the Earth

The seraphim in Isaiah 6 do not merely cry that God is holy. They add:

*"the whole earth is full of his glory." — **Isaiah 6:3***

That statement may seem surprising. Isaiah is living in a nation marked by corruption, injustice, and coming judgment. The earth does not appear full of glory to ordinary sight. Yet heaven sees what earth often misses. God's glory is not absent because sinners refuse to acknowledge it. The world remains His. His wisdom, power, providence, judgment, patience, and purposes are everywhere at work.

Habakkuk looks ahead to a day when this glory will be universally recognized:

*"For the earth shall be filled with the knowledge of the glory of the LORD, as the waters cover the sea." — **Habakkuk 2:14***

The glory already belongs to God. The future promise is that the knowledge of that glory will fill the earth openly and unmistakably. Rebellion will not have the final word. Ignorance will not endure forever. The day is coming when God's worth will be known on a scale creation has not yet seen.

This promise is echoed in Numbers 14:21:

"But as truly as I live, all the earth shall be filled with the glory of the LORD."
— Numbers 14:21

God swears by His own life. His glory will fill the earth. Human rebellion may delay the visible triumph of that glory in history, but it cannot prevent it. The purposes of God do not finally bend before unbelief.

This has implications for prophecy, mission, and hope. The future of the world is not the endless triumph of disorder. It is the public vindication of God's glory. The nations will not forever rage without answer. The name of the LORD will be exalted. The kingdom of Christ will not remain hidden. Every knee shall bow. Every tongue shall confess that Jesus Christ is Lord, to the glory of God the Father.

God Acts for His Glory

One of the clearest biblical truths, and one often neglected in modern theology, is that God acts for His own glory.

Human beings tend to become uncomfortable with this. If a man constantly seeks his own praise, we call it vanity, because no man is worthy of ultimate praise. Self-exaltation in a creature is ugly because it claims a weight the creature does not possess. But God is not a creature. He alone is infinitely worthy. For Him to prize His own glory above all else is not vanity. It is truth.

If God treated anything as more worthy than Himself, He would deny reality.

The Lord says through Isaiah:

"I am the LORD: that is my name: and my glory will I not give to another, neither my praise to graven images." **— Isaiah 42:8**

Again:

"For mine own sake, even for mine own sake, will I do it: for how should my name be polluted? and I will not give my glory unto another." — **Isaiah 48:11**

God's jealousy for His glory is not insecurity. It is righteousness. He knows His own worth truly. He knows that all good, beauty, truth, life, and blessedness flow from Him. To allow His glory to be permanently given to idols would be to permit a lie to stand at the center of reality.

This also explains why God's saving acts so often have His name and glory as their stated purpose.

When He promises to restore Israel after judgment, He says:

"Therefore say unto the house of Israel, Thus saith the Lord GOD; I do not this for your sakes, O house of Israel, but for mine holy name's sake, which ye have profaned among the heathen, whither ye went." — **Ezekiel 36:22**

He continues:

"And I will sanctify my great name, which was profaned among the heathen, which ye have profaned in the midst of them; and the heathen shall know that I am the LORD, saith the Lord GOD, when I shall be sanctified in you before their eyes." — **Ezekiel 36:23**

God's mercy toward Israel serves the vindication of His name. His faithfulness to covenant promises is bound up with His glory. If He abandoned His Word, the nations would misunderstand His character. When He restores, He displays who He is.

This is not a cold motive. It is the highest possible good. The glory of God and the good of His people are not enemies. His people are blessed precisely because He is glorified in faithfulness, mercy, power, and truth. Their salvation would lose its certainty if it rested finally on their worthiness. It stands firm because God acts for His name's sake.

David understood this:

"He restoreth my soul: he leadeth me in the paths of righteousness for his name's sake." — **Psalm 23:3**

The Shepherd guides His sheep for His name's sake. That does not make His care impersonal. It makes His care dependable. His reputation as a faithful Shepherd stands behind His leading.

The believer's hope is strengthened when he sees that God's purposes are anchored in God's glory. He will not fail to complete what He has purposed, because failure would contradict His own name.

The Glory of God in Judgment

Many people are willing to speak of God's glory in creation and salvation but hesitate to connect it with judgment. Scripture does not hesitate.

When God delivered Israel from Egypt, He repeatedly said He would get honor upon Pharaoh and upon his host:

"And I will harden Pharaoh's heart, that he shall follow after them; and I will be honoured upon Pharaoh, and upon all his host; that the Egyptians may know that I am the LORD." — **Exodus 14:4**

After the sea closed over Pharaoh's army, Moses and the children of Israel sang:

"Who is like unto thee, O LORD, among the gods? who is like thee, glorious in holiness, fearful in praises, doing wonders?" — **Exodus 15:11**

God's judgment upon Egypt revealed His glory because it revealed His holiness, justice, faithfulness to His oppressed people, and power over arrogant rulers. Pharaoh had exalted himself against the Lord. Judgment answered that rebellion.

The same pattern appears in Ezekiel's prophecies against Gog:

"And I will magnify myself, and sanctify myself; and I will be known in the eyes of many nations, and they shall know that I am the LORD." — **Ezekiel 38:23**

God's judgment magnifies His name. It shows that evil does not rival Him successfully. It shows that His patience is not weakness. It shows that His promises are not empty.

Revelation carries this theme to its final form. When Babylon falls, heaven rejoices:

*"Alleluia; Salvation, and glory, and honour, and power, unto the Lord our God: For true and righteous are his judgments: for he hath judged the great whore, which did corrupt the earth with her fornication, and hath avenged the blood of his servants at her hand." — **Revelation 19:1–2***

The glory of God is praised in connection with His righteous judgment. Heaven does not regard divine wrath as an embarrassment to be explained away. It sees what redeemed creatures on earth often struggle to remember: the judgment of God is glorious because it is true and righteous.

This truth must be held carefully. Human beings can speak of judgment crudely, vindictively, or with little evidence of sorrow over the lost. Such speech does not reflect the heart of God rightly. Yet the abuse of a doctrine does not justify its denial. God's glory is displayed when He saves. His glory is also displayed when He judges. Both are true because both proceed from His perfect character.

The Glory of God in Mercy

If judgment reveals God's glory, mercy reveals it no less.

When Moses asked to see God's glory, the Lord proclaimed His goodness and mercy. When Christ came into the world, the angels announced:

*"Glory to God in the highest, and on earth peace, good will toward men." — **Luke 2:14***

The incarnation is a display of divine glory. John writes:

"And the Word was made flesh, and dwelt among us, and we beheld his glory, the glory as of the only begotten of the Father, full of grace and truth." — **John 1:14**

Grace and truth again appear together, as goodness and truth did in Exodus 34. The glory of the Son is not simply brightness seen with natural eyes. Many looked upon Jesus during His earthly ministry and did not recognize Him. His glory was seen in who He was: the eternal Word made flesh, full of grace and truth.

He reveals glory when He turns water into wine at Cana:

"This beginning of miracles did Jesus in Cana of Galilee, and manifested forth his glory; and his disciples believed on him." — **John 2:11**

He reveals glory when He raises Lazarus. Before doing so, He tells Martha:

"Said I not unto thee, that, if thou wouldest believe, thou shouldest see the glory of God?" — **John 11:40**

He reveals glory in compassion, provision, healing, authority over death, and the awakening of faith. The glory of God is not reserved for cataclysmic displays of power. It appears in mercy toward the needy and life given where death had entered.

Most of all, the glory of God is revealed at the cross.

As Judas goes out to betray Him, Jesus says:

"Now is the Son of man glorified, and God is glorified in him." — **John 13:31**

The cross looks like shame to the world. It looks like defeat, humiliation, and weakness. Yet Jesus says this is the hour of glory. Why? Because at the cross, the character of God is displayed with unparalleled fullness. His holiness confronts sin. His justice is satisfied. His love gives the Son. His mercy opens salvation to the guilty. His wisdom accomplishes redemption through what men intended for evil. His faithfulness fulfills promise. His truth stands.

Nothing reveals God's glory more clearly than the crucified Christ.

This is one reason the gospel cannot be reduced to human benefit. Salvation is indeed for sinners, and its blessings are immeasurable. But the ultimate aim of redemption is the glory of God. Paul says believers are predestinated, redeemed, and sealed:

"to the praise of the glory of his grace." — **Ephesians 1:6**

Again:

"That we should be to the praise of his glory, who first trusted in Christ." — **Ephesians 1:12**

And again:

"unto the praise of his glory." — **Ephesians 1:14**

Salvation is not man-centered at its deepest level. It is God-centered. The redeemed are saved by grace, through Christ, unto the praise of God's glory. That does not reduce the tenderness of salvation. It gives it its highest meaning.

The Glory of Christ

The glory of God and the glory of Christ cannot be separated.

Isaiah saw the Lord high and lifted up. John says Isaiah saw Christ's glory and spoke of Him. On the Mount of Transfiguration, the veil of Christ's ordinary appearance is briefly drawn back:

"And was transfigured before them: and his face did shine as the sun, and his raiment was white as the light." — **Matthew 17:2**

Peter, James, and John see a glimpse of the glory that belongs to the Son. Peter later writes:

"For he received from God the Father honour and glory, when there came such a voice to him from the excellent glory, This is my beloved Son, in whom I am well pleased." — **2 Peter 1:17**

The resurrection and exaltation of Christ also reveal His glory. After His suffering, He enters into glory. The Father highly exalts Him. He sits at the right hand of the Majesty on high. Stephen, just before martyrdom, sees:

"the glory of God, and Jesus standing on the right hand of God." — **Acts 7:55**

The glorified Christ is not merely restored to life. He is publicly vindicated and enthroned. His glory will be unveiled before the world at His return:

"When the Son of man shall come in his glory, and all the holy angels with him, then shall he sit upon the throne of his glory." — **Matthew 25:31**

The first coming revealed glory through humility, incarnation, service, suffering, and resurrection. The second coming will reveal glory in majesty, kingship, judgment, and visible dominion.

No doctrine of Christ is adequate if it sees only one side. The babe in Bethlehem is the King of glory. The suffering servant is the returning Judge. The Lamb slain is the Lion of the tribe of Judah. The glory veiled in His first coming will be displayed openly in His second.

The Glory of God and Human Pride

God's glory exposes the absurdity of human pride.

Man is often impressed with himself. He boasts in wisdom, strength, riches, influence, beauty, achievement, knowledge, or moral superiority. Scripture repeatedly answers such boasting by directing attention back to God.

Jeremiah records the Lord's words:

"Let not the wise man glory in his wisdom, neither let the mighty man glory in his might, let not the rich man glory in his riches: But let him that glorieth glory in this, that he understandeth and knoweth me, that I am the LORD which exercise lovingkindness, judgment, and righteousness, in the earth: for in these things I delight, saith the LORD." — **Jeremiah 9:23–24**

Human boasting shrinks before the knowledge of God. Wisdom, strength, and wealth are not meaningless, but they are not ultimate. The only rightful boast is that God has made Himself known.

Paul takes up the same theme:

"That, according as it is written, He that glorieth, let him glory in the Lord." — **I Corinthians 1:31**

The cross especially humiliates human pride. God saves not through the wisdom of the world, not through the strength of the mighty, not through human righteousness, but through Christ crucified. The one who is saved cannot finally glory in himself. He must glory in the Lord.

Pride is not merely improper self-esteem. It is a glory problem. It assigns weight to the creature that belongs to the Creator. It is therefore deeply opposed to worship. The proud man wants significance without dependence, achievement without gratitude, praise without reference to God. The glory of God shatters that illusion.

Nebuchadnezzar learned this. Standing in Babylon, he boasted:

"Is not this great Babylon, that I have built for the house of the kingdom by the might of my power, and for the honour of my majesty?" — **Daniel 4:30**

Before the words left his mouth, judgment fell. He was driven from men until he learned:

"that the most High ruleth in the kingdom of men, and giveth it to whomsoever he will." — **Daniel 4:32**

When his reason returned, Nebuchadnezzar blessed the Most High and said:

"those that walk in pride he is able to abase." — **Daniel 4:37**

The glory of God will eventually humble all pride. The only question is whether we bow willingly now or are brought low by His hand.

The Glory of God and the Life of His People

God's people are called to live for His glory.

Paul writes:

"Whether therefore ye eat, or drink, or whatsoever ye do, do all to the glory of God." — **1 Corinthians 10:31**

The command is sweeping. Ordinary actions matter. Eating and drinking, activities so common they seem spiritually neutral, are brought under the call to glorify God. The Christian life is not divided neatly between sacred moments and disposable moments. All of life belongs to Him.

To live for God's glory means more than attaching religious language to our preferences. It means ordering life around His worth. It means asking whether our conduct reflects the character of the God whose name we bear. It means that truth matters, holiness matters, love matters, obedience matters, because all of them display or obscure His glory before others.

Jesus says:

"Let your light so shine before men, that they may see your good works, and glorify your Father which is in heaven." — **Matthew 5:16**

Good works are not performed to gather praise for the self. They are meant to direct attention toward the Father. Christian ethics is doxological. Holiness in the believer should make God's character more visible, not draw ultimate admiration to the believer.

This also means sin among God's people profanes His name. David's sin with Bathsheba gave "great occasion to the enemies of the LORD to blaspheme." Israel's rebellion caused God's name to be profaned among the nations. Paul warns that hypocrisy among Jews led to the name of God being blasphemed among the Gentiles. The conduct of God's people matters because they bear association with His name.

That truth should not drive believers into despair, but it should sober them. The glory of God is not a vague concept for worship services. It is implicated in daily obedience.

From Glory to Glory

The gospel not only reveals God's glory. It transforms believers by it.

Paul writes:

"But we all, with open face beholding as in a glass the glory of the Lord, are changed into the same image from glory to glory, even as by the Spirit of the Lord." — 2 Corinthians 3:18

Transformation comes through beholding. As believers look to Christ in the gospel, the Spirit conforms them increasingly to His image. The glory that once terrified sinners apart from grace now becomes the means by which redeemed sinners are changed.

This does not mean believers become glorious in the same independent sense that God is glorious. His glory is essential and underived. Ours is received, reflected, and creaturely. But salvation does include glorification. Those whom God justifies, He also glorifies. Christ will change our vile body, that it may be fashioned like unto His glorious body. When He appears, we shall be like Him, for we shall see Him as He is.

The future of the redeemed is not merely escape from pain. It is participation in the unveiled glory of God through Christ.

Jesus prays:

"Father, I will that they also, whom thou hast given me, be with me where I am; that they may behold my glory, which thou hast given me: for thou lovedst me before the foundation of the world." — **John 17:24**

The eternal joy of the saints is to behold the glory of Christ. This is the fulfillment of every redeemed desire. The heart was made for God. Its rest is found not in lesser gifts detached from Him, but in the vision of His glory.

Revelation describes the New Jerusalem:

"And the city had no need of the sun, neither of the moon, to shine in it: for the glory of God did lighten it, and the Lamb is the light thereof." — **Revelation 21:23**

The glory of God is not one feature of the eternal state. It is its light. The Lamb is its lamp. What creation now reflects in part, the redeemed world will know without obstruction. There will be no temple there, for the Lord God Almighty and the Lamb are the temple of it. There will be no night. His servants shall serve Him, and they shall see His face.

The story of redemption moves toward unveiled glory.

The God Whose Glory Must Be Recovered

The church cannot recover the full character of God while treating His glory as an ornamental theme. His glory is central. He creates for it. He judges for it. He saves for it. He keeps covenant for it. He sends His Son for it. He sanctifies His people for it. He will fill the earth with the knowledge of it.

Where God's glory is diminished, theology turns inward. Salvation becomes primarily about personal fulfillment. Worship becomes primarily about emotional experience. Preaching becomes primarily about human improvement. Doctrine becomes primarily useful insofar as it meets felt needs. The center shifts from God's worth to man's benefit.

But the Bible begins elsewhere and ends elsewhere.

"In the beginning God…" — **Genesis 1:1**

"Alleluia: Salvation, and glory, and honour, and power, unto the Lord our God." — **Revelation 19:1**

God is the beginning. God is the end. God is the center. His glory is not served by making Him useful to our self-centered purposes. We are redeemed to see that all things are from Him, through Him, and to Him.

The glory of God humbles us, but it does not crush the redeemed. It gathers us into worship. It pulls our eyes away from small things. It restores proportion. It teaches us that the universe is not finally about our comfort, our reputation, our preferences, or our plans. It is about the God who is infinitely worthy.

- He is holy, and His holiness shines.
- He is good, and His goodness shines.
- He is just, and His justice shines.
- He is merciful, and His mercy shines.
- He is glorious because every perfection of His being is excellent beyond measure.

The whole earth is full of His glory, even where men refuse to see it.

And one day, they will not be able to look away.

Chapter 14 — God Is Eternal and Self-Existent

Everything we know in this world began.

Every person has a first moment. Every tree emerged from a seed. Every mountain rose through processes God set in motion. Every nation had a beginning. Every star was called into being. The oldest ruins are still young compared with time itself, and time itself is not eternal.

But God never began.

Before the first dawn, before the first angel worshiped, before the first word of creation sounded into the void, God was. Not waiting to become. Not developing toward fullness. Not emerging from some reality older than Himself. He simply is.

Moses begins Psalm 90 with one of the most majestic declarations in Scripture:

"Lord, thou hast been our dwelling place in all generations. Before the mountains were brought forth, or ever thou hadst formed the earth and the world, even from everlasting to everlasting, thou art God." — **Psalm 90:1–2**

The sentence does not say that God lasts a very long time. It says He is God **from everlasting to everlasting**. There is no point behind Him where He was not. There is no point ahead of Him where He will cease to be. His existence is not stretched across time the way ours is. He is eternal.

That truth is easy to confess and nearly impossible to imagine. We can speak the words, but our minds instinctively ask what came before. Before our birth, there were parents. Before them, ancestors. Before a house, there was a builder. Before a book, an author. Before an event, causes. We live in a world of sequence and dependence, so we search for origins.

God has no origin.

He is the origin of all else.

The God Who Is

When Moses stood before the burning bush and asked what name he should give the children of Israel, God answered:

*"I AM THAT I AM: and he said, Thus shalt thou say unto the children of Israel, I AM hath sent me unto you." — **Exodus 3:14***

This name is inexhaustible. It reveals God's faithfulness, His presence with His people, and His covenant constancy. But it also reveals something deeper about His being. God does not say, "I came to be." He says, **"I AM."**

Creatures become. God is.

A child becomes a man. A seed becomes a tree. A nation becomes powerful and then declines. Human understanding grows, weakens, and can be lost. Even angels are created beings who owe their existence to God. Everything outside of God has received being. God alone possesses life in Himself.

Jesus says of the Father:

*"For as the Father hath life in himself; so hath he given to the Son to have life in himself." — **John 5:26***

The phrase **"life in himself"** is astonishing. Created beings have life, but not in themselves. Their life is sustained. Breath is given. Heartbeats continue because God permits them. If He withdraws His hand, creatures return to dust. God does not receive life from another. Life belongs to Him inherently.

John writes of the Son:

*"In him was life; and the life was the light of men." — **John 1:4***

The Son is not merely alive. He is the source of life. This fits what John has already said:

*"All things were made by him; and without him was not any thing made that was made." — **John 1:3***

If all created things were made through the Son, then the Son cannot be numbered among created things. He shares the divine self-existence. The eternal Word is not part of the universe. The universe exists through Him.

God's self-existence is sometimes called **aseity**, though the theological term matters less than the truth itself: God depends on nothing outside Himself for His being, life, joy, strength, wisdom, or perfection.

- He does not need a source.
- He does not require support.
- He does not survive by receiving.
- He does not endure because something stronger preserves Him.

He is.

The Folly of Asking Who Made God

One of the most common questions raised against belief in God is, "If God made everything, who made God?" The question sounds penetrating until we recognize that it misunderstands what Christians mean by God.

We do not say that **everything** has a cause. We say that everything that **begins to exist** requires explanation beyond itself. God did not begin to exist. He is not one more object inside the chain of caused realities. He is the uncaused Creator, the eternal One upon whom all caused things depend.

If God needed a maker, then that maker would be God instead. A dependent god is no God at all.

Scripture never tries to explain God by appealing to something prior. It simply begins:

*"In the beginning God created the heaven and the earth." — **Genesis 1:1***

The first verse of the Bible does not place God inside the beginning. He is already there when the beginning begins. Time, space, matter, and created order enter existence by His act. God is not a being located at the earliest point on a timeline. He is the eternal Creator of the timeline itself.

This does not mean we fully comprehend eternity. We do not. But it does mean Christianity is not embarrassed by the question of ultimate origin. A world of contingent things cannot explain itself. Matter cannot be its own final cause if it is not eternal and self-existent. Time cannot generate its own beginning. The universe points beyond itself to One who does not receive being, but gives it.

Paul told the Athenians:

"God that made the world and all things therein, seeing that he is Lord of heaven and earth, dwelleth not in temples made with hands; Neither is worshipped with men's hands, as though he needed any thing, seeing he giveth to all life, and breath, and all things." — **Acts 17:24–25**

Those last words should stop us: **"he giveth to all life, and breath, and all things."** Every breath is borrowed. Every moment is received. Every creature lives on divine generosity. God alone needs nothing.

The Eternal God Before Creation

The opening line of Genesis can become so familiar that we miss what it implies. Before the heavens and the earth, God existed in full perfection. He was not awaiting creation in order to become Creator in some fulfilled sense. He freely chose to create. The act revealed His power and wisdom, but it did not complete Him.

This connects directly to the doctrine of the Trinity we considered earlier. Father, Son, and Holy Ghost were eternally full before the world began. Jesus speaks of the glory He possessed with the Father:

"And now, O Father, glorify thou me with thine own self with the glory which I had with thee before the world was." — **John 17:5**

He also speaks of the Father's love for Him:

*"for thou lovedst me before the foundation of the world." — **John 17:24***

Before creation, there was glory. Before angels, there was love. Before human worship, there was divine blessedness. God did not create to escape loneliness or acquire meaning. He created from abundance.

That matters because poor theology often makes man seem too necessary to God. It speaks as though God needed someone to love, needed someone to praise Him, or needed redemption in order to complete His own purpose of being loving. Scripture says otherwise. God is love eternally because the triune God eternally exists. God is glorious eternally because glory belongs to His being. God is blessed eternally because nothing lacking exists in Him.

Creation is not God filling a deficiency. It is God displaying His glory.

The redeemed should find great comfort in this. A needy god would be unstable in love. He would give in order to receive something He lacks. But the true God gives from fullness. His grace is free because He is self-sufficient. His love is steady because it does not arise from need. His mercy is not desperation. His covenant faithfulness is not a bargain by which He secures something missing in Himself.

He is eternally full. Therefore His generosity is truly gracious.

God Is Not Bound by Time

Because God is eternal, His relation to time is unlike ours.

We move through time one moment after another. Yesterday is gone. Tomorrow is unknown. We remember imperfectly, anticipate uncertainly, and exist only in the present instant as it passes. Time masters us. We cannot speed it, stop it, reverse it, or escape it. Even the strongest man is carried toward death by it.

God is not carried by time.

Scripture says:

*"But, beloved, be not ignorant of this one thing, that one day is with the Lord as a thousand years, and a thousand years as one day." — **2 Peter 3:8***

Peter is not giving a mathematical formula by which prophetic "days" should always be converted into thousand-year periods. He is explaining why the apparent delay of Christ's return should not be mistaken for slowness in God. The Lord does not experience time with creaturely impatience or limitation. A thousand years do not weary Him. One day does not constrain Him.

Psalm 90 says similarly:

*"For a thousand years in thy sight are but as yesterday when it is past, and as a watch in the night." — **Psalm 90:4***

What overwhelms human perspective does not strain God. Centuries that seem immense to us are not immense to Him. He does not forget promises because time has passed. He does not lose track of justice because generations come and go. He does not abandon His purposes because fulfillment takes longer than human expectation.

This truth matters deeply for doctrine and for faith.

Scoffers in Peter's day mocked the promise of Christ's return:

*"Where is the promise of his coming? for since the fathers fell asleep, all things continue as they were from the beginning of the creation." — **2 Peter 3:4***

They treated delay as disproof. Peter answers by reminding them of God's past judgment in the flood, God's present preservation of the world for coming judgment, and God's different relation to time. The Lord's apparent delay is not failure. It is longsuffering.

"The Lord is not slack concerning his promise, as some men count slackness; but is longsuffering to us-ward, not willing that any should perish, but that all should come to repentance." — **2 Peter 3:9**

Only the eternal God can delay without weakness. His patience is not inability. His promise is not fading. His timing is governed by perfect wisdom, not by pressure from the clock.

The Ancient of Days

Daniel's vision gives us a striking title for God:

"I beheld till the thrones were cast down, and the Ancient of days did sit, whose garment was white as snow, and the hair of his head like the pure wool: his throne was like the fiery flame, and his wheels as burning fire." — **Daniel 7:9**

The title **"Ancient of days"** does not mean God has aged. Aging belongs to creatures. It marks the passage of time upon weakness. God does not grow old. The title communicates eternal majesty, absolute precedence, and judicial authority. Kingdoms rise like beasts from the sea, but above them sits One before whom all empires are recent and temporary.

Daniel continues:

"A fiery stream issued and came forth from before him: thousand thousands ministered unto him, and ten thousand times ten thousand stood before him: the judgment was set, and the books were opened." — **Daniel 7:10**

Human power loves to imagine itself permanent. Babylon, Persia, Greece, Rome, and every empire after them have carried that illusion. God's eternity exposes it. Nations that appear immovable are brief. Rulers who demand worship are dust. Systems that boast of inevitability vanish. The Ancient of days remains.

Isaiah says:

"Behold, the nations are as a drop of a bucket, and are counted as the small dust of the balance: behold, he taketh up the isles as a very little thing." — **Isaiah 40:15**

Again:

"All nations before him are as nothing; and they are counted to him less than nothing, and vanity." — **Isaiah 40:17**

These verses are not meant to imply that people are worthless or that God is indifferent to nations. Scripture everywhere shows His concern with justice among them and His purposes for them. The point is proportion. Against the eternal God, the grandest earthly powers are not grand. They cannot threaten Him. They cannot delay His counsel. They cannot outlast His throne.

This matters whenever Christians are tempted to interpret God through the turbulence of history. Political upheaval, cultural decay, persecution, war, and the apparent advance of evil can make the world feel unstable. It is unstable. God is not. The Ancient of days still sits.

The Everlasting God and Human Frailty

Psalm 90 not only declares God eternal; it places His eternity beside human brevity.

"Thou turnest man to destruction; and sayest, Return, ye children of men." — **Psalm 90:3**

"Thou carriest them away as with a flood; they are as a sleep: in the morning they are like grass which groweth up. In the morning it flourisheth, and groweth up; in the evening it is cut down, and withereth." — **Psalm 90:5–6**

Man is grass. He flourishes briefly. He fades quickly. Even seventy or eighty years, Moses says, are filled with labor and sorrow and pass swiftly away. He then prays:

"So teach us to number our days, that we may apply our hearts unto wisdom." — **Psalm 90:12**

God's eternity should teach us to count our days rightly.

A life lived as though this world were permanent is foolish. Ambition without reference to eternity is foolish. Delayed repentance is foolish. Hoarding, boasting, and making ultimate what will soon disappear are foolish. The eternal God puts human life in its proper frame.

James writes:

"For what is your life? It is even a vapour, that appeareth for a little time, and then vanisheth away." — **James 4:14**

That statement is not meant to strip life of meaning. It is meant to rescue us from false meaning. Life matters intensely because it is lived before God and moves toward eternity. The brevity of life does not make it meaningless. It makes wisdom urgent.

Moses' prayer in Psalm 90 is therefore not despairing. After reflecting on human frailty under divine eternity, he asks God to satisfy His people with mercy, to make them glad, to establish the work of their hands. Meaning is not found by pretending our days are endless. It is found by receiving our days from the eternal God and living them under His mercy.

The Eternal God as Refuge

God's eternity does not only humble us. It shelters us.

Moses begins Psalm 90:

"Lord, thou hast been our dwelling place in all generations." — **Psalm 90:1**

Generations come and go, but God remains the dwelling place of His people. Abraham lived in tents. Israel wandered in the wilderness. David fled from enemies. The faithful have often lacked visible stability. Yet God Himself has been their home.

Moses says elsewhere:

"The eternal God is thy refuge, and underneath are the everlasting arms." — **Deuteronomy 33:27**

That is one of the most tender statements in Scripture. The God whose eternity overwhelms the mind stoops to become the refuge of His people. His arms are everlasting. They do not tire. They do not fail. They do not lower the believer midway through suffering. What rests upon God rests upon One who cannot collapse.

This is why divine eternity belongs in a book on God's character, not merely in a philosophical discussion of time. It changes how we trust Him. Human supports fail because human beings fail. Friends die. Parents die. Leaders fail. Churches can disappoint. Bodies weaken. Economies shift. Plans dissolve. But God remains.

The psalmist says:

"My flesh and my heart faileth: but God is the strength of my heart, and my portion for ever." — **Psalm 73:26**

"Forever" matters. A temporary refuge may comfort briefly. God is the portion that cannot be outlived. His eternity makes Him an eternal inheritance.

God's Eternal Purposes

Because God is eternal, His purposes do not arise as reactions to circumstances He failed to anticipate. He does not improvise redemption after sin catches Him by surprise. He does not form His plans under pressure. Scripture speaks of purposes and promises reaching back before the foundation of the world.

Paul writes that God:

*"hath saved us, and called us with an holy calling, not according to our works, but according to his own purpose and grace, which was given us in Christ Jesus before the world began." — **2 Timothy 1:9***

Titus speaks of:

"eternal life, which God, that cannot lie, promised before the world began." **— Titus 1:2**

Peter says Christ was:

"foreordained before the foundation of the world, but was manifest in these last times for you." — **1 Peter 1:20**

The cross was not God's emergency response to Eden. Redemption was purposed before the world began and revealed in history at the appointed time. This does not make sin unreal or human choices irrelevant. It means evil never placed God in a position of helpless reaction. His wisdom stretches beyond the beginning. His grace was not conceived after the fall. His purposes stand in eternity.

Paul writes in Ephesians that God works:

"according to the purpose of him who worketh all things after the counsel of his own will." — **Ephesians 1:11**

The eternal God is not surprised by history. That is a comfort when history surprises us.

Many believers struggle when events seem to derail what they thought God was doing. A diagnosis interrupts plans. A death reshapes a family. A betrayal alters a future. A ministry collapses. A prayer remains unanswered longer than expected. In such moments, it can seem as though life has spun outside divine intention.

The eternal God has not been overtaken.

That does not mean we always know what He is doing. Often we do not. Job did not know. Joseph could only understand later that what his brothers meant for evil, God meant for good. The disciples could not comprehend the cross while it unfolded before them. But God's eternal purpose gives the believer reason to trust that no event has forced Him into a corner.

His counsel is not fragile. His wisdom is not late. His grace is not improvised. His purposes are not aging toward failure.

The Eternal Son

The eternity of God must include the eternity of Christ.

The Son did not begin at Bethlehem. His human nature began in the womb of Mary, but His person did not. The Word was already in the beginning with God and was God. He speaks of glory with the Father before the world was. He declares:

*"Before Abraham was, I am." — **John 8:58***

The grammar is striking. Jesus does not merely say, "Before Abraham was, I was," though that alone would have claimed preexistence. He says, **"I am,"** echoing the divine self-revelation of Exodus. His hearers understood the claim. They took up stones to cast at Him.

Micah's prophecy of the Messiah's birth in Bethlehem also speaks of His eternal origin:

*"But thou, Bethlehem Ephratah, though thou be little among the thousands of Judah, yet out of thee shall he come forth unto me that is to be ruler in Israel; whose goings forth have been from of old, from everlasting." — **Micah 5:2***

The ruler to be born in Bethlehem is not a merely human king. His goings forth are from everlasting.

The writer of Hebrews applies Psalm 102's language about the eternal Creator directly to the Son:

"And, Thou, Lord, in the beginning hast laid the foundation of the earth; and the heavens are the works of thine hands: They shall perish; but thou remainest; and they all shall wax old as doth a garment; And as a vesture shalt thou fold them up, and they shall be changed: but thou art the same, and thy years shall not fail." — **Hebrews 1:10–12**

Creation ages. The Son remains. His years shall not fail.

This matters for salvation. If Christ were merely a creature, even the highest creature, He could not save eternally. A finite savior cannot secure infinite redemption. But Hebrews says:

"Wherefore he is able also to save them to the uttermost that come unto God by him, seeing he ever liveth to make intercession for them." — **Hebrews 7:25**

He ever lives. His priesthood does not pass to another because He continues forever. The believer's hope rests upon a living Savior whose life cannot be overcome by death.

The Eternal Spirit

Scripture also speaks of the Holy Spirit in eternal terms. Hebrews says Christ:

"through the eternal Spirit offered himself without spot to God." — **Hebrews 9:14**

The Spirit is not temporary divine influence. He is eternal. He was present in creation, moving upon the face of the waters. He spoke through the prophets. He overshadowed Mary. He descended upon Christ. He inspired Scripture. He indwells believers. He will raise their mortal bodies.

The eternal Spirit applies the benefits of the eternal Son's sacrifice according to the eternal purpose of the Father. Salvation is the work of the eternal God from beginning to end.

God's Eternity and His Unchanging Character

God's eternity is closely related to His immutability, which we will consider more fully in the next chapter. Yet the distinction matters. God is eternal in that He has no beginning or end. He is unchanging in that His being, character, purposes, and promises do not fluctuate. The truths belong together because one who moves from one condition to another is marked by temporality and development. God does not.

James says there is with the Father:

"no variableness, neither shadow of turning." — **James 1:17**

The eternal God does not become better, wiser, kinder, or more faithful over time. He does not progress toward perfection. He is eternally perfect. His love is not younger than His justice. His mercy did not arise later than His holiness. His wrath against evil is not a temporary mood generated by creation's fall. Everything that belongs to His character belongs to Him eternally.

This protects us from imagining that God was somehow severe in the Old Testament and became gracious in the New. The gospel reveals grace more fully, but grace did not newly arise in God. He was gracious in Eden, in the calling of Abraham, in the deliverance from Egypt, in the restoration of David, in the promises of the prophets. Christ does not introduce mercy into a previously merciless God. He reveals in history the mercy eternally belonging to God's character.

Likewise, judgment in Revelation is not a late shift away from the love of Christ. The Lamb's wrath does not contradict His eternal love. Both belong to the unchanging, eternal character of God.

The God Who Outlasts All Things

Psalm 102 sets human weakness beside divine permanence. The writer laments that his days are consumed like smoke and wither like grass. Then he turns to God:

*"But thou, O LORD, shalt endure for ever; and thy remembrance unto all generations." — **Psalm 102:12***

Later he says:

*"Of old hast thou laid the foundation of the earth: and the heavens are the work of thy hands. They shall perish, but thou shalt endure: yea, all of them shall wax old like a garment; as a vesture shalt thou change them, and they shall be changed: But thou art the same, and thy years shall have no end." — **Psalm 102:25–27***

The heavens seem enduring to us. God calls them garments that will wear out. Creation is vast, but not eternal in itself. God alone endures absolutely.

That gives eternal significance to what otherwise seems fleeting. The believer's labor in the Lord is not in vain because it is connected to the purposes of the eternal God. The sufferings of this present time are not worthy to be compared with the glory to be revealed. A cup of cold water given in Christ's name is not forgotten. Prayers offered in weakness are heard by the One who does not forget. Faithfulness hidden from the world is remembered in heaven.

The eternal God gives permanence to obedience.

He also exposes the vanity of rebellion. Sin promises urgency. It presses the soul with the importance of the moment. Take now. Enjoy now. Assert now. Delay repentance. Secure yourself. But the eternal God sees the end from the beginning. What sin treats as weighty often disappears almost immediately. What God calls weighty endures forever.

John writes:

*"And the world passeth away, and the lust thereof: but he that doeth the will of God abideth for ever." — **I John 2:17**￼*

The contrast is sharp. The world with all its lusts is passing. The will of God abides. Wisdom means living in view of what lasts.

The Comfort and Terror of Eternity

God's eternity is comfort to the redeemed and terror to the unrepentant.

For the redeemed, it means their salvation rests in One who cannot die, fail, forget, or diminish. His mercy is from everlasting to everlasting upon them that fear Him. His kingdom is everlasting. His covenant faithfulness does not expire. Their inheritance is incorruptible, undefiled, and that fadeth not away.

For the unrepentant, it means there is no escaping Him by outlasting Him. Human beings sometimes live as though delay equals safety. Judgment has not come yet, so it must not come. Conscience dulls. The body remains strong. Life continues. But every human life is brief, and the eternal God waits without weakening.

Daniel says of Him:

*"his dominion is an everlasting dominion, and his kingdom is from generation to generation." — **Daniel 4:34***

Rebellion can resist Him for a season. It cannot outlive His dominion.

The eternity of God gives solemn force to the words of Hebrews:

*"It is a fearful thing to fall into the hands of the living God." — **Hebrews 10:31***

He is living. He is eternal. He cannot be dismissed as though time erodes His claims.

The Eternal God and the Fullness of His Character

The eternal self-existence of God strengthens everything else we will say about Him.

- His holiness is eternal holiness.
- His glory is eternal glory.
- His goodness is eternal goodness.
- His righteousness is eternal righteousness.
- His love is eternal love.
- His truth is eternal truth.
- His faithfulness is eternal faithfulness.
- His wisdom is eternal wisdom.

Nothing in God is temporary, acquired, or fragile.

He did not become just when moral creatures appeared. He did not become merciful only after sin entered the world. He did not become sovereign when creation gave Him something to rule. He did not become loving when He made humanity. All that He is, He is eternally.

That means God's character is not reactive in the way human character often is. Human beings become patient through trials, merciful through remembered weakness, wise through experience. God does not learn patience. He is longsuffering. He does not develop mercy. He is merciful. He does not acquire wisdom through observation. He is infinitely wise.

This should steady our theology. We are not dealing with a God whose character is under construction. We are not tracing divine improvement across Scripture. We are witnessing the unfolding revelation of the One who has always been perfectly Himself.

The Bible moves from Genesis to Revelation, but God does not move from immaturity to maturity within it. He reveals more. He does not become more.

From Everlasting to Everlasting

The eternal God stands at the beginning of all things and remains beyond their end. He is before creation, above history, present in every generation, and unchanged by the passage of ages. His name is I AM. His throne does not age. His purposes do not decay. His promises do not expire. His arms are everlasting.

This truth humbles the proud, comforts the weary, steadies the faithful, and gives seriousness to every human life.

We are not eternal by nature. We are dependent creatures whose days are like grass. Yet the eternal God has made Himself our refuge in Christ. He offers everlasting life to those who believe. He brings mortal sinners into fellowship with the One who inhabits eternity.

Isaiah says:

*"For thus saith the high and lofty One that inhabiteth eternity, whose name is Holy; I dwell in the high and holy place, with him also that is of a contrite and humble spirit, to revive the spirit of the humble, and to revive the heart of the contrite ones." — **Isaiah 57:15***

The One who inhabits eternity dwells with the humble.

That sentence gathers much of this chapter into one astonishing truth. God's eternity does not make Him inaccessible to the contrite. His transcendence does not forbid His nearness. The everlasting God stoops to revive broken hearts without ceasing to be high and holy.

- He is eternal.
- He is self-existent.
- He is the source of all life and the refuge of all who trust Him.

From everlasting to everlasting, He is God.

Chapter 15 — God Is Unchanging

Everything around us changes.

Bodies weaken. Nations rise and fall. Friendships deepen or fracture. Convictions that seemed immovable in one generation are dismissed in the next. Human moods shift. Human plans fail. Human promises sometimes bend under pressure. Even the strongest things in this world carry the marks of instability.

God does not.

He is not developing, improving, declining, or becoming something He was not before. His being does not change. His character does not change. His purposes do not change. His promises do not change. The God who revealed Himself to Moses is the same God who raised Christ from the dead, the same God who now keeps His people, and the same God who will fulfill every word He has spoken.

He says through Malachi:"For I am the LORD, I change not; therefore ye sons of Jacob are not consumed." — **Malachi 3:6**

The immediate comfort of the verse is easy to miss. Israel's survival rests upon God's immutability. If His covenant faithfulness fluctuated with their obedience, they would already have been destroyed. But because He does not change, His promises stand. Their hope is not found in their consistency, but in His.

God Does Not Become Better

Human beings may change for the better. A foolish man may become wise. A cruel man may learn tenderness. A weak man may grow strong. We need improvement because we are unfinished and flawed.

God does not improve.

To improve would mean that something was previously lacking. Scripture will not allow that. His works are perfect. His wisdom is infinite. His holiness is absolute. His goodness is without deficiency. He cannot become more righteous, more faithful, more loving, or more glorious than He already is.

James writes:

"Every good gift and every perfect gift is from above, and cometh down from the Father of lights, with whom is no variableness, neither shadow of turning."
— James 1:17

The imagery is striking. Created lights shift. Shadows move. The angle of the sun changes. Seasons pass. But in God there is no variableness, no shadow produced by turning, no alteration in His perfection.

This matters because some people read Scripture as though God Himself matures across the biblical story. They imagine a severe God in the Old Testament who gradually gives way to a gentler God in the New. But the Bible does not present divine development. It presents progressive revelation of an unchanging God.

The God who judged Egypt is the God who sent His Son. The God who forgave David is the God who forgives sinners through Christ. The God who declared Himself merciful and just in Exodus 34 is the God whose mercy and justice meet at the cross.

Christ does not replace a former version of God. He reveals the same God more fully.

God Does Not Become Worse

God cannot decline.

Human beings grow weary. Their patience wears thin. Their judgments can be clouded by anger, fear, or fatigue. Their love can cool. Their courage can fail. Their memories fade. Their priorities shift. No such instability exists in God.

The psalmist says:

"Of old hast thou laid the foundation of the earth: and the heavens are the work of thy hands. They shall perish, but thou shalt endure: yea, all of them shall wax old like a garment; as a vesture shalt thou change them, and they shall be changed: But thou art the same, and thy years shall have no end." — **Psalm 102:25–27**

Creation ages. God does not. The heavens themselves will be changed, but He remains the same. Hebrews applies this passage to the Son, confirming that Christ shares this divine immutability:

"They shall perish; but thou remainest; and they all shall wax old as doth a garment; And as a vesture shalt thou fold them up, and they shall be changed: but thou art the same, and thy years shall not fail." — **Hebrews 1:11–12**

The Savior who keeps His people does not weaken. His priesthood does not decay. His intercession does not lose effectiveness. His love does not erode with time. The believer's security rests in an unchanging Christ.

God's Purposes Do Not Fail

Because God does not change, His purposes do not collapse.

Isaiah records the Lord's words:

"Remember the former things of old: for I am God, and there is none else; I am God, and there is none like me, Declaring the end from the beginning, and from ancient times the things that are not yet done, saying, My counsel shall stand, and I will do all my pleasure." — **Isaiah 46:9–10**

God's counsel stands because God stands. He does not form plans based on partial knowledge and then revise them when new information arrives. He does not intend one thing and discover later that circumstances have made it impossible. His purposes are wise from the beginning and certain to the end.

The cross proves this. Men acted wickedly in condemning Christ, yet Peter says He was delivered:

*"by the determinate counsel and foreknowledge of God." — **Acts 2:23***

Human rebellion did not derail God's plan. It became the very setting in which His redemptive purpose was accomplished.

This does not make evil good. It does not make sinners innocent. But it does mean that no act of rebellion can overthrow God's final purpose. His counsel does not tremble before history.

God's Promises Do Not Shift

The immutability of God gives strength to every promise He makes.

Numbers says:

*"God is not a man, that he should lie; neither the son of man, that he should repent: hath he said, and shall he not do it? or hath he spoken, and shall he not make it good?" — **Numbers 23:19***

God does not speak hastily. He does not promise under one set of emotions and later reconsider. His Word is fixed because His character is fixed.

The writer of Hebrews makes the same point when discussing God's promise to Abraham:

*"Wherein God, willing more abundantly to shew unto the heirs of promise the immutability of his counsel, confirmed it by an oath: That by two immutable things, in which it was impossible for God to lie, we might have a strong consolation, who have fled for refuge to lay hold upon the hope set before us." — **Hebrews 6:17–18***

The believer's consolation is strong because God's counsel is immutable and God cannot lie. Hope is not wishful thinking. It is confidence anchored in the unchanging character of God.

This has broad doctrinal importance. When God makes covenant promises, His immutability matters. When He declares future judgment, His immutability matters. When Christ promises eternal life to His sheep, His immutability matters. When Scripture speaks of resurrection, restoration, and the return of Christ, those promises rest upon the God who cannot become less faithful than He was when He spoke them.

What About Passages Where God "Repents"?

Scripture sometimes says that God "repented" or "turned" from a course of action. After Nineveh humbled itself, for example:

*"And God saw their works, that they turned from their evil way; and God repented of the evil, that he had said that he would do unto them; and he did it not." — **Jonah 3:10***

At first glance, such passages may seem to challenge divine immutability. But they do not describe a change in God's character. They describe a change in His dealings with people whose posture toward Him has changed.

God had warned Nineveh of judgment. Nineveh repented. The God who is just toward the unrepentant is also merciful toward the repentant. His response changes because the situation changes, not because His character changes.

Jeremiah explains this principle plainly:

*"At what instant I shall speak concerning a nation, and concerning a kingdom, to pluck up, and to pull down, and to destroy it; If that nation, against whom I have pronounced, turn from their evil, I will repent of the evil that I thought to do unto them." — **Jeremiah 18:7–8***

God's warnings often carry a call to repentance. When repentance occurs, mercy follows. That is not inconsistency. It is perfect consistency with His revealed character.

The same is true in the opposite direction. If God promises blessing to a people who then turn to evil, He may withhold the announced blessing. Again, His character has not shifted. He remains righteous in both mercy and judgment.

God's Immutability and Prayer

If God does not change, why pray?

Because prayer is not an attempt to correct God's wisdom or alter His character. Prayer is one of the means through which the unchanging God accomplishes His purposes. He commands prayer. He responds to prayer. He incorporates the cries of His people into the unfolding of His will.

Moses intercedes for Israel after the golden calf. Hezekiah prays when told to set his house in order. The early church prays for Peter's deliverance. In each case, God truly responds. Yet His response does not mean He has become more merciful, more informed, or more faithful than He was before. It means His unchanging character is active within time.

Prayer matters because God has ordained it to matter.

The immutability of God should not discourage prayer. It should encourage it. We pray to One whose goodness will not fail, whose wisdom will not falter, whose promises will not loosen, and whose fatherly character will not suddenly turn uncertain.

The Comfort of an Unchanging God

God's immutability is not an abstract doctrine reserved for theological textbooks. It is deeply pastoral.

When everything around us shifts, God does not. When emotions fluctuate, God does not. When circumstances alter, God does not. When the world grows darker, God does not. When we feel weak, He remains strong. When we are confused, He remains wise. When we sin and confess, He remains faithful and just to forgive. When we suffer, He remains good. When death approaches, He remains eternal life for those who are in Christ.

The psalmist says:

"My covenant will I not break, nor alter the thing that is gone out of my lips."
— Psalm 89:34

That single verse could steady a trembling heart. God does not alter His Word. He does not revise His faithfulness. He does not wake one day less committed to His promises than before.

The believer's confidence rests there.

- Not in the steadiness of our emotions.
- Not in the strength of our circumstances.
- Not in the predictability of the world.

In the God who changes not.

The God Who Is Always Himself

God's immutability gives weight to the entire study of His character. Every attribute we consider in this book is unchanging.

His holiness will never become less pure. His justice will never become less exact. His mercy will never become less compassionate. His love will never become less steadfast. His truth will never become less reliable. His wisdom will never become less perfect. His glory will never fade.

He is not one God in creation, another in redemption, and another in judgment. He is the same God in all His works. His acts differ because His purposes unfold in history, but His character does not vary.

That is why He can be trusted.

*"Jesus Christ the same yesterday, and to day, and for ever." — **Hebrews 13:8***

The unchanging God is not static in the sense of lifelessness. He acts. He speaks. He creates. He judges. He saves. He answers prayer. He enters history in the incarnation. But in all His acts, He remains perfectly and eternally Himself.

And because He does, faith has a foundation that cannot move.

Chapter 16 — God Is Good

Few truths are stated more simply in Scripture than this:

"The LORD is good." — **Nahum 1:7**

The sentence is brief, but it carries immense weight. God is good in Himself. He does good in all His works. He is the source of every true good His creatures receive. Nothing cruel, corrupt, selfish, or morally defective exists in Him. His goodness is not one pleasant trait among others. It is the perfection of His nature expressed in kindness, generosity, wisdom, holiness, justice, mercy, and truth.

When Scripture says God is good, it does not mean merely that He is agreeable to us. It does not mean He always gives what we want, protects us from every pain, or arranges life according to our immediate preferences. Divine goodness is not measured by human comfort.

God is good because He is perfectly excellent in all that He is and all that He does.

The psalmist declares:

"Thou art good, and doest good; teach me thy statutes." — **Psalm 119:68**

His goodness belongs first to His being: **"Thou art good."** Then it appears in His action: **"and doest good."** God does good because God is good. His works flow from His character.

The Source of All Good

Every good thing originates in God.

James writes:

"Every good gift and every perfect gift is from above, and cometh down from the Father of lights, with whom is no variableness, neither shadow of turning." **— James 1:17**

The verse follows a warning not to blame God for temptation. Evil does not come from Him. Good does. The God who cannot be tempted with evil is the giver of every good and perfect gift.

Life is His gift. Breath is His gift. Food, rain, friendship, beauty, work, rest, laughter, intelligence, skill, family, and every lawful pleasure come from His hand. Even in a fallen world marked by sorrow and corruption, traces of His generosity remain everywhere.

Paul told the people of Lystra that God:

"left not himself without witness, in that he did good, and gave us rain from heaven, and fruitful seasons, filling our hearts with food and gladness." — **Acts 14:17**

Rain and harvest are not spiritually trivial. They testify to divine goodness. Food does more than sustain survival; it gives gladness. God's common kindness reaches even those who do not acknowledge Him.

Jesus says:

"for he maketh his sun to rise on the evil and on the good, and sendeth rain on the just and on the unjust." — **Matthew 5:45**

God's goodness extends broadly across the world. The wicked breathe His air, eat food from His earth, enjoy relationships made possible by His design, and live under a patience they do not deserve. Common grace does not save, but it reveals that God is not stingy, bitter, or eager to withhold all kindness from rebels.

His goodness is abundant.

The psalmist says:

"The LORD is good to all: and his tender mercies are over all his works." — **Psalm 145:9**

That verse must not be reduced to universal salvation or the denial of judgment. The same psalm speaks of God destroying the wicked. But His goodness is genuinely displayed throughout creation. His mercies are evident in the life He gives, the order He sustains, and the blessings He lavishes upon a world that has not earned them.

God's Goodness in Creation

The opening chapter of Genesis repeatedly declares God's creation good.

Light is good. The divided waters, the dry land, the vegetation, the heavenly lights, the creatures of sea and sky, the animals of the earth—all are pronounced good. After the creation of man and woman, Scripture says:

"And God saw every thing that he had made, and, behold, it was very good." **— Genesis 1:31**

Creation reflects the goodness of its Maker. The world was not born from chaos, conflict among gods, or an accident without meaning. It was made by wisdom and declared good by God Himself.

Sin has marred creation, but it has not erased every mark of goodness. The beauty of the natural world, the bond between parent and child, the dignity of work, the delight of music, the satisfaction of learning, the capacity for friendship—all of these still testify that creation came from a good God.

This matters because some religious thought has treated the material world as inherently corrupt or inferior. Scripture does not. Matter is not evil. The body is not evil. Marriage is not evil. Food is not evil. Creation is fallen because of sin, but its origin is good.

Paul warns against those who forbid what God created to be received with thanksgiving:

"For every creature of God is good, and nothing to be refused, if it be received with thanksgiving." **— 1 Timothy 4:4**

The goodness of creation calls for gratitude. Gifts become idolatrous when they replace God, but they are properly enjoyed when received from God and returned to Him in thanksgiving.

God's Goodness and His Commands

Because God is good, His commandments are good.

This truth is often resisted. Fallen human beings instinctively treat commands as restrictions upon joy. We assume that freedom means self-rule and that obedience means loss. Scripture presents the opposite. God's law reflects God's goodness. His commands teach His creatures how life ought to be lived before Him.

Moses told Israel:

"And now, Israel, what doth the LORD thy God require of thee, but to fear the LORD thy God, to walk in all his ways, and to love him, and to serve the LORD thy God with all thy heart and with all thy soul, To keep the commandments of the LORD, and his statutes, which I command thee this day for thy good?" — **Deuteronomy 10:12–13**

"For thy good." God's commands are not arbitrary tests of submission. They are holy instructions from the good God. They protect what is good, expose what is destructive, and direct His people into paths of righteousness.

The psalmist says:

"The law of the LORD is perfect, converting the soul: the testimony of the LORD is sure, making wise the simple. The statutes of the LORD are right, rejoicing the heart: the commandment of the LORD is pure, enlightening the eyes." — **Psalm 19:7–8**

The law rejoices the heart because truth is good. It enlightens the eyes because God's way is not oppression. It is wisdom.

This helps us resist a modern assumption that God's moral boundaries are obstacles to flourishing. His commands regarding truth, sexuality, worship, justice, marriage, forgiveness, and purity do not arise from cold control. They arise from goodness. A culture that calls God's commands harmful does not understand either His goodness or the ruin caused by sin.

God's Goodness and Discipline

If God is good, why does He discipline His people?

Because His goodness is not indulgence.

A parent who never corrects a child is not more loving than one who disciplines wisely. Neglect may feel gentle in the moment, but it leaves ruin untouched. God's goodness does not allow His children to remain comfortably attached to what destroys them.

Hebrews says:

"For whom the Lord loveth he chasteneth, and scourgeth every son whom he receiveth." — **Hebrews 12:6**

The passage continues:

"Now no chastening for the present seemeth to be joyous, but grievous: nevertheless afterward it yieldeth the peaceable fruit of righteousness unto them which are exercised thereby." — **Hebrews 12:11**

Discipline may be painful. Scripture does not pretend otherwise. But its purpose is good: "the peaceable fruit of righteousness." God's discipline is not condemning wrath toward His redeemed children. It is fatherly correction flowing from love.

David understood that affliction could serve good ends:

"Before I was afflicted I went astray: but now have I kept thy word." — **Psalm 119:67**

And again:

"It is good for me that I have been afflicted; that I might learn thy statutes."
— Psalm 119:71

Not every suffering is direct discipline for a specific sin, and we must not assume that it is. Job's friends erred badly at that point. But Scripture does teach that God can use affliction for the good of His people. He may expose idols, deepen faith, teach dependence, refine obedience, and drive the soul toward Himself.

His goodness is sometimes severe precisely because He will not abandon His children to destruction.

God's Goodness in Suffering

The goodness of God becomes hardest to confess when life hurts.

It is easy to say God is good when prayers are answered as hoped, when health is strong, when family is secure, and when the path ahead appears bright. The confession is tested when grief enters, when loss lingers, when injustice stands unanswered, or when God's providence feels hidden.

Scripture does not dismiss that struggle. The Psalms are filled with cries from the afflicted. Job sits in ashes. Habakkuk trembles before coming devastation. Paul speaks openly of being troubled, perplexed, persecuted, and cast down. Biblical faith is not denial of sorrow.

Yet Scripture refuses to conclude from suffering that God is not good.

Joseph's life is one of the clearest examples. Betrayed by his brothers, sold into slavery, falsely accused, and imprisoned, he endured years in which God's goodness may have been difficult to see. But at the end, he could say:

"But as for you, ye thought evil against me; but God meant it unto good, to bring to pass, as it is this day, to save much people alive." **— Genesis 50:20**

Joseph does not call evil good. His brothers meant evil. Their sin remains sin. But God, without becoming the author of evil, governed the same events toward a good purpose far beyond Joseph's immediate understanding.

Romans 8:28 expresses the same confidence for believers:

*"And we know that all things work together for good to them that love God, to them who are the called according to his purpose." — **Romans 8:28***

The verse does not say all things are good. Death is not good in itself. Betrayal is not good. Disease is not good. Sin is not good. But God works all things together for the good of His people. The surrounding context defines that good as conformity to the image of Christ and final glorification.

God's goodness is not fragile. It does not disappear in the presence of suffering. Sometimes it is seen through deliverance. Sometimes through sustaining grace. Sometimes only in hindsight. Sometimes its full meaning waits for eternity. But the character of God does not change when circumstances become dark.

Nahum's declaration comes in a chapter filled with judgment:

*"The LORD is good, a strong hold in the day of trouble; and he knoweth them that trust in him." — **Nahum 1:7***

The day is troubled. Judgment is coming. Yet the Lord is good and a stronghold to those who trust Him. Divine goodness is not the denial of trouble. It is the refuge of God's people within it.

God's Goodness and Judgment

Some assume that judgment cannot be good. Scripture teaches otherwise.

If God is good, He must oppose evil. A goodness that never confronts cruelty, abuse, idolatry, murder, deceit, oppression, and rebellion would not be moral goodness at all. It would be indifference.

The Lord says:

"For the LORD is righteous, he loveth righteousness; his countenance doth behold the upright." — **Psalm 11:7**

The same psalm says:

"Upon the wicked he shall rain snares, fire and brimstone, and an horrible tempest: this shall be the portion of their cup." — **Psalm 11:6**

God's love of righteousness and His judgment of wickedness belong together. His goodness does not prevent judgment. His goodness requires that evil not be treated as morally weightless.

The cross confirms this. God's goodness toward sinners did not lead Him to ignore sin. It led Him to provide His Son. Mercy was given through a righteous atonement. Divine goodness is not softness. It is holy generosity joined to perfect justice.

When final judgment comes, heaven will not regard it as contradiction of God's goodness. Revelation says:

"Alleluia; Salvation, and glory, and honour, and power, unto the Lord our God: For true and righteous are his judgments." — **Revelation 19:1–2**

The goodness of God will be vindicated in His judgment because His judgments are true and righteous.

God's Goodness Revealed in Christ

The goodness of God is most beautifully displayed in Jesus Christ.

Peter summarized the earthly ministry of Jesus by saying He:

*"went about doing good, and healing all that were oppressed of the devil; for God was with him." — **Acts 10:38***

Christ healed the sick, fed the hungry, restored the outcast, opened blind eyes, cleansed lepers, raised the dead, welcomed children, forgave sinners, and taught truth. His life was not merely powerful. It was good.

When the rich young ruler called Him "Good Master," Jesus answered:

*"Why callest thou me good? there is none good but one, that is, God." — **Mark 10:18***

Jesus was not denying His own goodness. He was pressing the man to think about what he had said. If Jesus is truly good in the ultimate sense, then the young man is standing before more than a teacher. He is standing before God in the flesh.

The goodness of God reaches its highest expression at the cross. Paul writes:

*"But God commendeth his love toward us, in that, while we were yet sinners, Christ died for us." — **Romans 5:8***

The good God does not merely give rain, bread, health, and earthly joys. He gives His Son for His enemies. He provides salvation for those who had no claim upon Him. He opens eternal life through the death and resurrection of Christ.

No charge of divine harshness can stand unchanged before Calvary. The God who judges sin is the God who, in immeasurable goodness, provided a Savior for sinners.

Taste and See

The goodness of God is not merely a doctrine to affirm. It is a reality to be trusted and experienced.

David says:

"O taste and see that the LORD is good: blessed is the man that trusteth in him." — **Psalm 34:8**

To taste and see is to discover through faith that God is exactly as His Word declares. His goodness is not always perceived immediately by sight. It is trusted, embraced, and increasingly recognized as we walk with Him.

The believer learns over time that God's commands were good, even when obedience was costly. His denials were good, even when desire resisted them. His discipline was good, even when it hurt. His timing was good, even when waiting seemed long. His promises were good, even when fulfillment remained unseen.

The final proof will come in glory. When every providence is understood rightly, when every tear is wiped away, when every wrong is judged, when every promise is fulfilled, the redeemed will not find one act of God lacking in goodness.

They will confess what Scripture already declares:

"O give thanks unto the LORD; for he is good: for his mercy endureth for ever." — **Psalm 136:1**

God is good.

- He is good in creation.
- Good in commandment.
- Good in discipline.
- Good in suffering.
- Good in judgment.
- Good in salvation.
- Good in every purpose He has ordained.

And because He is good, He can be trusted even before we understand.

Chapter 17 — God Is Righteous

God is not merely powerful enough to do as He pleases. He is righteous in all that He pleases.

That distinction matters. Power alone does not guarantee goodness. A tyrant may possess power and use it wickedly. A fallen man may achieve authority and bend it toward pride, exploitation, or revenge. But God's will is never arbitrary because God Himself is perfectly righteous. He does not merely establish what is right by command. He is right in His being, right in His judgments, right in His laws, and right in every act of His hand.

The psalmist says:

"The LORD is righteous in all his ways, and holy in all his works." — **Psalm 145:17**

Not some of His ways. All of them.

- His mercy is righteous.
- His wrath is righteous.
- His patience is righteous.
- His judgments are righteous.
- His salvation is righteous.

Nothing God does can be charged with moral error. He cannot act crookedly because there is no crookedness in Him.

The Righteous God

The word **righteous** speaks of what is straight, just, morally right, and perfectly aligned with the standard of truth. In God, righteousness is not conformity to a law outside Himself. There is no higher moral authority above Him to which He must answer. His own holy nature is the source and measure of righteousness.

Moses declares:

"He is the Rock, his work is perfect: for all his ways are judgment: a God of truth and without iniquity, just and right is he." — **Deuteronomy 32:4**

The verse joins truth, justice, and righteousness. God is "without iniquity." There is nothing morally twisted in Him. He is "just and right." His actions are never merely forceful; they are always morally perfect.

Abraham appealed to this truth when the Lord revealed the coming judgment of Sodom. He asked:

"Shall not the Judge of all the earth do right?" — **Genesis 18:25**

The question assumes its own answer. The Judge of all the earth will do right. Abraham does not accuse God. He reasons from God's known character. Divine judgment cannot be unjust because God Himself is righteous.

This truth remains essential whenever Scripture confronts us with difficult judgments. There are passages that humble the reader, scenes where God's severity exceeds what modern instinct expects. The right response is not to reshape God until He matches our sensibilities. It is to remember that our moral sight is partial, while His is perfect. Whatever God does, He does rightly.

God Loves Righteousness

God is not neutral toward righteousness. He loves it.

"For the righteous LORD loveth righteousness; his countenance doth behold the upright." — **Psalm 11:7**

Righteousness is not an impersonal ideal God enforces from duty. It delights Him because it accords with His own nature. He loves what is true, upright, faithful, pure, and just because He is all of those things perfectly.

The same psalm reveals that His love of righteousness includes opposition to wickedness:

"The LORD trieth the righteous: but the wicked and him that loveth violence his soul hateth." — **Psalm 11:5**

Modern readers may recoil at such language, but Scripture does not apologize for it. A righteous God cannot regard violence, deceit, oppression, and rebellion with moral indifference. If He loves righteousness, He must oppose wickedness. The two are inseparable.

This helps us understand why divine righteousness is good news for the oppressed. If God were merely kind but not righteous, victims of evil would have no guarantee that wrongs will be answered. If He were powerful but morally indifferent, strength would provide no hope. But because God is righteous, injustice will not stand forever. Every hidden act is seen. Every lie is known. Every abuse of power will meet the Judge of all the earth.

The righteous God is the refuge of those who suffer under unrighteousness.

God's Righteous Law

God's law reflects God's righteousness.

The psalmist says:

"The statutes of the LORD are right, rejoicing the heart: the commandment of the LORD is pure, enlightening the eyes." — **Psalm 19:8**

Again:

"Thy righteousness is an everlasting righteousness, and thy law is the truth." — **Psalm 119:142**

His commandments are righteous because they arise from His righteous character. They are not arbitrary restrictions imposed upon creation. They reveal the shape of moral reality as God designed it.

This becomes important in an age that increasingly treats moral boundaries as oppressive unless they align with individual desire. Scripture presents the opposite view. God's commands are not threats to human flourishing. Sin is. His commandments guard life, preserve truth, honor covenant, protect the vulnerable, and direct creatures toward what is fitting before their Maker.

When God forbids false witness, He reflects His own truthfulness. When He forbids adultery, He reflects His faithfulness. When He commands justice for the poor and the stranger, He reflects His own righteousness. When He condemns idolatry, He reflects the truth that He alone is God.

The law is righteous because the Lawgiver is righteous.

Paul writes:

"Wherefore the law is holy, and the commandment holy, and just, and good." **— Romans 7:12**

The problem is never with God's law. The problem is with sin in man. Fallen hearts resist what is righteous because righteousness exposes rebellion. That is why human beings often call evil good and good evil. Their moral judgment has been damaged by sin.

Isaiah warns:

"Woe unto them that call evil good, and good evil; that put darkness for light, and light for darkness; that put bitter for sweet, and sweet for bitter!" **— Isaiah 5:20**

God's righteousness stands over against every moral inversion. No culture, legislature, court, scholar, pastor, or individual can redefine righteousness against Him and remain right.

Righteousness and Judgment

Because God is righteous, His judgments are righteous.

David says:

"The judgments of the LORD are true and righteous altogether." **— Psalm 19:9**

The heavenly multitude in Revelation declares:

"Great and marvellous are thy works, Lord God Almighty; just and true are thy ways, thou King of saints." — **Revelation 15:3**

And again:

"Even so, Lord God Almighty, true and righteous are thy judgments." — **Revelation 16:7**

Judgment is often treated as though it stands in tension with divine goodness. Scripture presents it as an expression of divine righteousness. God judges because He is right. He condemns wickedness because wickedness deserves condemnation. He vindicates the righteous because truth must prevail.

This is not mere theological abstraction. It matters deeply for doctrine. Final judgment cannot be denied without weakening God's righteousness. If unrepentant evil were never answered, the moral order of the universe would remain unresolved. The cries of martyrs, the wounds of the oppressed, the hidden crimes of the powerful, and the blasphemies of the rebellious would finally be treated as though they carried no lasting moral weight.

Scripture says otherwise.

"Because he hath appointed a day, in the which he will judge the world in righteousness by that man whom he hath ordained; whereof he hath given assurance unto all men, in that he hath raised him from the dead." — **Acts 17:31**

The resurrection of Christ guarantees a day of righteous judgment. The gospel does not erase the Judge. It announces that the Judge has risen, salvation is offered now, and judgment is certain.

Righteousness and Salvation

God's righteousness is not only seen in condemnation. It is also seen in salvation.

At first that may seem surprising. We often think of mercy and grace when we think of salvation, and rightly so. But Paul insists that the gospel reveals **the righteousness of God**:

"For therein is the righteousness of God revealed from faith to faith: as it is written, The just shall live by faith." — **Romans 1:17**

Later he explains that God set forth Christ as a propitiation:

"To declare, I say, at this time his righteousness: that he might be just, and the justifier of him which believeth in Jesus." — **Romans 3:26**

The cross proves that God does not save by abandoning righteousness. He saves in a way that displays it.

Sin must be judged. The guilty cannot be declared righteous by mere denial of guilt. God's moral perfection cannot be set aside.

Therefore Christ bears sin. He stands in the place of sinners. He receives judgment. He sheds His blood. Through Him, God justifies the ungodly without ceasing to be righteous.

This is one of the great glories of the gospel. The believer is not saved by a divine compromise. He is saved through a divine accomplishment in which mercy and righteousness meet perfectly.

The psalmist anticipated such a harmony:

"Mercy and truth are met together; righteousness and peace have kissed each other." — **Psalm 85:10**

The fullest realization of that verse is found at the cross. Peace with God comes through righteousness satisfied in Christ.

The Righteousness God Provides

The gospel not only preserves God's righteousness. It provides righteousness for sinners who have none of their own.

Isaiah says:

*"But we are all as an unclean thing, and all our righteousnesses are as filthy rags." — **Isaiah 64:6***

Even what fallen man presents as righteousness cannot make him acceptable before the Holy God. His obedience is fractured, his motives mixed, his heart stained by sin. If he is to stand before God, righteousness must come from God.

Jeremiah prophesies of the coming King:

*"And this is his name whereby he shall be called, THE LORD OUR RIGHTEOUSNESS." — **Jeremiah 23:6***

Paul declares the fulfillment in Christ:

*"But of him are ye in Christ Jesus, who of God is made unto us wisdom, and righteousness, and sanctification, and redemption." — **I Corinthians 1:30***

The righteousness by which believers stand before God is not self-generated. It is found in Christ. Paul says:

*"And be found in him, not having mine own righteousness, which is of the law, but that which is through the faith of Christ, the righteousness which is of God by faith." — **Philippians 3:9***

This doctrine protects the gospel from every form of self-salvation. Man does not climb to God through moral effort. He receives righteousness through faith in Christ. Salvation is not God pretending the sinner is righteous. It is God uniting the sinner to the Righteous One.

That is why justification is not merely pardon. It is a righteous declaration grounded in Christ's finished work.

Righteousness and the Believer's Life

The God who justifies also transforms.

Grace does not leave believers indifferent to righteousness. Those who have received the righteousness of Christ are called to walk in righteousness. John writes:

*"Little children, let no man deceive you: he that doeth righteousness is righteous, even as he is righteous." — **I John 3:7***

John is not teaching salvation by works. He is saying that righteous conduct reveals the life of the righteous God at work in His people. A profession of faith that makes peace with unrighteousness should not be trusted easily.

Paul tells believers:

*"Being filled with the fruits of righteousness, which are by Jesus Christ, unto the glory and praise of God." — **Philippians I:II***

Righteousness in the believer is the fruit of Christ's work, not the basis of acceptance. But it is real fruit. The God who saves His people by grace does not train them to love what He hates. He teaches them to walk in newness of life.

This also means Christians should care deeply about justice, honesty, faithfulness, purity, and upright conduct. Righteousness is not a peripheral concern. It reflects the character of God. A church that defends doctrine while tolerating dishonesty, cruelty, or exploitation contradicts the God it claims to worship.

The Righteous God Can Be Trusted

God's righteousness gives stability to faith.

We may not always understand His providence. We may struggle with why the wicked prosper for a season, why the righteous suffer, why prayers seem delayed, or why evil is permitted to continue. The psalmists wrestled with these questions. So did Habakkuk. Yet faith returns again and again to the same foundation: God is righteous.

"Righteous art thou, O LORD, and upright are thy judgments." — **Psalm 119:137**

When circumstances seem confusing, His character is not. He will never do wrong. He will never mistreat His people. He will never judge unjustly. He will never fail to distinguish truth from falsehood or good from evil.

The believer may not yet see the whole path, but he knows the One who walks it with perfect righteousness.

God is righteous.

- His ways are right.
- His judgments are right.
- His law is right.
- His salvation is right.
- His promises are right.
- His future kingdom will be right.

And because He is righteous, no trust placed in Him will ever prove misplaced.

Chapter 18 — God Is Just

Righteousness and justice belong closely together, but they are not identical in emphasis.

God's **righteousness** speaks of the perfect moral uprightness of His nature and ways. God's **justice** speaks of that righteousness applied in judgment, reward, punishment, and the ordering of all things according to what is right.

Because God is righteous, He is just. He never judges falsely. He never punishes unfairly. He never overlooks evil through indifference or favors the powerful because they are powerful. His justice is not delayed by ignorance, corrupted by partiality, or weakened by fear. He sees all things exactly as they are and will render to every matter its true moral weight.

Moses declares:

"A God of truth and without iniquity, just and right is he." — **Deuteronomy 32:4**

Abraham asks:

"Shall not the Judge of all the earth do right?" — **Genesis 18:25**

The answer is certain. He will.

Justice Belongs to God's Throne

Justice is not a secondary concern in God's rule. It is foundational to His reign.

The psalmist says:

"Justice and judgment are the habitation of thy throne: mercy and truth shall go before thy face." — **Psalm 89:14**

God's throne is not built upon raw power. It is established in justice and judgment. He reigns rightly. Every act of His government is morally perfect.

This matters because human authority is often unreliable. Judges can be bribed. Rulers can oppress. Institutions can protect the guilty and crush the weak. Those with power may use it to shield themselves from consequences. Human justice is frequently slow, partial, or corrupted.

God's justice is never any of those things.

"For the LORD your God is God of gods, and Lord of lords, a great God, a mighty, and a terrible, which regardeth not persons, nor taketh reward: He doth execute the judgment of the fatherless and widow, and loveth the stranger, in giving him food and raiment." — **Deuteronomy 10:17–18**

The great and mighty God is not indifferent to the vulnerable. His justice reaches toward the fatherless, the widow, and the stranger. Scripture never presents justice as a cold abstraction. It matters because real wrongs happen to real people, and God sees.

God Does Not Show Partiality

Human beings are easily swayed by appearance. Wealth, charm, status, tribe, education, and influence can distort judgment. God is not moved by any of them.

Peter says:

"Of a truth I perceive that God is no respecter of persons." — **Acts 10:34**

Paul writes:

"But glory, honour, and peace, to every man that worketh good, to the Jew first, and also to the Gentile: For there is no respect of persons with God." — *Romans 2:10–11*

God's justice is not tribal. It is not sentimental. It is not manipulated by religious privilege. Israel's covenant history did not exempt the nation from judgment when it persisted in rebellion. The churches of Revelation were not protected from Christ's rebukes because they bore His name. Judgment begins at the house of God because privilege heightens responsibility.

God is just toward all.

This should sober anyone who assumes religious familiarity can substitute for obedience. It should also comfort anyone who has suffered under human systems that favored others unjustly. God's courtroom cannot be bought. His verdicts cannot be bent.

Justice and the Punishment of Evil

Justice requires that evil be answered.

This is increasingly difficult for modern people to accept when the subject is God's judgment. Many want a God who forgives, but they do not want a God who condemns. Yet a judge who never punishes evil is not more loving. He is unjust.

Imagine a human court where murder, abuse, betrayal, exploitation, and violence are continually dismissed without consequence. No one would call that compassion. We would call it corruption. Why, then, would we imagine that God becomes better by refusing to judge what is evil?

Scripture says:

"The LORD trieth the righteous: but the wicked and him that loveth violence his soul hateth. Upon the wicked he shall rain snares, fire and brimstone, and an horrible tempest: this shall be the portion of their cup." — **Psalm 11:5–6**

These are severe words, but severity is not injustice when directed toward real wickedness by the perfectly just God. His judgment is not emotional excess. It is moral truth enacted.

Paul warns:

"But after thy hardness and impenitent heart treasurest up unto thyself wrath against the day of wrath and revelation of the righteous judgment of God; Who will render to every man according to his deeds." — **Romans 2:5–6**

The final judgment will be the revelation of God's righteous judgment. Much that is hidden now will be exposed then. Motives concealed from men will be known. Secret sins will not remain secret. False reputations will fall away. God will judge truly.

Justice and Delayed Judgment

Because judgment is often delayed, people mistake delay for absence.

Ecclesiastes says:

"Because sentence against an evil work is not executed speedily, therefore the heart of the sons of men is fully set in them to do evil." — **Ecclesiastes 8:11**

When consequences do not come immediately, sinners assume they may never come. The patience of God is interpreted as indifference. But Scripture warns that divine delay is not divine neglect.

Peter writes that the Lord is longsuffering, giving space for repentance, and then immediately says:

"But the day of the Lord will come as a thief in the night." — **2 Peter 3:10**

God's justice does not weaken while He waits. His patience gives opportunity for repentance. If that patience is despised, judgment becomes more solemn, not less certain.

The world often asks why God allows wickedness to continue. Scripture gives part of the answer: He is patient. He is merciful. He delays judgment while calling sinners to repentance. But Scripture also insists that the delay has an end. The just God will not allow evil to endure forever.

Justice and the Cross

The cross is the greatest demonstration that God's justice cannot simply be set aside.

If God could forgive sin by ignoring guilt, there would have been no need for Christ to die. The cross reveals that sin must be dealt with. Divine love does not erase divine justice. It provides a righteous way for sinners to be saved.

Paul says God set forth Christ:

"to be a propitiation through faith in his blood, to declare his righteousness for the remission of sins that are past, through the forbearance of God; To declare, I say, at this time his righteousness: that he might be just, and the justifier of him which believeth in Jesus." — **Romans 3:25–26**

That final phrase is central: **"just, and the justifier."**

God does not justify by becoming less just. He justifies through the atoning blood of Christ. The guilt of sin is not denied. It is borne. The sentence is not forgotten. It falls upon the willing Substitute.

Isaiah foretold:

"But he was wounded for our transgressions, he was bruised for our iniquities: the chastisement of our peace was upon him; and with his stripes we are healed." — **Isaiah 53:5**

Justice and mercy meet at Calvary. The saved sinner never stands before God as one whose guilt was casually dismissed. He stands as one whose guilt was answered in Christ.

This protects the gospel from sentimentality. Mercy is not God pretending that evil is smaller than it is. Mercy is God providing salvation at infinite cost while remaining perfectly just.

Justice and Forgiveness

The justice of God also gives assurance to believers who confess their sins.

John writes:

"If we confess our sins, he is faithful and just to forgive us our sins, and to cleanse us from all unrighteousness." — **I John I:9**

At first, we might expect John to say God is merciful to forgive. He is. But John says He is **faithful and just** to forgive. Why just? Because Christ has truly dealt with the sins of His people. God does not demand payment twice. He does not condemn those whose guilt has been borne by the Son. Forgiveness is righteous because the cross is sufficient.

This gives the believer a firmer foundation than emotion. When he confesses sin, he does not plead for God to abandon justice in order to show mercy. He comes through Christ, trusting the justice of God that has already been satisfied in Christ's work.

God's justice is not the enemy of the redeemed. In Christ, it becomes part of their assurance.

Justice and God's Promises

Because God is just, He will not fail to vindicate what is right, fulfill what He has promised, or reward faithfulness according to His Word.

Paul says:

"For God is not unrighteous to forget your work and labour of love, which ye have shewed toward his name." — **Hebrews 6:10**

God does not overlook faithful service. Human beings may forget it. Churches may fail to see it. Sacrifices may pass unnoticed by those who benefit from them. But God is not unrighteous to forget.

This is not salvation by works. It is the justice of God toward the labor of His redeemed people. He sees. He remembers. He will reward rightly.

Likewise, when believers suffer unjustly, they are commanded not to take vengeance into their own hands:

"Dearly beloved, avenge not yourselves, but rather give place unto wrath: for it is written, Vengeance is mine; I will repay, saith the Lord." — **Romans 12:19**

The command to release personal vengeance rests on the certainty of divine justice. Christians are not asked to pretend evil does not matter. They are asked to entrust justice to the only One who can administer it perfectly.

The Justice of God and Final Hope

A world without final justice would be unbearable.

If death ends all things and there is no judgment beyond history, then many evils remain forever unanswered. The righteous suffer and are forgotten. The wicked prosper and escape. Truth loses in public and is never vindicated. Scripture refuses that conclusion.

"Because he hath appointed a day, in the which he will judge the world in righteousness by that man whom he hath ordained." — **Acts 17:31**

The appointed Judge is Jesus Christ. The One who offered Himself for sinners will also judge the world in righteousness. The gospel does not eliminate final judgment. It announces the way of salvation before that judgment comes.

For those in Christ, judgment is no terror of condemnation. He has borne their guilt. For those who reject Him, judgment will reveal the full seriousness of sin and the perfect justice of God.

Revelation shows heaven praising Him:

"Great and marvellous are thy works, Lord God Almighty; just and true are thy ways, thou King of saints." — **Revelation 15:3**

No one in eternity will discover injustice in God. Every verdict will be right. Every sentence deserved. Every act of mercy glorious. Every act of judgment true.

The God Who Will Do Right

God's justice is not a doctrine to be tolerated uneasily. It is one of the reasons He is worthy of trust.

- Because He is just:
- evil will not triumph forever,
- truth will not remain buried,
- the oppressed will not be forgotten,
- the guilty will not escape by power or influence,
- the believer's sins will not be counted against him if Christ has borne them,

and every promise of God will be fulfilled with perfect righteousness.

The Judge of all the earth will do right.

He always has.

He always does.

He always will.

Chapter 19 — God Is True

God does not merely tell the truth. He is true.

There is no falsehood in Him, no deception, no exaggeration, no hidden corruption beneath His words. He does not mislead by accident or design. He does not speak from partial knowledge. He does not promise what He cannot perform, threaten what He will never do, or reveal Himself in ways meant to confuse those who humbly receive His Word.

Moses declares:

"He is the Rock, his work is perfect: for all his ways are judgment: a God of truth and without iniquity, just and right is he." — **Deuteronomy 32:4**

God is **"a God of truth."** His truthfulness is not a policy He follows. It is part of His very character. He speaks truth because He is truth. His Word is trustworthy because He is trustworthy.

This matters for everything. If God were not true, faith would have no foundation. Prayer would become guesswork. Promise would become uncertain. Scripture would lose its authority. Doctrine would become unstable. Hope would become wishful thinking.

But God is true.

God Cannot Lie

Scripture does not merely say that God usually tells the truth. It says He cannot lie.

Paul writes of:

"eternal life, which God, that cannot lie, promised before the world began." **— Titus 1:2**

The writer of Hebrews says:

*"it was impossible for God to lie." — **Hebrews 6:18***

This impossibility does not indicate weakness in God. It reveals perfection. God cannot lie for the same reason He cannot be evil, unjust, foolish, or unholy. Falsehood would contradict His nature.

Human beings lie for many reasons. They lie to escape consequences, gain advantage, hide shame, manipulate others, protect pride, or maintain control. None of those motives can exist in God. He has no weakness to hide, no ignorance to cover, no guilt to conceal, no fear of exposure, no need to manipulate reality. He is the Lord of reality.

Balaam, for all his corruption, spoke truly when he said:

*"God is not a man, that he should lie; neither the son of man, that he should repent: hath he said, and shall he not do it? or hath he spoken, and shall he not make it good?" — **Numbers 23:19***

God's truthfulness is tied directly to His faithfulness. If He has spoken, He will make it good. His words are not like human intentions, sincere in the moment but vulnerable to weakness, forgetfulness, or change. What God says stands.

God's Word Is Truth

Because God is true, His Word is truth.

Jesus prayed:

*"Sanctify them through thy truth: thy word is truth." — **John 17:17***

He did not say merely that God's Word contains true ideas, though it does. He said, **"thy word is truth."** Scripture bears the character of the God who gave it. It is reliable because He is reliable.

The psalmist says:

"Thy word is true from the beginning: and every one of thy righteous judgments endureth for ever." — **Psalm 119:160**

Again:

"The words of the LORD are pure words: as silver tried in a furnace of earth, purified seven times." — **Psalm 12:6**

God's words are pure. They do not need human correction. They do not become more trustworthy when filtered through the moral assumptions of the age. They do not wait for our approval before they become authoritative. The church does not stand over Scripture as editor. It stands under Scripture as servant.

This has direct importance for the theme of this book. If God is true, then His self-revelation must be received as true. We are not free to accept the attributes we prefer and reinterpret the rest until they become more agreeable. When Scripture declares His holiness, it is true. When it declares His mercy, it is true. When it declares His wrath, it is true. When it declares His faithfulness to covenant promises, it is true.

A partial God is often produced by partial trust in God's Word.

Truth and Interpretation

God's truthfulness also shapes how we interpret Scripture.

Because God is true, His revelation is not deceitful. Because He is wise, His words are not careless. Because He is orderly, His speech does not collapse into confusion. The Bible contains symbol, poetry, prophecy, parable, type, and vision, but none of these forms makes God's speech untrue.

A symbol is not a lie. A parable is not a trick. A prophecy is not an empty container for whatever meaning later readers prefer.

The question is always: **What has God actually said, in the form He chose to say it?**

This guards us from two opposite errors. One error refuses to recognize figurative language where Scripture clearly uses it. The other error turns figurative language into permission to dissolve the text's meaning. Both mishandle truth. Literal and figurative language are both truthful when interpreted according to the intent of the passage.

Jesus treated Scripture's wording as reliable. When answering the Sadducees on the resurrection, He reasoned from God's words to Moses:

*"I am the God of Abraham, and the God of Isaac, and the God of Jacob? God is not the God of the dead, but of the living." — **Matthew 22:32***

His argument depends on the exact force of what God said. He did not treat Scripture as vague religious material. He treated it as God's truthful speech.

That should sober every interpreter. To handle Scripture loosely is to forget whose words we are handling.

Christ Is the Truth

The truthfulness of God is revealed supremely in Jesus Christ.

Jesus says:

*"I am the way, the truth, and the life: no man cometh unto the Father, but by me." — **John 14:6***

He does not merely teach truth as a prophet might. He is the truth. In Him, God's self-revelation becomes personal, visible, and embodied. Every word He speaks is true. Every promise He makes is sure. Every warning He gives is faithful.

John says of the incarnate Word:

"And the Word was made flesh, and dwelt among us, and we beheld his glory, the glory as of the only begotten of the Father, full of grace and truth." — **John 1:14**

Grace and truth are not enemies in Christ. He is full of both. His grace does not require Him to soften truth. His truth does not make Him harsh. He can expose sin with perfect honesty and receive repentant sinners with perfect mercy.

This is why any version of Christianity that separates Jesus from truth is false at the root. Christ cannot be made into a symbol of affirmation detached from His own words. He is not available as a gentle religious figure who blesses whatever men decide to call good. He is the Truth who says, "No man cometh unto the Father, but by me."

His exclusivity is not arrogance. It is reality spoken by the One who cannot lie.

Truth and the Gospel

The gospel depends upon the truthfulness of God.

If God's warnings about sin are not true, the cross is unnecessary. If His promises are not true, faith has no ground. If the resurrection is not true, Christianity collapses. Paul says plainly:

"And if Christ be not raised, your faith is vain; ye are yet in your sins." — **1 Corinthians 15:17**

Christian hope is not built on inspiring myth. It rests on truth in history: Christ died for our sins according to the Scriptures, was buried, and rose again the third day according to the Scriptures.

The gospel also reveals God as true to His promises. What He promised through the prophets, He fulfilled in Christ. Paul writes:

"For all the promises of God in him are yea, and in him Amen, unto the glory of God by us." — **2 Corinthians 1:20**

Christ is not God's change of plan. He is the confirmation of God's truth. The promises are not weakened in Him. They find their certainty in Him.

This gives the believer confidence. Salvation does not rest on shifting inward feelings. It rests on the truthful God who has spoken in His Son, given His gospel, and promised eternal life to those who believe.

Truth and Human Falsehood

The truthfulness of God exposes the falsehood of man.

Paul writes:

"let God be true, but every man a liar." — **Romans 3:4**

This is not saying every human statement is false. It means that when human claims stand against God's Word, God is true and man is wrong. No amount of scholarship, popularity, sincerity, or cultural pressure can make falsehood true.

This is a necessary correction in every age. Human beings often want truth to bend. We want sin renamed, judgment softened, promises revised, identity self-created, and righteousness redefined. But reality does not yield to rebellion. God is true whether men agree with Him or not.

Truth is not cruel because it refuses to flatter us. It is mercy when God tells us what is real before judgment falls.

The prophets often sounded severe because they told the truth. Jesus sounded severe when He called men to repentance because He told the truth. The apostles sounded exclusive when they proclaimed salvation in Christ alone because they told the truth. False comfort may feel kind for a moment, but it destroys. Truth wounds only to heal when received in repentance and faith.

Truth and Worship

God must be worshiped in truth.

Jesus told the woman at the well:

*"But the hour cometh, and now is, when the true worshippers shall worship the Father in spirit and in truth: for the Father seeketh such to worship him. God is a Spirit: and they that worship him must worship him in spirit and in truth." — **John 4:23–24***

Sincerity alone is not enough. Zeal alone is not enough. Beauty, emotion, music, and tradition are not enough. Worship must be governed by truth because the God worshiped is true.

This means false ideas about God corrupt worship. If we worship a god of our own preferences while using biblical language, we are not worshiping rightly. To worship God truthfully, we must receive Him as He reveals Himself.

The more fully we know His character, the more rightly we worship. His truth does not reduce devotion. It purifies it.

Truth and the Christian Life

Because God is true, His people must be truthful.

Paul writes:

*"Wherefore putting away lying, speak every man truth with his neighbour: for we are members one of another." — **Ephesians 4:25***

Lying is not a small social defect. It contradicts the character of God. The devil is called "a liar, and the father of it." Christ is truth. The Christian cannot belong to the God of truth and make peace with deceit.

This applies to more than spoken lies. It includes exaggeration, manipulation, hypocrisy, flattery, false appearances, doctrinal dishonesty, and the refusal to confess sin plainly. Truthfulness should mark the people of God because truth belongs to the character of God.

A church that tolerates lies for the sake of reputation has forgotten God. A teacher who bends Scripture to protect a system has forgotten God. A believer who hides sin under religious appearance has forgotten God. The God we worship is true.

The Truth That Sets Free

Jesus said:

"And ye shall know the truth, and the truth shall make you free." — **John 8:32**

Truth frees because lies enslave. Sin lies about pleasure, autonomy, identity, and consequence. False religion lies about God. Self-righteousness lies about man. Despair lies about mercy. The gospel tells the truth: God is holy, man is guilty, Christ is sufficient, grace is real, repentance is necessary, judgment is coming, and eternal life is found in the Son.

That truth may first humble us. It may expose us. It may strip away illusions we preferred to keep. But the wound is mercy. God's truth leads out of darkness.

No one is helped by a false god, a false gospel, a false peace, or a false hope. The truth of God is not our enemy. It is the light by which we see everything else rightly.

The God Who Cannot Lie

God is true.

- His Word is true.
- His promises are true.
- His warnings are true.
- His judgments are true.
- His gospel is true.
- His Son is the truth.

This gives weight to every doctrine and stability to every hope. The believer does not stand on religious imagination. He stands on the Word of the God who cannot lie.

When everything in the world feels uncertain, God remains true. When cultures redefine reality, God remains true. When false teachers twist Scripture, God remains true. When our emotions tremble, God remains true.

And because He is true, all who trust Him will find that not one word of His has failed.

Chapter 20 — God Is Faithful

God is true in what He says. He is faithful in what He keeps.

Faithfulness is truthfulness carried through time. It is the steadfastness of God to His Word, His covenant, His promises, His people, and His own name. He does not merely speak accurately in the moment. He remains committed to what He has spoken. He does not forget, weaken, drift, reconsider, or fail.

Moses declares:

"Know therefore that the LORD thy God, he is God, the faithful God, which keepeth covenant and mercy with them that love him and keep his commandments to a thousand generations." — **Deuteronomy 7:9**

That phrase matters: **"the faithful God."** Faithfulness is not simply something God sometimes does. It belongs to who He is. He is the covenant-keeping God. He binds Himself by His Word and never proves false to it.

Human faithfulness is often fragile. We mean well and fail. We promise and forget. We commit and grow weary. Our love can cool, our strength can collapse, our memory can fail, and our courage can falter. But God is not like man. What He says, He does. What He promises, He keeps. Whom He loves, He does not abandon.

Faithful to His Name

God's faithfulness is rooted first in Himself.

He does not remain faithful because His people are worthy of such steadfastness. He remains faithful because He is God. His name, character, and glory are bound up with the keeping of His Word.

When Israel sinned grievously, Moses pleaded with God on the basis of His promise and reputation among the nations:

"Remember Abraham, Isaac, and Israel, thy servants, to whom thou swarest by thine own self, and saidst unto them, I will multiply your seed as the stars of heaven, and all this land that I have spoken of will I give unto your seed, and they shall inherit it for ever." — **Exodus 32:13**

Moses understood that God's covenant promises mattered. Israel's sin was real and deserved judgment, but God's faithfulness to His oath was also real. The hope of the people did not rest upon their stability, but upon God's.

Later, through Ezekiel, the Lord says:

"I do not this for your sakes, O house of Israel, but for mine holy name's sake." — **Ezekiel 36:22**

That is not coldness. It is hope. If God's faithfulness rested finally on man's worthiness, no sinner would be secure. But because God acts for His holy name, His promises stand on stronger ground than human performance.

Faithful to His Covenant

The Bible's story is filled with covenant, and covenant depends upon faithfulness.

God promised Abraham seed, land, blessing, and a future through which all families of the earth would be blessed. Centuries passed. Abraham died. Isaac died. Jacob died. Israel went down into Egypt and suffered bondage. Yet God had not forgotten.

Exodus says:

*"And God heard their groaning, and God remembered his covenant with Abraham, with Isaac, and with Jacob. And God looked upon the children of Israel, and God had respect unto them." — **Exodus 2:24–25***

The word **remembered** does not mean God had previously forgotten. It means He turned His covenant commitment into action at the appointed time. His faithfulness may not always move according to human expectation, but it never fails.

Joshua later testified:

*"There failed not ought of any good thing which the LORD had spoken unto the house of Israel; all came to pass." — **Joshua 21:45***

That sentence should teach us how to think about God's promises. Not one good thing failed. The fulfillment of God's Word may involve long waiting, discipline, testing, and unexpected paths. But His covenant faithfulness is never uncertain.

This is why doctrines that casually dissolve God's covenant promises should be handled with great care. God does not speak empty words. He does not make covenant commitments lightly. Fulfillment in Christ is richer than human expectation, but it is not less faithful to what God said.

Faithful Even When His People Fail

God's faithfulness does not mean He ignores sin. He disciplines, corrects, judges, and warns. But He does not cease to be faithful when His people are unfaithful.

Paul writes:

*"If we believe not, yet he abideth faithful: he cannot deny himself." — **2 Timothy 2:13***

This verse is not permission for unbelief. The surrounding passage includes real warnings. But it reveals something essential: God's faithfulness is not a fragile response to ours. He cannot deny Himself. His character cannot collapse because man is unstable.

Israel's history proves this repeatedly. The people grumbled, rebelled, worshiped idols, despised prophets, and broke covenant. God judged them severely. Yet He preserved a remnant, sent prophets, remembered His promises, and brought forth Christ according to His Word.

The book of Lamentations was written amid devastation, yet in the middle of grief we read:

"It is of the LORD'S mercies that we are not consumed, because his compassions fail not. They are new every morning: great is thy faithfulness." **— Lamentations 3:22–23**

That confession does not come from a comfortable life untouched by sorrow. It rises from ruins. The city has fallen. Judgment has come. Yet the prophet still says, **"great is thy faithfulness."**

God's faithfulness is not proved only when life is easy. Sometimes it is confessed through tears by those who know that judgment has been deserved and mercy has not been exhausted.

Faithful in Temptation

God is faithful in the daily struggles of His people.

Paul writes:

"There hath no temptation taken you but such as is common to man: but God is faithful, who will not suffer you to be tempted above that ye are able; but will with the temptation also make a way to escape, that ye may be able to bear it." **— I Corinthians 10:13**

The promise is not that temptation will be light. It is not that obedience will feel easy. It is that God is faithful. He does not abandon His people to temptation as though they were left alone before powers greater than His grace. He provides a way of escape, not always from the presence of temptation, but from surrender to it.

This truth removes excuses. No believer can honestly say God left him no path of obedience. The path may be costly, humbling, and painful to the flesh, but it is real. God's faithfulness stands behind every command to flee sin, endure trial, resist the devil, and walk in holiness.

At the same time, this promise comforts the weak. The believer fighting sin is not fighting without divine faithfulness beneath him. God sees. God provides. God sustains.

Faithful to Forgive

God is faithful when His children confess their sins.

John writes:

"If we confess our sins, he is faithful and just to forgive us our sins, and to cleanse us from all unrighteousness." — I John 1:9

This is not cheap comfort. Confession means bringing sin into the light before God without excuse or disguise. But when the believer confesses, he does not meet a God whose mercy must be coaxed out of reluctance. He meets the faithful God who has provided Christ, promised forgiveness, and will not despise the blood of His Son.

God is faithful and just to forgive because Christ's sacrifice is sufficient. The believer's assurance does not rest upon the intensity of his regret, though sorrow for sin is real. It rests upon the faithfulness of God to His own gospel.

This matters because guilt can make the soul suspicious of God. After repeated failure, the believer may wonder whether God's patience has finally ended. But the remedy is not to minimize sin. It is to confess it honestly and trust the faithful God who cleanses from all unrighteousness.

Faithful to Preserve His People

God's faithfulness also secures the believer's final hope.

Paul writes to the Thessalonians:

*"And the very God of peace sanctify you wholly; and I pray God your whole spirit and soul and body be preserved blameless unto the coming of our Lord Jesus Christ. Faithful is he that calleth you, who also will do it." — **I Thessalonians 5:23–24***

The command to holiness is real, but final preservation rests upon God's faithfulness. He calls, sanctifies, preserves, and completes His work.

Paul says elsewhere:

*"Being confident of this very thing, that he which hath begun a good work in you will perform it until the day of Jesus Christ." — **Philippians 1:6***

God does not begin salvation and then leave its completion uncertain. He does not awaken faith only to abandon His own work halfway. The Christian's perseverance matters, but it is upheld by God's preserving faithfulness.

This does not produce carelessness in true faith. It produces confidence, endurance, and worship. The sheep continue because the Shepherd keeps them. The saints persevere because God preserves.

Faithful in Suffering

Suffering often tempts believers to question God's faithfulness.

Pain narrows vision. Waiting stretches faith. Prayers that seem unanswered can make the soul wonder whether God has forgotten. Scripture answers not by denying sorrow, but by directing us back to God's character.

Peter writes:

"Wherefore let them that suffer according to the will of God commit the keeping of their souls to him in well doing, as unto a faithful Creator." — I Peter 4:19

That title is beautiful: **"a faithful Creator."** The One who made His people is faithful to keep them. They may suffer according to His will, but their souls are not unsafe in His hands.

Christ Himself entrusted His spirit to the Father while suffering on the cross. The path of obedience led through agony, but not abandonment. The resurrection vindicated the faithfulness of God.

The believer may not understand every trial, but he may commit his soul to the faithful Creator. God's faithfulness does not always remove suffering quickly. It keeps His people through suffering until His purpose is complete.

Faithful to His Warnings

God's faithfulness includes His warnings.

This is often neglected. We gladly speak of God keeping comforting promises, but His truthfulness also means He will do what He has warned. Judgment delayed is not judgment canceled unless God Himself grants repentance and mercy according to His Word.

Noah preached while the ark was preparing. The flood still came. Prophets warned Israel and Judah. Exile still came. Jesus warned Jerusalem. Destruction still came.

The same faithful God who promises salvation in Christ also warns of wrath for those who reject Him. He is faithful to mercy and faithful to judgment because He is faithful to Himself.

This should make preaching sober. It is unfaithful to God to proclaim His promises while muting His warnings. The full character of God requires both.

Faithful to Finish All Things

The faithfulness of God extends to the end of history.

The return of Christ, the resurrection of the dead, the judgment of the wicked, the restoration of all things, and the new creation do not rest on human optimism. They rest on the faithful God.

John writes in Revelation:

*"And I saw heaven opened, and behold a white horse; and he that sat upon him was called Faithful and True, and in righteousness he doth judge and make war." — **Revelation 19:11***

Christ Himself is called **Faithful and True**. The One who came in humility will return in glory. The promises of God will not dissolve into symbolism detached from reality. The King will come. The kingdom will be established. Evil will be judged. The bride will be made ready. The dwelling of God will be with men.

The final pages of Scripture are not wishful poetry. They are the faithful God declaring the end He will bring to pass.

Great Is Thy Faithfulness

God is faithful.

- Faithful to His name.
- Faithful to His covenant.
- Faithful when His people fail.
- Faithful in temptation.
- Faithful to forgive.
- Faithful to preserve.
- Faithful in suffering.
- Faithful to warn.
- Faithful to finish what He began.

This truth steadies the whole Christian life. We are not saved by our consistency, but by His. We are not kept by the strength of our grip, but by the faithfulness of His hand. We are not hoping in a God who may grow weary of His promises. We are hoping in the faithful God.

"Let us hold fast the profession of our faith without wavering; for he is faithful that promised." — **Hebrews 10:23**

That is the call. Hold fast.

- Not because the world is stable.
- Not because the flesh is strong.
- Not because suffering is light.
- Not because obedience is easy.

Hold fast because He is faithful that promised.

Chapter 21 — God Is Love

Few statements in Scripture are more precious, and few are more often misused, than this:

"God is love." — I John 4:8

The words are simple. Their meaning is not shallow.

John does not say that love is God. He says God is love. Love does not define God from outside Himself, as though human feelings could sit in judgment over Him. God defines love. Whatever love truly is, it must be understood from His character, His Word, and His works.

This matters because love is one of the easiest attributes to distort. In many minds, love has been reduced to affirmation, tolerance, emotional warmth, or the refusal to judge. But if God is love, then love must be holy, righteous, truthful, faithful, wise, and good. God's love is never separated from the rest of His character.

- His love does not cancel His holiness.
- His love does not deny His justice.
- His love does not silence His truth.
- His love does not make sin harmless.

God's love is not sentimental weakness. It is the holy, self-giving, covenant-keeping goodness of God toward His people, revealed supremely in Jesus Christ.

Love Belongs Eternally to God

God did not become loving after He created the world.

This is important. If God were a solitary person, love would require creation in order to become active. He would need someone outside

Himself in order to love. But the true God is Father, Son, and Holy Ghost. Before the world began, the Father loved the Son in the fellowship of the Spirit.

Jesus prayed:

"Father, I will that they also, whom thou hast given me, be with me where I am; that they may behold my glory, which thou hast given me: for thou lovedst me before the foundation of the world." — **John 17:24**

Before creation, there was love. Before angels sang, before Adam breathed, before the first promise was given, the Father loved the Son. God's love is not a response to loneliness. It belongs to His eternal life.

This protects us from imagining that God created because He lacked something. He did not need creatures in order to love. He created from fullness, not deficiency. His love toward us is therefore grace. It is not God using us to complete Himself. It is the overflowing generosity of the God who is already perfect in Himself.

God's Love Revealed in Giving His Son

The clearest revelation of God's love is not found by looking inward at human emotion. It is found at the cross.

John writes:

"In this was manifested the love of God toward us, because that God sent his only begotten Son into the world, that we might live through him." — **I John 4:9**

God's love was **manifested**. It was shown. It entered history. It took visible form in the sending of the Son.

John continues:

"Herein is love, not that we loved God, but that he loved us, and sent his Son to be the propitiation for our sins." — **I John 4:10**

This is one of the most important verses in Scripture for defining love. Love begins with God, not with man. It acts toward the undeserving. It sends the Son. It deals with sin through propitiation.

That last word matters. God's love does not ignore wrath against sin. It provides the sacrifice by which wrath is satisfied. The cross does not show love by pretending sin is small. It shows love by revealing that God gave His Son to bear what sinners deserved.

Paul says the same:

"But God commendeth his love toward us, in that, while we were yet sinners, Christ died for us." — **Romans 5:8**

God loved us while we were sinners. Not while we were attractive, obedient, or spiritually impressive. His love moved toward enemies, rebels, and the ungodly. That does not mean He approved of our sin. It means His love was strong enough to save us from it.

The Love of Christ

The love of God is revealed in the love of Christ.

Paul writes:

"the Son of God, who loved me, and gave himself for me." — **Galatians 2:20**

Christ's love is not vague goodwill. It is personal, costly, and sacrificial. He gave Himself. He did not merely give teaching, miracles, example, or comfort. He gave His life.

Jesus says:

"Greater love hath no man than this, that a man lay down his life for his friends." — **John 15:13**

The cross is the measure of divine love. Any definition of love that cannot make sense of the cross is false. At Calvary, love bleeds. Love obeys the Father. Love bears guilt. Love suffers shame. Love saves.

This is why Christian love cannot be reduced to niceness. Christ was not merely nice. He was truthful, holy, compassionate, patient, severe when needed, tender to the broken, and unyielding toward hypocrisy. His love was never detached from righteousness.

The same Jesus who wept over Jerusalem also pronounced judgment upon it. The same Jesus who welcomed sinners also told them to repent. The same Jesus who forgave also warned of hell. The love of Christ is full, not flattened.

God's Love Is Holy Love

Because God is holy, His love is holy.

This must be said plainly. God does not love the way fallen man often loves. Human love can become selfish, possessive, indulgent, cowardly, or blind. It may excuse evil in the name of loyalty. It may avoid hard truth to preserve comfort. It may confuse desire with goodness.

God's love has no such impurity.

He loves what is good for His creatures, and the greatest good is Himself. Therefore His love does not lead people away from holiness. It draws them toward it. He does not love His children by leaving them enslaved to sin. He loves them by redeeming, cleansing, disciplining, and transforming them.

Hebrews says:

"For whom the Lord loveth he chasteneth, and scourgeth every son whom he receiveth." — **Hebrews 12:6**

That verse will sound strange to anyone who thinks love means avoiding all pain. But a father who loves his child corrects what would destroy him. God's discipline is not the contradiction of His love. It is one expression of it.

Christ's love for the church has the same goal:

"Christ also loved the church, and gave himself for it; That he might sanctify and cleanse it with the washing of water by the word, That he might present it to himself a glorious church, not having spot, or wrinkle, or any such thing; but that it should be holy and without blemish." — **Ephesians 5:25–27**

Christ loves His bride by making her holy. He does not love her spots and wrinkles. He removes them. He does not cherish sin in His people. He cleanses it away.

God's Love Is Covenant Love

The love of God is often expressed in Scripture as steadfast covenant mercy.

God set His love upon Israel, not because the nation was great, but because He chose to love and keep His promise.

"The LORD did not set his love upon you, nor choose you, because ye were more in number than any people; for ye were the fewest of all people: But because the LORD loved you, and because he would keep the oath which he had sworn unto your fathers..." — **Deuteronomy 7:7–8**

God's love is not explained by Israel's worthiness. It is bound to His gracious choice and covenant oath. He loved because He loved. He kept because He had sworn.

This covenant love runs throughout Scripture. It is patient with weakness, but not indifferent to rebellion. It forgives, restores, warns, disciplines, and keeps promise. Israel's unfaithfulness did not make God unfaithful. His love endured through judgment and restoration because His covenant purpose stood.

The same is true for believers in Christ. The New Covenant is secured not by human strength but by the blood of the Son. God's love is not a passing affection that evaporates when His people stumble. It is steadfast, purposeful, and faithful.

Paul asks:

"Who shall separate us from the love of Christ?" — **Romans 8:35**

After naming tribulation, distress, persecution, famine, nakedness, peril, and sword, he concludes:

"For I am persuaded, that neither death, nor life, nor angels, nor principalities, nor powers, nor things present, nor things to come, Nor height, nor depth, nor any other creature, shall be able to separate us from the love of God, which is in Christ Jesus our Lord." — **Romans 8:38–39**

That is covenant security. God's love in Christ is stronger than every created threat.

The Love of God and the World

John 3:16 is perhaps the most familiar verse in the Bible:

"For God so loved the world, that he gave his only begotten Son, that whosoever believeth in him should not perish, but have everlasting life." — **John 3:16**

The verse reveals the wideness of God's saving love. The world in John is not morally attractive. It is fallen, darkened, rebellious, and guilty. Yet God loved the world in this way: He gave His only begotten Son.

But the verse must be allowed to finish its own sentence. God's love gives the Son so that believers should not perish. It does not say that love means all are saved regardless of faith. It does not say that perishing is unreal. In fact, the greatness of the love is seen precisely because perishing is real and the gift of the Son is necessary.

John continues:

*"He that believeth on him is not condemned: but he that believeth not is condemned already, because he hath not believed in the name of the only begotten Son of God." — **John 3:18***

God's love does not erase the distinction between belief and unbelief. It provides salvation in Christ and calls sinners to come.

Love and Hatred of Evil

The fact that God is love does not mean He loves everything.

Scripture says:

*"Ye that love the LORD, hate evil." — **Psalm 97:10***

Those who love God must hate evil because God Himself is opposed to it. Love for righteousness requires hatred of what destroys righteousness. Love for the oppressed requires hatred of oppression. Love for truth requires hatred of lies. Love for holiness requires hatred of sin.

A love that refuses to hate evil is not biblical love. It is moral confusion.

This is important in a time when love is often used as an argument against repentance. People speak as though love requires God to affirm whatever a person desires. Scripture speaks differently. God's love rescues sinners from darkness. It does not rename darkness as light.

Jesus loved the rich young ruler, and He confronted his idol. The text says:

"Then Jesus beholding him loved him, and said unto him, One thing thou lackest…" — **Mark 10:21**

Love told the truth. Love exposed what stood between the man and eternal life. Love did not flatter him into destruction.

God's Love Poured Into His People

God not only loves His people; He makes His love known to them.

Paul writes:

"the love of God is shed abroad in our hearts by the Holy Ghost which is given unto us." — **Romans 5:5**

The believer does not merely infer God's love from a distance. The Holy Ghost bears witness to it within the heart. This inward assurance is not detached from the objective work of Christ, for Paul immediately points to the death of Christ for sinners. The Spirit applies to the heart what the Son accomplished in history.

God's love also creates love in His people.

John writes:

"We love him, because he first loved us." — **I John 4:19**

Christian love is responsive before it is active. We love because we have been loved. God's love is the fountain; ours is the stream. This means loveless Christianity is a contradiction. A person may hold correct doctrine in many areas, but if hatred, cruelty, bitterness, and pride rule the heart, he is not reflecting the God he claims to know.

John says:

"Beloved, if God so loved us, we ought also to love one another." — I John 4:11

The logic is simple and searching. If God loved us at such cost, we cannot withhold love from His people.

The God Whose Love Must Not Be Reduced

God is love.

But that sentence must be protected from the age that wants to use it against everything else God has revealed. God's love is not permission to edit His holiness, silence His justice, dismiss His wrath, or soften His truth. The Bible never pits love against the full character of God.

- The God who is love is the God who is light.
- The Father who loves is the Father who disciplines.
- The Son who loves is the Son who warns.
- The Spirit who sheds abroad God's love is the Holy Spirit.

Love is not less beautiful because it is holy. It is more beautiful. A love that lies would be corrupt. A love that ignores evil would be unjust. A love that refuses to save from sin would be cruel. God's love is better than the sentimental substitutes men invent.

- It is eternal love.
- Holy love.
- Covenant love.
- Saving love.
- Truthful love.
- Sacrificial love.
- Unfailing love.

And it is known supremely here:

"Hereby perceive we the love of God, because he laid down his life for us…"
— I John 3:16

At the cross, the love of God is not merely announced. It is displayed.

The sinner who wants to know whether God is loving must look there. The believer who fears he has been forgotten must look there. The church tempted to redefine love must look there.

God is love, and Calvary tells us what that means.

Chapter 22 — God Is Merciful

Mercy is God's goodness toward the miserable, the guilty, the helpless, and the undeserving.

Grace emphasizes God's favor freely given. Mercy emphasizes God's compassion toward those in need and His willingness to withhold deserved judgment. The two often stand together because sinners need both. We need grace because we have no merit. We need mercy because we are guilty, weak, broken, and exposed.

When God proclaimed His name to Moses, mercy came near the front of His own description:

"The LORD, The LORD God, merciful and gracious, longsuffering, and abundant in goodness and truth." — **Exodus 34:6**

God did not allow man to invent this description. He declared it Himself. Mercy is not a human wish projected onto heaven. It belongs to the revealed character of God.

That matters because guilty people often wonder whether mercy is reluctant in God. We imagine He must be persuaded into compassion, as though judgment were natural to Him but mercy had to be dragged from Him. Scripture will not allow that. God is just, and He will not clear the guilty apart from atonement. But He is also merciful. Mercy is not foreign to Him.

The Tender Mercy of God

Scripture often speaks of God's mercy with warmth and tenderness.

David says:

"Like as a father pitieth his children, so the LORD pitieth them that fear him. For he knoweth our frame; he remembereth that we are dust." — **Psalm 103:13–14**

God is not ignorant of human frailty. He knows what we are made of. He remembers our weakness even when we forget it. His mercy is not harsh pity from a distance, but fatherly compassion toward dust-bound children.

The same psalm says:

"The LORD is merciful and gracious, slow to anger, and plenteous in mercy. He will not always chide: neither will he keep his anger for ever." — **Psalm 103:8–9**

God's mercy is plentiful. He is not miserly with compassion. He does not delight in endless accusation against those who fear Him. He is slow to anger, not because sin is small, but because mercy is real.

This does not mean God's mercy abolishes His holiness. Psalm 103 also says:

"But the mercy of the LORD is from everlasting to everlasting upon them that fear him, and his righteousness unto children's children; To such as keep his covenant, and to those that remember his commandments to do them." — **Psalm 103:17–18**

Mercy and reverence belong together. The merciful God is still the holy God. His mercy does not train His people to despise His commandments. It draws them into grateful obedience.

Mercy Toward Sinners

The mercy of God is seen most clearly when He receives repentant sinners.

David had sinned grievously. He did not come before God with excuses, comparisons, or claims of personal worth. He pleaded for mercy:

"Have mercy upon me, O God, according to thy lovingkindness: according unto the multitude of thy tender mercies blot out my transgressions." — **Psalm 51:1**

David understood that his only hope was not the smallness of his sin but the greatness of God's mercy. He asked God to blot out transgressions according to the multitude of His tender mercies.

The tax collector in Jesus' parable stood far off and would not lift up his eyes to heaven. His prayer was short:

"God be merciful to me a sinner." — **Luke 18:13**

Jesus said that man went down to his house justified rather than the self-confident Pharisee. The sinner who cast himself upon mercy found acceptance. The religious man who stood upon his own righteousness did not.

This is the way of salvation. No one enters God's favor by proving himself worthy. The door is mercy. The proud miss it because they do not think they need it. The broken find it because they know they do.

Mercy and the Incarnation

The coming of Christ is the great visitation of divine mercy.

When Zacharias prophesied at the birth of John the Baptist, he said God had acted:

"To perform the mercy promised to our fathers, and to remember his holy covenant." — **Luke 1:72**

He continued:

"Through the tender mercy of our God; whereby the dayspring from on high hath visited us." — **Luke 1:78**

The incarnation is mercy promised, mercy remembered, mercy visiting. God did not look upon a dark world with indifference. He sent the Dayspring from on high. Christ came because God is merciful.

During His earthly ministry, Jesus embodied this mercy. He had compassion on the multitudes because they fainted and were scattered abroad as sheep having no shepherd. He touched lepers. He gave sight to the blind. He wept at the tomb of Lazarus. He received sinners. Again and again, desperate people cried, **"Have mercy on me,"** and He did.

Two blind men cried:

*"Thou son of David, have mercy on us." — **Matthew 9:27***

The Canaanite woman cried:

*"Have mercy on me, O Lord, thou son of David." — **Matthew 15:22***

Blind Bartimaeus cried:

*"Jesus, thou son of David, have mercy on me." — **Mark 10:47***

Those cries were not treated as interruptions. Mercy answered them. Christ revealed the heart of God toward the helpless who call upon Him.

Mercy and the Cross

God's mercy does not bypass justice. It provides atonement.

Paul writes:

*"But God, who is rich in mercy, for his great love wherewith he loved us, Even when we were dead in sins, hath quickened us together with Christ, by grace ye are saved." — **Ephesians 2:4–5***

God is **rich in mercy**. He did not show mercy to people who were merely confused or unfortunate. He showed mercy to those dead in sins. Mercy came to the spiritually dead and made them alive together with Christ.

Peter says:

"Blessed be the God and Father of our Lord Jesus Christ, which according to his abundant mercy hath begotten us again unto a lively hope by the resurrection of Jesus Christ from the dead." — **I Peter 1:3**

New birth is according to abundant mercy. Hope is mercy's fruit. The resurrection of Christ is mercy's triumph.

Yet this mercy is never separated from the blood of Christ. God does not forgive by pretending sin does not deserve judgment. Mercy reaches sinners through the sacrifice of the Son. The mercy seat in the tabernacle pointed toward this reality. Blood was sprinkled there because guilty people needed more than sympathy. They needed atonement.

Hebrews says Christ was made like unto His brethren:

"that he might be a merciful and faithful high priest in things pertaining to God, to make reconciliation for the sins of the people." — **Hebrews 2:17**

Christ is merciful, and His mercy makes reconciliation through sacrifice. The cross is not mercy softened by justice, nor justice softened by mercy. It is God's merciful provision of a just salvation.

Mercy in the Believer's Weakness

God's mercy does not end at conversion. His people continue to need mercy.

Hebrews invites believers:

"Let us therefore come boldly unto the throne of grace, that we may obtain mercy, and find grace to help in time of need." — **Hebrews 4:16**

The invitation is astonishing. The throne is still a throne, but because of Christ it is a throne of grace to His people. We come not because we are strong, but because we are needy. We come to obtain mercy.

This mercy is needed in temptation, sorrow, failure, confusion, weariness, and fear. The believer does not outgrow dependence. He does not graduate from mercy into self-sufficiency. The longer he walks with God, the more clearly he sees his need.

Paul understood this. He never forgot that his ministry existed because of mercy:

"And I thank Christ Jesus our Lord, who hath enabled me, for that he counted me faithful, putting me into the ministry; Who was before a blasphemer, and a persecutor, and injurious: but I obtained mercy…" — **1 Timothy 1:12–13**

Paul's apostleship did not erase his memory of mercy. It deepened it. He knew what he had been and what God had done.

A church that forgets mercy becomes hard. It may remain doctrinally precise in some areas, but if it forgets what sinners are and what God has done for them, it will become proud, impatient, and severe in ways God Himself is not.

Mercy and Repentance

God's mercy calls sinners to return.

Isaiah says:

*"Let the wicked forsake his way, and the unrighteous man his thoughts: and let him return unto the LORD, and he will have mercy upon him; and to our God, for he will abundantly pardon." — **Isaiah 55:7***

Mercy does not tell the wicked to remain comfortably in his way. It calls him to forsake it. Mercy is not the denial of repentance. It is the reason repentance is not hopeless.

This is vital. Some distort mercy into permission. Others, seeing the seriousness of sin, despair of returning at all. Scripture corrects both. The wicked must forsake his way. And when he returns to the LORD, he finds abundant pardon.

The prodigal son came home with no claim to deserve restoration. He had wasted his inheritance and dishonored his father. Yet the father saw him, had compassion, ran, embraced him, and kissed him. That parable is not meant to make sin light. It is meant to show mercy as astonishing.

The son came home confessing. The father received him rejoicing.

Mercy and Judgment

Mercy is meaningful because judgment is deserved.

If there were no guilt, mercy would be unnecessary. If there were no judgment, mercy would lose its urgency. Scripture's mercy is not sentimental escape from moral reality. It is God's compassion toward those who deserve wrath.

This is why men should not presume upon mercy while refusing repentance. Mercy is not owed. God says:

"I will have mercy on whom I will have mercy, and I will have compassion on whom I will have compassion." — **Romans 9:15**

Mercy is sovereign. It is free. No sinner can demand it as a right. The proper response is humility, gratitude, repentance, and faith.

At the same time, the freeness of mercy should not make sinners hesitant to come. Scripture repeatedly invites the guilty to seek the Lord. The publican found mercy. David found mercy. Paul found mercy. The dying thief found mercy. No sinner who comes to God through Christ will find Him lacking in compassion.

Mercy Required of God's People

Those who receive mercy must show mercy.

Jesus says:

*"Blessed are the merciful: for they shall obtain mercy." — **Matthew 5:7***

He also says:

*"Be ye therefore merciful, as your Father also is merciful." — **Luke 6:36***

Mercy in believers does not mean moral compromise. It does not mean calling evil good or refusing to confront sin. God's mercy never does that. But it does mean compassion toward the weak, patience toward the struggling, readiness to forgive the repentant, generosity toward the needy, and humility toward sinners.

James warns:

*"For he shall have judgment without mercy, that hath shewed no mercy; and mercy rejoiceth against judgment." — **James 2:13***

A merciless heart has not understood mercy. The forgiven servant who refuses to forgive his fellow servant exposes that he has not grasped the mercy shown to him.

The church should be a place where truth is not sacrificed and mercy is not absent. If truth disappears, sinners are not helped. If mercy disappears, sinners are crushed without hope. God gives both.

His Mercy Endureth for Ever

Psalm 136 repeats one refrain again and again:

"for his mercy endureth for ever."

Creation is mentioned, and the refrain follows. Deliverance from Egypt is mentioned, and the refrain follows. The overthrow of kings is mentioned, and the refrain follows. God's remembrance of His people in low estate is mentioned, and the refrain follows.

His mercy endureth for ever.

The repetition teaches the soul to see mercy everywhere in God's works. Mercy is not brief. It does not flicker and vanish. It endures because God endures. His people may pass through discipline, sorrow, waiting, and weakness, but His mercy is not exhausted.

Jeremiah confessed this amid ruins:

"It is of the LORD'S mercies that we are not consumed, because his compassions fail not. They are new every morning: great is thy faithfulness." **— Lamentations 3:22–23**

New every morning. Not because yesterday's mercy failed, but because today's need is met by fresh compassion from the same faithful God.

The God Rich in Mercy

God is merciful.

He sees the afflicted. He pities the weak. He receives the repentant. He forgives the guilty through Christ. He helps His children in need. He calls sinners to return. He teaches His people to show mercy because they have obtained mercy.

Mercy does not make God less holy. It shows the tenderness of His holiness toward those He saves. Mercy does not make sin less serious. It reveals that God Himself has provided the answer to sin in the blood of His Son.

The sinner should not presume upon mercy. But neither should he despair of it.

The throne is a throne of grace. The High Priest is merciful and faithful. The Father is rich in mercy. The Son has died and risen. The invitation stands:

Come boldly.

Obtain mercy.

Chapter 23 — God Is Gracious

Grace is God's favor freely given to the undeserving.

Mercy looks upon misery and guilt with compassion. Grace gives blessing where no blessing has been earned. Mercy withholds what sin deserves. Grace gives what sinners could never deserve. The two are closely joined, but grace especially humbles man because it strips away every claim of merit.

When God proclaimed His name to Moses, He declared Himself:

"The LORD, The LORD God, merciful and gracious, longsuffering, and abundant in goodness and truth." — **Exodus 34:6**

God is gracious. This is not a New Testament invention, as though grace appeared only after the cross. Grace belongs to God's revealed character from the beginning. He clothed Adam and Eve after their sin. He spared Noah and his family. He called Abraham from idolatry. He delivered Israel from bondage. He forgave David. He restored the remnant. He promised a Savior before man ever sought one.

Grace is not God becoming kind after centuries of severity. Grace is the heart of God revealed fully in Jesus Christ.

A simple way many Christians have remembered grace is through the teaching acronym:

G.R.A.C.E. — God's Riches At Christ's Expense

Hal Lindsey used this phrase memorably, and while no acronym can fully define a doctrine as rich as grace, this one captures something true and important. Grace gives the sinner riches he did not earn, and those riches come only through the cost paid by Christ. The favor is free to us, but it was not cheap. It came through the blood of the Son of God.

Grace Is Not Earned

The first thing grace destroys is boasting.

If grace could be earned, it would no longer be grace. Paul states this plainly:

"And if by grace, then is it no more of works: otherwise grace is no more grace. But if it be of works, then is it no more grace: otherwise work is no more work." — **Romans 11:6**

Grace and works cannot occupy the same ground as the basis of salvation. If salvation is by grace, it is not payment for human achievement. If it is by works, it is not grace. Paul does not allow a blended foundation.

This offends human pride. Man wants to contribute something that gives him ground to boast. He wants to believe his morality, sincerity, effort, religious background, knowledge, service, or suffering gives him some claim upon God. Grace says otherwise. The sinner brings need, guilt, and empty hands.

Paul writes:

"For by grace are ye saved through faith; and that not of yourselves: it is the gift of God: Not of works, lest any man should boast." — **Ephesians 2:8–9**

Salvation is a gift. Faith receives; it does not purchase. Grace saves; works do not. The result is that boasting is excluded. No redeemed person will stand before God and say, "I made the difference." All glory belongs to the God who saves by grace.

Grace Comes Through Christ

John writes:

"For the law was given by Moses, but grace and truth came by Jesus Christ." — **John 1:17**

This does not mean the Old Testament lacked grace or truth. God was always gracious and true. The point is that grace and truth come to their fullest revelation in Christ. He is the eternal Word made flesh, full of grace and truth. In Him, God's gracious purpose takes visible, saving form.

Paul says:

"For ye know the grace of our Lord Jesus Christ, that, though he was rich, yet for your sakes he became poor, that ye through his poverty might be rich." — **2 Corinthians 8:9**

The incarnation is grace. The eternal Son took upon Himself true humanity. The Lord of glory humbled Himself. He entered poverty, weakness, rejection, suffering, and death for those who had no riches before God.

The cross is grace at its highest cost.

Sinners are not saved because God overlooks their guilt. They are saved because Christ bore it. Grace is free to us, but it was not cheap. It comes through blood. Paul writes:

"In whom we have redemption through his blood, the forgiveness of sins, according to the riches of his grace." — **Ephesians 1:7**

Grace is rich because the redemption it gives is immeasurable. Forgiveness, adoption, justification, reconciliation, inheritance, and eternal life flow from the riches of God's grace in Christ.

Grace Justifies the Ungodly

The gospel is astonishing because grace comes not to the worthy, but to the ungodly.

Paul says:

"But to him that worketh not, but believeth on him that justifieth the ungodly, his faith is counted for righteousness." — **Romans 4:5**

God justifies the ungodly. That sentence must be handled carefully. It does not mean God declares sin acceptable. It means God declares righteous the sinner who believes in Christ because Christ's righteousness is counted to him. The ungodly person is not justified by remaining ungodly, but by being united to the Righteous One through faith.

This is grace.

Religion built on human merit says, "Improve yourself until God receives you." The gospel says, "Come to Christ, because you cannot make yourself righteous." Grace does not wait for the sinner to become worthy. It saves the unworthy and begins to transform them.

Paul never forgot this. He wrote:

"But by the grace of God I am what I am: and his grace which was bestowed upon me was not in vain." — **I Corinthians 15:10**

Paul had been a blasphemer, persecutor, and injurious. Grace did not merely pardon him; it made him a servant of Christ. Yet even his labor as an apostle was grace at work in him. He continues:

"but I laboured more abundantly than they all: yet not I, but the grace of God which was with me." — **I Corinthians 15:10**

Grace does not produce passivity. It produces humbled obedience.

Grace Teaches Holiness

Grace is often distorted into permission to sin. Scripture teaches the opposite.

Paul asks:

"What shall we say then? Shall we continue in sin, that grace may abound? God forbid. How shall we, that are dead to sin, live any longer therein?" — **Romans 6:1–2**

Grace does not make peace with sin. It delivers from sin's dominion. The person who uses grace as an excuse for rebellion has not understood grace at all.

Titus says:

"For the grace of God that bringeth salvation hath appeared to all men, Teaching us that, denying ungodliness and worldly lusts, we should live soberly, righteously, and godly, in this present world." — **Titus 2:11–12**

Grace teaches. It trains the redeemed to deny ungodliness and worldly lusts. It forms sober, righteous, godly lives. Grace is not indulgence. It is divine favor that saves sinners and then trains them to live as those who belong to God.

This matters in the church. A message that speaks often of grace but rarely of repentance, obedience, holiness, or transformation is not preaching grace fully. Grace forgives, but it also disciplines. Grace comforts, but it also commands. Grace receives the sinner, but it does not leave him chained to the sins that were destroying him.

The same grace that justifies also sanctifies.

Grace Strengthens the Weak

Grace is not only for conversion. It is the believer's daily supply.

Paul pleaded with the Lord three times that his thorn in the flesh might depart. The Lord answered:

"My grace is sufficient for thee: for my strength is made perfect in weakness." **— 2 Corinthians 12:9**

God did not remove the thorn. He gave sufficient grace. That answer was not less loving than deliverance. It taught Paul that divine strength is displayed in human weakness.

This is deeply important. Grace does not always mean escape from pain. Sometimes grace sustains obedience while pain remains. Sometimes grace gives endurance rather than removal. Sometimes grace makes weakness the stage upon which Christ's strength is seen.

Paul's response was not resentment. He said:

"Most gladly therefore will I rather glory in my infirmities, that the power of Christ may rest upon me." **— 2 Corinthians 12:9**

Only grace can teach a man to speak that way.

The believer who feels weak should not conclude that God's grace is absent. Weakness may be the very place where grace becomes most evident.

The Throne of Grace

Because of Christ, believers may come boldly before God.

Hebrews says:

"Let us therefore come boldly unto the throne of grace, that we may obtain mercy, and find grace to help in time of need." **— Hebrews 4:16**

The throne is not less holy than it was in Isaiah's vision. The difference is that Christ, our great High Priest, has opened the way. The holy throne is now a throne of grace for those who come through Him.

We come in need. We come with confession. We come under pressure, temptation, sorrow, fear, and weakness. And there, through Christ, we find grace to help.

This should keep believers from hiding from God when they most need Him. Shame often drives the soul into distance. Grace calls the soul near. The answer to need is not withdrawal, but approach through the blood of Christ.

Grace and Humility

Grace is received by the humble, not the proud.

Peter writes:

"God resisteth the proud, and giveth grace to the humble." — **I Peter 5:5**

Pride is not a small flaw. It sets itself against the way of grace. The proud man cannot receive grace rightly because he does not want to be needy. He wants recognition, not mercy. He wants credit, not gift. He wants God's help without surrendering his self-importance.

The humble man knows he has no claim. He does not bargain with God. He bows. And to such a man God gives grace.

This principle should shape the whole Christian life. We begin by grace, continue by grace, serve by grace, endure by grace, repent by grace, and will be glorified by grace. There is no point where the believer outgrows dependence.

Grace and Gratitude

Grace creates gratitude.

A person who thinks he has earned blessing may become proud or entitled. A person who knows he has received grace becomes thankful. He sings differently. He prays differently. He treats others differently. He becomes slower to despise sinners because he remembers what he himself has received.

Paul asks:

"For who maketh thee to differ from another? and what hast thou that thou didst not receive? now if thou didst receive it, why dost thou glory, as if thou hadst not received it?" — **I Corinthians 4:7**

That question cuts deeply. What do we possess that we did not receive? Life, breath, salvation, gifts, knowledge, opportunities, endurance, repentance, faith—all are received. Grace leaves no room for self-exaltation.

The church that truly understands grace should be serious about holiness and rich in gratitude. It should be humble without being weak, joyful without being shallow, and firm without being proud.

The God of All Grace

Peter calls Him:

"the God of all grace." — **I Peter 5:10**

That title gathers the doctrine beautifully. Grace begins in God. Grace comes through Christ. Grace is applied by the Spirit. Grace saves the guilty, strengthens the weak, humbles the proud, teaches holiness, and brings the saints home.

Peter continues:

"But the God of all grace, who hath called us unto his eternal glory by Christ Jesus, after that ye have suffered a while, make you perfect, stablish, strengthen, settle you." — **I Peter 5:10**

Grace does not mean the absence of suffering. Peter says, "after that ye have suffered a while." But suffering is not the end. The God of all grace will perfect, establish, strengthen, and settle His people.

That is the hope of every believer. The grace that called us will not fail before glory.

Grace Upon Grace

God is gracious.

- He gives where nothing has been earned.
- He saves those who cannot save themselves.
- He justifies the ungodly through Christ.
- He teaches His people to deny sin.
- He supplies strength in weakness.
- He welcomes the needy to His throne.
- He humbles pride and fills the empty-handed.

Grace is not softness. It is not permission. It is not God pretending sinners are better than they are. Grace tells the truth about our guilt and then gives Christ as the answer.

John writes:

*"And of his fulness have all we received, and grace for grace." — **John 1:16***

Grace upon grace. Grace for the beginning, grace for the road, grace for repentance, grace for endurance, grace for death, grace for resurrection, grace for glory.

The Christian life is not merely helped by grace. It is grace from first to last.

Chapter 24 — God Is Patient and Longsuffering

God is not quick-tempered.

That does not mean He is indifferent to sin. It does not mean His wrath is uncertain, His holiness relaxed, or His justice asleep. It means God is slow to anger. He bears long with sinners. He delays deserved judgment. He gives space for repentance. He endures rebellion with a patience that should astonish us.

When God proclaimed His name to Moses, He said:

"The LORD, The LORD God, merciful and gracious, longsuffering, and abundant in goodness and truth." — **Exodus 34:6**

Longsuffering belongs to God's revealed character. He is not impulsive. He does not strike in rash anger. His judgments are never emotional outbursts. Before judgment falls, Scripture often shows warning, patience, repeated calls to repentance, and mercy extended beyond what man would expect.

The patience of God is one reason sinners are alive today.

God's Patience Before the Flood

The days of Noah reveal both God's patience and His judgment.

Genesis says:

"And GOD saw that the wickedness of man was great in the earth, and that every imagination of the thoughts of his heart was only evil continually." — **Genesis 6:5**

That is a devastating description. Human corruption had filled the earth. Yet judgment did not fall instantly. God warned. Noah prepared the ark. Peter later says:

"the longsuffering of God waited in the days of Noah, while the ark was a preparing." — **I Peter 3:20**

God waited.

That waiting did not mean judgment would never come. The flood came exactly as God said. But before it came, His longsuffering was displayed. The same history teaches two truths that must never be separated: God is patient, and God will judge.

Patience is not the denial of judgment. It is the delay of judgment for a righteous purpose.

God's Patience with Israel

Israel's history is one long testimony to the patience of God.

The people grumbled in the wilderness. They doubted His promises. They worshiped idols. They rejected His commandments. They despised His prophets. Yet God did not cast them away at the first provocation.

Nehemiah summarizes Israel's history this way:

"Yet many years didst thou forbear them, and testifiedst against them by thy spirit in thy prophets: yet would they not give ear…" — **Nehemiah 9:30**

God "forbare" them many years. He testified against them. He sent prophets. He warned before He judged.

The exile did not come because God was impatient. It came after generations of covenant rebellion. His patience had been despised.

This should correct the way many people read Old Testament judgment. They see the judgment and assume harshness. Scripture often shows that judgment came only after extraordinary patience. The question is not why God judged so severely, but why He endured so long.

Slow to Anger

The refrain appears throughout Scripture:

*"The LORD is gracious, and full of compassion; slow to anger, and of great mercy." — **Psalm 145:8***

To be slow to anger does not mean God never becomes angry. It means His anger is never reckless, petty, or uncontrolled. His wrath is holy opposition to evil, not the loss of self-control.

Human anger is often corrupted by pride. We become angry because we are embarrassed, inconvenienced, ignored, wounded in ego, or denied what we wanted. God's anger is not like that. He is slow to anger because He is perfect in patience. When His wrath comes, it comes with truth, righteousness, and justice.

This is why God's patience should never be mistaken for weakness. A weak ruler may delay judgment because he cannot act. God delays because He is longsuffering. No sinner is safe because judgment has not yet come. Delay is mercy, not inability.

Patience and Repentance

God's patience has a purpose.

Paul writes:

*"Or despisest thou the riches of his goodness and forbearance and longsuffering; not knowing that the goodness of God leadeth thee to repentance?" — **Romans 2:4***

The goodness, forbearance, and longsuffering of God are meant to lead sinners to repentance. Every day of delayed judgment is not permission to continue in sin. It is an invitation to turn.

But fallen man often twists patience into presumption. Because God does not strike immediately, sinners imagine He never will. Ecclesiastes says:

*"Because sentence against an evil work is not executed speedily, therefore the heart of the sons of men is fully set in them to do evil." — **Ecclesiastes 8:11***

This is one of the great dangers of delayed judgment. The patience that should produce repentance can be abused into deeper rebellion. Sinners mistake mercy for absence, silence for approval, and time for safety.

But the clock is not proof that judgment has vanished. It is proof that God has been patient.

The Patience of Christ

The patience of God is seen beautifully in Jesus Christ.

He endured misunderstanding from His disciples, hatred from His enemies, hypocrisy from religious leaders, unbelief from the crowds, and cruelty from sinners. He was reviled, yet He did not respond with sinful anger. Peter writes:

*"Who, when he was reviled, reviled not again; when he suffered, he threatened not; but committed himself to him that judgeth righteously." — **I Peter 2:23***

Christ's patience was not passivity. He spoke truth. He rebuked hypocrisy. He warned of judgment. But He did not act from wounded pride or uncontrolled anger. His endurance was holy.

Paul saw himself as a living display of Christ's longsuffering:

*"Howbeit for this cause I obtained mercy, that in me first Jesus Christ might shew forth all longsuffering, for a pattern to them which should hereafter believe on him to life everlasting." — **I Timothy 1:16***

Paul had been a blasphemer, persecutor, and injurious. Yet Christ showed him mercy. His conversion became a pattern: if Christ showed longsuffering to Paul, no sinner should assume he is beyond the reach of mercy if he will come.

The Lord Is Not Slack

The patience of God is central to understanding the apparent delay of Christ's return.

Peter writes:

"The Lord is not slack concerning his promise, as some men count slackness; but is longsuffering to us-ward, not willing that any should perish, but that all should come to repentance." — **2 Peter 3:9**

Scoffers interpret delay as failure. Peter interprets delay as longsuffering.

The Lord has not forgotten His promise. He is not late. He is not uncertain. He is patient. The delay of judgment means salvation is still being offered. Repentance is still being called for. The gospel is still going out.

But Peter immediately adds:

"But the day of the Lord will come as a thief in the night…" — **2 Peter 3:10**

Again, patience and judgment stand together. Longsuffering is real, and the day of the Lord will come. No biblical doctrine of God's patience should ever weaken the certainty of His coming judgment.

Patience in the Life of God's People

Because God is patient, His people must learn patience.

Paul lists longsuffering among the fruit of the Spirit:

"But the fruit of the Spirit is love, joy, peace, longsuffering, gentleness, goodness, faith." — **Galatians 5:22**

Christian patience is not natural temperament alone. Some people are calmer than others by personality, but biblical longsuffering is deeper. It is the Spirit-formed ability to endure wrong, delay, weakness, and provocation without sinful retaliation.

Paul urges believers:

"With all lowliness and meekness, with longsuffering, forbearing one another in love." — **Ephesians 4:2**

The church needs longsuffering because people are difficult, immature, wounded, sinful, and slow to grow. Without patience, correction becomes harsh, leadership becomes domineering, marriage becomes brittle, parenting becomes exasperating, and Christian fellowship becomes easily fractured.

This does not mean sin should never be confronted. God's patience does not mean He refuses correction. But correction without patience rarely reflects the character of God.

Patience and Hope

God's people also need patience while waiting for His promises.

James writes:

"Be patient therefore, brethren, unto the coming of the Lord. Behold, the husbandman waiteth for the precious fruit of the earth, and hath long patience for it, until he receive the early and latter rain." — **James 5:7**

The believer waits because God's timing is wise. The farmer cannot force the harvest by anxiety. He waits for what he cannot control. So the Christian waits for the Lord, trusting that delay does not mean failure.

James continues:

*"Be ye also patient; stablish your hearts: for the coming of the Lord draweth nigh." — **James 5:8***

Patience does not weaken expectation. It strengthens the heart while expectation remains. The coming of the Lord is certain. Therefore His people can endure.

The Danger of Despising Patience

God's patience is one of the most abused attributes in Scripture.

Sinners use it to postpone repentance. Believers sometimes use it to make peace with sins they should confess. False teachers use it to dull the warnings of Scripture. Mockers use it to deny the coming judgment.

But patience is not permission.

The same God who waited in the days of Noah brought the flood. The same God who bore long with Israel sent them into exile. The same Christ who wept over Jerusalem also foretold its destruction. The same Lord who is longsuffering will return in flaming judgment.

To despise patience is spiritually dangerous because patience is mercy with time attached to it. It is not owed. It is not endless in its present form. It is given so that men might repent.

The God Who Waits Without Weakness

God is patient and longsuffering.

- He waits without weakness.
- He delays without forgetfulness.
- He warns without cruelty.
- He endures sinners without approving sin.

- He gives time for repentance without surrendering justice.

His patience should humble us. It should lead sinners to repentance. It should teach believers to endure. It should make the church gentle with the weak and sober toward the rebellious. It should deepen our gratitude that God did not strike us down in the days of our ignorance.

If God had not been longsuffering, none of us would be saved.

Every believer is living proof that the Lord is slow to anger and plenteous in mercy.

Chapter 25 — God Is Kind

God's kindness is His generous goodness expressed in tenderness, patience, provision, and care toward His creatures.

Kindness is easy to underestimate. We may think of it as softness, politeness, or a pleasant disposition. But in Scripture, the kindness of God carries deep theological weight. It is not weakness. It is not mere niceness. It is the gracious inclination of God to do good, to show compassion, to provide, to lead sinners toward repentance, and to treat His people with tenderness they do not deserve.

Paul writes:

"But after that the kindness and love of God our Saviour toward man appeared, Not by works of righteousness which we have done, but according to his mercy he saved us..." — **Titus 3:4–5**

The coming of salvation in Christ is described as the appearing of God's kindness and love. That means kindness is not a minor attribute. It belongs to the saving revelation of God.

- The God who judges evil is kind.
- The God who commands holiness is kind.
- The God who disciplines His children is kind.
- The God who reigns with absolute sovereignty is kind.

If we lose His kindness, we will misread His authority, His commands, His providence, and even His correction.

The Kindness of God in Creation

God's kindness is visible in the world He made and sustains.

He did not create a bare world fit only for survival. He filled it with beauty, order, abundance, taste, color, sound, relationship, and joy. Bread nourishes, but it also satisfies. Water sustains life, but it also refreshes. The earth bears fruit, flowers, shade, fragrance, and wonder. Even after the fall, creation continues to display the generous hand of God.

Paul told the people of Lystra that God:

"left not himself without witness, in that he did good, and gave us rain from heaven, and fruitful seasons, filling our hearts with food and gladness." — **Acts 14:17**

That is kindness. God gives rain. He gives fruitful seasons. He fills hearts with food and gladness. These gifts are so common that men easily forget they are gifts at all. But Scripture teaches us to see daily provision as evidence of God's kind hand.

Jesus says the Father:

"maketh his sun to rise on the evil and on the good, and sendeth rain on the just and on the unjust." — **Matthew 5:45**

God's kindness reaches even His enemies. The unjust man may deny God, mock His Word, and misuse His gifts, yet still wake beneath sunlight he did not create and eat food from a world he does not sustain. Such kindness should lead to repentance. Too often, it leads only to presumption.

Kindness and Repentance

God's kindness is not meant to make sinners comfortable in sin. It is meant to lead them out of it.

Paul asks:

"Or despisest thou the riches of his goodness and forbearance and longsuffering; not knowing that the goodness of God leadeth thee to repentance?" — **Romans 2:4**

The word translated **goodness** carries the idea of kindness. God's kind patience toward sinners has a moral purpose. It is not approval. It is summons. Every breath given to the unrepentant is a kindness calling him to turn before judgment comes.

This should correct a dangerous misunderstanding. Because God is kind, many assume He will not judge. Scripture says the opposite. The kindness of God makes continued rebellion more serious, not less. To sin under judgment is dreadful. To sin under kindness is shameful.

A man who receives years of patience, provision, warnings, and opportunities to repent cannot claim God was harsh with him. If judgment finally comes, it will come after kindness was despised.

Paul later warns:

"Behold therefore the goodness and severity of God: on them which fell, severity; but toward thee, goodness, if thou continue in his goodness: otherwise thou also shalt be cut off." — **Romans 11:22**

Goodness and severity must be beheld together. God's kindness is real, but it must not be used to deny His severity. The full character of God includes both.

The Kindness of God in Christ

The kindness of God is most fully revealed in Jesus Christ.

He did not move through the world as a distant moral inspector. He drew near to the weak, the sick, the sinful, and the forgotten. His kindness did not flatter sin, but it did welcome the broken who came to Him.

Matthew says:

*"But when he saw the multitudes, he was moved with compassion on them, because they fainted, and were scattered abroad, as sheep having no shepherd." — **Matthew 9:36**

Christ saw need truly. He was not annoyed by human weakness. He was moved with compassion. The weary, diseased, demon-oppressed, hungry, grieving, and guilty found in Him the kindness of God in flesh.

He touched lepers when others withdrew. He received children when the disciples would have sent them away. He restored Peter after denial. He spoke hope to the thief beside Him. He fed the multitudes before sending them home. He wept at Lazarus's tomb even though He knew He was about to raise him.

None of this kindness made Him morally soft. He rebuked hypocrisy. He warned of hell. He called sinners to repentance. But His severity was never cruelty, and His tenderness was never compromise.

That is the pattern of divine kindness.

Kindness in Salvation

Salvation itself is an act of divine kindness.

Paul tells the Ephesians that God raised believers with Christ and seated them in heavenly places:

*"That in the ages to come he might shew the exceeding riches of his grace in his kindness toward us through Christ Jesus." — **Ephesians 2:7**

Eternity will display the riches of God's grace in kindness toward His people. The redeemed will never exhaust the wonder of it. They will forever be living evidence that God has been kind through Christ Jesus.

This kindness is undeserved. Ephesians 2 has already described sinners as dead in trespasses and sins, walking according to the course of this world, and by nature children of wrath. Then come the words, **"But God."** The kindness shown in salvation is not God rewarding spiritual promise. It is God making the dead alive.

The gospel is not merely rescue from punishment. It is the overflowing kindness of God toward those who deserved wrath and received mercy.

Kindness and Discipline

God's kindness does not disappear when He disciplines His children.

This is difficult to feel in the moment. Discipline hurts. Correction exposes. Trials can press deeply into the heart. But if God's discipline is fatherly, then it is kind even when it is severe.

David says:

"Let the righteous smite me; it shall be a kindness: and let him reprove me; it shall be an excellent oil…" — **Psalm 141:5**

If even righteous human correction can be called kindness, how much more the correction of God? He does not wound His children carelessly. He corrects to restore, humble, cleanse, and protect.

A parent who allows a child to destroy himself is not kind. A physician who refuses to tell the truth about disease is not kind. A shepherd who never pulls the sheep back from danger is not kind. Real kindness may hurt when it rescues.

So it is with God. His kindness is not indulgence. He is kind enough to disturb false peace, expose hidden sin, frustrate destructive plans, and call His children back from paths that would ruin them.

The Kindness Required of God's People

Because God is kind, His people must be kind.

Paul commands:

"And be ye kind one to another, tenderhearted, forgiving one another, even as God for Christ's sake hath forgiven you." — **Ephesians 4:32**

Christian kindness is not mere personality. It is imitation of God. It is shaped by the forgiveness we have received in Christ. The believer who has been treated with divine kindness has no right to become harsh, bitter, cruel, or needlessly severe toward others.

This does not mean Christians should avoid truth. Biblical kindness does not lie. It does not excuse evil. It does not flatter rebellion. But it speaks and acts with a heart shaped by mercy. It remembers weakness. It refuses unnecessary harshness. It forgives the repentant. It bears patiently with the immature. It helps the needy without contempt.

Paul lists kindness among the qualities of God's servants:

"By pureness, by knowledge, by longsuffering, by kindness, by the Holy Ghost, by love unfeigned." — **2 Corinthians 6:6**

A doctrinally serious church should not be an unkind church. Truth and kindness belong together because both belong to God.

The Danger of Unkind Religion

Religion can become cruel while defending true things.

This is one of the subtle dangers among those who care about doctrine. A man may defend holiness in an unholy spirit. He may defend truth with a cruel tongue. He may speak of grace without graciousness, mercy without tenderness, and righteousness without patience. Such a man may be right in the sentence and wrong in the spirit.

Jesus exposed this kind of religion often. The Pharisees could be exact about details and blind to the weightier matters of the law. They could tithe mint and anise and cummin while neglecting judgment, mercy, and faith. They could load burdens on others and refuse to move them with one of their fingers.

That was not the character of God.

God's kindness should shape how truth is carried. There is a time for rebuke. There is a time for sharp warning. Scripture gives us both. But even rebuke must arise from faithfulness to God and love for souls, not from delight in severity.

The servant of the Lord must not strive, Paul says, but be gentle unto all men, apt to teach, patient, in meekness instructing those that oppose themselves. That does not weaken truth. It adorns it.

Kindness That Will Be Remembered Forever

God's kindness toward His people is not temporary.

Isaiah records the Lord's words:

"For the mountains shall depart, and the hills be removed; but my kindness shall not depart from thee, neither shall the covenant of my peace be removed, saith the LORD that hath mercy on thee." — **Isaiah 54:10**

Mountains seem permanent. Hills appear immovable. Yet God says His kindness is more secure than both. His covenant peace will not be removed.

This promise was spoken to Zion in the context of restoration, but it reveals the character of God toward His covenant people. His kindness is not a mood. It is steadfast. It remains when visible supports tremble.

The believer in Christ can rest in this same God. The kindness of God has appeared in the Savior. It will be displayed in the ages to come. It will not depart from those who are His.

The God Who Is Kind

God is kind.

- He gives rain and fruitful seasons.
- He fills hearts with food and gladness.
- He delays judgment and calls sinners to repentance.
- He comes near in Christ.
- He saves by grace.
- He disciplines His children for their good.
- He teaches His people to treat others with tenderness and forgiveness.
- His kindness is not weakness.
- His kindness is not moral compromise.
- His kindness is not sentimental softness.

It is holy kindness. Righteous kindness. Patient kindness. Saving kindness. Covenant kindness.

The sinner should not despise it.

The believer should not doubt it.

The church should not fail to reflect it.For after all our sin, all our need, all our weakness, and all our wandering, this remains true:

God has been kind.

Chapter 26 — God Is All-Knowing

God knows all things.

That statement is simple, but its reach is endless. God knows every fact, every thought, every motive, every event, every possibility, every hidden sin, every secret grief, every future day, and every purpose of His own will. Nothing is hidden from Him. Nothing surprises Him. Nothing must be reported to Him. Nothing is discovered by Him after the fact.

His knowledge is perfect, immediate, complete, and eternal.

John says:

"God is greater than our heart, and knoweth all things." — **I John 3:20**

There is no qualification attached to that sentence. God knows all things. Not most things. Not merely all things presently visible. All things.

Theologians call this **omniscience**, but the doctrine is not difficult to state. God knows everything because He is God. He is the Creator of all things, the sustainer of all things, the Lord of all history, and the One before whom every creature is fully exposed.

Nothing Is Hidden from Him

The writer of Hebrews says:

"Neither is there any creature that is not manifest in his sight: but all things are naked and opened unto the eyes of him with whom we have to do." — **Hebrews 4:13**

That verse is both comforting and terrifying. Every creature is manifest before Him. Every hidden thing is open. God does not merely see outward behavior. He sees the person entire.

David says:

"O LORD, thou hast searched me, and known me. Thou knowest my downsitting and mine uprising, thou understandest my thought afar off." — **Psalm 139:1–2**

God knows the sitting down and the rising up. He knows the movements of ordinary life. But He also understands the thought afar off. Before the thought is expressed, before it is explained, before another person could detect it, God knows.

David continues:

"For there is not a word in my tongue, but, lo, O LORD, thou knowest it altogether." — **Psalm 139:4**

The tongue has not yet spoken, and God already knows. Words do not inform Him. They reveal us before others, but not before Him.

This should end all pretense. Human beings can hide from one another. We can polish appearances, choose careful language, conceal motives, and manage reputation. But there is no theater before God. He sees the heart.

God Knows the Heart

Scripture repeatedly tells us that God knows the heart of man.

When Samuel was sent to anoint one of Jesse's sons, he was impressed by outward appearance. God corrected him:

"Look not on his countenance, or on the height of his stature; because I have refused him: for the LORD seeth not as man seeth; for man looketh on the outward appearance, but the LORD looketh on the heart." — **I Samuel 16:7**

Man sees appearance. God sees the heart.

This means God's knowledge is not shallow. He does not judge merely by visible action, public reputation, emotional expression, religious performance, or the opinion of others. He knows what is underneath.

Solomon prayed:

"for thou, even thou only, knowest the hearts of all the children of men." — **I Kings 8:39**

God alone knows every human heart perfectly. We do not even know our own hearts fully. Jeremiah says:

"The heart is deceitful above all things, and desperately wicked: who can know it? I the LORD search the heart, I try the reins, even to give every man according to his ways, and according to the fruit of his doings." — **Jeremiah 17:9–10**

The human heart is deceitful, but God is not deceived by it. He searches it. He tries the reins. He sees through self-justification, religious masking, hidden bitterness, false humility, envy, lust, fear, pride, and unbelief.

This truth should humble us. It should also make us honest in prayer. We do not come to God by pretending. We come to the One who already knows us completely.

God Knows the Future

God not only knows what is present and hidden. He knows what is future.

Through Isaiah, the Lord declares:

"I am God, and there is none like me, Declaring the end from the beginning, and from ancient times the things that are not yet done, saying, My counsel shall stand, and I will do all my pleasure." — **Isaiah 46:9–10**

God declares the end from the beginning because the end is not uncertain to Him. He does not guess. He does not project trends. He does not wait to see how history turns out. He knows, governs, and fulfills His purpose.

This is one reason prophecy matters. Predictive prophecy is not religious fortune-telling. It is the truthful God revealing what He knows and what He will bring to pass. When God names Cyrus before Cyrus is born, foretells judgment before it falls, promises Messiah before He comes, or declares the return of Christ before the world sees Him, He is showing that history is open before Him.

Human beings live forward. God knows the end from the beginning.

David says:

*"Thine eyes did see my substance, yet being unperfect; and in thy book all my members were written, which in continuance were fashioned, when as yet there was none of them." — **Psalm 139:16***

Before David's days unfolded, God knew them. The life of a man is not a mystery to the One who formed him.

This does not make human choices unreal. Scripture holds human responsibility and divine knowledge together without embarrassment. Men choose, act, believe, rebel, repent, obey, and disobey. God knows all of it perfectly, without learning and without uncertainty.

God's Knowledge and Wisdom

God's knowledge must be distinguished from mere information.

A person may possess many facts and still be foolish. God's knowledge is never like that. He knows all things truly, and He orders all things wisely. His knowledge is joined to His wisdom, righteousness, goodness, and sovereignty.

Paul bursts into worship:

"O the depth of the riches both of the wisdom and knowledge of God! how unsearchable are his judgments, and his ways past finding out!" — **Romans 11:33**

God's judgments are unsearchable not because they are irrational, but because they are deeper than human tracing. His ways are past finding out not because they are confused, but because finite minds cannot exhaust infinite wisdom and knowledge.

This matters when providence is difficult. We see fragments. God knows the whole. We see the moment. God knows the end from the beginning. We see one thread. God knows the entire tapestry.

Joseph could not have understood all that God was doing when he was betrayed, enslaved, falsely accused, and imprisoned. But God knew. The cross itself is the greatest example. The disciples saw catastrophe. God knew redemption. Men saw defeat. God knew resurrection.

Faith does not require us to understand everything God knows. It requires us to trust the God who knows.

God's Knowledge and Sin

Because God knows all things, no sin is truly secret.

Moses warned:

"be sure your sin will find you out." — **Numbers 32:23**

Sin may remain hidden from men for a season, but it is never hidden from God. Every secret action, every private indulgence, every whispered slander, every concealed injustice, every inward lust, every dishonest motive is already seen.

Ecclesiastes says:

"For God shall bring every work into judgment, with every secret thing, whether it be good, or whether it be evil." — **Ecclesiastes 12:14**

This is a fearful truth. It strips away the false comfort of concealment. The question is not whether sin will be known. It is whether it will be confessed and covered by the blood of Christ before judgment.

David models the right response:

"Search me, O God, and know my heart: try me, and know my thoughts: And see if there be any wicked way in me, and lead me in the way everlasting." — **Psalm 139:23–24**

The God who knows the heart should not be avoided. He should be invited to search, expose, cleanse, and lead. His knowledge becomes mercy when it brings us to repentance.

God's Knowledge and Comfort

God's omniscience also comforts His people.

He knows their griefs. He knows their weakness. He knows their frame. He sees what others miss. He understands tears that cannot be explained. He knows the prayer that never becomes articulate speech.

Jesus says:

"your Father knoweth what things ye have need of, before ye ask him." — **Matthew 6:8**

Prayer does not inform God of needs He did not know. Prayer brings the child before the Father who already knows and cares. That should not discourage prayer. It should strengthen it. We do not pray to awaken God's attention. We pray because His attention is already perfect.

Jesus also says:

*"But the very hairs of your head are all numbered." — **Matthew 10:30***

The point is not trivia. It is care. God's knowledge reaches even what we consider insignificant. If He knows the hairs of our head, He is not careless with the wounds of our soul.

Many believers suffer because they feel unseen. They obey quietly. They endure burdens privately. They labor without recognition. They grieve without words. The all-knowing God sees. Not one faithful act is unnoticed. Not one tear is misplaced. Not one sigh is unintelligible to Him.

Christ Knows His Sheep

The knowledge of God is revealed tenderly in Christ's knowledge of His people.

Jesus says:

*"I am the good shepherd, and know my sheep, and am known of mine." — **John 10:14***

This is not bare awareness. It is covenant knowledge, shepherding knowledge, loving knowledge. Christ knows those who belong to Him. He knows their names, their dangers, their weakness, their wanderings, and their need.

He also knows false profession. At the judgment, He will say to some:

*"I never knew you: depart from me, ye that work iniquity." — **Matthew 7:23***

They had religious activity. They had words. They had claims. But they did not belong to Him. The all-knowing Christ cannot be deceived by outward profession.

This should sober the hypocrite and comfort the believer. Christ is not fooled by religious performance, but neither does He lose one true sheep in the crowd. He knows His own.

The God Before Whom We Live

God is all-knowing.

That means all life is lived before His face. There is no private world sealed off from Him, no hidden chamber of the heart beyond His sight, no future outside His knowledge, no sorrow beneath His notice, and no faithful obedience forgotten by Him.

This doctrine should produce reverence, honesty, repentance, trust, and comfort.

Reverence, because God sees all. Honesty, because pretense is useless. Repentance, because hidden sin is already known. Trust, because God knows the path we cannot see. Comfort, because the Father knows our need before we ask.

The all-knowing God is not cold surveillance. He is the holy, wise, merciful, faithful God who knows perfectly. To the unrepentant, that knowledge is terrifying. To the redeemed, it is safety.

David says:

"Such knowledge is too wonderful for me; it is high, I cannot attain unto it."
— Psalm 139:6

We cannot attain unto it. We cannot master the mystery of omniscience. But we can worship.

God knows all things.

And because He does, nothing true will be lost, nothing evil will remain hidden, nothing faithful will be forgotten, and nothing His people need is unknown to Him.

Chapter 27 — God Is All-Powerful

God is all-powerful.

Nothing is too hard for Him. Nothing can overpower Him, restrain Him, exhaust Him, or force Him to act against His will. He does not possess great power merely in comparison with creatures. His power is unlimited, underived, and perfectly governed by His wisdom, holiness, goodness, and truth.

The Lord asked Abraham:

"Is any thing too hard for the LORD?" — **Genesis 18:14**

The question answers itself. Sarah was barren. Abraham was old. The promise of a son seemed impossible from a human standpoint. But God's promise did not depend upon human possibility. Isaac was born because the Lord is not limited by what man can do.

Jeremiah later confessed:

"Ah Lord GOD! behold, thou hast made the heaven and the earth by thy great power and stretched out arm, and there is nothing too hard for thee." — *Jeremiah 32:17*

Creation is the first great display of divine power. The heavens and the earth exist because God willed them into being. He did not struggle against preexisting chaos as though creation were difficult. He spoke, and it was so.

The Almighty God

One of God's names is **Almighty**.

The Lord appeared to Abram and said:

"I am the Almighty God; walk before me, and be thou perfect." — **Genesis 17:1**

This came in the context of promise. Abram was to become the father of many nations, though the promise seemed beyond natural fulfillment. God's power stood behind God's Word.

The title appears again and again in Scripture. Job says:

"I know that thou canst do every thing, and that no thought can be withholden from thee." — **Job 42:2**

Job had questioned, grieved, and wrestled in deep suffering. But when God revealed His majesty, Job confessed that God can do everything He purposes. No plan of God can be restrained.

This does not mean God can do what contradicts His own nature. He cannot lie. He cannot sin. He cannot deny Himself. Such "inabilities" are not weaknesses. They are perfections. God's power is not the ability to become false, wicked, or foolish. It is His unlimited ability to accomplish all His holy will.

Power in Creation

The Bible begins with God's power.

"In the beginning God created the heaven and the earth." — **Genesis 1:1**

No explanation is given for where God found material, because He did not need material. No struggle is described, because no rival power resisted Him. No tool is named, because His Word was sufficient.

Psalm 33 says:

"By the word of the LORD were the heavens made; and all the host of them by the breath of his mouth." — **Psalm 33:6**

And again:

"For he spake, and it was done; he commanded, and it stood fast." — **Psalm 33:9**

Creation obeyed His voice. Light came. Waters divided. Dry land appeared. Stars filled the heavens. Life entered the sea, sky, and earth. Man was formed from the dust and given breath. Everything that exists outside of God depends on His power.

This should humble every creature. We are not self-sustaining. We do not own our existence. The God who made all things by His power holds all things by that same power.

Power in Providence

God's power did not cease after creation.

He upholds what He made. The universe is not running independently while God watches from a distance. Scripture says of Christ:

"upholding all things by the word of his power." — **Hebrews 1:3**

All things are upheld. Every star, every sea, every atom, every creature, every breath remains dependent upon the sustaining power of God.

Paul told the Athenians:

"For in him we live, and move, and have our being." — **Acts 17:28**

That is true of every creature, whether acknowledged or not. The skeptic who denies God does so with breath God gives, a mind God sustains, and a life held together by divine power.

This means God is never absent from His creation. He is distinct from it, not contained within it, and not identical to it. Yet He is actively sustaining it. His power is near enough that every heartbeat depends upon Him.

Power Over Nations

God's power rules over kings and kingdoms.

Nebuchadnezzar learned this after being humbled by the Lord. When his reason returned, he confessed:

"all the inhabitants of the earth are reputed as nothing: and he doeth according to his will in the army of heaven, and among the inhabitants of the earth: and none can stay his hand, or say unto him, What doest thou?" — **Daniel 4:35**

No one can stay His hand. No empire is too great for Him. No ruler is beyond His reach. Pharaoh, Nebuchadnezzar, Belshazzar, Herod, Caesar, and every ruler since have lived under God's power whether they knew it or not.

This is a comfort in unstable times. Nations appear strong. Governments boast. Evil men rise. Laws change. Cultures rebel. Yet God's throne is not threatened by earthly power. He sets up kings and removes them. He accomplishes His purpose through, over, and sometimes against the rulers of the earth.

Psalm 2 asks:

"Why do the heathen rage, and the people imagine a vain thing?" — **Psalm 2:1**

The nations rage, but their rage is vain. The Lord is not anxious in heaven. He is not outmatched by rebellion. The King He has set upon Zion will reign.

Power in Salvation

The salvation of sinners requires divine power.

Sin does not leave man merely uninformed. It leaves him dead in trespasses and sins. A dead man does not need advice alone. He needs life.

Paul says believers know:

"what is the exceeding greatness of his power to us-ward who believe, according to the working of his mighty power, Which he wrought in Christ, when he raised him from the dead…" — **Ephesians 1:19–20**

The same mighty power that raised Christ from the dead is at work toward believers. Salvation is resurrection power. God takes those dead in sins and makes them alive together with Christ.

This should destroy spiritual pride. No one saves himself. No sinner gives himself life. No human will, religious effort, moral improvement, or intellectual seriousness can raise the dead. Salvation is of the Lord.

It should also strengthen hope. The hardest sinner is not too hard for God. The longest rebellion is not beyond His power. The chains of addiction, hatred, unbelief, pride, false religion, and despair are not stronger than the God who raises the dead.

Power in Weakness

God's power often appears most clearly through human weakness.

Paul pleaded for his thorn in the flesh to depart. The Lord answered:

"My grace is sufficient for thee: for my strength is made perfect in weakness." — **2 Corinthians 12:9**

God did not remove the weakness. He displayed power through it. Paul then said:

*"Most gladly therefore will I rather glory in my infirmities, that the power of Christ may rest upon me." — **2 Corinthians 12:9***

This is not the way men naturally think. We assume power is displayed best through visible strength, success, influence, health, and ability. God often chooses the weak things of the world to confound the mighty. He uses clay vessels so the excellency of the power may be of God and not of us.

The cross itself is the supreme example. To the world, Christ crucified looked like weakness and defeat. Yet Paul calls the gospel:

*"the power of God unto salvation to every one that believeth." — **Romans 1:16***

God's power is not always displayed the way pride expects. It is displayed according to divine wisdom.

Power and Resurrection

The resurrection of Christ is the great declaration of God's power in history.

Men condemned Him. Soldiers crucified Him. A stone sealed the tomb. Guards stood watch. But death could not hold Him.

Peter preached:

*"Whom God hath raised up, having loosed the pains of death: because it was not possible that he should be holden of it." — **Acts 2:24***

It was not possible for death to hold Him. Christ's resurrection reveals power over the grave, over sin, over Satan, and over every enemy of God's purpose.

That same power guarantees the resurrection of His people. Paul says:

"And God hath both raised up the Lord, and will also raise up us by his own power." — I Corinthians 6:14

The Christian hope is not vague survival after death. It is bodily resurrection by the power of God. The same God who formed man from dust can raise the dead from dust. No grave is too old. No body is too lost. No decay is too complete. God is able.

Power and Final Judgment

God's power will also be displayed in final judgment.

Many sinners mistake God's patience for weakness. Because judgment does not fall immediately, they assume it never will. But the Lord who delays judgment is fully able to execute it.

Jesus said:

"And fear not them which kill the body, but are not able to kill the soul: but rather fear him which is able to destroy both soul and body in hell." — Matthew 10:28

God's power is not only comforting. It is terrifying to those who remain in rebellion. No creature can resist Him in the day of judgment. No hiding place will remain. No power will intervene. No accusation against God will stand.

Revelation says:

"Alleluia: for the Lord God omnipotent reigneth." — Revelation 19:6

The omnipotent God reigns. His kingdom will come. Evil will fall. Christ will triumph. The new creation will appear. Every enemy will be put under His feet.

Power Governed by Character

God's power must never be separated from His character.

Power without goodness would be dreadful. Power without wisdom would be unstable. Power without justice would be tyranny. Power without love would be cold dominion. But God's power is holy power, wise power, good power, righteous power, faithful power.

This is why His omnipotence is comfort to His people. The God who can do all His will is the God whose will is perfectly good. His power does not make Him dangerous to those who trust Him. It makes Him a refuge.

The psalmist says:

"God is our refuge and strength, a very present help in trouble." — **Psalm 46:1**

Not merely refuge, but strength. Not distant strength, but present help. The power that upholds the stars also sustains the trembling believer.

The God for Whom Nothing Is Too Hard

God is all-powerful.

- He created all things.
- He sustains all things.
- He rules nations.
- He raises the dead.
- He saves sinners.
- He strengthens the weak.
- He will judge evil.
- He will bring His kingdom to completion.

This power should humble us, sober us, and comfort us.

It humbles us because we are dependent creatures. It sobers us because no rebellion can succeed against Him. It comforts us because no promise of God can fail for lack of strength.

The question still stands:

"Is any thing too hard for the LORD?" — **Genesis 18:14**

No.

- Not creation.
- Not providence.
- Not salvation.
- Not resurrection.
- Not judgment.
- Not the fulfillment of every promise He has made.

The Lord God omnipotent reigneth.

Chapter 28 — God Is Everywhere Present

God is not confined.

He is not limited by distance, contained by temples, restricted to heaven, or absent from any corner of creation. He is fully present everywhere, not by being spread thin across the universe, but because He is God. No place can contain Him, and no place can exclude Him.

Solomon understood this when he prayed at the dedication of the temple:

"But will God indeed dwell on the earth? behold, the heaven and heaven of heavens cannot contain thee; how much less this house that I have builded?" **— I Kings 8:27**

The temple was real and holy. God chose to put His name there. Yet Solomon knew the building did not contain God. Even the heaven of heavens cannot contain Him.

God's presence is not like ours. We are present in one place and absent from another. To move here is to leave there. We occupy space because we are creatures. God made space. He is not trapped inside it.

Where Shall I Flee?

David speaks of God's presence with awe:

"Whither shall I go from thy spirit? or whither shall I flee from thy presence?" **— Psalm 139:7**

The question has no answer. There is nowhere to flee.

"If I ascend up into heaven, thou art there: if I make my bed in hell, behold, thou art there. If I take the wings of the morning, and dwell in the uttermost

*parts of the sea; Even there shall thy hand lead me, and thy right hand shall hold me." — **Psalm 139:8–10***

Heaven is not too high. The depths are not too low. The farthest sea is not too remote. God is there.

For the rebellious, this is terrifying. There is no hidden place where sin escapes His sight. No darkness conceals from Him. David says:

"Yea, the darkness hideth not from thee; but the night shineth as the day: *the darkness and the light are both alike to thee." — **Psalm 139:12***

Secret sin is not secret before God. The darkness may hide a man from other men, but it does not hide him from the Lord.

For the redeemed, the same truth is comfort. The believer cannot be abandoned to a place where God is absent. Suffering may feel lonely, but God is there. The hospital room, the prison cell, the quiet grief no one else understands, the wilderness season, the valley of the shadow of death— none of these places are beyond His presence.

God Is Near and High

God's omnipresence does not mean He is everything. The Bible does not teach that God and creation are the same. He is present everywhere, but He remains distinct from what He has made.

Jeremiah records the Lord's words:

*"Am I a God at hand, saith the LORD, and not a God afar off? Can any hide himself in secret places that I shall not see him? saith the LORD. Do not I fill heaven and earth? saith the LORD." — **Jeremiah 23:23–24***

God fills heaven and earth, yet He is not heaven and earth. He is near and far, immanent and transcendent. He is present with His creation while remaining Lord over it.

This guards us from two opposite errors. One error makes God distant, as though He created the world and then withdrew from it. The other collapses God into the world, as though every tree, star, and human soul were part of Him. Scripture rejects both. God is not absent. God is not creation. He is the living Lord who fills heaven and earth.

Isaiah holds the same truths together:

*"For thus saith the high and lofty One that inhabiteth eternity, whose name is Holy; I dwell in the high and holy place, with him also that is of a contrite and humble spirit, to revive the spirit of the humble, and to revive the heart of the contrite ones." — **Isaiah 57:15***

The high and holy God dwells with the humble. His nearness does not lessen His majesty. His majesty does not prevent His nearness.

God's Presence in Judgment

God's presence is not always comforting.

Adam and Eve hid among the trees after their sin, but the Lord came walking in the garden. Cain could not escape the voice of his brother's blood crying from the ground. Jonah fled from the presence of the Lord, but the Lord found him in the sea.

The prophet Amos gives a severe warning:

*"Though they dig into hell, thence shall mine hand take them; though they climb up to heaven, thence will I bring them down: And though they hide themselves in the top of Carmel, I will search and take them out thence; and though they be hid from my sight in the bottom of the sea, thence will I command the serpent, and he shall bite them." — **Amos 9:2–3***

No height, depth, mountain, sea, or hidden place can shield the guilty from God. His omnipresence makes judgment unavoidable.

This should sober every sinner. To reject God is not to get away from Him. It is to stand before Him unreconciled. Hell itself is not a place where God ceases to be God. It is the place where His righteous judgment is known without the comfort of His saving favor.

God's Presence with His People

God's presence is one of the greatest promises given to His people.

When Moses feared going forward without the Lord, God said:

"My presence shall go with thee, and I will give thee rest." — **Exodus 33:14**

Moses knew that Israel's distinction was not military strength, wisdom, or numbers. It was the presence of God. Without Him, they were nothing.

David could walk through death's shadow because God was with him:

"Yea, though I walk through the valley of the shadow of death, I will fear no evil: for thou art with me; thy rod and thy staff they comfort me." — **Psalm 23:4**

The valley was still dark. Death still cast its shadow. But the Shepherd was present. That was enough.

God's presence does not always remove danger. It makes His people safe within His purpose. Daniel's friends were thrown into the fiery furnace, and the fire was real. Yet Nebuchadnezzar saw a fourth walking with them. Daniel was cast into the lions' den, but God sent His angel and shut the lions' mouths. Paul suffered greatly, yet the Lord stood with him.

The promise is not that believers will never pass through fire or flood. It is that God will be with them.

"When thou passest through the waters, I will be with thee; and through the rivers, they shall not overflow thee: when thou walkest through the fire, thou

shalt not be burned; neither shall the flame kindle upon thee." — **Isaiah 43:2**

God With Us in Christ

The presence of God reaches its greatest revelation in Jesus Christ.

Matthew says Christ's birth fulfilled the word:

"Behold, a virgin shall be with child, and shall bring forth a son, and they shall call his name Emmanuel, which being interpreted is, God with us." — **Matthew 1:23**

God with us.

Not merely God above us, though He is. Not merely God around us, though He fills heaven and earth. In Christ, God comes near in human flesh. The eternal Son dwells among men. John writes:

"And the Word was made flesh, and dwelt among us, and we beheld his glory..." — **John 1:14**

The tabernacle pointed to God dwelling among His people. The temple represented His covenant presence. But Christ is the true and living presence of God among men.

This makes the incarnation astonishing. The God whom heaven cannot contain took upon Himself a true human nature. He walked roads, entered homes, touched lepers, ate with sinners, wept at a grave, and slept in a storm-tossed boat. God was not distant from human weakness. In Christ, He came near.

The Spirit's Indwelling Presence

After His resurrection and ascension, Christ did not leave His people as orphans. He gave the Holy Spirit.

Jesus said:

*"And I will pray the Father, and he shall give you another Comforter, that he may abide with you for ever." — **John 14:16***

The Spirit's presence is not temporary. He abides with believers forever. Paul says:

*"Know ye not that ye are the temple of God, and that the Spirit of God dwelleth in you?" — **I Corinthians 3:16***

This is not poetic exaggeration. God dwells in His people by His Spirit. The church is His temple. The believer's body is the temple of the Holy Ghost. This gives dignity to Christian life and seriousness to Christian holiness.

No Christian lives alone. No act of obedience is performed apart from God's presence. No sin is merely private. The Spirit of God dwells within those who belong to Christ.

That should comfort us and sober us.

The Presence of God in the Church

Jesus also promises His presence to His gathered people:

*"For where two or three are gathered together in my name, there am I in the midst of them." — **Matthew 18:20***

This does not mean Christ is absent elsewhere. It means He is present in a special covenantal way with His people gathered in His name. The church does not gather merely to discuss God from a distance. It gathers before Him and with Him in the midst.

That should shape worship. Carelessness in the assembly is not a small matter if God is present. Prayer is not empty speech if God is present. Preaching is not human performance if God is present through His Word and Spirit. Fellowship is not merely social if Christ is in the midst of His people.

The presence of God gives weight to the church.

The Final Dwelling of God with Man

The story of Scripture moves toward the full enjoyment of God's presence.

Sin drove man from Eden. The tabernacle and temple gave covenant signs of God dwelling among His people. Christ came as Emmanuel. The Spirit indwells the church. Yet the final hope is still greater.

Revelation says:

"Behold, the tabernacle of God is with men, and he will dwell with them, and they shall be his people, and God himself shall be with them, and be their God." — **Revelation 21:3**

That is the great end of redemption: God with His people, His people with God. No veil. No curse. No exile. No distance produced by sin. His servants shall serve Him, and they shall see His face.

The presence of God is heaven's joy.

The God Who Is Near

God is everywhere present.

- No sinner can hide from Him.
- No suffering saint is forgotten by Him.
- No place is beyond His reach.
- No prayer is spoken outside His hearing.
- No church gathers outside His sight.
- No grave can remove His people from His power.

His presence terrifies the unrepentant because they cannot escape Him. His presence comforts the redeemed because they cannot be separated from Him.

The God who fills heaven and earth has come near in Christ, dwells in His people by the Spirit, and will one day dwell with them in unveiled glory.

The believer's hope is not merely that God will send help from far away.

God Himself is with us.

Chapter 29 — God Is Wise

God knows all things, but wisdom is more than knowledge.

Knowledge sees what is true. Wisdom orders what is true toward the right end. A man may know many facts and still live foolishly. He may understand details and miss the meaning of them. He may have information without judgment, intelligence without righteousness, skill without holiness.

God is not merely all-knowing. He is wise.

Paul calls Him:

*"God only wise." — **Romans 16:27***

That does not mean no creature can possess any wisdom. Scripture commands men to seek wisdom, and God gives wisdom to His people. But all creaturely wisdom is received, limited, and dependent. God's wisdom is original, infinite, and perfect. He never misjudges. He never overlooks. He never chooses poorly. He never acts without the fullest knowledge of what is best.

His wisdom is not separate from His goodness, holiness, justice, and love. He is wise in all that He is and all that He does.

Wisdom in Creation

Creation displays the wisdom of God.

The psalmist says:

*"O LORD, how manifold are thy works! in wisdom hast thou made them all: the earth is full of thy riches." — **Psalm 104:24***

The world is not merely powerful. It is ordered. The heavens move with precision. The earth brings forth life. Creatures are fitted to their places. Seasons come and go. Systems interlock in ways that exceed human understanding. The smallest details and the largest structures both testify that God's works are wise.

Proverbs speaks of wisdom in connection with creation:

*"The LORD by wisdom hath founded the earth; by understanding hath he established the heavens." — **Proverbs 3:19***

God did not create clumsily. He did not experiment, fail, and revise. He founded the earth by wisdom. Every created thing depends upon divine thought before it depends upon physical process.

This should shape how we look at the world. Creation is not random noise. It is not meaningless matter. It is the work of the wise God. Even where sin has brought corruption, suffering, decay, and death, the underlying wisdom of the Creator remains visible.

Wisdom in Providence

God's wisdom also governs His providence.

This is often harder to see than wisdom in creation. We can look at the order of the heavens and marvel. But when providence wounds us, delays us, or confuses us, we may struggle to believe God is wise.

Yet Scripture teaches that God orders all things according to perfect counsel.

Paul says God works:

*"all things after the counsel of his own will." — **Ephesians 1:11***

That counsel is not impulsive. It is not uncertain. It is not forced upon God by circumstances. He governs according to wisdom deeper than human sight.

Joseph's life shows this clearly. His brothers sold him into slavery. Potiphar's wife falsely accused him. Prison swallowed years of his life. At many points, the path would have looked meaningless or cruel. Yet at the end Joseph said:

"But as for you, ye thought evil against me; but God meant it unto good, to bring to pass, as it is this day, to save much people alive." — **Genesis 50:20**

Joseph does not call evil good. His brothers meant evil. But God, in wisdom, governed even their evil toward a good purpose. The wise God does not become the author of sin, but He is never defeated by it.

That truth does not answer every question we might ask in suffering. It does something better. It gives us a God worthy of trust when answers remain hidden.

Wisdom Hidden from Man

God's wisdom often confounds human expectation.

Isaiah records the Lord's words:

"For my thoughts are not your thoughts, neither are your ways my ways, saith the LORD. For as the heavens are higher than the earth, so are my ways higher than your ways, and my thoughts than your thoughts." — **Isaiah 55:8–9**

This passage is sometimes used vaguely, as though it simply means life is confusing. In context, it speaks of God's abundant mercy toward the wicked who return to Him. His mercy exceeds human instinct. His thoughts are higher than ours not because He is irrational, but because His wisdom is greater.

God's wisdom may humble us because it does not always match what we would have chosen. He may delay when we would hurry. He may allow weakness where we would prefer visible strength. He may sanctify through affliction when we would choose ease. He may accomplish His greatest purposes through what appears to be loss.

The wise response is not to accuse Him, but to trust Him.

Job learned this. He wanted explanations for his suffering. God answered by revealing His majesty in creation and providence. Job was brought to confession:

*"I know that thou canst do every thing, and that no thought can be withholden from thee." — **Job 42:2***

Job did not receive every detail he may have wanted. He received a clearer sight of God. Sometimes the deepest answer to the mystery of providence is not an explanation but a revelation of the One who rules it.

Wisdom in the Cross

The wisdom of God is most astonishing at the cross.

To human eyes, the crucifixion looked like defeat. Israel's leaders rejected the Messiah. Rome condemned Him. The disciples scattered. The promised King was nailed to a tree. Nothing about that hour looked like wisdom to the world.

Yet Paul writes:

*"But we preach Christ crucified, unto the Jews a stumblingblock, and unto the Greeks foolishness; But unto them which are called, both Jews and Greeks, Christ the power of God, and the wisdom of God." — **I Corinthians 1:23–24***

The cross is the wisdom of God.

There God accomplished what no human mind could have devised. He judged sin and saved sinners. He upheld righteousness and justified the ungodly. He fulfilled prophecy through the actions of wicked men. He defeated the powers of darkness through the suffering of the Son. He turned shame into glory and death into life.

Paul says:

"Because the foolishness of God is wiser than men; and the weakness of God is stronger than men." — **I Corinthians 1:25**

There is no foolishness in God. Paul is speaking from the standpoint of human judgment. What men call foolish in God is wiser than the highest wisdom of men.

Every theology that is embarrassed by the cross is foolish. Every gospel that tries to make Christianity respectable by softening blood, substitution, wrath, and resurrection has lost divine wisdom. The cross is not a problem to be solved. It is the wisdom of God displayed in history.

Christ the Wisdom of God

God's wisdom is not merely a plan. It is revealed in a Person.

Paul says Christ Jesus:

"of God is made unto us wisdom, and righteousness, and sanctification, and redemption." — **I Corinthians 1:30**

In Christ are hidden all treasures of wisdom and knowledge:

"In whom are hid all the treasures of wisdom and knowledge." — **Colossians 2:3**

To know Christ is not to step away from wisdom into mere religious feeling. It is to come to the One in whom divine wisdom is fully revealed. He teaches the truth of God. He reveals the Father. He exposes the human heart. He fulfills the promises. He brings salvation. He will judge the world rightly.

The world often presents Christ as one religious teacher among many. Scripture presents Him as the wisdom of God. To reject Him is not intellectual courage. It is folly.

Wisdom Given to God's People

The wise God gives wisdom to His people.

James writes:

*"If any of you lack wisdom, let him ask of God, that giveth to all men liberally, and upbraideth not; and it shall be given him." — **James 1:5***

God does not mock the humble who ask for wisdom. He gives liberally. This is a great mercy, because we constantly need wisdom. We need it for suffering, temptation, parenting, marriage, church life, decisions, speech, correction, patience, discernment, and obedience.

But biblical wisdom begins with reverence.

*"The fear of the LORD is the beginning of wisdom: and the knowledge of the holy is understanding." — **Proverbs 9:10***

A man may be educated and still be a fool if he does not fear the Lord. Wisdom is not merely the ability to analyze life. It is the ability to live rightly before God.

This means the church must not confuse cleverness with wisdom. Clever men can mishandle Scripture. Gifted teachers can become proud. Skilled leaders can act foolishly if they do not fear God. True wisdom bows before the Lord and receives His Word.

Wisdom and the Word of God

God's wisdom is given through Scripture.

Paul told Timothy:

*"And that from a child thou hast known the holy scriptures, which are able to make thee wise unto salvation through faith which is in Christ Jesus." — **2 Timothy 3:15***

The Scriptures make men wise unto salvation. They reveal Christ. They expose sin. They teach righteousness. They correct false paths. They train the people of God for obedience.

Psalm 19 says:

*"The testimony of the LORD is sure, making wise the simple." — **Psalm 19:7***

The simple do not need the world's approval to become wise. They need the sure testimony of the Lord. Scripture gives a wisdom that cannot be produced by fallen human speculation.

This is why careless handling of Scripture is foolish. The Word of God is not raw material for human creativity. It is the wisdom of God given to His people. To ignore it, twist it, or submit it to the spirit of the age is to exchange wisdom for folly.

The Wise God Can Be Trusted

God is wise.

- He made all things wisely.
- He governs all things wisely.
- He saves sinners wisely.

- He reveals truth wisely.
- He gives wisdom to those who ask.
- He orders the lives of His people with wisdom deeper than their sight.

This doctrine should quiet anxiety and humble pride.

Anxiety assumes that if we cannot see the way, perhaps there is no way. Wisdom answers that God sees what we cannot. Pride assumes that our judgment is sufficient to evaluate God. Wisdom answers that His thoughts are higher than ours.

The believer does not always understand what God is doing. He does not need to pretend that he does. Faith is not pretending pain makes sense when it does not. Faith is trusting the wise God when sense is beyond reach.

Paul's worship should become ours:

"To God only wise, be glory through Jesus Christ for ever. Amen." — **Romans 16:27**

God is wise.

And because He is wise, not one act of His will prove foolish, not one promise will fail through miscalculation, not one providence will be wasted, and not one redeemed life will arrive at glory by accident.

Chapter 30 — God Is Sovereign

God reigns.

He does not merely influence history, react to human choices, or hope His purposes succeed. He rules over all things with supreme authority. His will cannot be overthrown. His counsel cannot be defeated. His throne is not threatened by angels, nations, demons, kings, sinners, or time.

The psalmist declares:

"The LORD hath prepared his throne in the heavens; and his kingdom ruleth over all." — **Psalm 103:19**

That last word matters: **all**.

God's sovereignty is His absolute right and power to govern all things according to His holy will. He rules creation, providence, nations, salvation, judgment, and the final end of history. Nothing exists outside His authority.

This truth humbles man deeply. It also comforts the believer greatly.

The Lord Reigns

Scripture does not present God as struggling to become King. He is King.

"The LORD reigneth; let the earth rejoice; let the multitude of isles be glad thereof." — **Psalm 97:1**

His reign is not bad news for creation. It is the reason creation can rejoice. The world is not finally ruled by chance, chaos, Satan, political power, or human rebellion. The Lord reigns.

Nebuchadnezzar learned this after God humbled him:

"And all the inhabitants of the earth are reputed as nothing: and he doeth according to his will in the army of heaven, and among the inhabitants of the

earth: and none can stay his hand, or say unto him, What doest thou?" — **Daniel 4:35**

No one can stay His hand. No creature can summon God into court as though He were accountable to a higher throne. He is not one ruler among many. He is the Most High.

This does not mean God rules as a tyrant. His sovereignty is not raw force. It is holy, wise, righteous, good, and faithful sovereignty. The One who rules all things is the same God whose character we have been tracing. His power cannot be separated from His goodness. His authority cannot be separated from His justice. His decrees cannot be separated from His wisdom.

Sovereign Over Creation

God's sovereignty begins with creation because He made all things.

"The earth is the LORD'S, and the fulness thereof; the world, and they that dwell therein." — **Psalm 24:1**

Ownership belongs to the Creator. God does not rule the world by seizure, as though creation were someone else's possession. He rules what He made. Every creature owes Him existence, breath, obedience, and worship.

Paul says:

"For of him, and through him, and to him, are all things: to whom be glory for ever. Amen." — **Romans 11:36**

All things are **of** Him as source, **through** Him as sustainer, and **to** Him as final end. Nothing has independent meaning apart from Him. The universe is not centered on man. It is centered on God.

This corrects one of the most common errors of fallen thinking. Man imagines himself as owner, judge, and goal. He asks whether God fits his plans, approves his desires, and serves his happiness. Scripture reverses the entire arrangement. Man belongs to God.

God is not useful because He fits into our story. We exist for His glory.

Sovereign Over Nations

God rules the nations.

Earthly governments may not acknowledge Him, but they remain under His hand. Their borders, rulers, rise, decline, and final accountability are not outside His dominion.

Daniel says:

"Blessed be the name of God for ever and ever: for wisdom and might are his: And he changeth the times and the seasons: he removeth kings, and setteth up kings." — **Daniel 2:20–21**

History is not random movement. God changes times and seasons. He removes kings and sets up kings. The rulers of the earth may boast, scheme, oppress, and imagine themselves untouchable, but they govern only by permission.

Paul told the Athenians that God:

"hath made of one blood all nations of men for to dwell on all the face of the earth, and hath determined the times before appointed, and the bounds of their habitation." — **Acts 17:26**

Nations have appointed times and boundaries under God. This does not make every ruler righteous or every national act good. Scripture condemns wicked rulers often. But even wicked rulers are not beyond God's government. Pharaoh resisted and was judged. Nebuchadnezzar boasted and was humbled. Herod received praise as a god and was struck down.

The sovereignty of God is a warning to proud nations and a comfort to His people. No empire owns the future. No ruler can cancel God's promises. No law can dethrone Christ.

Sovereign Over Human Plans

Human beings make real plans and real choices, but they do not control the final outcome.

Proverbs says:

"There are many devices in a man's heart; nevertheless the counsel of the LORD, that shall stand." — **Proverbs 19:21**

Again:

"A man's heart deviseth his way: but the LORD directeth his steps." — **Proverbs 16:9**

This does not make human planning meaningless. Scripture encourages wisdom, diligence, counsel, labor, and responsibility. But man's plans are subordinate. God directs the steps.

James rebukes arrogant planning:

"Go to now, ye that say, To day or to morrow we will go into such a city, and continue there a year, and buy and sell, and get gain: Whereas ye know not what shall be on the morrow." — **James 4:13–14**

Then he gives the proper posture:

"For that ye ought to say, If the Lord will, we shall live, and do this, or that." — **James 4:15**

"If the Lord will" is not a religious phrase to sprinkle over self-confidence. It is a confession of reality. We do not control tomorrow. God does.

Sovereign Without Being the Author of Evil

The sovereignty of God must be handled carefully.

Scripture teaches that God rules over all things. It also teaches that God is holy, righteous, and not the author of sin. He governs even evil acts without becoming evil, approving evil, or removing creaturely responsibility.

The clearest example is the cross. Peter preached that Jesus was delivered: "by the determinate counsel and foreknowledge of God," yet he immediately told his hearers:

*"ye have taken, and by wicked hands have crucified and slain." — **Acts 2:23***

Both truths stand together. The cross happened according to God's determinate counsel. The men who crucified Christ acted wickedly. God's sovereignty did not make their sin righteous. Their sin did not overthrow God's sovereignty.

Joseph said the same to his brothers:

*"But as for you, ye thought evil against me; but God meant it unto good." — **Genesis 50:20***

One event. Two intentions. They meant evil. God meant good. God did not become the author of their sin, but He ruled over it for His saving purpose.

This is mystery, but it is not contradiction. Scripture never asks us to protect God's sovereignty by making Him morally responsible for evil. Nor does it ask us to protect His holiness by denying His rule over history. The full character of God requires both.

Sovereign in Salvation

Salvation belongs to the Lord.

Jonah confessed from the belly of the fish:

"Salvation is of the LORD." — **Jonah 2:9**

Sinners do not rescue themselves. Dead men do not raise themselves. Blind men do not give themselves sight. The gospel is not God helping the spiritually strong finish what they began. It is God saving those who could not save themselves.

Jesus said:

"No man can come to me, except the Father which hath sent me draw him: and I will raise him up at the last day." — **John 6:44**

And again:

"All that the Father giveth me shall come to me; and him that cometh to me I will in no wise cast out." — **John 6:37**

These words are humbling and comforting. They humble because salvation begins with God's gracious initiative. They comfort because everyone given by the Father comes to the Son, and everyone who comes to the Son is received.

God's sovereignty in salvation does not make the gospel invitation meaningless. Christ calls sinners to come. The apostles preached repentance and faith. Men are responsible to believe. Yet behind every true response is the gracious work of God.

No saved person will boast in heaven that he made himself to differ. The song of the redeemed will be praise to the Lamb.

Sovereign Over Suffering

God's sovereignty is often most precious when life hurts.

If suffering were outside God's rule, then pain would be meaningless chaos. If God were sovereign but not good, suffering would be terrifying. But the

God who rules is also wise, loving, faithful, and merciful. That does not make suffering easy. It makes trust possible.

Job suffered deeply, yet he confessed:

"The LORD gave, and the LORD hath taken away; blessed be the name of the LORD." — **Job 1:21**

Job did not understand the heavenly scene. He did not know all that God was doing. But he knew that his life was not governed by accident.

Later, after much anguish, God did not answer every question Job raised. He revealed His majesty. Job was brought to humility before the sovereign Lord.

This is often how faith survives suffering. Not by receiving every explanation, but by seeing again that God is God.

The believer may say, "I do not understand this." Scripture allows that. But he cannot say, "God has lost control." The Lord reigns even in the dark.

Sovereign Over the End

God's sovereignty guarantees the final outcome of history.

The world does not end in uncertainty. Christ will return. The dead will be raised. Evil will be judged. Israel's promises will be fulfilled according to God's faithfulness. The nations will be brought under the rule of the King. The bride will be presented without spot or wrinkle. The new creation will come.

Revelation declares:

"The kingdoms of this world are become the kingdoms of our Lord, and of his Christ; and he shall reign for ever and ever." — **Revelation 11:15**

That is not possibility. It is certainty.

The same book shows heaven crying:

"Alleluia: for the Lord God omnipotent reigneth." — **Revelation 19:6**

God's sovereignty is not merely a doctrine for present comfort. It is the guarantee that all things are moving toward the end He has ordained.

- No rebellion will remain unresolved.
- No promise will remain unfulfilled.
- No enemy will remain unconquered.
- No tear of the redeemed will remain unwiped.

The King will finish what He began.

The Right Response to Sovereignty

The sovereignty of God should produce humility, trust, obedience, and worship.

Humility, because we are not in control. Trust, because God is. Obedience, because His authority is absolute. Worship, because His rule is glorious.

Sovereignty should not make believers passive. Scripture never reasons that way. Because God reigns, His people pray, preach, obey, work, endure, and hope. Divine sovereignty establishes human responsibility; it does not erase it.

Paul knew God had many people in Corinth, and that truth encouraged him to keep preaching. Joseph believed God meant his suffering for good, and that truth enabled him to forgive. Christ knew the Father's will, and He obeyed all the way to the cross.

The doctrine of sovereignty is not meant to produce cold speculation. It is meant to bring the soul low before God and steady it beneath His rule.

The Lord Reigneth

God is sovereign.

- He rules creation.
- He rules nations.
- He rules human plans.
- He rules salvation.
- He rules suffering.
- He rules the end of history.

His sovereignty is not harsh because He is good. It is not reckless because He is wise. It is not corrupt because He is holy. It is not unstable because He is faithful.

The throne is occupied.

That is terror to the proud, comfort to the afflicted, strength to the obedient, and hope to the church.

"The LORD reigneth; let the earth rejoice." — **Psalm 97:1**

Chapter 31 — God Is Jealous for His Name

God is jealous.

That statement can sound strange until we understand it biblically. Human jealousy is often sinful because it is rooted in insecurity, envy, possessiveness, pride, or fear of loss. God's jealousy is nothing like that. He is not insecure. He is not threatened. He does not envy another. He lacks nothing.

God's jealousy is His holy zeal for His own glory, name, worship, covenant, and people. He will not share the honor that belongs to Him alone. He will not treat idolatry as harmless. He will not allow His name to be profaned forever. He is jealous because He is God, and because no rival deserves what belongs only to Him.

The Lord says:

"I am the LORD: that is my name: and my glory will I not give to another, neither my praise to graven images." — **Isaiah 42:8**

If God gave His glory to another, He would be approving a lie. If He allowed idols to receive worship as though they were equal to Him, He would be denying reality. His jealousy is not moral weakness. It is truth defending what is infinitely worthy.

The Jealous God

The second commandment warns Israel not to make or bow down to idols. Then God gives the reason:

"For I the LORD thy God am a jealous God..." — **Exodus 20:5**

Later Moses says:

"For thou shalt worship no other god: for the LORD, whose name is Jealous, is a jealous God." — **Exodus 34:14**

This is not a passing description. God's name is Jealous. He is the God who tolerates no rival for His people's worship.

That is because worship is not a small matter. To worship is to ascribe worth. It is to bow the heart before what is ultimate. Idolatry does not merely break a rule; it insults God's glory by giving created things the honor due to the Creator.

The jealousy of God protects the truth that He alone is God.

Jealousy and Covenant Love

God's jealousy is not detached from His love. It is bound to it.

Israel's idolatry is often described in marital terms. The Lord had entered covenant with His people. He had redeemed them from Egypt, carried them through the wilderness, given them His law, and set His name among them. When they turned to idols, Scripture describes it as spiritual adultery.

The Lord says through Jeremiah:

"Surely as a wife treacherously departeth from her husband, so have ye dealt treacherously with me, O house of Israel, saith the LORD." — **Jeremiah 3:20**

A husband who is indifferent to his wife's adultery is not loving. Covenant love is rightly jealous. It protects the exclusivity of the relationship. God's jealousy over His people is the jealousy of a covenant Lord who will not treat spiritual treachery as a minor offense.

This helps us understand why idolatry receives such severe attention in Scripture. Idolatry is not religious variety. It is betrayal. It gives the heart to another. It takes the name, gifts, and mercy of God and lays them before false gods.

The Profaning of God's Name

God is jealous not only because idols rob Him of worship, but because His name is profaned when His people live falsely.

Through Ezekiel, the Lord says that Israel profaned His holy name among the heathen:

*"And when they entered unto the heathen, whither they went, they profaned my holy name, when they said to them, These are the people of the LORD, and are gone forth out of his land." — **Ezekiel 36:20***

Israel's sin caused the nations to misunderstand God. Their exile appeared to the heathen as though the Lord were weak, unfaithful, or unable to keep His people. So God promised restoration:

*"Therefore say unto the house of Israel, Thus saith the Lord GOD; I do not this for your sakes, O house of Israel, but for mine holy name's sake, which ye have profaned among the heathen, whither ye went." — **Ezekiel 36:22***

God acts for His holy name. That does not make Him cold toward His people. It gives them hope. If their future rested only on their worthiness, there would be no future. But God's own name is bound to His promises.

His jealousy for His name secures His faithfulness.

Jealousy and Worship

God's jealousy demands exclusive worship.

Jesus said:

*"Thou shalt worship the Lord thy God, and him only shalt thou serve." — **Matthew 4:10***

That word **only** cannot be softened. God does not accept a divided throne. He is not one devotion among many. He is not the highest item on a list that still allows idols beneath Him. He alone is God.

This reaches deeper than carved images. Anything can become an idol when it receives the trust, affection, fear, obedience, or ultimate weight that belongs to God. Money can become an idol. Family can become an idol. Nation, success, comfort, ministry, knowledge, reputation, pleasure, and even theological systems can become idols.

The heart is skilled at manufacturing rivals.

God's jealousy confronts every one of them. He will not bless the lie that something created can bear the weight of deity. He loves His people too much to let idols destroy them quietly.

Christ and Divine Jealousy

The jealousy of God is seen in Christ.

When Jesus entered the temple and found it corrupted by buying and selling, He drove out those who had turned His Father's house into a house of merchandise. John records:

"And his disciples remembered that it was written, The zeal of thine house hath eaten me up." — **John 2:17**

Christ's zeal was holy. He was not defending personal pride. He was consumed with honor for His Father's house. Worship had been profaned. The place of prayer had been turned into a market. The Son acted with the jealousy of God for pure worship.

This same Christ receives worship rightly because He is God the Son. The Father's jealousy for His glory does not exclude the Son; it includes Him.

The glory of God is revealed in the face of Jesus Christ. To honor the Son is to honor the Father. To reject the Son is to dishonor the Father.

Jesus says:

"That all men should honour the Son, even as they honour the Father. He that honoureth not the Son honoureth not the Father which hath sent him." **— John 5:23**

The jealous God will not accept worship that refuses His Son.

Jealousy and the Church

The New Testament applies the language of jealousy to the church.

Paul writes to the Corinthians:

"For I am jealous over you with godly jealousy: for I have espoused you to one husband, that I may present you as a chaste virgin to Christ." **— 2 Corinthians 11:2**

Paul's jealousy was godly because it reflected Christ's claim upon His people. The church belongs to Christ. She is not free to flirt with false gospels, false christs, worldly wisdom, or spiritual corruption.

This matters deeply for doctrine. False teaching is not merely an intellectual mistake. It can be spiritual seduction. A false gospel leads the bride away from devotion to Christ. A distorted view of God alters worship. A compromised message can dress unfaithfulness in religious language.

Paul feared that the Corinthians would be corrupted from the simplicity that is in Christ. That danger remains. The church must not treat doctrinal faithfulness as optional, because Christ is jealous for His bride.

The Jealousy of the Lamb

The jealousy of Christ also helps us understand His protection of His people.

He gave Himself for the church. He purchased her with His blood. He sanctifies and cleanses her. He will present her to Himself glorious, without spot or wrinkle. His love is covenant love, and covenant love is rightly jealous.

This does not mean Christ is harsh with His bride. It means He will not abandon her to rivals. He will not make peace with what defiles her. He will not share her with idols. The Bridegroom's love includes holy jealousy.

That truth will matter later when we consider the Bridegroom, His bride, and the wrath of the Lamb. Christ's relationship to His church must be interpreted through the fullness of His character. He does not love His bride casually. He does not cleanse her indifferently. He is faithful, holy, and jealous for the one He has redeemed.

God's Jealousy and Our Good

God's jealousy is good news for His people.

If God were not jealous, He would allow us to give ourselves to what destroys us. He would watch quietly while idols stole our hearts. He would let false gods promise life while leading us into death. But because He is jealous, He confronts our divided worship.

This confrontation may be painful. Idols do not leave easily. The heart resents losing what it has trusted. But the jealousy of God is mercy when it tears down false refuges.

The Lord is not cruel when He exposes idols. He is rescuing worship from lies.

James warns believers:

"Ye adulterers and adulteresses, know ye not that the friendship of the world is enmity with God? whosoever therefore will be a friend of the world is the enemy of God." — **James 4:4**

Then he asks:

"Do ye think that the scripture saith in vain, The spirit that dwelleth in us lusteth to envy?" — **James 4:5**

The wording is difficult, but the point of the passage is clear: God does not treat spiritual adultery lightly. He claims His people wholly. Friendship with the world is not harmless because the God who dwells among His people is jealous for them.

The Danger of Provoking God to Jealousy

Scripture warns against provoking God to jealousy.

Moses says of Israel:

"They provoked him to jealousy with strange gods, with abominations provoked they him to anger." — **Deuteronomy 32:16**

Paul uses Israel's history to warn the Corinthian church against idolatry:

"Do we provoke the Lord to jealousy? are we stronger than he?" — **I Corinthians 10:22**

That question should silence presumption. Are we stronger than He? Can we flirt with idols and imagine God will not answer? Can we bring the table of the Lord and the table of demons together? Can we claim Christ while giving our deepest allegiance elsewhere?

The jealous God is not mocked.

This warning is needed because modern religion often treats divided loyalty gently. Scripture does not. God is patient, merciful, gracious, and kind, but He is not indifferent to rivals. He will have His people's worship.

Zeal for God's Name in His People

Because God is jealous for His name, His people should care about His name.

Jesus taught us to pray:

*"Our Father which art in heaven, Hallowed be thy name." — **Matthew 6:9***

The first request is not about our needs. It is about God's name being hallowed. To hallow His name is to regard it as holy, to honor Him as He is, to desire that He be known, worshiped, obeyed, and glorified.

A believer who has no concern for the honor of God's name has not understood the heart of prayer. God's glory should matter to us. His reputation should matter. His worship should matter. His Word should matter. His people's conduct should matter because they bear His name.

This is not about defending God as though He were weak. It is about loving what He loves.

The God Who Will Sanctify His Name

God's jealousy guarantees that His name will finally be sanctified before all creation.

The world may blaspheme now. Idols may be praised now. False gods may gather worship now. The wicked may mock. The nations may rage. Even God's own people may sometimes profane His name by disobedience.

But it will not remain so.

The Lord says:

*"And I will sanctify my great name, which was profaned among the heathen, which ye have profaned in the midst of them; and the heathen shall know that I am the LORD, saith the Lord GOD, when I shall be sanctified in you before their eyes." — **Ezekiel 36:23**

God will vindicate His name. He will show that He is the Lord. His promises will stand. His enemies will be judged. His people will be cleansed. His glory will fill the earth.

The jealousy of God moves history toward worship.

The God Whose Name Is Jealous

God is jealous for His name.

He will not give His glory to another. He will not share His worship with idols. He will not treat spiritual adultery as harmless. He will not allow His name to be profaned forever. He will not abandon His bride to rivals.

- His jealousy is holy.
- His jealousy is righteous.
- His jealousy is loving.
- His jealousy is faithful.

This truth should search us. What rivals have we tolerated? What idols have we renamed as necessities? What loyalties have competed with Christ? What parts of our worship have become divided?

The jealous God does not ask for a corner of the heart. He claims the whole.

And He is worthy of it.

Chapter 32 — God Is Wrathful Against Evil

God's wrath is one of the most rejected truths about His character.

Many people can accept a God who loves, forgives, heals, comforts, and provides. But wrath sounds harsh to modern ears. It seems to belong to an older and less acceptable way of speaking about God. Some try to remove it. Others soften it until it becomes little more than natural consequence. Still others treat it as though wrath belongs to the Father but not to the Son.

Scripture will not allow any of these reductions.

God is wrathful against evil because He is holy, righteous, just, good, and true. His wrath is not a flaw in His character. It is the necessary opposition of His holy nature to all that is wicked, corrupt, cruel, idolatrous, false, and rebellious.

Paul writes:

"For the wrath of God is revealed from heaven against all ungodliness and unrighteousness of men, who hold the truth in unrighteousness." — **Romans 1:18**

The wrath of God is not revealed against weakness as weakness, grief as grief, or ignorance as ignorance. It is revealed against ungodliness and unrighteousness. It is God's settled opposition to evil.

If God were not wrathful against evil, He would not be good.

Wrath Is Not Human Temper

The wrath of God must not be confused with sinful human anger.

Human anger is often impatient, proud, selfish, excessive, and poorly aimed. We become angry when our pride is injured, our comfort is interrupted, our preferences are denied, or our control is threatened. Even when our anger has a righteous cause, sin can easily corrupt it.

God's wrath is never like that.

His wrath is not emotional instability. It is not loss of control. It is not cruelty. It is not divine irritation. God does not lash out. He does not overreact. He does not punish beyond what is right. His wrath is holy, measured, true, and just.

Nahum says:

*"The LORD is slow to anger, and great in power, and will not at all acquit the wicked." — **Nahum 1:3***

Both truths stand together. He is slow to anger, and He will not acquit the wicked. His patience is real, but it does not erase His wrath. His wrath is certain, but it is not rash.

This matters because many objections to divine wrath are really objections to a caricature. People imagine God as though He were a fallen man with infinite power and a short temper. But Scripture reveals the opposite. God's wrath is the response of perfect holiness to evil.

Wrath and Holiness

God's wrath arises from His holiness.

Habakkuk says:

"Thou art of purer eyes than to behold evil, and canst not look on iniquity..." **— *Habakkuk 1:13***

God sees evil, but He cannot look upon it with approval. He cannot become morally comfortable with sin. His holiness burns against it.

This is why wrath cannot be removed from God without damaging every other doctrine. If God is holy, He must oppose what is unholy. If He is righteous, He must oppose unrighteousness. If He is good, He must oppose what destroys goodness. If He is love, He must oppose what corrupts, enslaves, and ruins those He made.

A god who never becomes wrathful against evil is not loving. He is morally indifferent.

We understand this instinctively in human terms. If someone watches abuse, murder, exploitation, betrayal, and cruelty without moral outrage, we do not praise him as loving. We call him corrupt or cowardly. Yet many want a God who does exactly that on a cosmic scale.

The Bible gives us a better God.

- His wrath means evil matters.
- His wrath means victims are not forgotten.
- His wrath means holiness is not an empty word.
- His wrath means justice will be done.

Wrath Revealed in History

Scripture gives many historical displays of God's wrath.

The flood came upon a world filled with violence and corruption. Sodom and Gomorrah were judged for grievous wickedness. Egypt was struck with plagues after Pharaoh hardened himself against the Lord. Israel itself experienced judgment when it turned from God to idols. Jerusalem fell under judgment after repeated warnings were despised.

These accounts are not comfortable reading, but they are necessary. They teach us that God does not merely dislike evil in theory. He judges it in history.

Paul says Israel's wilderness judgments were written for our warning:

"Now all these things happened unto them for ensamples: and they are written for our admonition, upon whom the ends of the world are come." — **1 Corinthians 10:11**

Judgment texts are not embarrassments to hide. They are warnings to hear.

At the same time, the history of God's wrath almost always shows His patience first. Noah's generation had warning while the ark was preparing. Egypt saw plague after plague before final destruction. Israel received prophets for generations before exile. Jerusalem heard Christ Himself weep and warn before the city fell.

God's wrath is not impulsive. It comes after patience has been despised.

The Wrath of the Lamb

The New Testament does not remove divine wrath. It reveals it even more clearly.

Some people imagine Jesus as though He were opposed to the wrath of God. But Jesus warned of hell, spoke of judgment, rebuked hypocrisy, cleansed the temple, and declared coming wrath upon unrepentant cities. The gentle Savior is also the righteous Judge.

Revelation gives one of the most striking phrases in Scripture:

"And said to the mountains and rocks, Fall on us, and hide us from the face of him that sitteth on the throne, and from the wrath of the Lamb: For the great day of his wrath is come; and who shall be able to stand?" — **Revelation 6:16–17**

The wrath is the wrath of the Lamb.

That phrase should correct every shallow view of Christ. The Lamb who was slain is not morally indifferent to evil. The One who gave Himself for sinners will judge those who refuse repentance. His wrath is not contrary to His love. It is the wrath of the holy Savior against all that opposes God.

This is important for the whole structure of biblical doctrine. The same Christ who loves His bride also brings wrath upon a rebellious world. The same Christ who bore wrath for His people will execute wrath upon His enemies. We must not divide Him.

Wrath and the Cross

The cross is the clearest proof that God's wrath against sin is real.

If sin could be forgiven by simple dismissal, Christ did not need to die. If wrath were only a metaphor for bad consequences, the blood of the Son of God becomes unnecessary. But Scripture says Christ bore the curse, suffered for sins, and was set forth as a propitiation.

Paul writes:

*"Whom God hath set forth to be a propitiation through faith in his blood, to declare his righteousness for the remission of sins that are past, through the forbearance of God." — **Romans 3:25***

Propitiation means that God's wrath is dealt with through sacrifice. At the cross, wrath is not denied. It is satisfied. Sin is not ignored. It is judged. The guilty are not excused apart from justice. They are saved because Christ stands in their place.

Isaiah says:

*"But he was wounded for our transgressions, he was bruised for our iniquities: the chastisement of our peace was upon him; and with his stripes we are healed." — **Isaiah 53:5***

The cross is love, mercy, grace, justice, righteousness, wisdom, and wrath all displayed together. God's love provides the Son. God's wrath against sin falls upon the willing Substitute. God's justice is upheld. God's mercy saves.

A cross without wrath is not the biblical cross.

Wrath and Unbelief

The wrath of God remains upon those who reject the Son.

John says:

*"He that believeth on the Son hath everlasting life: and he that believeth not the Son shall not see life; but the wrath of God abideth on him." — **John 3:36***

The verse is plain. Everlasting life is in the Son. Those who reject the Son remain under wrath.

This is not because God delights in destruction. Scripture says He has no pleasure in the death of the wicked. But unbelief is not a small matter. To reject Christ is to reject God's appointed Savior, despise the blood of the covenant, and refuse the only refuge from judgment.

The gospel is urgent because wrath is real. Evangelism loses its biblical seriousness when wrath is muted. If sinners are merely unhappy, unfulfilled, or confused, the gospel becomes therapy. If sinners are guilty before the holy God and wrath is coming, the gospel is rescue.

The church must not be ashamed of this. Warnings are mercy when danger is real.

Saved from Wrath

The believer's hope is not that wrath does not exist. His hope is that Christ has delivered him from it.

Paul writes:

"Much more then, being now justified by his blood, we shall be saved from wrath through him." — **Romans 5:9**

Again, to the Thessalonians:

"Jesus, which delivered us from the wrath to come." — **I Thessalonians 1:10**

And again:

"For God hath not appointed us to wrath, but to obtain salvation by our Lord Jesus Christ." — **I Thessalonians 5:9**

These promises are precious because wrath is real. Christ does not merely improve the believer's life. He delivers him from the wrath to come.

This also distinguishes fatherly discipline from condemning wrath. God may discipline His children. He may correct, chasten, expose, and humble them. But He does not pour condemning wrath upon those whose sins have been borne by Christ. The believer may suffer in this world, but he is not under the wrath from which Christ has delivered him.

That distinction matters for assurance, for suffering, and for eschatology. The church belongs to the Bridegroom who gave Himself for her. She is not appointed to wrath.

Wrath and Final Judgment

The wrath of God will be fully revealed in final judgment.

Paul speaks of:

"the day of wrath and revelation of the righteous judgment of God." — **Romans 2:5**

Revelation describes the final judgment with terrifying clarity. Books are opened. The dead stand before God. Those not found written in the book of life are cast into the lake of fire.

This is not symbolic of nothing. Whatever imagery is involved, the reality is dreadful. Final judgment is the irreversible answer of the holy God to unrepentant evil.

Jesus Himself warned:

"And these shall go away into everlasting punishment: but the righteous into life eternal." — **Matthew 25:46**

Everlasting punishment and life eternal stand together in the same sentence. We do not honor Christ by softening what He said.

The doctrine of final wrath is heavy. It should never be handled with coldness or delight in the destruction of the wicked. But it must be handled. To remove it is to contradict Christ, weaken the gospel, and distort the character of God.

The Right Response to Wrath

The right response to God's wrath is not embarrassment. It is repentance, faith, reverence, and gratitude.

Repentance, because sin is not safe. Faith, because Christ is the only refuge. Reverence, because God is holy. Gratitude, because believers have been delivered at infinite cost.

The wrath of God should also produce seriousness in preaching. Paul said:

"Knowing therefore the terror of the Lord, we persuade men..." — **2 Corinthians 5:11**

The terror of the Lord did not make Paul silent. It made him persuasive. He pleaded with sinners because judgment was real and reconciliation was offered.

A church that cannot speak of wrath will eventually lose the wonder of grace. We cannot understand the greatness of salvation if we no longer know what we have been saved from.

The Holy God Against Evil

God is wrathful against evil.

His wrath is not sinful anger.

It is not cruelty.

It is not instability.

It is not opposed to love.

It is the holy response of the righteous God to all that is evil.

Because God is wrathful, sin matters.

Because God is wrathful, justice will come.

Because God is wrathful, the cross was necessary.

Because God is wrathful, Christ's deliverance is glorious.

The sinner should flee to Christ.

The believer should worship with trembling gratitude.

The church should preach the whole counsel of God.

For the same Scripture that says God is love also says:

"For our God is a consuming fire." — **Hebrews 12:29**

Chapter 33 — God Is a Consuming Fire

Scripture does not allow us to make God small.

He is merciful, gracious, longsuffering, good, kind, and full of compassion. But He is also holy, righteous, jealous, wrathful against evil, and a consuming fire. If we remove the truths that make us tremble, we are no longer describing the God of the Bible.

Hebrews says:

"For our God is a consuming fire." — **Hebrews 12:29**

That verse is not addressed to pagans only. It appears in a warning to those who have received greater revelation and greater privilege. The writer of Hebrews has just said:

"Wherefore we receiving a kingdom which cannot be moved, let us have grace, whereby we may serve God acceptably with reverence and godly fear." — **Hebrews 12:28**

Grace does not remove reverence. The kingdom cannot be moved, but the God who gives it is still a consuming fire. The redeemed do not fear condemnation in Christ, but they must never lose godly fear.

A fire can warm, purify, illuminate, and consume. Scripture uses the imagery of fire to reveal God's presence, His holiness, His judgment, His purification, and His glory. The point is not that God is destructive in some careless sense. The point is that He is not safe for sin, not manageable by man, and not to be approached lightly.

The Fire of His Presence

When Moses first encountered the Lord, he saw a bush burning with fire, yet the bush was not consumed.

"And the angel of the LORD appeared unto him in a flame of fire out of the midst of a bush: and he looked, and, behold, the bush burned with fire, and the bush was not consumed." — **Exodus 3:2**

The sign was arresting. Fire was present, but the bush remained. The holy God was revealing Himself, and Moses was told:

"Draw not nigh hither: put off thy shoes from off thy feet, for the place whereon thou standest is holy ground." — **Exodus 3:5**

The ground was not holy in itself. It was holy because God was there. His presence changed the place. Moses could not approach casually. Before God sent him to Pharaoh, He taught him reverence.

This pattern matters. God's nearness is mercy, but His nearness is never common. When He comes near, the proper response is not casual familiarity but worship.

The Fire of Sinai

At Sinai, God's presence was marked by fire, smoke, trembling, and fear.

"And mount Sinai was altogether on a smoke, because the LORD descended upon it in fire: and the smoke thereof ascended as the smoke of a furnace, and the whole mount quaked greatly." — **Exodus 19:18**

Israel was not allowed to treat the mountain as ordinary. Boundaries were set. Warnings were given. The people trembled.

Later Moses reminded them:

"And ye came near and stood under the mountain; and the mountain burned with fire unto the midst of heaven, with darkness, clouds, and thick darkness." — **Deuteronomy 4:11**

Then he warned:

"Take heed unto yourselves, lest ye forget the covenant of the LORD your God... For the LORD thy God is a consuming fire, even a jealous God." — **Deuteronomy 4:23–24**

The consuming fire is connected to covenant faithfulness and the danger of idolatry. God's fire is not random. It is the burning holiness of the jealous God who will not share His people with idols.

Sinai teaches that revelation is not light entertainment. When God speaks, His people should tremble, listen, and obey.

The Fire of Judgment

God's fire also reveals judgment.

When Nadab and Abihu offered strange fire before the Lord, Scripture says:

"And there went out fire from the LORD, and devoured them, and they died before the LORD." — **Leviticus 10:2**

The next verse explains the meaning:

"I will be sanctified in them that come nigh me, and before all the people I will be glorified." — **Leviticus 10:3**

God will be treated as holy by those who draw near. Their sin was not merely a procedural mistake. They approached God in a way He had not commanded. The judgment was severe because the lesson was serious: worship is governed by God's holiness, not human invention.

This same theme continues throughout Scripture. Fire falls in judgment on Sodom. Fire consumes the murmurers at Taberah. Fire is associated with the coming day of the Lord. John the Baptist says of Christ:

"Whose fan is in his hand, and he will throughly purge his floor, and gather his wheat into the garner; but he will burn up the chaff with unquenchable fire." — **Matthew 3:12**

Christ is not only Savior. He is Judge. The chaff will not remain forever mixed with the wheat. The consuming fire of God's judgment will make the final distinction.

The Fire That Purifies

Yet fire in Scripture is not only destructive. It also purifies.

Malachi asks:

"But who may abide the day of his coming? and who shall stand when he appeareth? for he is like a refiner's fire, and like fullers' soap." — **Malachi 3:2**

The refiner's fire burns to cleanse. It removes dross. It purifies what is precious. This is a different image than the burning of chaff, but both reveal the same holy God. His fire destroys what is wicked and purifies what belongs to Him.

Peter applies refining imagery to the trials of believers:

"That the trial of your faith, being much more precious than of gold that perisheth, though it be tried with fire, might be found unto praise and honour and glory at the appearing of Jesus Christ." — **1 Peter 1:7**

The believer's trials are not meaningless heat. Under God's hand, they refine faith. They expose impurities, deepen trust, strip away false confidence, and prepare praise for the appearing of Christ.

This helps us understand why God's holiness may feel painful in the lives of His people. He is not consuming them in wrath. Christ has borne that.

But He does purify them. He burns away what does not belong in His children.

Fire and the Works of Believers

Paul also speaks of fire testing the works of believers.

*"Every man's work shall be made manifest: for the day shall declare it, because it shall be revealed by fire; and the fire shall try every man's work of what sort it is." — **1 Corinthians 3:13***

Some work will endure as gold, silver, and precious stones. Some will burn as wood, hay, and stubble. The issue is not condemnation of the believer, for Paul says the man himself may be saved, "yet so as by fire." The issue is the testing of labor before God.

This is sobering. Not everything done in religious language will endure. Not every ministry effort, sermon, sacrifice, program, book, argument, or visible success will survive divine evaluation. God's fire tests quality, motive, faithfulness, and truth.

The consuming fire should make us serious about how we build.

The Fire of God and the Cross

If God is a consuming fire, then the cross becomes even more astonishing.

At Calvary, the holy judgment of God against sin fell upon the willing Substitute. Christ did not merely experience human cruelty. He bore sin before the holy God. He stood where sinners deserved to stand.

Isaiah says:

*"Yet it pleased the LORD to bruise him; he hath put him to grief: when thou shalt make his soul an offering for sin..." — **Isaiah 53:10***

The consuming fire did not consume the guilty believer because Christ bore judgment in his place. This is why grace should never produce casualness. The believer has not escaped judgment because sin was overlooked. He has been saved because sin was judged in Christ.

The cross teaches us to fear God rightly and love Him deeply. It shows how terrible sin is and how great mercy is.

Serving with Reverence and Godly Fear

Hebrews draws the practical conclusion clearly:

*"let us have grace, whereby we may serve God acceptably with reverence and godly fear: For our God is a consuming fire." — **Hebrews 12:28–29***

Grace enables acceptable service. Reverence and godly fear shape that service. The consuming fire does not drive believers away from God; Christ has opened the way. But it does drive irreverence, presumption, and careless worship out of the soul.

This is badly needed in the church. Familiar language about God can become too familiar. Worship can become performance. Preaching can become technique. Doctrine can become argument detached from awe. Prayer can become routine. Holiness can become optional.

But our God is a consuming fire.

That sentence should stand over the pulpit, the prayer closet, the Lord's Table, the home, the study, the ministry, and the secret life.

The Fire of Final Judgment

Scripture ends with a sober vision of final judgment.

*"And whosoever was not found written in the book of life was cast into the lake of fire." — **Revelation 20:15***

This is dreadful language. It should not be spoken lightly. But it must be spoken, because Christ and His apostles spoke of final judgment plainly.

The consuming fire means evil will not be allowed to remain. Sin will not be domesticated in the new creation. Rebellion will not be permitted to stain eternity. The same God who dwells with His people forever will judge everything that opposes His holy kingdom.

For those in Christ, this is not a threat of condemnation. Their names are written in the book of life. For those outside Christ, it is the most urgent warning imaginable.

Flee to the Savior before the day of fire comes.

The God We Must Not Treat Lightly

God is a consuming fire.

- He appeared in fire to Moses.
- He descended in fire at Sinai.
- He judged with fire.
- He purifies with fire.
- He tests works by fire.
- He will bring final judgment by fire.

This truth does not cancel His mercy. It makes mercy weightier. It does not erase His love. It makes the cross more glorious. It does not push the redeemed away. It teaches them to draw near with reverence.

A reduced view of God cannot handle this doctrine. It wants warmth without holiness, nearness without trembling, grace without fear, and worship without weight. Scripture gives us something better.

The God who is merciful and gracious is also a consuming fire.

Therefore let us worship.

Let us tremble.

Let us give thanks that in Christ, the fire that would have consumed us has become the holy presence that purifies us, keeps us, and will one day bring us into a kingdom that cannot be moved.

PART FOUR

The Character of God
as the Guardrail of Doctrine

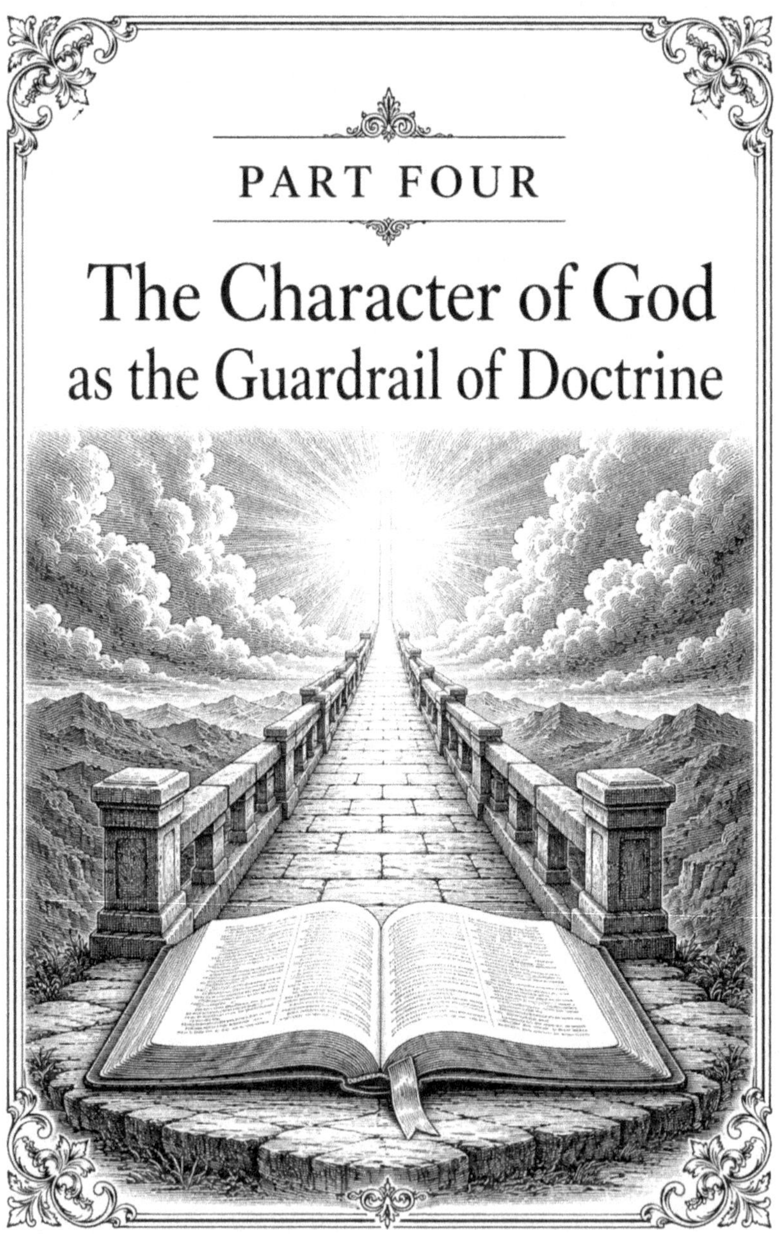

Chapter 34 — Love Without Holiness Is Not God's Love

A distorted doctrine often begins with a true statement used wrongly.

"God is love" is true. It is gloriously true. No Christian should ever speak as though that sentence needs to be softened, hidden, or balanced by something more severe in order to make God safer. The Bible says it plainly:

"He that loveth not knoweth not God; for God is love." — I John 4:8

But true words can be mishandled. They can be lifted out of the full witness of Scripture, filled with meanings Scripture never gave them, and then used against the very God who spoke them. This is what often happens with the love of God.

Instead of allowing God to define love, men define love for themselves and then require God to conform to it.

That is where distortion begins.

When love is separated from holiness, it ceases to be God's love. It becomes sentiment, permission, indulgence, affirmation, or emotional comfort detached from truth. It may still use biblical language. It may still speak warmly of Jesus. It may still sound compassionate. But it is not the love revealed in Scripture.

God's love is holy love.

That means His love never blesses evil, never lies to sinners, never makes peace with darkness, never calls rebellion harmless, and never saves people by leaving them unchanged. The God who is love is also light:

"This then is the message which we have heard of him, and declare unto you, that God is light, and in him is no darkness at all." — I John 1:5

The doctrinal guardrail is simple: any view of love that requires God to set aside His holiness is not biblical love.

When Love Is Redefined as Affirmation

One of the most common distortions of love is the idea that love means affirmation.

In this view, to love someone is to approve of his desires, validate his choices, avoid moral correction, and remove the burden of guilt. Any call to repentance feels unloving. Any warning about judgment sounds hateful. Any boundary placed around obedience feels oppressive. Love becomes the refusal to say anything that might wound.

That definition is not from Scripture.

It is from a culture that wants comfort without repentance and acceptance without holiness.

If love means affirmation, then much of the Bible becomes a problem. The prophets become unloving. John the Baptist becomes unloving. The apostles become unloving. Jesus Himself becomes unloving, because He constantly told sinners the truth.

He said:

"except ye repent, ye shall all likewise perish." — **Luke 13:3**

He said:

"go, and sin no more." — **John 8:11**

He said:

"If ye love me, keep my commandments." — **John 14:15**

These are not the words of someone whose love can be reduced to affirmation. Christ loved sinners too much to flatter them into destruction.

This matters for doctrine because once love is redefined as affirmation, entire categories of biblical teaching become difficult to accept. Sin must be softened. Repentance must be minimized. Judgment must be avoided. Church discipline must be treated as cruel. Biblical holiness must be recast as legalism. The cross itself begins to change shape, because if love means simple acceptance, then atonement becomes unnecessary.

A love that merely affirms cannot explain why Christ had to die.

False Assurance Built on Partial Love

A reduced view of love often produces false assurance.

People are told that because God loves them, they have nothing to fear, no need to repent, no reason to examine themselves, and no danger in continuing in sin. The love of God is presented as though it guarantees safety regardless of response to Christ.

But Scripture never uses God's love that way.

God's love is the reason He sent His Son:

"For God so loved the world, that he gave his only begotten Son, that whosoever believeth in him should not perish, but have everlasting life." — **John 3:16**

The verse is often quoted, but its full force is often missed. God's love gives the Son so that those who believe should not perish. The danger is real. Perishing is real. The gift of the Son is necessary because sinners are not safe apart from Him.

A few verses later, John writes:

"He that believeth on him is not condemned: but he that believeth not is condemned already, because he hath not believed in the name of the only begotten Son of God." — **John 3:18**

The love of God does not erase the distinction between belief and unbelief. It does not remove condemnation from those who reject the Son. It provides salvation in Christ and calls sinners to believe.

False assurance tells people, "God loves you, therefore you are safe." Biblical assurance says, "God has loved sinners by giving His Son; therefore flee to Christ, believe on Him, and find life."

Those are not the same message.

The first comforts people apart from repentance and faith. The second brings them to the Savior.

Grace Detached from Holiness

Another distortion appears when grace is preached as forgiveness without transformation.

This error often appeals to love. God loves sinners, so He forgives. God is gracious, so He accepts. God is merciful, so He does not require change. Holiness then becomes optional, perhaps admirable, but not necessary to the Christian life.

The New Testament rejects that entirely.

Paul asks:

"What shall we say then? Shall we continue in sin, that grace may abound? God forbid. How shall we, that are dead to sin, live any longer therein?" — **Romans 6:1–2**

Grace does not leave the believer at peace with sin. It unites him to Christ in His death and resurrection. It frees him from sin's dominion. It teaches him to deny ungodliness and worldly lusts.

The love of Christ has the same purpose. Paul says:

"Christ also loved the church, and gave himself for it; That he might sanctify and cleanse it with the washing of water by the word, That he might present

*it to himself a glorious church, not having spot, or wrinkle, or any such thing; but that it should be holy and without blemish." — **Ephesians 5:25–27**result

This passage is one of the strongest correctives to sentimental love. Christ loves the church by giving Himself for her. But His purpose is not merely that she be forgiven. He sanctifies her. He cleanses her. He presents her holy.

The Bridegroom does not love His bride by leaving her defiled.

This has direct doctrinal importance. Any gospel that promises forgiveness while making holiness unnecessary has divided Christ's love from Christ's purpose. The Savior who justifies also sanctifies. The love that pardons also purifies.

Preaching That Removes Warning

When love is separated from holiness, preaching loses its edge.

Warnings begin to sound unkind. Hell becomes embarrassing. Judgment is pushed to the margins. The fear of the Lord is replaced with therapeutic reassurance. Sermons become careful never to make hearers feel the weight of sin too deeply.

But biblical preaching has always included warning because biblical love cares about danger.

Paul said:

*"Knowing therefore the terror of the Lord, we persuade men..." — **2 Corinthians 5:11**

He did not see a contradiction between persuasion and love. He warned because judgment was real. He pleaded because reconciliation was offered. To remain silent about danger would have been unloving.

Jesus Himself warned constantly. He warned of hell. He warned of false teachers. He warned of self-deception. He warned religious people who assumed they were safe. He warned cities that rejected the light given to them. His warnings were not failures of tenderness. They were expressions of holy love.

A preacher who never warns may seem gentle, but he is not more loving than Christ.

This does not mean warnings should be delivered harshly, coldly, or with delight in judgment. A man can speak true things in an ungodly spirit. But the abuse of warning does not cancel the duty to warn. Love does not remove warning. Love purifies it.

The church must recover preaching that can say both, "Come unto me," and "Flee from the wrath to come."

Discipline Mistaken for Cruelty

The same distortion affects church discipline and personal correction.

If love means never causing discomfort, then discipline will always appear unloving. But Scripture says the opposite. God disciplines His children because He loves them:

"For whom the Lord loveth he chasteneth, and scourgeth every son whom he receiveth." — **Hebrews 12:6**

This is not condemning wrath against the believer. It is fatherly correction. It is painful, but it is loving. It aims at life, holiness, and restoration.

The church must learn from the Father's character. Discipline should never be vindictive. It should never be used to protect pride, control people, or punish those who ask hard questions. But when sin is serious and unrepented of, refusing correction is not love.

Paul commanded the Corinthians to deal with open immorality in the church. Their tolerance was not compassion. It was arrogance. They had mistaken permissiveness for grace. Paul's correction was severe, but it aimed at salvation and purity.

A church that refuses discipline because it wants to be loving has misunderstood love. It may preserve appearances for a while, but it will fail sinners, weaken holiness, and dishonor Christ.

Holy love restores where there is repentance. It also confronts when confrontation is necessary.

A Jesus Without Holiness

A reduced doctrine of love also produces a reduced Jesus.

Many are willing to speak of Jesus as compassionate, welcoming, gentle, and forgiving. All of that is true. But if those truths are isolated from His holiness, the Jesus being described is not the Jesus of Scripture.

The biblical Jesus touches lepers and rebukes demons.

- He receives sinners and exposes hypocrisy.
- He weeps over Jerusalem and announces its judgment.
- He forgives the guilty and commands repentance.
- He blesses the meek and warns the self-righteous.
- He lays down His life and will return to judge the living and the dead.

The same apostle John who leaned on Jesus' breast also fell at His feet as dead when he saw Him glorified:

*"And when I saw him, I fell at his feet as dead." — **Revelation 1:17***

Christ is tender, but He is not tame. He is meek and lowly in heart, but He is also holy and true. He is the Lamb slain, and He is the Lamb whose wrath terrifies the kings of the earth.

A doctrine of love that cannot account for the full Christ is false.

The Cross Corrects Sentimental Love

The cross is the great correction to every shallow definition of love.

At the cross, God does not say sin is harmless. He does not say guilt is imaginary. He does not say holiness can be set aside because love is present. He gives His Son.

Paul writes:

*"But God commendeth his love toward us, in that, while we were yet sinners, Christ died for us." — **Romans 5:8***

The love of God is displayed toward sinners, but it is displayed through death. Christ dies because sin is real, guilt is real, wrath is real, justice is real, and love is real.

A sentimental view of love cannot explain Calvary. If love means simple acceptance, then the cross is excessive. If holiness is not necessary, then blood is unnecessary. If judgment is not real, then propitiation becomes meaningless.

But if God's love is holy, the cross becomes the perfect revelation of His character. There, love does not cancel holiness. Love provides the sacrifice holiness requires. Love does not deny justice. Love gives the Son who bears judgment in the sinner's place.

The cross is not God choosing love over holiness.

It is holy love saving sinners.

Doctrines Protected by Holy Love

When God's love is kept holy, several doctrines are protected.

The doctrine of sin is protected, because love does not require us to minimize evil.

The doctrine of repentance is protected, because love calls sinners out of death.

The doctrine of the cross is protected, because love saves through atonement, not denial.

The doctrine of sanctification is protected, because love cleanses those it redeems.

The doctrine of church discipline is protected, because love seeks restoration and purity.

The doctrine of final judgment is protected, because love does not make God indifferent to evil.

The doctrine of Christ is protected, because the Savior remains both compassionate and holy.

This is why the full character of God matters. If one attribute is isolated, doctrine bends. Love separated from holiness produces a different gospel, a different church, and eventually a different God.

The Love That Saves

God's love is better than the counterfeit.

The world's version of love may feel gentle for a moment, but it cannot save. It cannot cleanse guilt. It cannot free from sin. It cannot explain the cross. It cannot prepare anyone to stand before God. It can only comfort sinners while leaving them in danger.

God's love does more.

- It tells the truth.
- It sends the Son.
- It bears the cost.
- It calls to repentance.
- It forgives through blood.
- It disciplines children.
- It sanctifies the bride.
- It warns before judgment.
- It brings sinners into everlasting life.

That is love worthy of God.

Not love without holiness.

Not holiness without love.

Holy love.

And because God's love is holy, it is strong enough to save sinners without lying to them.

Chapter 35 — Mercy Without Justice Is Not God's Mercy

Mercy is one of the most comforting truths in Scripture.

The sinner needs mercy. The weak need mercy. The guilty need mercy. The broken, ashamed, fearful, and weary need mercy. If God were not merciful, no man could stand before Him with hope.

But mercy can be distorted.

That happens when mercy is separated from justice. When men speak of God's mercy as though it means He simply overlooks guilt, ignores evil, dismisses judgment, or forgives without atonement, they are no longer speaking of biblical mercy. They are speaking of something softer, thinner, and far less glorious.

God's mercy is not moral carelessness.

It is not His willingness to pretend sin does not matter. It is not emotional tenderness at the expense of righteousness. It is not forgiveness without blood, pardon without justice, or compassion without truth.

When God proclaimed His name to Moses, He declared Himself:

"The LORD, The LORD God, merciful and gracious, longsuffering, and abundant in goodness and truth, Keeping mercy for thousands, forgiving iniquity and transgression and sin..."

But the same declaration continues:

"and that will by no means clear the guilty..." — **Exodus 34:6–7**

That is the guardrail. God forgives iniquity, transgression, and sin. Yet He will by no means clear the guilty. His mercy is real, but it is never unjust.

A doctrine of mercy that cannot account for justice is not the mercy of God.

The Temptation of Crossless Mercy

The human heart wants mercy without reckoning.

It wants forgiveness without confession, pardon without repentance, salvation without substitution, and comfort without the exposure of guilt. It wants God to be merciful in a way that costs nothing, confronts nothing, and judges nothing.

That kind of mercy is attractive because it keeps man from being humbled.

If God can simply wave away guilt, then sin is not as serious as Scripture says. If forgiveness requires no atonement, then the cross becomes unnecessary. If justice can be set aside whenever mercy appears, then God's righteousness becomes flexible.

But Scripture never presents mercy that way.

The mercy seat in the tabernacle was not an empty symbol of divine softness. Blood was sprinkled there. The Day of Atonement did not teach Israel that God forgives because guilt is insignificant. It taught that guilty people can live only because God provides atonement.

*"For the life of the flesh is in the blood: and I have given it to you upon the altar to make an atonement for your souls: for it is the blood that maketh an atonement for the soul." — **Leviticus 17:11***

Mercy required blood because justice mattered.

This is why crossless mercy cannot save. It may comfort feelings for a moment, but it cannot remove guilt. It cannot cleanse the conscience. It cannot answer the holiness of God. It cannot silence the accusation of sin.

Only mercy through atonement can do that.

When Forgiveness Becomes Sentiment

A reduced doctrine of mercy often turns forgiveness into sentiment.

People speak as though God forgives because He is kindhearted enough not to insist on justice. Forgiveness becomes divine emotional generosity, as if God simply decides not to make an issue of sin. The sinner is comforted, but the moral problem remains unanswered.

That is not the gospel.

The gospel does not say God forgives because guilt is easy to dismiss. It says God forgives because Christ has borne sin. Paul writes:

"Whom God hath set forth to be a propitiation through faith in his blood, to declare his righteousness for the remission of sins that are past, through the forbearance of God; To declare, I say, at this time his righteousness: that he might be just, and the justifier of him which believeth in Jesus." — **Romans 3:25–26**

God is **just, and the justifier**.

That phrase must govern every doctrine of mercy. God does not justify sinners by denying justice. He justifies through Christ, whose blood declares God's righteousness even while providing forgiveness.

This protects mercy from becoming sentimental. Forgiveness is warm, but it is not weightless. It is tender, but not careless. It is free to the sinner, but not cheap. The mercy of God comes to us through the wounds of the Son.

A mercy that bypasses the cross is not kinder than the gospel. It is weaker than the gospel.

Repentance Removed from Mercy

Mercy is also distorted when repentance is treated as unnecessary.

Some speak as though calling sinners to repent somehow contradicts mercy. They think mercy means God receives people while leaving their rebellion unnamed and untouched. But Scripture does not separate mercy from return.

Isaiah says:

"Let the wicked forsake his way, and the unrighteous man his thoughts: and let him return unto the LORD, and he will have mercy upon him; and to our God, for he will abundantly pardon." — **Isaiah 55:7**

The mercy is abundant. The pardon is real. But the wicked is called to forsake his way, and the unrighteous man his thoughts. Mercy is not God blessing the road of rebellion. Mercy is God receiving the sinner who returns.

This does not mean repentance earns mercy. It does not. Repentance is not payment. It is the sinner turning from sin and coming empty-handed to the God who pardons. But where there is no turning, no confession, no surrender, no coming to God, the word **mercy** is being emptied of its biblical meaning.

The prodigal son was received with compassion, but he came home. The publican was justified, but he cried, "God be merciful to me a sinner." David found mercy, but he confessed his transgression. Paul obtained mercy, but the mercy that saved him made him a servant of Christ.

Mercy does not leave a man proudly defending the sin that made mercy necessary.

Universal Mercy and the Denial of Judgment

Another distortion appears when mercy is used to deny final judgment.

The argument may sound compassionate: if God is merciful, surely He will not judge forever. Surely His mercy means all will finally be saved. Surely wrath, hell, and everlasting punishment cannot remain once divine mercy is fully known.

But this reasoning begins with a partial God.

It isolates mercy from holiness, justice, truth, and wrath. It assumes mercy must erase judgment in order to be real. Scripture teaches otherwise.

The same Bible that says God is rich in mercy also says:

*"And these shall go away into everlasting punishment: but the righteous into life eternal." — **Matthew 25:46***

The same Christ who receives sinners also warns of hell. The same apostle who magnifies grace also speaks of the day of wrath and revelation of the righteous judgment of God. The same book of Revelation that shows the Lamb's redeemed people also shows the lake of fire.

We are not free to make mercy the attribute that cancels every warning God has given.

Biblical mercy is not universal pardon apart from Christ. It is saving compassion given through Christ to those who believe. Mercy is offered widely, sincerely, and richly. The gospel is to be preached to every creature. Sinners are invited to come. But mercy despised does not abolish judgment.

If final judgment is denied in the name of mercy, then mercy has been turned against the truthfulness of God.

Mercy and the Victims of Evil

Mercy without justice also fails the oppressed.

This point is often missed. People imagine mercy without judgment as though it were generous to everyone. But if God never judges evil, then what becomes of those crushed by evil? What becomes of the murdered, abused, betrayed, enslaved, slandered, persecuted, and forgotten? What becomes of martyrs whose blood cries from the ground?

A mercy that refuses justice is not merciful to victims.

Scripture does not treat the cries of the oppressed as spiritually inferior. The souls under the altar cry:

*"How long, O Lord, holy and true, dost thou not judge and avenge our blood on them that dwell on the earth?" — **Revelation 6:10***

They appeal to God as **holy and true**. They are not asking Him to become cruel. They are asking Him to do right.

If God's mercy meant He would never judge, then evil would have the final word over its victims. The wicked could destroy and then be excused without repentance, without atonement, without justice. That is not mercy. It is injustice against those who suffered.

The Judge of all the earth must do right, and His mercy never requires Him to abandon that.

The Cross Protects Mercy from Injustice

The cross is the answer to every false mercy.

At Calvary, God shows that He is more merciful than sinners dared hope and more just than sinners wanted to admit. He does not save by lowering the standard. He saves by giving the Son. He does not ignore guilt. He lays it upon Christ. He does not clear the guilty by denial. He justifies the ungodly through faith because Christ has borne their judgment.

Isaiah says:

*"All we like sheep have gone astray; we have turned every one to his own way; and the LORD hath laid on him the iniquity of us all." — **Isaiah 53:6***

That is mercy with justice.

The iniquity is real. The wandering is real. The substitution is real. The Lord lays the iniquity upon the Servant, and sinners are healed by His stripes.

This protects the gospel from two errors. The first error makes God merciful by pretending justice does not matter. The second makes God just in a way that leaves sinners without hope. The cross rejects both. God is just, and He is the justifier. He condemns sin and saves sinners. He upholds righteousness and pours out mercy.

No other mercy can save.

Mercy and Assurance

This also matters for assurance.

If mercy were merely God's decision to overlook sin, the believer could never be fully settled. Has God truly overlooked it? Will He continue to overlook it? What if the guilt returns? What if mercy gives way to judgment later?

But biblical assurance rests on something stronger than divine leniency.

It rests on Christ's finished work.

John writes:

*"If we confess our sins, he is faithful and just to forgive us our sins, and to cleanse us from all unrighteousness." — **I John 1:9***

Faithful and just. Not merely gentle. Not merely willing. Faithful and just.

God forgives the confessing believer because Christ has paid for sin. Justice does not threaten the one who is in Christ; justice confirms that the same guilt will not be charged twice. The believer is not safe because God has decided to ignore justice. He is safe because justice has been satisfied by the Savior.

This gives mercy backbone. It can bear the weight of a guilty conscience because it rests on blood, not mood.

Doctrines Protected by Just Mercy

When mercy is kept together with justice, several doctrines are protected.

The doctrine of atonement is protected, because mercy comes through sacrifice, not through denial.

The doctrine of repentance is protected, because mercy calls sinners to return rather than blessing rebellion.

The doctrine of final judgment is protected, because mercy does not erase God's righteous warnings.

The doctrine of assurance is protected, because forgiveness rests on Christ's finished work.

The doctrine of God's holiness is protected, because mercy does not make sin morally light.

The doctrine of pastoral care is protected, because sinners are offered real pardon, and victims are not told that justice no longer matters.

This is why the full character of God matters. If mercy is isolated, doctrine bends. The gospel becomes softer at first, then weaker, then false. It loses the cross as necessity and keeps it only as symbol.

But the cross is not a symbol only. It is the place where mercy comes righteously.

The Mercy That Saves

God's mercy is better than sentimental mercy.

Sentimental mercy can comfort, but it cannot cleanse. It can soothe guilt, but it cannot remove it. It can avoid judgment, but it cannot satisfy justice. It can sound loving, but it cannot save.

God's mercy can.

- It comes through Christ.
- It is purchased by blood.
- It calls sinners to repentance.
- It forgives the guilty.
- It vindicates the oppressed.
- It satisfies justice.
- It gives assurance to the believer.
- It glorifies the God who is both merciful and righteous.

Mercy without justice is not God's mercy.

God's mercy is holy mercy. Righteous mercy. Cross-shaped mercy.

And because it is just, it is strong enough to save.

Chapter 36 — Wrath Without Goodness Is Not God's Wrath

Wrath is one of the easiest doctrines to distort.

Some distort it by denying it. Others distort it by preaching it wrongly. The first error removes wrath because it seems too severe. The second keeps wrath but speaks of it in a way that makes God seem cruel, unstable, or harsh in a merely human sense.

Both errors misrepresent God.

God is wrathful against evil, but His wrath is not detached from His goodness. It is not divine rage. It is not the uncontrolled anger of a wounded ego. It is not cruelty with infinite power behind it. God's wrath is His holy, righteous, and good opposition to evil.

That word **good** matters.

If God is good, then His wrath is good. Not because evil is good, and not because judgment is light, but because God's wrath is the morally perfect answer of the good God to what is wicked. His wrath means evil matters. His wrath means cruelty will not be ignored. His wrath means lies, violence, idolatry, blasphemy, abuse, and rebellion will not have the final word.

Paul writes:

"For the wrath of God is revealed from heaven against all ungodliness and unrighteousness of men, who hold the truth in unrighteousness." — **Romans 1:18**

God's wrath is aimed. It is not random. It is revealed against ungodliness and unrighteousness. Wrath without goodness would be monstrous. But goodness without wrath would be moral indifference.

The God of Scripture is neither monstrous nor indifferent.

When Wrath Is Preached Without Tears

One of the most dangerous distortions of wrath happens among those who believe the doctrine but speak of it without the spirit of Scripture.

Wrath can be preached accurately in vocabulary and wrongly in tone. A man may say true things about judgment, hell, repentance, and condemnation, yet say them with a spirit that sounds more like personal irritation than holy grief. He may warn sinners, but seem pleased that they are in danger. He may defend hell, but appear untouched by the horror of men perishing.

That does not reflect the heart of God.

The Lord says through Ezekiel:

"As I live, saith the Lord GOD, I have no pleasure in the death of the wicked; but that the wicked turn from his way and live: turn ye, turn ye from your evil ways; for why will ye die, O house of Israel?" — **Ezekiel 33:11**

God's wrath is real, but He does not delight in the death of the wicked as though destruction were His pleasure. He calls them to turn and live.

Jesus Himself wept over Jerusalem even while announcing judgment:

"And when he was come near, he beheld the city, and wept over it." — **Luke 19:41**

Then He spoke of the city's coming destruction. Tears and judgment stood together in the same Savior.

That should shape every preacher, teacher, parent, pastor, and Christian who speaks of wrath. We must not soften what God has said. But neither should we speak in a way that makes wrath sound like personal vengeance, theological excitement, or cold satisfaction. Biblical warning carries urgency, grief, truth, and love.

A doctrine of wrath without goodness may be severe, but it is not faithful.

Wrath Is Not Cruelty

Cruelty delights in pain for its own sake. God does not.

Cruelty punishes beyond what is right. God never does.

Cruelty is often driven by malice, insecurity, pride, or revenge. None of those exists in God.

This distinction is necessary because many people hear the wrath of God as though it means divine cruelty. They imagine God angry in the way sinful men are angry, only stronger. But Scripture does not present God that way. His wrath is not the opposite of goodness. It is goodness opposing evil.

Nahum holds this together:

"The LORD is slow to anger, and great in power, and will not at all acquit the wicked…" — **Nahum 1:3**

A few verses later, the prophet says:

"The LORD is good, a strong hold in the day of trouble; and he knoweth them that trust in him." — **Nahum 1:7**

Nahum does not apologize for placing these truths near one another. The Lord is slow to anger. He will not acquit the wicked. The Lord is good. All three are true.

A god who acquits evil without justice would not be good. A god who punished cruelly would not be good. The true God judges evil rightly, patiently, and without moral defect.

The Goodness of Wrath Against Evil

There are evils in this world that should make the heart cry out for judgment.

Murder. Abuse. Human trafficking. False worship that devours generations. Exploitation of the poor. Betrayal of the innocent. Blasphemy against the holy God. Persecution of the righteous. Corruption hidden behind power. Lies that ruin souls.

If God looked upon these things forever without wrath, He would not be good.

The Bible does not ask us to view wrath as an embarrassing doctrine to be smuggled quietly into theology. It presents God's judgment as part of the hope of the world. The Judge of all the earth will do right. Evil will not remain unresolved. The cries of the afflicted will not echo forever without answer.

The martyrs under the altar cry:

"How long, O Lord, holy and true, dost thou not judge and avenge our blood on them that dwell on the earth?" — **Revelation 6:10**

They do not appeal to God's cruelty. They appeal to His holiness and truth. They know that a holy and true God must answer evil.

This is where many modern instincts fail. They want God's goodness to mean He will never judge. But to those who have suffered under evil, goodness without judgment is not comfort. It is abandonment.

God's wrath is good because evil is evil.

Wrath and Patience Belong Together

God's wrath must also be understood alongside His patience.

He is not quick-tempered. He is not eager to strike. Scripture repeatedly says He is slow to anger. Before judgment falls, He often warns, waits, sends messengers, exposes sin, and gives space for repentance.

Paul writes:

"Or despisest thou the riches of his goodness and forbearance and longsuffering; not knowing that the goodness of God leadeth thee to repentance?" — **Romans 2:4**

Notice the language: goodness, forbearance, longsuffering. God's patience is meant to lead sinners to repentance. Wrath does not come because God lacked patience. Wrath comes when patience has been despised.

Paul continues:

"But after thy hardness and impenitent heart treasurest up unto thyself wrath against the day of wrath and revelation of the righteous judgment of God." **— Romans 2:5**

The sinner who refuses repentance is not proving that wrath is absent. He is storing it up.

This guards us from two errors. We must not use God's patience to deny His wrath. But we also must not speak of His wrath as though patience were absent. The God who judges is the God who warned. The God who condemns is the God who called. The God who pours out wrath is the God who gave time for repentance.

Wrath without patience would distort God's goodness. Patience without final wrath would deny God's justice.

The Cross Shows Wrath and Goodness Together

The cross is where the goodness of God's wrath is most clearly seen.

That may sound strange until we remember what happened there. At Calvary, God did not pretend sin was harmless. He did not forgive by ignoring guilt. He did not set aside justice as though mercy required Him to become less righteous. He gave His Son.

The cross shows that wrath is real because sin had to be judged.

The cross shows that goodness is real because God provided the sacrifice.

Paul says:

"But God commendeth his love toward us, in that, while we were yet sinners, Christ died for us." **— Romans 5:8**

He then says:

"Much more then, being now justified by his blood, we shall be saved from wrath through him." — **Romans 5:9**

Christ saves us from wrath. That means wrath is not imaginary, and salvation is not vague improvement. The believer is delivered from the righteous judgment his sin deserved because Christ bore judgment in his place.

Wrath without goodness cannot explain the cross. It would make Calvary appear cruel.

Goodness without wrath cannot explain the cross either. It would make Calvary unnecessary.

But when wrath and goodness are held together, the cross becomes glorious. God hates evil enough to judge it, and loves sinners enough to provide His Son.

The Wrath of the Lamb

One of the clearest guardrails against a distorted doctrine of wrath is the phrase:

"the wrath of the Lamb." — **Revelation 6:16**

The Lamb is not cruel. The Lamb is the One who was slain. The Lamb is the Redeemer. The Lamb purchased His people with His blood. Yet Scripture speaks of His wrath.

This means wrath cannot be opposed to the character of Christ. It belongs to His righteous judgment. The gentle and lowly Savior is also the holy King. The One who says, "Come unto me," also warns the unrepentant. The One who lays down His life for His sheep also judges His enemies.

A doctrine of wrath that makes Christ seem unlike Himself is wrong. But a doctrine of Christ that has no room for wrath is also wrong.

The Lamb's wrath is the holy wrath of the Savior against everything that defies God, corrupts creation, persecutes His people, and rejects His grace. It is not a contradiction of His love. It is His goodness answering evil.

When Wrath Is Detached from the Gospel

Another distortion happens when wrath is preached without the gospel.

A message may speak much of judgment and little of Christ. It may expose sin but not proclaim the Savior. It may terrify the conscience but not open the door of mercy. It may warn of hell but fail to say with equal clarity that Christ saves sinners who come to Him.

That is not apostolic preaching.

Paul warned of judgment, but he also preached reconciliation. He knew the terror of the Lord, and therefore he persuaded men. He preached Christ crucified. He declared that sinners could be justified freely by God's grace through the redemption that is in Christ Jesus.

Wrath is not meant to stand alone as the whole message. It is part of the truth that makes the gospel urgent. The warning prepares the soul to see the glory of the refuge.

John the Baptist cried, "Who hath warned you to flee from the wrath to come?" But he also pointed to Jesus and said:

*"Behold the Lamb of God, which taketh away the sin of the world." — **John 1:29***

That is the pattern. Wrath is coming. The Lamb has come. Flee to Him.

Wrath and the Believer

The believer must understand wrath rightly for assurance.

Christians are not appointed to wrath. Paul writes:

*"For God hath not appointed us to wrath, but to obtain salvation by our Lord Jesus Christ." — **I Thessalonians 5:9***

This does not mean believers will never suffer. It does not mean they will never be disciplined. It does not mean they will escape all hatred, persecution, grief, or tribulation in the broad sense. But it does mean that the condemning wrath of God is not appointed for those who are in Christ.

This distinction matters. Fatherly discipline is not condemning wrath. Suffering under God's providence is not the same as being the object of divine wrath. The believer's sins were borne by Christ. There is therefore now no condemnation to them which are in Christ Jesus.

A distorted view of wrath can torment tender consciences by making every hardship feel like God's condemnation. But the gospel teaches something better. God may correct His children, but He does not pour out wrath upon those for whom Christ has borne wrath.

The cross settles that.

Doctrines Protected by Good Wrath

When wrath is held together with goodness, several doctrines are protected.

The doctrine of God's holiness is protected, because wrath is seen as His holy opposition to evil.

The doctrine of final judgment is protected, because judgment is not cruelty but righteous goodness answering sin.

The doctrine of the cross is protected, because Christ saves from real wrath through real atonement.

The doctrine of evangelism is protected, because warning sinners becomes an act of love rather than embarrassment.

The doctrine of assurance is protected, because believers know they are delivered from wrath through Christ.

The doctrine of pastoral tone is protected, because wrath must be preached with patience, grief, urgency, and gospel hope.

This is why the full character of God matters. Wrath isolated from goodness distorts God into something harsh. Goodness isolated from wrath distorts God into someone morally indifferent. Scripture gives us the living God, whose wrath is holy and whose goodness is never weak.

The Wrath We Must Recover

The church must recover the wrath of God, but it must recover it biblically.

- Not wrath as cruelty.
- Not wrath as rage.
- Not wrath preached with cold delight.
- Not wrath detached from tears, patience, or the cross.

The wrath of the good God.

- Wrath that opposes evil because evil is evil.
- Wrath that comes after patience has been despised.
- Wrath that vindicates the oppressed.
- Wrath that makes the cross necessary.
- Wrath from which Christ saves His people.
- Wrath that will one day cleanse creation of all rebellion.

The sinner should fear this wrath and flee to Christ.

The believer should give thanks that Jesus has delivered him from the wrath to come.

The preacher should warn with tears and point clearly to the Lamb.

God's wrath is not the enemy of His goodness. It is His goodness burning against evil.

And because God is good, evil will not stand forever.

Chapter 37 — Sovereignty Without Wisdom Is Not God's Sovereignty

God is sovereign.

That truth should steady the soul. It should humble pride, strengthen faith, deepen worship, and give courage in a world that often appears chaotic. The throne is not empty. History is not loose. Evil is not ultimate. God reigns.

But sovereignty can be mishandled.

It is possible to speak of God's control in a way that makes Him sound unlike Himself. Some speak of sovereignty as though God were only exercising power, as though His rule could be separated from His wisdom, goodness, righteousness, mercy, patience, and faithfulness. Others hear sovereignty and imagine fatalism, as if human choices, prayer, obedience, evangelism, suffering, and moral responsibility no longer truly matter.

Both errors distort God.

God's sovereignty is not raw control. It is not cold determinism. It is not blind force. It is not divine machinery moving history without heart, purpose, or moral beauty.

God's sovereignty is wise sovereignty.

Paul says God works:

*"all things after the counsel of his own will." — **Ephesians 1:11***

That word **counsel** matters. God's will is not reckless. His rule is not careless. His decree is not detached from thought, purpose, wisdom, or character. He rules according to perfect counsel. He knows the end from the beginning. He knows every means by which His purposes will be accomplished. He knows every creature, every motive, every event, and every hidden connection in the whole story of history.

A doctrine of sovereignty that does not sound wise is not yet biblical sovereignty.

When Sovereignty Becomes Fatalism

One distortion of sovereignty is fatalism.

Fatalism says, "What will happen will happen, so nothing matters." Prayer does not matter. Evangelism does not matter. Obedience does not matter. Warning does not matter. Human choices are swallowed by inevitability.

That is not Scripture.

The Bible teaches God's absolute rule, but it never uses that truth to erase human responsibility. God ordains ends, but He also ordains means. He commands prayer and answers it. He commands preaching and saves through it. He commands obedience and uses it. He warns sinners, calls them to repent, and holds them accountable for their response.

When Paul was in Corinth, the Lord told him:

"Be not afraid, but speak, and hold not thy peace: For I am with thee, and no man shall set on thee to hurt thee: for I have much people in this city." — ***Acts 18:9–10***

The sovereignty of God did not make Paul stop preaching. It made him keep preaching. God had people in the city, and the means by which they would be gathered was Paul's continued witness.

That is biblical sovereignty. It does not weaken action. It establishes it.

A fatalistic view says, "If God has chosen to work, He will do it without me." A biblical view says, "Because God rules, my obedience is not wasted."

When Sovereignty Weakens Prayer

Another distortion appears when sovereignty is used to make prayer seem unnecessary.

The reasoning sounds logical at first: if God already knows all things, has purposed all things, and governs all things, why pray? But Scripture never reasons that way. The sovereign God commands His people to pray, and He truly works through their prayers.

James says:

"The effectual fervent prayer of a righteous man availeth much." — **James 5:16**

That sentence must be allowed to stand. Prayer avails much. It does not inform God of what He did not know. It does not overpower His will. It does not make man sovereign. But it matters because God has ordained prayer as a real means in His wise rule.

Moses interceded for Israel. Hannah prayed for a son. Elijah prayed and rain stopped, then prayed again and rain came. Daniel prayed according to the prophetic word of Jeremiah. The early church prayed, and Peter was delivered from prison.

In each case, God was sovereign. In each case, prayer mattered.

Sovereignty without wisdom may make prayer feel meaningless. Biblical sovereignty makes prayer hopeful. We are not praying into chaos. We are not trying to persuade a reluctant deity. We are coming before the wise Father who rules all things and has invited His children to ask.

When Sovereignty Flattens Human Responsibility

Scripture holds God's sovereignty and human responsibility together.

The cross is the clearest example. Peter preached that Jesus was delivered:

"by the determinate counsel and foreknowledge of God,"

and then immediately said:

*"ye have taken, and by wicked hands have crucified and slain." — **Acts 2:23***

God's counsel was determinate. The hands of men were wicked.

The cross did not happen outside God's sovereign plan. It was not an accident repaired by resurrection. Yet those who betrayed, condemned, mocked, and crucified Christ were guilty. God's sovereignty did not make their sin innocent. Human wickedness did not make God's plan uncertain.

This guards us from two errors. We must not deny God's rule in order to preserve human responsibility. But we must also not speak of God's rule in a way that makes human responsibility unreal.

Scripture gives us both. Man chooses, and God reigns. Man sins willingly, and God remains holy. Man is accountable, and God's counsel stands.

A doctrine that cannot say all of that has become smaller than the Bible.

When Sovereignty Becomes Cold in Suffering

Few places require greater care than the doctrine of sovereignty in suffering.

It is true that God rules over suffering. Not one trial enters the believer's life outside His providence. That truth can be a deep comfort. But if spoken carelessly, it can sound like a stone laid on a wounded heart.

Some people use sovereignty as a blunt instrument. Someone grieves, and they say, "God is in control," as though that alone is the whole ministry needed. The statement is true. It may even be necessary. But truth can be spoken at the wrong time, in the wrong manner, without the tenderness Scripture itself models.

God's sovereignty is not cold.

The God who rules suffering also knows our frame. He remembers that we are dust. Christ wept at the tomb of Lazarus even though He knew He would raise him. The Spirit helps our infirmities when we know not what we should pray for as we ought.

A biblical doctrine of sovereignty does not forbid lament. Job lamented. David lamented. Jeremiah lamented. The psalms are filled with cries from the afflicted. Faith does not require us to pretend suffering does not hurt. It teaches us to bring suffering before the God who reigns.

Joseph could say in the end:

"But as for you, ye thought evil against me; but God meant it unto good, to bring to pass, as it is this day, to save much people alive." — **Genesis 50:20**

But Joseph did not say that from the bottom of the pit on the first day. He said it after years of providence had unfolded. The truth was real the whole time, but the wisdom became clearer later.

When ministering to sufferers, we must hold sovereignty together with compassion. God rules wisely, but He also draws near tenderly.

When Sovereignty Is Used to Avoid Obedience

Another distortion appears when sovereignty becomes an excuse for passivity.

If God is sovereign, some reason, then perhaps obedience is less urgent. Perhaps evangelism can be neglected. Perhaps repentance can be delayed.

Perhaps holiness can be treated casually because God will do what He has planned.

Scripture does not permit this.

The sovereign God commands obedience. His rule is the reason obedience matters, not the reason it may be avoided. Jesus says:

"If ye love me, keep my commandments." — **John 14:15**

Paul says believers are God's workmanship, created in Christ Jesus unto good works. Peter calls believers to holiness. James commands hearers to be doers of the word. None of these commands are weakened by sovereignty.

God's sovereignty establishes the seriousness of His commands. The King has spoken. His people obey.

Even in evangelism, divine sovereignty strengthens rather than cancels responsibility. Paul endured all things for the elect's sakes, that they might obtain salvation in Christ Jesus. He did not say election made missionary labor unnecessary. He said it made endurance worthwhile.

A sovereignty that produces laziness is not the sovereignty of Scripture.

When Sovereignty Ignores God's Promises

Sovereignty can also be misused in the interpretation of God's promises.

Some treat God's sovereignty as though it gives permission to detach fulfillment from what God actually said. Because God is sovereign, they reason, He can fulfill promises in ways that bear little resemblance to the words originally spoken. Covenant commitments can be spiritualized beyond recognition. Specific promises can be dissolved into general blessing. The faithfulness of God can be blurred under the claim that He has the right to do whatever He wants.

But God's sovereignty does not cancel His truthfulness.

The sovereign God is also faithful. He does not use His power to escape His promises. He uses His power to keep them.

Balaam spoke truly when he said:

"God is not a man, that he should lie; neither the son of man, that he should repent: hath he said, and shall he not do it? or hath he spoken, and shall he not make it good?" — **Numbers 23:19**

God's sovereignty means He is able to make good on what He has spoken. It does not mean His words can be treated loosely.

This matters for prophecy, covenant theology, Israel, the church, the kingdom, resurrection, judgment, and the return of Christ. The full character of God guards interpretation. His sovereignty must be read together with His truthfulness, order, wisdom, and faithfulness. Fulfillment in Christ is richer than human expectation, but it is never less faithful than God's own words.

A doctrine that uses sovereignty to weaken promise has misunderstood sovereignty.

When Sovereignty Makes God Morally Flat

Perhaps the most serious distortion occurs when sovereignty is spoken of in a way that flattens God's moral character.

This happens when people emphasize control so strongly that God's goodness, grief over evil, patience, compassion, justice, and mercy seem to disappear. God becomes the explanation for everything, but in a way that makes Him sound morally distant from everything.

Scripture does not speak that way.

God rules over evil, but He hates evil. God ordains judgment, but He takes no pleasure in the death of the wicked. God disciplines His children, but He does so as a Father. God permits suffering, but He is near to the brokenhearted. God governs all things, but He remains holy, righteous, merciful, and good.

The cross again keeps us from error. There God's determinate counsel is fulfilled through wicked hands. But God is not morally implicated in their wickedness. He is holy. They are guilty. His purpose is saving. Their motives are evil. The one event displays both human responsibility and divine wisdom.

If our doctrine of sovereignty makes God seem less holy than Scripture says, it is wrong. If it makes Him seem less good, it is wrong. If it makes Him seem less compassionate, it is wrong. Sovereignty does not swallow the rest of God's character. It operates in perfect harmony with it.

The Guardrail for Doctrine

Wise sovereignty protects doctrine from many distortions.

It protects prayer, because God's rule includes the prayers of His people as real means.

It protects evangelism, because God's saving purpose gives confidence that the gospel will bear fruit.

It protects responsibility, because God's counsel does not make human obedience or rebellion unreal.

It protects suffering, because pain is neither meaningless chaos nor cold machinery.

It protects prophecy, because the sovereign God is also truthful and faithful to His Word.

It protects worship, because the God who reigns is not merely powerful but wise, good, holy, and worthy.

It protects humility, because no creature sits above God as judge.

This is why the full character of God matters. Sovereignty isolated from wisdom becomes fatalism. Sovereignty isolated from goodness becomes terrifying. Sovereignty isolated from truthfulness becomes interpretive looseness. Sovereignty isolated from compassion becomes pastorally harmful.

But sovereignty held together with God's whole character becomes a refuge.

The Sovereignty We Must Recover

The church must recover biblical sovereignty.

- Not fatalism.
- Not cold determinism.
- Not control detached from compassion.
- Not power separated from promise.
- Not providence spoken without tears.
- Not decree severed from wisdom.

The sovereignty of the living God.

- The God who rules wisely.
- The God who keeps His promises.
- The God who hears prayer.
- The God who ordains means as well as ends.
- The God who judges evil without becoming evil.
- The God who governs suffering without ceasing to be tender.
- The God who works all things after the counsel of His own will.

This sovereignty humbles us without crushing us.

- It comforts us without making us passive.
- It steadies us without silencing lament.
- It strengthens obedience because the King is worthy.

God does not merely rule.

He rules wisely.

And because He does, His people can trust Him even when they cannot trace His hand.

Chapter 38 — The Cross: Where the Full Character of God Is Displayed

The cross is not one doctrine among many.

It is the place where the character of God is displayed with a fullness no human mind could have invented. If we look at the cross narrowly, we will distort it. If we see only love, we will miss holiness. If we see only wrath, we will miss mercy. If we see only justice, we will miss grace. If we see only human cruelty, we will miss divine wisdom. If we see only suffering, we will miss glory.

At Calvary, God is not partly revealed.

He is revealed in the fullness of His saving character.

Paul writes:

"But we preach Christ crucified, unto the Jews a stumblingblock, and unto the Greeks foolishness; But unto them which are called, both Jews and Greeks, Christ the power of God, and the wisdom of God." — *I Corinthians 1:23–24*

Christ crucified is the power of God and the wisdom of God. But the cross also reveals the holiness of God, the justice of God, the wrath of God, the love of God, the mercy of God, the grace of God, the faithfulness of God, and the truth of God.

This is why the cross must stand near the center of any study of God's character. It does not allow us to isolate one attribute and use it against the others. The cross gathers them together and shows that God is perfectly one in all He is.

The Cross Reveals the Holiness of God

The cross shows that sin cannot simply be dismissed.

If God were indifferent to sin, Christ would not have needed to die. If holiness could be set aside, atonement would be unnecessary. If guilt could be forgiven by divine overlooking, the blood of the Son of God would be excessive.

But the cross declares that God is holy.

The prophet Isaiah says:

*"But he was wounded for our transgressions, he was bruised for our iniquities: the chastisement of our peace was upon him; and with his stripes we are healed." — **Isaiah 53:5***

The language is moral and substitutionary. Transgressions. Iniquities. Chastisement. Healing through stripes. Sin is not treated as a minor weakness. It is guilt before God. It requires an answer.

This guards doctrine from a shallow view of forgiveness. God does not forgive by pretending sin is less sinful than it is. He forgives through sacrifice. His holiness is not lowered to make room for sinners. Sinners are cleansed and brought near through Christ.

A gospel that minimizes sin will always minimize the cross.

The cross teaches us not to do that.

The Cross Reveals the Justice of God

The cross also shows that God is just.

Paul makes this explicit:

"Whom God hath set forth to be a propitiation through faith in his blood, to declare his righteousness for the remission of sins that are past, through the forbearance of God; To declare, I say, at this time his righteousness: that he might be just, and the justifier of him which believeth in Jesus." — **Romans 3:25–26**

The phrase must never be rushed past: **"just, and the justifier."**

God justifies sinners. That is mercy beyond measure. But He does so while remaining just. The guilt is not ignored. The sentence is not forgotten. The moral order of God's universe is not bent around human need. Christ bears judgment in the place of His people.

This protects the doctrine of justification. The believer is not declared righteous because God has become lenient. He is declared righteous because Christ has provided a righteous basis for that declaration.

Justification is not legal fiction. It is not God pretending. It is the righteous verdict of God upon those who are in Christ.

The cross keeps mercy from becoming injustice and justice from leaving sinners hopeless.

The Cross Reveals the Wrath of God

The cross reveals wrath more deeply than any plague, flood, fire, or final warning.

There, the sinless Son bears sin. There, judgment falls. There, the cup is not avoided. There, the Holy One hangs under the weight of what sinners deserved.

In Gethsemane, Jesus prayed:

"O my Father, if it be possible, let this cup pass from me: nevertheless not as I will, but as thou wilt." — **Matthew 26:39**

The cup was not merely physical pain. Many martyrs have faced physical death with courage. Christ was facing something no martyr could bear for another—the judgment of God against sin.

Paul says:

*"For he hath made him to be sin for us, who knew no sin; that we might be made the righteousness of God in him." — **2 Corinthians 5:21***

Christ knew no sin. Yet He was made sin for us. He stood in the place of the guilty so that the guilty might stand righteous in Him.

If wrath is removed from the cross, the cross loses its saving depth. Christ becomes only an example of love, only a victim of injustice, only a symbol of solidarity with suffering. He is all righteousness, all compassion, all obedience, all love—but He is also the Substitute who bore wrath.

The church must not be ashamed of that. The believer's peace depends on it.

The Cross Reveals the Love of God

The wrath of God at the cross does not diminish love. It magnifies it.

Paul writes:

*"But God commendeth his love toward us, in that, while we were yet sinners, Christ died for us." — **Romans 5:8***

God does not merely claim love. He commends it. He displays it. He gives public proof of it in the death of Christ.

And the timing matters: **"while we were yet sinners."** God did not love us because we were lovely. He did not wait until we became righteous. He did not give His Son for people who had first made themselves worthy. Christ died for sinners.

John says:

*"Herein is love, not that we loved God, but that he loved us, and sent his Son to be the propitiation for our sins." — **I John 4:10***

Again, love and propitiation stand together. God's love is not the denial of wrath. It is the giving of His Son to bear wrath so that sinners might live.

This corrects sentimental love. The love of God is not mere approval, warmth, or kindness detached from holiness. It is costly, saving, holy love. It goes all the way to blood.

If we want to know what love is, we do not begin with human feeling. We look to the cross.

The Cross Reveals the Mercy of God

Mercy is God's compassion toward the guilty and miserable. At the cross, mercy reaches its deepest expression.

The sinner deserves judgment. The sinner has no claim. The sinner cannot repair the offense, cleanse the stain, or pay the debt. Yet God provides what the sinner lacks.

Peter writes:

*"Blessed be the God and Father of our Lord Jesus Christ, which according to his abundant mercy hath begotten us again unto a lively hope by the resurrection of Jesus Christ from the dead." — **I Peter 1:3***

The hope of the believer rests upon abundant mercy. But that mercy comes through the death and resurrection of Christ. It does not float above justice. It comes through the Savior who suffered and rose.

This protects mercy from becoming mere pity. God does not stand at a distance feeling sorry for sinners while leaving guilt untouched. He acts. He sends the Son. He provides the sacrifice. He opens the way of return.

At the cross, mercy has hands, wounds, blood, and victory.

The Cross Reveals the Grace of God

Grace gives what is not deserved.

At the cross, grace is not abstract. It is embodied in Christ crucified for those who had no merit before God.

Paul writes:

*"In whom we have redemption through his blood, the forgiveness of sins, according to the riches of his grace." — **Ephesians 1:7***

The riches of grace are seen in redemption through blood. Grace is free to us because it was costly to Christ. The sinner contributes nothing that earns salvation. He receives what Christ has accomplished.

This destroys boasting.

No one stands before the cross and says, "I made the difference." No one looks upon the crucified Son and claims salvation as wages. Grace silences pride because grace gives what only God could provide.

This is why works-righteousness is not a small mistake. It competes with the meaning of the cross. If man could make himself acceptable before God, Christ died in vain. If obedience could erase guilt, the cross is unnecessary. If human merit could secure righteousness, grace is no more grace.

But Scripture says:

*"For by grace are ye saved through faith; and that not of yourselves: it is the gift of God." — **Ephesians 2:8***

The cross is the gift of grace to the undeserving.

The Cross Reveals the Faithfulness of God

The cross did not appear suddenly in history as a divine afterthought.

It fulfilled what God had promised.

From the first promise that the seed of the woman would bruise the serpent's head, through the sacrifices, the Passover lamb, the priesthood, the suffering servant, and the prophetic witness, Scripture moved toward Christ. God had spoken, and God kept His Word.

Paul says:

"For all the promises of God in him are yea, and in him Amen, unto the glory of God by us." — 2 Corinthians 1:20

Christ is the great confirmation of God's promises. At the cross, God proves that He does not forget what He has spoken. Centuries may pass. Human expectation may fail. The path may seem strange. But God is faithful.

This matters for doctrine far beyond the cross itself. If God kept His promise concerning the suffering, death, and resurrection of Christ, then His other promises must not be handled lightly. The God who fulfills His Word through Christ is not less faithful after Christ. He is faithful in Christ.

The cross teaches us how seriously God takes His own Word.

The Cross Reveals the Wisdom of God

No human mind would have designed salvation this way.

The world would choose power without shame, victory without suffering, glory without humiliation. God chose the cross.

Paul writes:

"But God hath chosen the foolish things of the world to confound the wise; and God hath chosen the weak things of the world to confound the things which are mighty." — **I Corinthians 1:27**

The cross looked foolish to Greek wisdom and offensive to Jewish expectation. Yet it was the wisdom of God.

At the cross, God defeated Satan through apparent defeat. He conquered death through death. He brought life through the suffering of the Son. He exposed human sin and accomplished divine redemption in the same event. He fulfilled prophecy through the wicked actions of men who did not intend to fulfill prophecy.

Peter said Christ was delivered:

"by the determinate counsel and foreknowledge of God,"

yet those who crucified Him did so with:

"wicked hands." — **Acts 2:23**

There is the wisdom of God: human evil remained evil, and divine purpose remained holy. The same event displayed man's guilt and God's saving counsel.

The cross does not merely show that God is wiser than man. It shows that the wisdom of God often appears most clearly where human wisdom sees defeat.

The Cross Reveals the Sovereignty of God

At Calvary, the rulers of this world acted freely and wickedly, yet they did not overthrow God's plan.

Herod, Pontius Pilate, the Gentiles, and the people of Israel gathered against Christ. They were responsible for what they did. Yet the early church prayed:

"For to do whatsoever thy hand and thy counsel determined before to be done." — **Acts 4:28**

The cross was not God losing control. It was God accomplishing redemption through the very events His enemies intended for evil.

This is not fatalism. It is not God becoming morally responsible for sin. It is sovereign wisdom. God rules in such a way that even rebellion cannot escape serving His final purpose, while rebels remain guilty for their rebellion.

That truth gives the believer confidence. If God ruled at the cross, He rules everywhere. If the darkest event in history was also the place of redemption, then no darkness in the believer's life is beyond His wise sovereignty.

The cross is the strongest proof that God's rule is not threatened by evil.

The Cross Reveals the Truth of God

The cross also reveals that God tells the truth about sin, judgment, promise, and salvation.

Every warning about sin is vindicated there. Every sacrifice finds meaning there. Every prophetic word concerning the suffering Messiah is confirmed there. Every promise of redemption is shown to be trustworthy there.

Jesus Himself said after His resurrection:

*"Thus it is written, and thus it behoved Christ to suffer, and to rise from the dead the third day." — **Luke 24:46***

It was written. It had to be fulfilled. God's Word stood.

This corrects every doctrine that treats Scripture loosely. The cross came according to the Scriptures. Christ died for our sins according to the Scriptures. He rose again the third day according to the Scriptures. God's saving work honors God's written Word.

A church that loves the cross should love truth.

The Cross Guards Doctrine

The cross is the great guardrail of doctrine because it refuses to let us divide God.

- Love without holiness cannot explain it.
- Mercy without justice cannot explain it.
- Wrath without goodness cannot explain it.
- Sovereignty without wisdom cannot explain it.
- Grace without truth cannot explain it.
- Faithfulness without fulfillment cannot explain it.

Every reduced doctrine of God eventually produces a reduced doctrine of the cross.

If God is only love, the cross becomes unnecessary suffering.

If God is only wrath, the cross becomes terror without mercy.

If God is only justice, sinners have no hope.

If God is only mercy, blood becomes excessive.

If God is only sovereign power, Calvary becomes cold decree rather than holy redemption.

If God is only moral example, the atonement disappears.

But the God of Scripture is not partial.

At the cross, He shows Himself fully. Holy, loving, just, merciful, wrathful, gracious, wise, sovereign, faithful, true, and good.

This is why the church must never move away from the cross into a more respectable center. There is no better center. There is no deeper revelation of God's saving character.

The Cross and the Christian Life

The cross not only saves. It shapes the life of those who are saved.

Paul says:

*"I am crucified with Christ: nevertheless I live; yet not I, but Christ liveth in me: and the life which I now live in the flesh I live by the faith of the Son of God, who loved me, and gave himself for me." — **Galatians 2:20***

The believer does not move past the cross after conversion. He lives in its light. The cross teaches him humility because salvation was not earned. It teaches holiness because sin required blood. It teaches gratitude because Christ gave Himself. It teaches endurance because glory came through suffering. It teaches forgiveness because he has been forgiven. It teaches worship because God has revealed Himself there.

A cross-shaped life is not merely a life that remembers Jesus died. It is a life governed by the God revealed in that death.

The proud man has not understood the cross.

The careless man has not understood the cross.

The bitter man has not understood the cross.

The self-righteous man has not understood the cross.

The man who thinks sin is light has not understood the cross.

To stand at Calvary is to be humbled, cleansed, corrected, and summoned.

Behold the Lamb

John the Baptist saw Jesus and said:

*"Behold the Lamb of God, which taketh away the sin of the world." — **John 1:29***

That remains the call.

Behold Him.

- Not merely as example.
- Not merely as teacher.
- Not merely as martyr.
- Not merely as symbol.

Behold the Lamb of God.

There, the holy God deals with sin.

There, the just God justifies.

There, the wrathful God provides propitiation.

There, the loving God gives His Son.

There, the merciful God receives the guilty.

There, the gracious God gives what no sinner could earn.

There, the faithful God keeps His promises.

There, the wise God defeats evil through suffering.

There, the sovereign God rules even over the darkest hour.

There, the true God fulfills His Word.

The cross is not a contradiction in God.

It is the display of God.

And the more fully we know His character, the more deeply we will worship before the crucified and risen Christ.

Chapter 39 — The Bridegroom, His Bride, and the Wrath of the Lamb

Doctrine must be tested by the whole character of God.

This does not mean we build doctrine from sentiment. It does not mean we decide what God would or would not do based on human instinct. That would be dangerous. God defines Himself. Scripture governs our thinking. The text must rule.

But once God has revealed His character, His character becomes part of faithful interpretation. We are not free to interpret one passage in a way that makes God act contrary to what He has revealed elsewhere. The God who speaks is the God who acts. His Word and His ways cannot finally contradict His nature.

That principle becomes especially important when we consider Christ, His church, and the wrath revealed in the book of Revelation.

The New Testament presents Christ as the Bridegroom and the church as His bride. It also presents the end-time wrath in Revelation as the wrath of the Lamb. Those two truths must be held together carefully. If Christ has loved, purchased, cleansed, and betrothed His church to Himself, then any doctrine that places His bride under His eschatological wrath must be examined with great care.

Not dismissed carelessly.

Not accepted casually.

Examined carefully.

Because the Bridegroom does not relate to His bride the way He relates to His enemies.

Christ the Bridegroom

John the Baptist understood his own ministry in relation to Christ the Bridegroom. When his disciples worried that people were going to Jesus, John answered:

"He that hath the bride is the bridegroom: but the friend of the bridegroom, which standeth and heareth him, rejoiceth greatly because of the bridegroom's voice: this my joy therefore is fulfilled." — **John 3:29**

John was not the center. He was the friend of the Bridegroom. Christ was the One to whom the bride belonged.

Jesus also identified Himself with bridegroom imagery. When asked why His disciples did not fast as others did, He said:

"Can the children of the bridechamber mourn, as long as the bridegroom is with them? but the days will come, when the bridegroom shall be taken from them, and then shall they fast." — **Matthew 9:15**

Christ's presence was the presence of the Bridegroom. His removal would bring mourning. His return would bring joy.

The image is not decorative. It reveals relationship. The Bridegroom is not a distant ruler only. He is covenantally joined to the people He loves. He claims them, prepares them, cleanses them, and will bring them into joy.

The Church as the Bride

Paul's most direct teaching appears in Ephesians 5.

He writes:

"Husbands, love your wives, even as Christ also loved the church, and gave himself for it; That he might sanctify and cleanse it with the washing of water by the word, That he might present it to himself a glorious church, not having

*spot, or wrinkle, or any such thing; but that it should be holy and without blemish." — **Ephesians 5:25–27**

This passage does more than instruct husbands. It reveals Christ's relationship to the church.

- Christ loved the church.
- Christ gave Himself for the church.
- Christ sanctifies and cleanses the church.
- Christ will present the church to Himself glorious.

The direction of His action is unmistakable. His love moves toward sacrifice, cleansing, sanctification, and presentation. He does not give Himself for the church in order to abandon her to wrath. He gives Himself for her to make her holy and bring her to Himself.

Paul continues:

*"For no man ever yet hated his own flesh; but nourisheth and cherisheth it, even as the Lord the church: For we are members of his body, of his flesh, and of his bones." — **Ephesians 5:29–30**

Christ nourishes and cherishes the church. The language is tender and covenantal. It is not the language of judicial wrath against enemies. It is the language of union, care, and love.

This matters doctrinally. If the church is Christ's bride, body, and cherished possession, then we must be cautious about placing her under judgments described as the wrath of the Lamb.

The Bride Purchased by Blood

The church does not belong to Christ in a vague or sentimental way. She is purchased.

Paul told the Ephesian elders:

"Take heed therefore unto yourselves, and to all the flock, over the which the Holy Ghost hath made you overseers, to feed the church of God, which he hath purchased with his own blood." — **Acts 20:28**

The church was purchased at immeasurable cost. Christ did not merely choose an association. He bought His people by His blood. That purchase is not fragile. It is not uncertain. It is not temporary.

Peter speaks similarly of redemption:

"Forasmuch as ye know that ye were not redeemed with corruptible things, as silver and gold… But with the precious blood of Christ, as of a lamb without blemish and without spot." — **1 Peter 1:18–19**

The bride belongs to the Lamb because the Lamb gave Himself for her.

This is where character becomes doctrinally significant. The faithful Christ does not purchase His bride with blood and then treat her as the object of the wrath from which His blood delivers. The just Christ does not require payment twice. The loving Christ does not appoint His bride to the judicial wrath He bore for her. The holy Christ does discipline and purify His people, but discipline is not condemning wrath.

The distinctions matter.

The Wrath of the Lamb

Revelation 6 introduces a striking phrase:

"And said to the mountains and rocks, Fall on us, and hide us from the face of him that sitteth on the throne, and from the wrath of the Lamb: For the great day of his wrath is come; and who shall be able to stand?" — **Revelation 6:16–17**

This is not merely the wrath of an undefined deity. It is **the wrath of the Lamb**.

The Lamb is Christ. The Lamb is the One who was slain. The Lamb is the Redeemer. The Lamb is the Bridegroom. The Lamb purchased His people with His blood.

Therefore, when Revelation speaks of the wrath of the Lamb, we should not treat that wrath as though it were unrelated to Christ's covenant love for His church. The same Person who pours out wrath is the One who loves His bride.

That raises a serious interpretive question.

Is the church, as the bride of Christ, appointed to experience the eschatological wrath of her own Bridegroom?

That question cannot be answered by emotion. It must be answered by Scripture. But it is a legitimate question because Scripture itself gives us the categories: Bridegroom, bride, blood-bought church, and wrath of the Lamb.

Not Appointed to Wrath

Paul writes to the Thessalonians:

"For God hath not appointed us to wrath, but to obtain salvation by our Lord Jesus Christ." — I Thessalonians 5:9

This statement must be interpreted carefully, but it must not be weakened. Believers are not appointed to wrath. Their appointment is salvation through Christ.

Earlier, Paul says the Thessalonians had turned to God from idols:

"And to wait for his Son from heaven, whom he raised from the dead, even Jesus, which delivered us from the wrath to come." — I Thessalonians 1:10

Jesus delivers His people from the wrath to come.

416

That deliverance cannot be reduced to a vague spiritual idea with no eschatological significance. The Thessalonian context includes waiting for the Son from heaven. It includes the day of the Lord. It includes watchfulness, hope, and rescue. The believer's future is framed not by appointment to wrath, but by salvation through the returning Christ.

This does not mean believers are exempt from all suffering. Scripture says the opposite. Christians suffer tribulation, persecution, hatred, discipline, grief, and even martyrdom. But tribulation from the world is not the same as wrath from God. Persecution by the beast is not the same as the wrath of the Lamb. Fatherly discipline is not the same as judicial judgment.

A doctrine that confuses these categories will confuse the believer's hope.

Tribulation Is Not Always Wrath

This distinction is essential.

The word **tribulation** can refer broadly to pressure, affliction, persecution, or distress. Jesus told His disciples:

*"In the world ye shall have tribulation: ut be of good cheer; I have overcome the world." — **John 16:33**Christians should not expect ease in this age. The church has suffered from the beginning. The apostles were persecuted. Many believers have been imprisoned, tortured, and killed. Suffering does not mean Christ has failed His bride.*

But divine wrath is different.

Wrath is God's judicial response to evil. It is His holy anger against sin and rebellion. When Revelation speaks of the wrath of the Lamb and the great day of His wrath, it is not merely describing ordinary Christian suffering in a hostile world. It is describing judgment from heaven.

This is why the distinction matters in eschatology. If the church suffers under the hatred of the world, that is one thing. If the church is placed under the eschatological wrath of the Lamb, that is another. Scripture clearly teaches the first. The second must be proven, not assumed.

The Bride and Fatherly Discipline

Some might object that God does bring hardship upon His people. That is true. But Scripture gives a category for that: fatherly discipline.

Hebrews says:

*"For whom the Lord loveth he chasteneth, and scourgeth every son whom he receiveth." — **Hebrews 12:6***

Discipline may be painful. It may expose sin, humble pride, and correct wandering. But the passage itself says discipline flows from love and sonship. It is not condemnation. It is not wrath against enemies. It is the Father training His children.

Paul says:

*"There is therefore now no condemnation to them which are in Christ Jesus..." — **Romans 8:1***

No condemnation does not mean no correction. It means no judicial condemnation. The wrath due to the believer's sin has been borne by Christ.

Therefore, when we speak of God's dealings with the church, we must distinguish correction from condemnation, discipline from wrath, refinement from judgment, and persecution from divine fury. These are not interchangeable categories.

The Bridegroom may cleanse His bride. He may discipline His people. He may purify the church through trials. But His cleansing love is not the same as the wrath of the Lamb poured out upon a rebellious world.

The Bride in Revelation

Revelation itself presents the bride in glory.

John writes:

"Let us be glad and rejoice, and give honour to him: for the marriage of the Lamb is come, and his wife hath made herself ready." — **Revelation 19:7**

Then:

"Blessed are they which are called unto the marriage supper of the Lamb." **— Revelation 19:9**

The Lamb has a bride. The marriage comes. The wife is made ready. The scene is joy, union, celebration, and fulfillment.

Later, John sees the holy city, new Jerusalem:

"prepared as a bride adorned for her husband." — **Revelation 21:2**

The bridal imagery reaches its final consummation in the dwelling of God with His people.

This does not answer every eschatological timing question by itself. But it does provide a strong theological frame. The Lamb's bride is destined for marriage, glory, and dwelling with God. She is not characterized as the target of His wrath.

Any eschatological view must account for this.

A Doctrinal Guardrail, Not a Shortcut

The argument of this chapter should not be misunderstood.

The character of Christ as Bridegroom is not a shortcut that allows us to ignore the details of prophecy. We must still examine Revelation, Daniel, Matthew 24, 1 and 2 Thessalonians, 1 Corinthians 15, and the broader witness of Scripture carefully. Character reasoning does not replace exegesis.

But it does guard exegesis.

If an interpretation requires Christ to pour out His judicial wrath upon the bride He purchased, cleanses, nourishes, cherishes, and presents to Himself, that interpretation carries a burden of proof. It must show clearly from Scripture that this is what God teaches. It cannot simply assume that all end-time distress is the same category.

The full character of God forces careful distinctions.

Wrath is not discipline. Tribulation is not automatically divine judgment. Persecution by evil powers is not the same as the wrath of the Lamb. The bride is not the enemy. The Bridegroom is not indifferent to the covenant relationship He established by blood.

These distinctions do not settle every debate by themselves, but they keep doctrine from becoming careless.

The Church's Hope

The church's hope is not wrath, but Christ.

Paul writes:

*"Looking for that blessed hope, and the glorious appearing of the great God and our Saviour Jesus Christ." — **Titus 2:13***

The believer waits for the Savior. The bride waits for the Bridegroom. The church does not wait with dread that Christ will treat her as an object of condemning wrath. She waits for the One who loved her and gave Himself for her.

This hope should purify the church, not make her careless. John writes:

"And every man that hath this hope in him purifieth himself, even as he is pure." — I John 3:3

True hope produces holiness. The bride prepares. She watches. She keeps herself from idols. She endures suffering faithfully. She waits for her Lord.

But she waits as loved, purchased, and promised.

The Bridegroom Does Not Forget His Bride

Christ is not divided.

- He is the Lamb whose wrath terrifies the rebellious.
- He is the Bridegroom who loves His bride.
- He is the Judge of the earth.
- He is the Savior of His church.
- He is holy in judgment.
- He is faithful in covenant love.

A doctrine that emphasizes His wrath while forgetting His bride distorts Him. A doctrine that emphasizes His love while denying His wrath also distorts Him. The whole Christ must be kept together.

This is why the full character of God matters. It does not allow one truth to devour another. It teaches us to ask better questions, make better distinctions, and refuse interpretations that flatten the biblical witness.

The Lamb has wrath.

The Lamb also has a bride.

And the Lamb who purchased His bride with His own blood will not forget what He bought.

Chapter 40 — The Faithful God and the Promises He Keeps

God keeps His promises.

That sentence is simple, but it guards enormous portions of doctrine. If God is faithful, then His words cannot be treated lightly. His covenants cannot be handled as though they were temporary religious imagery. His promises cannot be dissolved whenever they become difficult to fit into a preferred system. His warnings cannot be softened. His prophetic declarations cannot be detached from His truthfulness.

The faithful God does not speak carelessly.

Moses said:

"God is not a man, that he should lie; neither the son of man, that he should repent: hath he said, and shall he not do it? or hath he spoken, and shall he not make it good?" — **Numbers 23:19**

That verse is a doctrinal guardrail. God is not like man. He does not speak beyond His ability, promise beyond His intention, or declare what He later abandons. What He has spoken, He will make good.

This matters because one of the easiest ways to distort doctrine is to speak highly of God's sovereignty while treating His promises loosely. But God's sovereignty does not make His words flexible. It guarantees their fulfillment. The God who rules all things is the God who keeps covenant.

When Promises Become Theological Clay

There is a subtle danger in theology: taking promises God has spoken and reshaping them until they fit a system more comfortably.

This can happen with prophecy. It can happen with covenant promises. It can happen with Israel, the church, the kingdom, resurrection, judgment, restoration, and the future hope of Scripture. The language of fulfillment may still be used, but the fulfillment described no longer bears clear relationship to what God actually said.

That is not careful interpretation. It is theological control.

To be clear, later revelation can deepen earlier revelation. Christ fulfills Scripture in ways that exceed what many may have expected. The New Testament reveals mysteries that were hidden in previous ages. Types, shadows, patterns, and promises find their fullness in Him.

But fulfillment does not mean contradiction. It does not mean God says one thing and does another. It does not mean concrete promises become unrelated abstractions. It does not mean covenant language can be emptied of its stated content because a theological system finds that easier.

The faithful God fulfills His Word more richly than man may have understood, but never less truthfully than He spoke.

The Promise to Abraham

God's covenant with Abraham is foundational to Scripture.

The Lord said:

"And I will make of thee a great nation, and I will bless thee, and make thy name great; and thou shalt be a blessing: And I will bless them that bless thee, and curse him that curseth thee: and in thee shall all families of the earth be blessed." — **Genesis 12:2–3**

Later He promised land:

"Unto thy seed have I given this land, from the river of Egypt unto the great river, the river Euphrates." — **Genesis 15:18**

These promises include nationhood, seed, blessing, land, and blessing to all families of the earth. The New Testament clearly shows that the blessing to the nations comes through Christ. Paul writes:

*"And if ye be Christ's, then are ye Abraham's seed, and heirs according to the promise." — **Galatians 3:29***

Gentile believers share in the blessing promised through Abraham because they belong to Christ. That is glorious fulfillment. But Gentile inclusion does not require us to say God has forgotten or canceled every particular promise connected to Abraham's physical descendants or the land He named. Inclusion is not erasure.

This is the guardrail: Christ expands blessing to the nations without making God unfaithful to the promises He made.

The Promise to David

God also made covenant promises to David.

He said:

*"And thine house and thy kingdom shall be established for ever before thee: thy throne shall be established for ever." — **2 Samuel 7:16***

This promise reaches its fulfillment in Christ, the Son of David. Gabriel told Mary:

*"He shall be great, and shall be called the Son of the Highest: and the Lord God shall give unto him the throne of his father David: And he shall reign over the house of Jacob for ever; and of his kingdom there shall be no end." — **Luke 1:32–33***

The promise did not disappear. It came to its rightful King. Jesus is not merely spiritually similar to David. He is David's Son and David's Lord. His throne is not temporary. His kingdom has no end.

The question is not whether Christ fulfills the Davidic promise. He does. The question is whether fulfillment in Christ allows the promise to be treated as something other than what God said. The angel's announcement does not weaken the language of throne, reign, house of Jacob, and kingdom. It confirms that God is keeping His Word.

A faithful God does not use messianic fulfillment to make His promises less reliable. He uses fulfillment to show they were more certain than anyone knew.

The Promise of the New Covenant

Jeremiah records one of the clearest covenant promises in the Old Testament:

"Behold, the days come, saith the LORD, that I will make a new covenant with the house of Israel, and with the house of Judah." — **Jeremiah 31:31**

The passage continues with promises of internal transformation, forgiveness, and covenant knowledge of God. The New Testament unquestionably connects the New Covenant to Christ's blood. Jesus said:

"This cup is the new testament in my blood, which is shed for you." — **Luke 22:20**

Believers in Christ receive New Covenant blessings. Forgiveness, the Spirit's work, and the knowledge of God come through the blood of Christ. Gentiles are brought near. The grace is astonishing.

But again, Gentile participation does not require denial of the covenant's named parties. Jeremiah says the covenant is made with the house of Israel and the house of Judah. The same chapter ties God's continuing commitment to Israel to the fixed order of sun, moon, and stars.

"If those ordinances depart from before me, saith the LORD, then the seed of Israel also shall cease from being a nation before me for ever." — **Jeremiah 31:36**

That is strong language.

A doctrine of fulfillment must be able to honor both realities: the church's real participation in New Covenant blessing through Christ and God's faithfulness to the words He spoke concerning Israel and Judah. We should not use one truth to erase the other.

The faithful God is able to fulfill all He has said.

When Spiritual Fulfillment Becomes Erasure

A major interpretive danger appears when the word **spiritual** is used to mean **less real** or **different from what God promised**.

Spiritual fulfillment is real fulfillment. Resurrection life in Christ is real. Forgiveness is real. The indwelling Spirit is real. Union with Christ is real. The heavenly inheritance is real. Spiritual does not mean imaginary, vague, or symbolic in the weak sense.

But spiritual fulfillment should not be used as a tool to erase concrete promises.

If God promises resurrection, spiritual life now does not cancel bodily resurrection later. If God promises a kingdom, spiritual reign in the present does not automatically cancel future reign. If God promises restoration, present gospel blessing does not necessarily exhaust every prophetic expectation. If God names Israel, Judah, Jerusalem, nations, land, and throne, those words should not be emptied unless Scripture itself clearly does so.

This is not a refusal to read the Bible theologically. It is a refusal to make God's faithfulness less than His words.

The faithful God may fulfill promises in layers, stages, and fullness beyond immediate expectation. But His fulfillment does not mock His speech.

The Faithfulness of God and Israel

Paul addresses Israel's future directly in Romans 11.

He asks:

"I say then, Hath God cast away his people? God forbid." — **Romans 11:1**

Later he says:

"For the gifts and calling of God are without repentance." — **Romans 11:29**

That verse must carry weight. God's gifts and calling are not revoked. Israel's unbelief is real. Gentile inclusion is real. The hardening in part is real. But Paul does not conclude that God is finished with Israel. He warns Gentiles against arrogance and points forward to mercy.

Whatever one's full eschatological structure, Romans 11 should restrain any theology that speaks as though God's covenant commitments to Israel have simply vanished. Paul's argument is rooted in the character of God. If God's Word to Israel failed, then confidence in any promise would be shaken.

But Paul insists God has not failed.

"For I would not, brethren, that ye should be ignorant of this mystery, lest ye should be wise in your own conceits; that blindness in part is happened to Israel, until the fulness of the Gentiles be come in." — **Romans 11:25**

The word **until** matters. Partial hardening is not presented as the final word. God's faithfulness continues to govern the story.

Promise and Prophecy

The faithfulness of God also guards how we read prophecy.

Prophecy may contain symbols, patterns, near and far fulfillments, typology, and apocalyptic imagery. We must read each genre carefully. But genre does not cancel truth. Symbolic language does not mean God is free to mean anything at all. Prophetic imagery still communicates something God intends.

The Lord says:

"Declaring the end from the beginning, and from ancient times the things that are not yet done, saying, My counsel shall stand, and I will do all my pleasure."
— Isaiah 46:10

God declares the end because He knows and governs the end. Prophecy is not divine poetry with no fixed referent. It is revelation from the faithful God.

This should make interpreters careful. We should not force every prophetic detail into wooden literalism where the text itself is clearly symbolic. But neither should we use symbolism as permission to detach fulfillment from the words given. Faithfulness requires attention to the text as God gave it.

If the prophecy is symbolic, interpret the symbol according to Scripture.

If the promise is covenantal, honor the covenant language.

If the fulfillment is expanded in Christ, rejoice in the expansion.

If the fulfillment is still future, do not collapse it prematurely.

The faithful God deserves careful readers.

The Promises of Christ to His Church

God's faithfulness is not only a matter of Israel and prophecy. It is precious to the church.

Jesus said:

"I will build my church; and the gates of hell shall not prevail against it." — **Matthew 16:18**

The church exists because Christ keeps that promise. Through persecution, corruption, weakness, opposition, and centuries of conflict, Christ continues to build. The church may be chastened, purified, corrected, and sometimes reduced in visible strength, but Christ will not fail in what He promised.

He also said:

"I give unto them eternal life; and they shall never perish, neither shall any man pluck them out of my hand." — **John 10:28**

That promise rests on the faithfulness of the Shepherd. Eternal life is not temporary life. The sheep are not secure because they are strong, but because His hand is.

If we trust Christ's promises to the church, we should also be careful with every promise God has spoken. We cannot defend assurance by appealing to God's faithfulness and then interpret other covenant promises as though faithfulness were flexible.

The character of God must be applied consistently.

The Danger of Selective Faithfulness

A subtle error arises when we want God's faithfulness for the promises we cherish but allow looseness with promises that trouble our system.

- We want assurance to mean assurance.

- We want resurrection to mean resurrection.
- We want eternal life to mean eternal life.
- We want forgiveness to mean forgiveness.
- We want Christ's return to mean Christ's return.
- We should. God is faithful.

But then we must not become careless when God speaks of Israel, covenant, land, throne, kingdom, restoration, judgment, or the nations. We do not honor God by trusting Him selectively. The same God speaks in all Scripture.

This does not mean all promises are addressed to the same people in the same way. They are not. We must distinguish Israel and the church, old covenant and new covenant, type and fulfillment, promise and application, near fulfillment and final fulfillment. Careful distinctions matter.

But distinctions are not excuses for unbelief. They are tools for faithfulness.

The question should always be: what did God say, to whom did He say it, what did He mean in context, how does later Scripture develop it, and how does Christ fulfill it without making God's earlier words untrue?

That is the work of faithful interpretation.

The Cross as Proof of Promise-Keeping

The cross proves that God keeps promises even when fulfillment comes through unexpected means.

Many expected Messiah to triumph, but few understood that He must first suffer. Yet after the resurrection, Jesus said:

"Ought not Christ to have suffered these things, and to enter into his glory?" — **Luke 24:26**

Then Luke tells us:

"And beginning at Moses and all the prophets, he expounded unto them in all the scriptures the things concerning himself." — **Luke 24:27**

The cross was not the failure of promise. It was the fulfillment of Scripture. God kept His Word through suffering before glory.

This should teach us humility. Fulfillment may be deeper than we first thought. It may include patterns we missed, types we did not understand, and timing we did not expect. But the surprise of fulfillment is not the cancellation of faithfulness. It is the unveiling of wisdom.

Christ's first coming fulfilled Scripture precisely, though not always according to common expectation. His second coming will do the same.

The faithful God has not become less faithful after the cross.

The Guardrail for Doctrine

The faithfulness of God protects doctrine in several ways.

It protects the gospel, because salvation rests on promises God has kept in Christ.

It protects assurance, because eternal life depends on Christ's faithful word.

It protects covenant theology from becoming careless with God's commitments.

It protects eschatology from dissolving prophecy into vague spiritual ideas.

It protects the doctrine of Scripture, because God's words are treated as reliable.

It protects worship, because praise grows deeper when God's works match His promises.

It protects humility, because interpreters must receive the text rather than control it.

When faithfulness is weakened, doctrine becomes unstable. Promises become elastic. Fulfillment becomes whatever the system needs. Warnings become negotiable. Hope becomes vague.

But when God's faithfulness is honored, Scripture gains weight. Every word matters because the God who spoke is faithful.

The God Who Makes Good His Word

God keeps His promises.

- He kept His promise to send the Seed of the woman.
- He kept His promise to bless the nations through Abraham.
- He kept His promise to raise up David's Son.
- He kept His promise to provide the suffering Servant.
- He kept His promise to pour out New Covenant blessing through Christ's blood.
- He will keep His promises concerning Israel.
- He will keep His promises to the church.
- He will keep His promises concerning judgment, resurrection, kingdom, and new creation.

Not one word of God will fall to the ground.

Joshua testified:

"There failed not ought of any good thing which the LORD had spoken unto the house of Israel; all came to pass." — **Joshua 21:45**

That is the testimony of Scripture. That will be the testimony of eternity.

The faithful God will make good everything He has spoken.

Chapter 41 — Fatherly Discipline Is Not Condemning Wrath

One of the most important doctrinal distinctions in the Christian life is the difference between **fatherly discipline** and **condemning wrath**.

If this distinction is lost, believers may begin to interpret every hardship as divine rejection. Suffering becomes evidence that God is angry in the same way He is angry with the wicked. Correction becomes condemnation. Trials become punishment in the ultimate sense. The conscience becomes unstable, and the believer's view of God becomes confused.

Scripture does not permit that confusion.

God does discipline His children. He corrects them. He chastens them. He exposes sin, humbles pride, removes idols, and trains them in holiness. But this discipline is not the wrath of a Judge condemning His enemies. It is the correction of a Father who loves His children.

That distinction matters because Christ has already borne the condemning wrath due to His people. The believer is not under condemnation.

Paul writes:

*"There is therefore now no condemnation to them which are in Christ Jesus, who walk not after the flesh, but after the Spirit." — **Romans 8:1***

No condemnation.

Those words must not be weakened. They do not mean the believer will never be corrected. They do not mean he will never suffer. They do not mean God will ignore sin in His children. But they do mean that the believer no longer stands under the judicial condemnation from which Christ has delivered him.

Fatherly discipline is real.

Condemning wrath is not appointed for those who are in Christ.

The Confusion That Harms Assurance

Many Christians struggle because they interpret God's dealings with them through fear rather than through Christ.

When they suffer, they wonder if God has turned against them. When trials come, they assume God is paying them back. When they fall into sin and then experience painful consequences, they imagine the cross has somehow become insufficient. Their assurance rises and falls with circumstances.

This is not spiritual sensitivity. It is doctrinal confusion.

The gospel does not teach that sin has no consequences in the believer's life. It does not teach that God will never bring painful correction. It does not teach that holiness is optional. But it does teach that Christ has borne the believer's guilt and condemnation.

If every painful providence is interpreted as condemning wrath, then Romans 8:1 loses its force. The believer may say "no condemnation" with his lips while living as though condemnation still hovers over every failure.

That is not the freedom of the gospel.

The believer needs to learn how to say two truths together: God may discipline me deeply, and God does not condemn me in Christ.

The Father Who Chastens

Hebrews gives the clearest teaching:

*"My son, despise not thou the chastening of the Lord, nor faint when thou art rebuked of him: For whom the Lord loveth he chasteneth, and scourgeth every son whom he receiveth." — **Hebrews 12:5–6***

The passage gives two dangers.

The first is despising discipline. A believer may shrug off correction, refuse repentance, harden his heart, or treat God's chastening as though it has no meaning.

The second is fainting under discipline. A believer may collapse in despair, believing God has rejected him.

Hebrews corrects both. Discipline should not be despised because it comes from the Lord. But it should not make the believer faint because it comes from love.

"For whom the Lord loveth he chasteneth…"

That sentence is the key. Discipline is not proof that God has stopped loving His child. It is proof that He does love him. The Father's correction is not abandonment. It is sonship.

Hebrews continues:

"If ye endure chastening, God dealeth with you as with sons; for what son is he whom the father chasteneth not?" — **Hebrews 12:7**

God deals with believers as sons. That does not make chastening easy. Hebrews admits:

"Now no chastening for the present seemeth to be joyous, but grievous…" — **Hebrews 12:11**

The Bible is honest. Discipline hurts. It can grieve deeply. But the verse continues:

"nevertheless afterward it yieldeth the peaceable fruit of righteousness unto them which are exercised thereby." — **Hebrews 12:11**

The aim is fruit. Discipline is purposeful. It is not God venting anger. It is not condemnation sneaking back into the Christian life. It is the Father training His children in righteousness.

Discipline Is Not Payment for Sin

This distinction must be pressed carefully.

When God disciplines His children, He is not requiring them to make additional payment for sins Christ failed to cover. That would deny the sufficiency of the cross.

Peter says Christ:

"his own self bare our sins in his own body on the tree…" — **I Peter 2:24**

If Christ bore our sins, then divine discipline is not God transferring the unpaid balance back onto the believer. The debt has not been partly paid by Christ and partly paid by suffering. The believer's pain is not atonement.

This matters pastorally. A Christian who thinks he is paying for sin through suffering will either despair or become strangely self-righteous. He may despair because the payment seems endless. Or he may begin to treat suffering as though it earns back God's favor.

Both are wrong.

Christ alone atones. Christ alone bears wrath for His people. Christ alone satisfies justice. Discipline may correct, expose, train, and restore, but it does not propitiate God. The blood of Christ has done that.

John writes:

"And he is the propitiation for our sins: and not for ours only, but also for the sins of the whole world." — **I John 2:2**

Propitiation belongs to Christ's work, not ours.

Consequences Are Not Always Condemnation

The believer may still experience consequences for sin.

David was forgiven, yet painful consequences followed his sin. Moses was faithful, yet he did not enter the land because of his disobedience. The Corinthians abused the Lord's Supper, and Paul says some were weak and sickly, and some slept. These are serious realities.

But consequences in the life of God's people must be understood through covenant relationship, not condemnation.

Paul writes to the Corinthians:

*"For if we would judge ourselves, we should not be judged. But when we are judged, we are chastened of the Lord, that we should not be condemned with the world." — **I Corinthians 11:31–32***

That last phrase is vital: **"that we should not be condemned with the world."**

God's chastening of His people is specifically distinguished from the condemnation of the world. He corrects His own so they will not be condemned with the world. The painful discipline is not the same as the final judgment of the wicked. It is God's fatherly intervention.

This helps us avoid shallow thinking. Forgiveness does not always remove every earthly consequence. But earthly consequences do not mean the believer is back under wrath. God may use consequences as part of His correcting mercy.

Discipline and Sanctification

The purpose of discipline is holiness.

Hebrews says earthly fathers chastened according to their own pleasure, but God chastens:

"for our profit, that we might be partakers of his holiness." — **Hebrews 12:10**

That is the goal: participation in holiness.

God's discipline is not merely behavior management. He is not simply trying to make His children more respectable. He is forming them according to His own holy character. He is removing what defiles, correcting what destroys, and training what reflects His Son.

This means discipline is often deeper than we first realize. We may want God to fix circumstances. He may be exposing pride. We may want relief from pressure. He may be teaching dependence. We may want quick forgiveness without transformation. He may be pressing the wound until repentance becomes honest.

The Father is not cruel in this. He is thorough.

A shallow mercy would leave the disease in place. A holy Father heals deeply, even when the healing hurts.

Suffering Is Not Always Discipline for Specific Sin

There is another error to avoid.

Not every suffering in the believer's life is discipline for a specific sin. Job's friends made this mistake. They assumed Job's suffering must be proof of hidden wickedness. They defended a simple moral equation: suffering means guilt; prosperity means favor.

God rebuked them.

Jesus corrected the same kind of thinking when His disciples asked about the man born blind:

"Master, who did sin, this man, or his parents, that he was born blind?" — **John 9:2**

Jesus answered:

"Neither hath this man sinned, nor his parents: but that the works of God should be made manifest in him." — **John 9:3**

The suffering was not traced to a particular sin in the way the disciples assumed.

This matters because some believers torment themselves by searching every hardship for a specific hidden cause. Self-examination is good. Humility is good. Asking the Lord to search the heart is good. But morbid speculation can become spiritually destructive.

The full character of God protects us here. He is wise. He is Father. He is faithful. He knows what He is doing. Sometimes He disciplines specific sin. Sometimes He refines faith. Sometimes He displays His works. Sometimes He teaches endurance. Sometimes He allows suffering for reasons hidden from us.

We should not assume more than Scripture allows.

The Cross and the Father's Hand

The cross stands behind the believer's confidence in discipline.

If God gave His Son for us, then His fatherly correction cannot be interpreted as hatred. Paul reasons this way:

"He that spared not his own Son, but delivered him up for us all, how shall he not with him also freely give us all things?" — **Romans 8:32**

The Father did not spare His own Son. He delivered Him up for His people. That act reveals the heart from which all His dealings with believers flow.

This does not mean every dealing is pleasant. The same chapter speaks of tribulation, distress, persecution, famine, nakedness, peril, and sword. Yet none of these separate believers from the love of God in Christ Jesus.

A Christian may be corrected severely and still be loved completely.

The cross proves it.

God's discipline is not the reversal of Calvary. It is one of the ways the benefits of Calvary are applied to the believer's life. The Son died to sanctify His people. The Father disciplines to make them partakers of His holiness. The Spirit works within them to produce fruit.

The triune God is not divided in the salvation of His people.

Eschatological Wrath and the Church

This distinction also matters for eschatology.

If believers are not appointed to wrath, then we must be careful when speaking about the church and end-time judgment. Paul writes:

"For God hath not appointed us to wrath, but to obtain salvation by our Lord Jesus Christ." — I Thessalonians 5:9

This promise does not mean the church will never suffer in the world. The New Testament repeatedly prepares believers for tribulation, persecution, and hatred. But suffering from the world is not the same as appointment to divine wrath.

This distinction should shape how we read prophetic passages. The wrath of God and the wrath of the Lamb belong to judicial judgment. The persecution of saints by wicked powers belongs to the hostility of the world against God's people. These categories may occur in the same period of history, but they should not be collapsed into one.

- The church may be refined.
- The church may be persecuted.
- The church may be disciplined.
- The church may be hated by the world.

But the church is not appointed to the condemning wrath from which Christ has delivered her.

Any doctrine that blurs this distinction risks weakening the believer's hope and confusing the work of Christ.

The Guardrail for Doctrine

The distinction between fatherly discipline and condemning wrath protects several doctrines.

It protects the sufficiency of the cross, because Christ has borne the believer's condemnation fully.

It protects assurance, because suffering does not mean the believer has fallen back under wrath.

It protects sanctification, because discipline is understood as loving correction toward holiness.

It protects pastoral care, because wounded believers are not crushed by careless accusations.

It protects repentance, because discipline is taken seriously without being mistaken for rejection.

It protects eschatology, because divine wrath and worldly tribulation are not treated as identical.

When this distinction is lost, doctrine becomes unstable. The believer's conscience is shaken. The cross seems incomplete. The Father's love appears uncertain. Suffering becomes impossible to interpret rightly.

But when the distinction is kept, the Christian can receive correction without despair.

The Father Who Corrects, Not the Judge Who Condemns

God disciplines His children.

He does not do so because Christ failed to satisfy justice. He does not do so because He has returned them to condemnation. He does not do so because His love has cooled.

He disciplines because He is Father.

- He corrects to restore.
- He wounds to heal.
- He exposes to cleanse.
- He humbles to save from pride.
- He chastens so His children may share His holiness.

The believer must not despise this discipline. But neither must he faint beneath it.

The Judge has already judged his sin in Christ.

The Father now trains him as a son.

Chapter 42 — The Shepherd Does Not Lose His Sheep

There are doctrines that become unstable when the character of Christ is not kept whole.

One of them is the security of the believer.

If Christ is treated merely as a helper, then salvation may seem fragile. If He is viewed only as an example, then the believer's hope rests too much upon imitation. If His love is separated from His power, we may wonder whether He desires to keep His people but cannot. If His power is separated from His faithfulness, we may wonder whether He can keep them but might not. If His holiness is separated from His mercy, wounded believers may fear that their failures will finally drive Him away.

But Scripture does not give us a partial Christ.

It gives us the Good Shepherd.

Jesus says:

"I am the good shepherd: the good shepherd giveth his life for the sheep." — **John 10:11**

That sentence is more than tenderness. It is doctrine. The Shepherd gives His life for the sheep. Their safety begins not with their grip on Him, but with His sacrifice for them.

Later in the same chapter He says:

"And I give unto them eternal life; and they shall never perish, neither shall any man pluck them out of my hand." — **John 10:28**

The Shepherd does not lose His sheep.

That truth is not an excuse for carelessness. It is not permission to sin. It is not a denial of warnings, discipline, endurance, or obedience. But it is a guardrail against every doctrine that makes salvation finally depend on the sheep being stronger than the Shepherd.

Security Begins with Christ, Not the Believer

Many Christians think of assurance by looking first at themselves.

They measure the strength of their faith, the consistency of their obedience, the sincerity of their repentance, the warmth of their affections, or the intensity of their prayers. Those things matter in their proper place. Scripture does call believers to examine themselves. Faith should bear fruit. Repentance should be real. Obedience is not optional.

But assurance does not begin there.

It begins with Christ.

Jesus says:

"My sheep hear my voice, and I know them, and they follow me." — **John 10:27**

The sheep hear and follow, but before the sentence moves to their safety, Jesus says, **"I know them."** The Shepherd's knowledge of His sheep is covenantal and personal. He does not merely know facts about them. He knows them as His own.

Then He gives eternal life.

Not temporary life. Not probationary life. Eternal life.

If eternal life can finally be lost, then the word **eternal** has been weakened. Jesus does not say, "I give unto them uncertain life." He says, **"I give unto them eternal life; and they shall never perish."**

The believer's hope rests in the Shepherd's gift, the Shepherd's knowledge, the Shepherd's hand, and the Shepherd's faithfulness.

The Father's Hand and the Son's Hand

Jesus continues:

"My Father, which gave them me, is greater than all; and no man is able to pluck them out of my Father's hand. I and my Father are one." — **John 10:29–30**

The security of the sheep is held in the hands of the Son and the Father. No created power is greater. No enemy can overpower the Shepherd. No accusation can surprise Him. No wolf is stronger than His hand.

This is not sentimental reassurance. It is Trinitarian security. The Father gives the sheep to the Son. The Son gives them eternal life. The Father and Son are one in the preservation of those who belong to Christ.

A doctrine that makes the sheep finally responsible for keeping themselves in the Shepherd's hand has inverted the image. Sheep are not strong. Shepherds are.

This does not make the sheep passive in the Christian life. They hear His voice. They follow Him. But their following is not what makes the Shepherd faithful. Their following is the evidence that they are His. Their preservation rests in Him.

Warnings Are Real

At this point, someone may object: Scripture contains warnings.

It does. The warnings are real, and we must not explain them away.

Believers are warned against unbelief, apostasy, hardness of heart, false teachers, love of the world, and continuing in sin. Churches are warned.

Professing believers are warned. The New Testament does not speak as though perseverance is unnecessary.

But warnings do not prove that the Shepherd loses true sheep. They are one of the means He uses to keep His sheep.

A father warns his child because the danger is real. A shepherd calls out because cliffs are real, wolves are real, wandering is real. The warning does not mean the shepherd is powerless. It means he actively guards the flock.

The same Christ who says His sheep shall never perish also tells His disciples to abide in Him. The same apostles who teach God's preserving grace also warn against falling away from an empty profession. These truths are not enemies.

- Warnings expose false assurance.
- Warnings awaken sleepy believers.
- Warnings call wandering sheep back.
- Warnings keep the church sober.
- Warnings are part of the Shepherd's care.

But they do not turn eternal life into a fragile arrangement.

False Profession Is Real

The New Testament also teaches that not everyone who appears to be Christ's sheep truly belongs to Him.

Jesus says:

"Not every one that saith unto me, Lord, Lord, shall enter into the kingdom of heaven; but he that doeth the will of my Father which is in heaven." — ***Matthew 7:21***

He then speaks of people who prophesied, cast out devils, and did many wonderful works in His name. His answer is terrifying:

*"I never knew you: depart from me, ye that work iniquity." — **Matthew 7:23***

He does not say, "I knew you once, but lost you." He says, **"I never knew you."**

This distinction is crucial. The doctrine of security does not teach that every person who makes a profession is saved no matter what fruit follows. It teaches that those truly known by Christ, given to Him by the Father, redeemed by His blood, and born of the Spirit will be kept by Him.

False profession must be exposed. Real faith must be encouraged. Those are not competing duties.

A careless version of eternal security says, "A prayer was prayed, so nothing else matters." That is not biblical assurance. Biblical assurance rests in Christ and is accompanied by the marks of His life in His people.

The Shepherd keeps His sheep. He does not promise security to goats who merely learned sheep-language.

Kept by the Power of God

Peter writes to suffering believers:

*"Who are kept by the power of God through faith unto salvation ready to be revealed in the last time." — **I Peter 1:5***

The believer is kept by the power of God.

That phrase should not be made small. The same God who created all things, raised Christ from the dead, rules nations, and will raise the dead at the last day keeps His people. Their preservation is not weak because they are weak. It is strong because God is strong.

Yet Peter says they are kept **through faith**. God's preserving power does not make faith unnecessary. It sustains faith. The believer continues believing because God keeps him. Again, God ordains the end and the means.

This guards against two errors.

One error says the believer must keep himself by his own power. That destroys assurance.

The other error says preservation does not involve continuing faith. That produces presumption.

Scripture says believers are kept by the power of God through faith. The keeping is divine. The faith is real. The salvation will be revealed in the last time.

The Intercession of Christ

The Shepherd keeps His sheep not only by power, but by priestly intercession.

Hebrews says:

"Wherefore he is able also to save them to the uttermost that come unto God by him, seeing he ever liveth to make intercession for them." — **Hebrews 7:25**

Christ saves to the uttermost. His saving work does not stop at conversion. He ever lives to make intercession for those who come unto God by Him.

This is a powerful answer to fear. The believer's failures are real. His weakness is real. His remaining sin is grievous. But Christ lives. His priesthood does not expire. His intercession does not fail. His sacrifice does not lose power.

Peter's life gives a concrete picture. Jesus told him:

"Simon, Simon, behold, Satan hath desired to have you, that he may sift you as wheat: But I have prayed for thee, that thy faith fail not." — **Luke 22:31–32**

Peter did fail grievously. He denied the Lord. But his faith did not finally fail because Christ had prayed for him. He was restored.

That is not permission to sin. Peter wept bitterly. Restoration was painful. But Christ's intercession was stronger than Peter's collapse.

The Shepherd does not abandon wounded sheep.

Nothing Shall Separate Us

Paul gives one of the strongest statements of security in Romans 8.

After declaring no condemnation in Christ, he asks:

"Who shall lay any thing to the charge of God's elect? It is God that justifieth." — **Romans 8:33**

If God justifies, no accusation can overturn His verdict.

Then:

"Who is he that condemneth? It is Christ that died, yea rather, that is risen again, who is even at the right hand of God, who also maketh intercession for us." — **Romans 8:34**

The death, resurrection, exaltation, and intercession of Christ all stand behind the believer's security.

Paul then asks:

"Who shall separate us from the love of Christ?" — **Romans 8:35**

He names tribulation, distress, persecution, famine, nakedness, peril, and sword. None of them can separate. He continues:

"For I am persuaded, that neither death, nor life, nor angels, nor principalities, nor powers, nor things present, nor things to come, Nor height, nor depth, nor any other creature, shall be able to separate us from the love of God, which is in Christ Jesus our Lord." — **Romans 8:38–39**

The list is comprehensive. Death cannot separate. Life cannot separate. Present things cannot separate. Future things cannot separate. No creature can separate.

The believer's security rests in the love of God in Christ Jesus our Lord.

Security and Holiness

Some fear that strong assurance will produce careless living.

False assurance can do that. Biblical assurance does not.

The same Shepherd who keeps His sheep also leads them. The same Christ who gives eternal life also calls His people to follow. The same grace that saves teaches believers to deny ungodliness and worldly lusts. The same Father who preserves His children disciplines them for holiness.

John writes:

"And every man that hath this hope in him purifieth himself, even as he is pure." — **I John 3:3**

True hope purifies. It does not produce indifference. A man who says, "I am secure, therefore sin does not matter," has not understood security. He has turned the Shepherd's faithfulness into an excuse to ignore the Shepherd's voice.

Christ does not keep His sheep by leaving them unchanged. He sanctifies them. He corrects them. He restores them. He leads them in paths of righteousness for His name's sake.

Security is not security in sin. It is security in Christ.

The Guardrail for Doctrine

The character of Christ guards the doctrine of security.

Because Christ is faithful, He will not abandon those given to Him.

Because Christ is powerful, no enemy can steal them from His hand.

Because Christ is just, He will not demand condemnation for sins He has already borne.

Because Christ is merciful, He restores wounded and wandering sheep.

Because Christ is holy, He does not preserve His people in order to leave them in corruption.

Because Christ is the Good Shepherd, His sheep are not finally lost.

When any of these truths are isolated, doctrine bends. If security is taught without holiness, it becomes presumption. If holiness is taught without security, assurance collapses. If warnings are taught without preservation, fear rules. If preservation is taught without warnings, carelessness grows.

The full character of God holds the doctrine together.

The Shepherd Who Keeps

The believer's hope is not that sheep are strong.

They are not.

They wander, stumble, fear, and often fail. Their understanding is limited. Their obedience is imperfect. Their strength is small.

But the Shepherd is strong.

- He gives His life for the sheep.
- He knows His own.
- He gives eternal life.
- He holds them in His hand.
- He intercedes for them.
- He restores them.
- He disciplines them.
- He leads them.
- He will bring them home.

The sheep follow because they are His.

And because they are His, they shall never perish.

Chapter 43 — Love Does Not Cancel Final Judgment

Final judgment is one of the doctrines most often softened in the name of love.

The reasoning usually sounds compassionate. God is love, therefore He surely will not judge forever. God is merciful, therefore hell must not be real in the way Scripture seems to say. God is good, therefore final condemnation must eventually give way to pardon. God is kind, therefore His warnings must be less severe than they sound.

But this is not how Scripture reasons.

The Bible never uses God's love to cancel His judgment. It never treats divine mercy as though it abolishes divine holiness. It never presents the compassion of Christ as a reason to doubt the warnings of Christ. The same God who delights in mercy also judges the wicked. The same Savior who receives sinners also speaks of everlasting punishment. The same Lamb who was slain also pours out wrath.

A doctrine of love that cannot account for final judgment is not biblical love.

It is a partial love, detached from holiness, justice, truth, wrath, and righteousness.

The Words of Jesus

No one spoke more clearly about final judgment than Jesus.

This must be faced honestly. Many people try to separate the gentle Jesus from the severe doctrine of hell, but the Gospels do not allow that division. Jesus warned of judgment repeatedly, plainly, and solemnly.

He said:

"And fear not them which kill the body, but are not able to kill the soul: but rather fear him which is able to destroy both soul and body in hell." — **Matthew 10:28**

He said:

"So shall it be at the end of the world: the angels shall come forth, and sever the wicked from among the just, And shall cast them into the furnace of fire: there shall be wailing and gnashing of teeth." — **Matthew 13:49–50**

He said:

"And these shall go away into everlasting punishment: but the righteous into life eternal." — **Matthew 25:46**

These are not the words of an unloving Christ. They are the words of the true Christ. His love does not make Him silent about judgment. His love makes Him truthful.

If our doctrine of love requires us to soften Jesus' warnings, then our doctrine of love is wrong.

Judgment and the Truthfulness of God

Final judgment must be held because God is true.

God does not threaten what He will never do. He does not warn merely for emotional effect. He does not speak terrifying words and then later reveal that they were never to be taken seriously. His warnings are not theatrical devices. They are truth.

Paul writes:

"But after thy hardness and impenitent heart treasurest up unto thyself wrath against the day of wrath and revelation of the righteous judgment of God; Who will render to every man according to his deeds." — **Romans 2:5–6**

The day of wrath is the revelation of God's righteous judgment. It is not the denial of His character. It is the unveiling of His character in judgment.

If final judgment is removed, God's warnings become unstable. The urgency of repentance weakens. The seriousness of sin fades. The cross loses part of its necessity. Evangelism becomes less rescue than invitation to personal improvement.

But Scripture presents judgment as certain because God is truthful.

The Judge of all the earth will do right, and He will do what He has said.

Judgment and the Love of God

God's love does not make judgment impossible.

This is where many modern instincts fail. They assume love and judgment are opposites. But righteous judgment can be an expression of love for what is good, true, holy, and just.

- Love for victims requires judgment against unrepentant evil.
- Love for truth requires judgment against lies.
- Love for holiness requires judgment against corruption.
- Love for creation requires judgment against everything that defiles it.
- Love for God's name requires judgment against blasphemy and idolatry.
- A love that never judges evil is not love. It is moral surrender.

The cross itself proves this. God's love did not lead Him to ignore judgment. It led Him to provide Christ, who bore judgment for sinners. If love canceled judgment, Calvary would be unnecessary. But Scripture says:

"Herein is love, not that we loved God, but that he loved us, and sent his Son to be the propitiation for our sins." — **I John 4:10**

Love sends the Son as propitiation. Love answers wrath through sacrifice. Love saves without denying judgment.

Final judgment is not contrary to the love displayed at the cross. It is the final outcome for those who refuse the only refuge God has provided in love.

The Cross and the Reality of Judgment

The cross is the strongest evidence that judgment is real.

If sin required the death of the Son of God, then sin cannot be treated lightly. If Christ bore wrath, then wrath is not imaginary. If the Father gave His Son to save sinners, then rejecting the Son is not a small matter.

Hebrews warns:

"Of how much sorer punishment, suppose ye, shall he be thought worthy, who hath trodden under foot the Son of God, and hath counted the blood of the covenant, wherewith he was sanctified, an unholy thing, and hath done despite unto the Spirit of grace?" — **Hebrews 10:29**

The gospel does not make judgment less serious. It makes rejection of grace more serious. Greater light brings greater accountability.

This is why preaching the love of God without warning of judgment is not faithful. The love of God is seen in the provision of Christ. But if men reject Christ, they reject the very mercy by which they must be saved.

The cross does not say, "Judgment no longer matters."

It says, "Judgment has fallen on Christ for all who take refuge in Him."

Outside of Him, judgment remains.

Universalism and the Problem of Scripture

One of the most direct distortions of love is universalism—the belief that all will finally be saved.

Its appeal is obvious. It seems emotionally satisfying. It appears to magnify mercy. It removes the horror of eternal judgment. It offers a final reconciliation without everlasting loss.

But it cannot survive the full testimony of Scripture.

Jesus speaks of a broad way that leads to destruction and a narrow way that leads to life. He speaks of foolish virgins shut out. He speaks of a rich man in torment. He speaks of outer darkness. He speaks of everlasting punishment. Revelation speaks of the lake of fire. Paul speaks of everlasting destruction from the presence of the Lord.

These passages cannot simply be brushed aside because they trouble us.

A theology that begins with the assumption that love must save all people will have to keep revising, softening, or reinterpreting texts until judgment no longer means what it plainly says. That is not submission to Scripture. It is the rule of human sentiment over revelation.

The question is not what we wish were true.

The question is what God has said.

Annihilation and the Weight of Jesus' Warning

Another view attempts to soften final judgment by teaching that the wicked will finally cease to exist rather than endure everlasting punishment.

This view often comes from a desire to take judgment seriously while avoiding the doctrine of eternal conscious punishment. It should be addressed with care, not caricature. Some who hold it are trying to honor Scripture as best they understand it.

Yet the strongest warnings of Jesus remain difficult for that view.

When Jesus says:

*"And these shall go away into everlasting punishment: but the righteous into life eternal." — **Matthew 25:46***

The parallel is sobering. Everlasting punishment stands opposite life eternal. The duration language should not be dismissed lightly.

Revelation also speaks of torment in severe terms:

*"And the smoke of their torment ascendeth up for ever and ever: and they have no rest day nor night..." — **Revelation 14:11***

Whatever interpretive questions surround apocalyptic imagery, the warning is dreadful. Scripture intends us to feel the terror of final judgment, not reduce it to something more acceptable to modern thought.

The doctrine is heavy. We should not speak of it glibly. But heaviness is not a reason to revise God's warnings. It is a reason to tremble.

Judgment and the Vindication of God

Final judgment also vindicates the character of God.

In this present age, evil often appears to win. The wicked prosper. The righteous suffer. Lies spread. The innocent are harmed. The powerful escape accountability. Martyrs die. The name of God is blasphemed. The world calls evil good and good evil.

If there is no final judgment, much of history remains morally unresolved.

Scripture gives a different end. God will judge.

John writes:

"And I saw a great white throne, and him that sat on it, from whose face the earth and the heaven fled away; and there was found no place for them. And I saw the dead, small and great, stand before God; and the books were opened…" — **Revelation 20:11–12**

No one is too small to be seen. No one is too great to be summoned. The dead stand before God. The books are opened. Hidden things are revealed. Every false refuge collapses.

This judgment is not an embarrassment to God's love. It is the final public vindication of His holiness, truth, justice, and righteousness.

The world will know that God was right.

Judgment and the New Creation

Final judgment is also necessary for the purity of the new creation.

Revelation says of the holy city:

"And there shall in no wise enter into it any thing that defileth, neither whatsoever worketh abomination, or maketh a lie: but they which are written in the Lamb's book of life." — **Revelation 21:27**

The new creation is not merely this world improved. It is a world cleansed of all defilement. No lie enters. No abomination enters. Nothing that corrupts, deceives, destroys, or profanes remains within it.

If God allowed unrepentant evil into the eternal state, heaven would not remain heaven. The curse would continue. The wounds of the old creation would be carried into the new.

Judgment is therefore part of God's mercy toward His redeemed creation. He removes what defiles. He brings His people into a world where righteousness dwells.

Love does not cancel this. Love requires it.

The Tone of the Doctrine

Because final judgment is so severe, it must be handled with reverence.

No Christian should speak of hell with delight. No preacher should use judgment as a weapon for personal anger. No teacher should describe the fate of the lost with cold satisfaction. If Christ wept over Jerusalem, His servants should not speak of judgment with dry eyes and hard hearts.

But neither should reverence become silence.

The apostles warned. Jesus warned. The prophets warned. To refuse warning in the name of compassion is not compassion. If judgment is real, warning is love.

Paul said:

"Knowing therefore the terror of the Lord, we persuade men..." — **2 Corinthians 5:11**

The terror of the Lord did not make him cruel. It made him persuasive. It moved him to plead, reason, preach, suffer, and call sinners to reconciliation.

That is the tone we need: sober, urgent, truthful, tearful, and centered on Christ.

The Guardrail for Doctrine

Love does not cancel final judgment.

That truth protects several doctrines.

It protects the truthfulness of Christ, because His warnings are received rather than softened.

It protects the holiness of God, because evil is not treated as eternally tolerable.

It protects the justice of God, because every wrong is answered.

It protects the cross, because Christ saves from real wrath.

It protects evangelism, because sinners are truly in danger and truly invited to flee to Christ.

It protects the hope of the new creation, because nothing defiling will enter.

It protects love itself, because love is kept holy, truthful, and morally serious.

If love is used to deny judgment, love has been severed from the God who is love. It becomes an argument against His own Word.

The full character of God does not allow that.

The Love That Warns

God is love.

- Therefore He sent His Son.
- Therefore He calls sinners to repentance.
- Therefore He delays judgment with longsuffering.
- Therefore He provides mercy through blood.
- Therefore He warns before wrath falls.

But love does not cancel judgment.

The same Christ who says, "Come unto me," also says to fear Him who can destroy both soul and body in hell. The same Savior who receives sinners will one day separate the wicked from among the just. The same Lamb who was slain will judge those who reject Him.

This should make us tremble.

It should also make us preach Christ with urgency.

Final judgment is real. But so is the Savior.

The door of mercy is open now.

Chapter 44 — The New Creation: The Character of God Delighting His People Forever

The final hope of Scripture is not merely escape.

It is not merely that sinners are forgiven, though forgiveness is necessary and glorious. It is not merely that pain ends, though the ending of pain is precious. It is not merely that death is defeated, though death must be swallowed up in victory.

The final hope is God dwelling with His redeemed people in a creation made new.

Revelation says:

*"And I heard a great voice out of heaven saying, Behold, the tabernacle of God is with men, and he will dwell with them, and they shall be his people, and God himself shall be with them, and be their God." — **Revelation 21:3***

That is the goal toward which redemption moves: **God with His people.**

The new creation is not an afterthought. It is the final display of God's character in redeemed creation. Everything sin has defiled will be cleansed. Everything God promised will be fulfilled. Every enemy will be removed. Every tear will be wiped away. Every redeemed creature will know, without obstruction, the goodness, holiness, glory, love, wisdom, justice, mercy, and faithfulness of God.

The full character of God will not merely be studied there.

It will be enjoyed forever.

A World Where God's Holiness Is No Longer Veiled

In this present age, God's holiness is often resisted.

Men call evil good and good evil. Sin is normalized. Purity is mocked. God's commands are treated as oppressive. Even within the redeemed, remaining sin resists holiness. We know God is holy, but we do not yet live in a world where every creature loves His holiness perfectly.

The new creation will be different.

John writes:

"And there shall in no wise enter into it any thing that defileth, neither whatsoever worketh abomination, or maketh a lie: but they which are written in the Lamb's book of life." — **Revelation 21:27**

Nothing defiling enters.

That sentence is not harsh to the redeemed. It is one of the greatest comforts imaginable. No corruption. No hidden evil. No temptation. No uncleanness. No betrayal. No lie. No profaning of what is holy. No private sin eating away at love. No darkness passing itself off as light.

God's holiness will no longer feel like a threat to His people, because His people will finally be made fully holy. They will not merely be declared righteous while still battling corruption. They will be transformed, glorified, and made fit for the presence of God.

The holiness that once exposed their sin will become the atmosphere of their joy.

A World Where Justice Is Finally Settled

The new creation comes after judgment.

That order matters. God does not bring His people into eternity by ignoring evil. He judges it. He removes it. He answers it. The new heavens and new earth are not built on unresolved injustice.

Revelation shows the great white throne before the final vision of the holy city. The books are opened. The dead are judged. Death and hell are cast into the lake of fire. Only then does John see the new heaven and new earth.

This means the peace of the eternal state is not shallow peace. It is peace after justice has been done.

In this present age, justice often appears delayed. The wicked prosper. The innocent suffer. The truth is buried. The proud escape earthly courts. But God has appointed a day when every hidden thing will be brought to light.

Paul says:

"Because he hath appointed a day, in the which he will judge the world in righteousness by that man whom he hath ordained…" — **Acts 17:31**

The new creation rests on the righteousness of that judgment. No one in eternity will wonder whether God overlooked evil. No redeemed voice will say that His court was unfair. Every verdict will be right. Every wrong will be answered. Every act of mercy will be seen as mercy. Every act of judgment will be seen as truth.

The Judge of all the earth will do right, and the world to come will shine with the settled peace of His justice.

A World Where Mercy Is Remembered Forever

The new creation will not make mercy obsolete.

The redeemed will not forget that they are redeemed. They will not stand in glory as though they had always belonged there by nature. They will know that they are in the city because of the Lamb.

John says nothing defiling enters, but only:

"they which are written in the Lamb's book of life." — **Revelation 21:27**

That phrase keeps mercy at the center of eternity. The inhabitants of the new creation are not those who were naturally undefiled. They are those whose names are written in the Lamb's book of life.

The Lamb will remain central.

Revelation says:

"And I beheld, and, lo, in the midst of the throne and of the four beasts, and in the midst of the elders, stood a Lamb as it had been slain…" — **Revelation 5:6**

The scars of redemption are not an embarrassment to glory. The Lamb is worshiped precisely as the Lamb who was slain. Heaven sings:

"Thou art worthy… for thou wast slain, and hast redeemed us to God by thy blood…" — **Revelation 5:9**

Mercy will never become a small subject to the redeemed. They will know forever that they are there because Christ shed His blood. The memory of sin will not bring shame in the old way, for guilt will be gone. But the knowledge of mercy will deepen worship forever.

Grace will not be forgotten in glory.

A World Where Love Is Perfected

In this life, love is real but imperfect.

Even among believers, love is mixed with weakness. We love God, yet not as we should. We love one another, yet often with impatience, selfishness, fear, pride, or dullness. We know the commandment. We taste the love of Christ. We are taught by the Spirit. Yet our love remains incomplete.

The new creation will be a world of perfected love because it will be a world of perfected holiness.

That matters. Love will not be made perfect by becoming less holy. It will be made perfect because sin is gone. No envy will corrupt it. No lust will counterfeit it. No bitterness will poison it. No pride will use it. No fear will distort it.

John writes:

"Beloved, now are we the sons of God, and it doth not yet appear what we shall be: but we know that, when he shall appear, we shall be like him; for we shall see him as he is." — **I John 3:2**

We shall be like Him. That does not mean believers become divine. It means they will be conformed to the image of Christ in glorified holiness. The love of God will be known, received, and reflected without the remaining corruption of the flesh.

The fellowship of the redeemed will be unlike anything known fully now. No suspicion. No betrayal. No selfish ambition. No manipulation. No coldness. No failure to love God with all the heart, soul, mind, and strength. No failure to love the neighbor rightly.

God's love will fill the life of His people, and His people will finally love Him without hindrance.

A World Where Truth Is Never Bent

The new creation will also be a world of truth.

Revelation says no one who makes a lie will enter. That is not a small detail. Lies have marked the fallen world from the garden onward. The serpent lied about God. Sinners lie about themselves. False prophets lie in God's name. Nations build identities on lies. Men suppress the truth in unrighteousness.

But the eternal city admits no lie.

The God of truth will dwell with a truthful people in a truthful world.

That should make us long for the new creation. Imagine a world where nothing is hidden under deception. No false teaching. No hypocrisy. No self-deception. No manipulation of words. No twisting of Scripture. No promises broken. No public narratives built to protect evil. No heart pretending to be what it is not.

Truth will not be fought there. It will be loved.

Jesus said:

"I am the way, the truth, and the life..." — **John 14:6**

The new creation will be centered on Him. Therefore it will be a world where truth is not merely known, but delighted in. Every creature in that redeemed order will live in agreement with reality as God defines it.

No one will ever again ask whether God really said.

A World Where God's Faithfulness Is Fully Vindicated

The new creation is the final proof that not one word of God fails.

Every promise will stand fulfilled. Every covenant purpose will reach its appointed end. Every prophecy God intended for that final state will be realized. Every hope He gave His people will prove more solid than the world that opposed it.

Peter writes:

*"Nevertheless we, according to his promise, look for new heavens and a new earth, wherein dwelleth righteousness." — **2 Peter 3:13**

According to His promise.

The new creation is not human optimism. It is not poetic longing. It is promise. And because God is faithful, His people look for it.

That phrase—**wherein dwelleth righteousness**—is beautiful. Righteousness will not merely visit. It will dwell. In this present age, righteousness is often contested, resisted, mocked, or persecuted. In the world to come, righteousness will be at home.

That is where history is going.

The faithful God who promised redemption will finish redemption. He who began a good work in His people will perform it until the day of Jesus Christ. He who promised eternal life before the world began will bring His people into the fullness of it.

The new creation will be God's faithfulness made visible.

A World Where God's Glory Is the Light

John writes:

*"And the city had no need of the sun, neither of the moon, to shine in it: for the glory of God did lighten it, and the Lamb is the light thereof." — **Revelation 21:23**

The glory of God will be the light of the city, and the Lamb will be its light.

Creation has always declared God's glory, but the new creation will be filled with that glory in a way this age has not yet known. No veil of sin. No blindness of unbelief. No idols stealing worship. No shadows cast by corruption. God's glory will not be argued for there. It will shine.

This is the answer to every man-centered view of salvation. God does not redeem merely to improve human circumstances. He redeems for His glory and for the joy of His people in His glory. The two belong together. God is glorified, and His people are satisfied in Him.

The Lamb is the light. That means the glory of the new creation is forever Christ-centered. The One who was crucified is the One who illuminates eternity. The wounds of the Lamb do not fade into the background of heaven's worship. They remain central to the glory of God revealed to His people.

The final world is not merely beautiful.

It is radiant with God.

A World Where Sovereignty Is No Longer Questioned

In this age, God's sovereignty is often questioned because history is painful and confusing.

Men ask why God allows evil, why He delays judgment, why the righteous suffer, why the wicked prosper, why prayers wait, why providence takes such strange paths. Some questions are answered in part. Others remain beyond us. We live by faith, not by sight.

In the new creation, faith will give way to sight.

The redeemed will not accuse God of mismanaging history. They will not discover that His wisdom failed. They will not look back and find that His sovereignty was careless. They will see that the Lord God omnipotent reigneth, and that His reign was always wise, holy, good, and faithful.

Revelation gives the worship of heaven:

*"Great and marvellous are thy works, Lord God Almighty; just and true are thy ways, thou King of saints." — **Revelation 15:3***

That song will not become less true in eternity. It will become more fully understood. God's works are great and marvelous. His ways are just and true.

The mysteries that humbled us will become reasons for worship. The providences we could not trace will be seen in the light of His wisdom. The delays that tested faith will be recognized as perfect. The sovereignty of God will not feel like a doctrine to defend. It will be the joy of the redeemed world.

The End of Death, Sorrow, Crying, and Pain

The new creation reveals God's compassion by the removal of all that has wounded His people.

Revelation says:

"And God shall wipe away all tears from their eyes; and there shall be no more death, neither sorrow, nor crying, neither shall there be any more pain: for the former things are passed away." — **Revelation 21:4**

This is not abstract theology. These words are tender.

God Himself wipes away tears. Death is gone. Sorrow is gone. Crying is gone. Pain is gone. The former things are passed away.

The God who is holy enough to exclude defilement is also tender enough to wipe tears. The God who judges evil is also the God who heals the grief of His people. His final world is not cold perfection. It is holy joy.

Every funeral points toward the need for this promise. Every hospital room, every grave, every lonely night of grief, every scar left by sin, every cry that seemed unheard—all of it will meet the compassion of God in the end.

He does not merely stop death.

He comforts His people.

The Full Character of God in the Final Hope

The new creation is not merely a location. It is the final display of the full character of God in redeemed fellowship with His people.

- His holiness is seen because nothing defiles.
- His justice is seen because evil has been judged.
- His mercy is seen because the redeemed are there by the Lamb's blood.
- His grace is seen because none earned the city.
- His love is seen because God dwells with His people.
- His truth is seen because no lie enters.
- His faithfulness is seen because every promise stands fulfilled.
- His wisdom is seen because all His ways are vindicated.
- His sovereignty is seen because His kingdom cannot be moved.
- His glory is seen because it gives light to the city.

This is why the final hope matters doctrinally. If our view of eternity is thin, our view of God will become thin. The biblical hope is not clouds, vague spirituality, or endless religious atmosphere. It is resurrection, creation renewed, righteousness dwelling, God present, the Lamb glorified, and the redeemed made whole.

The end of the story reveals the God who wrote it.

Behold, I Make All Things New

John records:

"And he that sat upon the throne said, Behold, I make all things new. And he said unto me, Write: for these words are true and faithful." — **Revelation 21:5**

True and faithful.

The promise of the new creation rests on the character of God. He will make all things new, and His words can be trusted. The world as it is now will not have the final word. Sin will not. Death will not. Satan will not. Sorrow will not. The grave will not.

God will.

- He will dwell with His people.
- He will wipe away every tear.
- He will remove every defiling thing.
- He will fill the city with His glory.
- He will make all things new.

The final hope of the believer is not merely that suffering ends.

It is that God remains, God reigns, God fulfills, God dwells, and God delights His people forever in the fullness of who He is.

PART FIVE

Living Before the
Full Character of God

Chapter 45 — Worshiping God for All That He Is

Doctrine should become worship.

If the study of God's character does not lead the heart to reverence, gratitude, humility, repentance, trust, and praise, then something has gone wrong. The aim is not merely to define God correctly. It is to know Him truly and worship Him rightly.

This matters because even sound doctrine can be handled in an unsound spirit. A man can defend God's holiness and remain proud. He can speak of sovereignty and become cold. He can explain grace and be ungracious. He can teach the love of God while lacking love for God. He can study divine attributes as though he were examining a subject beneath him rather than bowing before the Lord above him.

But God is not an object of study only.

He is the living God.

The right response to His character is worship.

David says:

"Give unto the LORD the glory due unto his name; worship the LORD in the beauty of holiness." — **Psalm 29:2**

There is glory due unto His name. Worship is not man's generous offering to God, as though God needed our approval. Worship is the creature giving rightful honor to the Creator. It is the redeemed heart answering the revelation of God with reverence and praise.

To know God as He is should make shallow worship impossible.

Worship Must Be Governed by Revelation

True worship begins with God's self-revelation.

We do not decide what God is like and then worship the image we have formed. That is idolatry, even if the image is mental rather than carved from wood or stone. The human heart is skilled at making a god who comforts its preferences, approves its desires, and avoids its fears.

Scripture does not permit that.

Jesus said:

*"God is a Spirit: and they that worship him must worship him in spirit and in truth." — **John 4:24***

Truth is not optional in worship. Sincerity alone is not enough. Emotion alone is not enough. Tradition alone is not enough. Beauty alone is not enough. Worship must answer the God who has revealed Himself.

This means worship must be corrected by Scripture. If our worship celebrates what God condemns, it is not true worship. If it hides the attributes of God that make us uncomfortable, it is not full worship. If it magnifies love while ignoring holiness, or mercy while ignoring justice, or nearness while ignoring glory, it becomes distorted.

The God we worship must be the God who is.

The Whole God Must Be Praised

Partial worship often comes from partial doctrine.

Some worship God almost entirely for His kindness but rarely tremble before His holiness. Others emphasize His majesty but speak little of His tenderness. Some rejoice in grace but rarely confess sin. Others speak much of judgment but little of mercy. Some delight in His nearness but lose the fear of His greatness. Others defend His transcendence but forget that He is Father to His children.

But Scripture does not divide God that way.

The seraphim cry:

"Holy, holy, holy, is the LORD of hosts: the whole earth is full of his glory." — **Isaiah 6:3**

The redeemed in Revelation sing:

"Great and marvellous are thy works, Lord God Almighty; just and true are thy ways, thou King of saints." — **Revelation 15:3**

The worship of heaven is not thin. It is full. God's holiness, glory, power, justice, truth, kingship, worthiness, redemption, and judgment are all praised.

That should shape the church now.

We should worship God for His love and for His holiness.

- For His mercy and for His justice.
- For His grace and for His truth.
- For His patience and for His wrath against evil.
- For His nearness and for His majesty.
- For His tenderness and for His consuming fire.

Not because these are competing sides of God, but because the one living God is all that He is perfectly.

Worship and the Fear of God

Worship without the fear of God becomes casual.

The fear of God is not the terror of a condemned man fleeing from judgment. For the believer, it is reverent awe, holy seriousness, trembling love, and humble awareness that God is God and we are not.

The psalmist says:

*"But as for me, I will come into thy house in the multitude of thy mercy: and in thy fear will I worship toward thy holy temple." — **Psalm 5:7***

Mercy and fear belong together. The psalmist comes because of mercy, but he worships in fear. Mercy does not make God less holy. Forgiveness does not make reverence unnecessary. Grace does not turn worship into casual familiarity.

This is badly needed in an age that often confuses intimacy with informality. God does bring His people near. Believers cry, "Abba, Father." They are loved, adopted, accepted in Christ, and invited to come boldly unto the throne of grace. But boldness is not irreverence. Nearness is not flippancy.

The throne of grace is still a throne.

The Father who receives us is still the Holy One.

Worship and Humility

The full character of God humbles worshipers.

Pride cannot survive long before the true God. His holiness exposes us. His wisdom surpasses us. His sovereignty lowers us. His grace removes boasting. His mercy reminds us that we had no claim. His glory reveals our smallness. His truth strips away self-deception.

When Isaiah saw the Lord, he did not congratulate himself for having a spiritual experience. He said:

*"Woe is me! for I am undone; because I am a man of unclean lips, and I dwell in the midst of a people of unclean lips: for mine eyes have seen the King, the LORD of hosts." — **Isaiah 6:5***

True worship does not inflate man. It undoes him.

But God does not undo His people to leave them destroyed. In Isaiah's vision, cleansing follows confession. The coal touches his lips. His iniquity is taken away. His sin is purged.

That is the pattern of biblical worship. God is exalted. Man is humbled. Sin is confessed. Grace is received. Service follows.

A church that never confesses sin in worship has likely lost sight of holiness. A church that never rejoices in grace has likely lost sight of mercy. A church that never bows has likely lost sight of glory.

Worship and Gratitude

To know God fully is to become thankful.

Every attribute gives reason for gratitude. We thank Him that He is holy, because His holiness means evil will not define eternity. We thank Him that He is just, because no wrong will remain unresolved. We thank Him that He is merciful, because we deserved judgment and received compassion. We thank Him that He is gracious, because salvation is gift. We thank Him that He is faithful, because His promises do not fail.

The psalmist says:

*"O give thanks unto the LORD; for he is good: for his mercy endureth for ever." — **Psalm 136:1***

His goodness and mercy become the ground of thanksgiving.

But gratitude should not be confined only to pleasant providences. The mature believer learns to thank God for who He is even when circumstances are painful. That does not mean pretending grief is not grief. It means God's character remains worthy when life is hard.

Habakkuk could say:

"Although the fig tree shall not blossom, neither shall fruit be in the vines; the labour of the olive shall fail, and the fields shall yield no meat; the flock shall be cut off from the fold, and there shall be no herd in the stalls: Yet I will rejoice in the LORD, I will joy in the God of my salvation." — **Habakkuk 3:17–18**

That is worship rooted in God, not merely in gifts.

Worship and the Word

God-centered worship must be Word-saturated.

If worship is governed by revelation, then Scripture must shape its content, language, priorities, and boundaries. God's people must sing truth, pray truth, hear truth, confess truth, and respond to truth.

Paul writes:

"Let the word of Christ dwell in you richly in all wisdom; teaching and admonishing one another in psalms and hymns and spiritual songs, singing with grace in your hearts to the Lord." — **Colossians 3:16**

The word of Christ dwelling richly leads to singing. Worship is not less heartfelt because it is doctrinal. It becomes more deeply heartfelt because truth gives the heart something worthy to answer.

Shallow lyrics produce shallow worship. Vague language produces vague affections. Songs that could be sung to a human lover, a general deity, or personal inspiration do not serve the church well. The people of God need worship that names the God of Scripture and praises Him according to what He has revealed.

The church should sing of the blood of Christ.

- The holiness of God.
- The mercy of God.
- The resurrection.
- The faithfulness of His promises.
- The return of Christ.
- The judgment of evil.
- The hope of glory.
- The triune God.

Worship teaches. Therefore worship must be true.

Worship and Obedience

Worship cannot be separated from obedience.

God is not honored by songs that rise from a life that refuses His commands. He is not impressed by raised hands while the heart clings to rebellion. He does not receive outward worship as a substitute for surrendered obedience.

Samuel told Saul:

*"Hath the LORD as great delight in burnt offerings and sacrifices, as in obeying the voice of the LORD? Behold, to obey is better than sacrifice, and to hearken than the fat of rams." — **I Samuel 15:22***

Obedience is better than sacrifice.

This does not mean worship must wait until we are sinless. If that were true, no one would worship. It means worship must not become a covering for rebellion. The worshiper who sins must come confessing, not pretending. He must come through blood, not through performance. He must come willing to be corrected by the God he praises.

Jesus said:

"If ye love me, keep my commandments." — **John 14:15**

Love for God has a shape. It obeys.

The man who sings of God's holiness while cherishing secret sin is being summoned by his own song to repent. The man who praises God's mercy while refusing mercy to others has not yet let worship search him deeply enough. The man who confesses Christ as Lord while disobeying His Word is using language that will testify against him unless he repents.

True worship offers the whole life.

Worship and the Church

Worship is personal, but it is not merely private.

God saves a people. He builds a church. He gathers His redeemed to praise Him together. Corporate worship is one of the great privileges of Christian life.

The psalmist says:

"O magnify the LORD with me, and let us exalt his name together." — **Psalm 34:3**

Together.

There is something fitting about the people of God joining their voices. The church is not a crowd of isolated worshipers who happen to stand in the same room. It is the body of Christ, the household of God, the redeemed assembly, the bride awaiting her Bridegroom.

Corporate worship reminds us that salvation is bigger than individual experience. We hear others confess the same Lord. We sing truths that are not dependent on our mood. We sit under the same Word. We come to the same table. We join the worship of saints across generations and anticipate the worship of heaven.

This should make worship serious, joyful, and humble. We are not attending a religious performance. We are gathering before God.

Worship and Suffering

The full character of God also teaches us to worship in suffering.

This is not natural. Pain narrows vision. Grief exhausts the heart. Fear makes God seem distant. But worship in suffering does not require the denial of sorrow. It requires bringing sorrow before the God who is worthy.

Job lost almost everything. Yet Scripture says:

*"Then Job arose, and rent his mantle, and shaved his head, and fell down upon the ground, and worshipped." — **Job 1:20***

He grieved. He tore his robe. He shaved his head. Then he worshiped.

This is not shallow praise. It is costly worship. It does not pretend the loss is small. It declares that God remains God in the ashes.

The suffering believer may worship through tears. He may worship with trembling voice. He may worship by simply refusing to curse God. He may worship by saying, "Though he slay me, yet will I trust in him." He may worship by clinging to promises when he feels nothing.

God is worthy in the valley as truly as on the mountain.

Worship and Joy

Reverence does not cancel joy.

Some people think serious worship must be joyless. That is false. The fear of God and the joy of the Lord belong together. The God who is holy is also good. The God who humbles us also saves us. The God who exposes sin also forgives it. The God whose glory overwhelms us also welcomes us in Christ.

The psalmist says:

"Serve the LORD with gladness: come before his presence with singing." —
Psalm 100:2

Gladness is commanded. Singing is fitting. Joy belongs in worship because God is delightful. He is not merely correct. He is beautiful. He is not merely powerful. He is good. He is not merely to be feared. He is to be loved.

Christian joy is not shallow excitement. It is gladness rooted in God's character and saving work. It can coexist with tears because it rests deeper than circumstance.

- A church that loses reverence becomes casual.
- A church that loses joy becomes cold.
- A church that loses truth becomes unstable.

The full character of God gives us all three: reverence, joy, and truth.

The Worship of Heaven

Earthly worship prepares us for heavenly worship.

Revelation gives repeated glimpses of worship around the throne. The living creatures say:

"Holy, holy, holy, Lord God Almighty, which was, and is, and is to come." —
Revelation 4:8

The elders say:

"Thou art worthy, O Lord, to receive glory and honour and power: for thou hast created all things, and for thy pleasure they are and were created." — **Revelation 4:11**

The redeemed sing to the Lamb:

"Thou art worthy… for thou wast slain, and hast redeemed us to God by thy blood…" — **Revelation 5:9**

Heaven's worship is God-centered, Christ-exalting, blood-conscious, holiness-filled, truth-saturated, and full of awe. It does not hide the character of God. It rejoices in it.

That is where the church is going.

Our worship now should be shaped by the worship that will never end. Not identical in form, because we remain on earth. But aligned in truth, reverence, joy, and Christ-centered praise.

The God Worthy of All Worship

God is worthy of worship because He is God.

- Not because He benefits us, though He does.
- Not because He saves us, though He has.
- Not because He comforts us, though He will.
- Not because He answers us, though He hears.

He is worthy because of who He is.

- Holy.
- Glorious.
- Eternal.
- Good.
- Righteous.

- Just.
- True.
- Faithful.
- Loving.
- Merciful.
- Gracious.
- Patient.
- Kind.
- Wise.
- Sovereign.
- Jealous for His name.
- Wrathful against evil.
- A consuming fire.
- Father, Son, and Holy Ghost.

The proper response is worship.

Not partial worship for a partial god.

Not shallow worship for a vague deity.

Not casual worship for a domesticated lord.

Whole worship for the whole God.

Let the church recover the full character of God, and her worship will deepen. Her songs will gain weight. Her prayers will gain reverence. Her preaching will gain force. Her repentance will become honest. Her joy will become stronger. Her hope will become clearer.

The more truly we know God, the more rightly we will worship Him.

And the more rightly we worship Him, the more our lives will confess that He alone is worthy.

Chapter 46 — Trusting the God Whose Character Cannot Fail

Trust is not built on ignorance.

Faith is sometimes spoken of as though it means believing without reason, resting without knowledge, or closing the eyes and hoping for the best. But biblical faith is not blind confidence in an unknown God. It is trust in the God who has revealed Himself.

The more truly we know His character, the more firmly we can trust Him.

This does not mean trust becomes easy. Faith often lives under pressure. It is tested by pain, delay, confusion, loss, fear, unanswered questions, and circumstances that seem to contradict what God has promised. The believer may know true doctrine and still tremble. He may believe God is good and still weep. He may confess God is sovereign and still feel the weight of uncertainty.

But faith has somewhere to stand.

It stands on the character of God.

David says:

*"And they that know thy name will put their trust in thee: for thou, LORD, hast not forsaken them that seek thee." — **Psalm 9:10***

They that know His name put their trust in Him. His name is not a mere label. It is the revelation of who He is. To know His name is to know His character, His ways, His faithfulness, His mercy, His power, His holiness, His covenant reliability.

Trust grows where God is known.

Trusting God When We Do Not Understand

There are times when God's ways are hidden from us.

We do not see the end. We do not know why a door closes, why a prayer waits, why a wound remains, why an enemy prospers, why a trial continues, or why obedience seems to lead into deeper hardship rather than relief. The mind reaches for answers and finds none that satisfy.

Scripture does not pretend this struggle is imaginary.

Job did not understand his suffering. Joseph did not understand the full meaning of the pit or the prison while he was in them. Habakkuk struggled with the violence and injustice around him. The psalmists repeatedly asked, "How long?" The disciples did not understand the cross as it unfolded before their eyes.

Faith is not the absence of questions.

Faith is trusting God when the questions remain unanswered.

Solomon writes:

"Trust in the LORD with all thine heart; and lean not unto thine own understanding. In all thy ways acknowledge him, and he shall direct thy paths."
— Proverbs 3:5–6

The command is not to abandon understanding altogether. Scripture calls us to wisdom. But our understanding must not become the foundation beneath God. We are not permitted to trust God only when His ways make immediate sense to us.

His wisdom is higher than ours.

There are times when the most faithful thing a believer can say is not, "I understand," but, "I know Him."

Trusting God's Goodness

God's goodness is one of the foundations of trust.

If God were powerful but not good, His sovereignty would terrify us. If He were wise but not good, His counsel could become a mystery to fear rather than a refuge. If He were holy but not good, His purity would only expose us. But God is good.

The psalmist says:

*"O taste and see that the LORD is good: blessed is the man that trusteth in him." — **Psalm 34:8***

The goodness of God does not mean life will always feel good. It does not mean every providence will be pleasant. It does not mean the believer will be spared grief, disappointment, betrayal, sickness, persecution, or death.

It means that God Himself is good in all His ways.

This distinction matters. Many believers stumble because they measure God's goodness by the immediate sweetness of their circumstances. When life is pleasant, they feel God must be good. When pain comes, they wonder if His goodness has changed.

But circumstances are not the measure of God's character.

The cross proves that. The darkest event in history was also the place where God displayed saving goodness beyond all measure. If we had stood at Calvary with only human sight, we might have seen defeat, injustice, abandonment, and horror. But God was accomplishing redemption.

The believer can trust God's goodness even when the present moment is bitter.

Trusting God's Wisdom

Trust also rests on God's wisdom.

We often want God to do what seems best to us. We bring Him our plans, our timing, our desired outcomes, and our preferred path. When He does not follow them, we are tempted to think He has failed to answer wisely.

But God sees what we cannot.

He sees the end from the beginning. He knows the hidden motives of hearts. He understands consequences generations beyond us. He knows which mercies would ruin us if given too soon. He knows which delays are necessary. He knows which losses will humble, purify, redirect, or deepen us. He knows what will glorify His name and conform His people to Christ.

Paul says:

"O the depth of the riches both of the wisdom and knowledge of God! how unsearchable are his judgments, and his ways past finding out!" — **Romans 11:33**

Unsearchable does not mean irrational. It means deeper than our searching can exhaust. His ways are not foolish because we cannot trace them. They are wise beyond us.

This humbles prayer. We may ask boldly, but we must not demand arrogantly. We may pour out desire, but we must yield to wisdom. We may plead for relief, but we must trust the Father when His answer is not what we expected.

Faith says, "Lord, I do not see what You see."

Trusting God's Faithfulness

Trust would collapse if God could change His mind in the way sinful men do.

People make promises and fail to keep them. They forget, weaken, deceive, exaggerate, or discover they do not have the power to do what they said. Even well-meaning people can fail because they are limited.

God is not like man.

*"Know therefore that the LORD thy God, he is God, the faithful God, which keepeth covenant and mercy with them that love him and keep his commandments to a thousand generations." — **Deuteronomy 7:9***

He is the faithful God.

That means His promises are not fragile. His covenant mercy is not unstable. His Word does not expire. His truthfulness does not weaken under pressure. His purposes do not decay with time.

This matters in seasons of delay. Waiting can make promises feel distant. Abraham waited. Israel waited. David waited. The prophets waited. The church waits for the return of Christ. Delay is not denial when the faithful God has spoken.

Peter says:

*"The Lord is not slack concerning his promise, as some men count slackness; but is longsuffering to us-ward, not willing that any should perish, but that all should come to repentance." — **2 Peter 3:9***

God is not slack. What men interpret as delay may be longsuffering. The timetable of God is not proof against His faithfulness. It is governed by His wisdom, patience, and purpose.

The believer can wait because God does not forget.

Trusting God's Power

A promise is only as secure as the one who makes it.

God is not only faithful in intention. He is almighty in power. He can do what He has said.

Jeremiah prayed:

"Ah Lord GOD! behold, thou hast made the heaven and the earth by thy great power and stretched out arm, and there is nothing too hard for thee." — **Jeremiah 32:17**

Nothing is too hard for Him.

That does not mean God will do everything we imagine. His power is not subject to human demand. But it does mean no circumstance is beyond His ability. No enemy is too strong. No providence is too tangled. No grave is too sealed. No promise is too difficult.

This is why Abraham could trust God concerning Isaac. Hebrews says Abraham accounted:

"that God was able to raise him up, even from the dead." — **Hebrews 11:19**

Faith looked beyond visible impossibility to the power of God.

Believers need that same confidence. When sin seems too strong, God is able. When the future seems closed, God is able. When the church seems weak, Christ is able to build it. When death comes, God is able to raise the dead.

Trust does not rest in likelihood.

It rests in the God with whom nothing is too hard.

Trusting God's Love

The love of God gives warmth to trust.

A believer may acknowledge God's sovereignty and still wonder whether God's heart is toward him. He may confess God's power and still fear that power will be used against him. The gospel answers that fear with the love of God in Christ.

Paul writes:

"He that spared not his own Son, but delivered him up for us all, how shall he not with him also freely give us all things?" — **Romans 8:32**

The cross is the believer's proof of love.

When circumstances seem to argue against God's love, Calvary speaks louder. God did not spare His own Son. He delivered Him up for us all. The believer may not understand a thousand providences, but he must not interpret them as though the cross had never happened.

God's love does not mean He gives every lesser thing we want. It means He has given the greatest gift. All other dealings with His children come from the God who gave His Son.

This does not remove grief. It anchors it.

The Christian may cry. He may lament. He may ask why. But he need not wonder whether God's love has disappeared. The cross has already answered that.

Trusting God's Holiness

Trusting God also means trusting His holiness.

At first, holiness may seem only frightening. God is pure, and we are not. He is light, and in Him is no darkness at all. His holiness exposes sin.

But once the sinner is in Christ, holiness becomes part of his confidence.

- Because God is holy, He will never deceive.

494

- Because God is holy, He will never act unjustly.

- Because God is holy, He will never become corrupt.

- Because God is holy, He will never compromise His promises.

- Because God is holy, He will finish the work of sanctifying His people.

The believer can trust God's holiness because it means there is no darkness in Him.

John writes:

"This then is the message which we have heard of him, and declare unto you, that God is light, and in him is no darkness at all." — I John 1:5

No darkness at all.

There are no hidden motives in God that contradict His revealed goodness. There is no secret injustice behind His providence. There is no lie beneath His promises. His holiness means He is perfectly trustworthy.

The holy God may correct us, but He will not wrong us.

Trusting God in Suffering

Suffering tests trust because it presses doctrine into the nerves.

It is one thing to say God is good when the table is full. It is another to say it beside a hospital bed, at a graveside, after betrayal, in financial ruin, during spiritual dryness, or while prayers seem unanswered.

But suffering does not create a new God.

The God who was faithful before the trial remains faithful in the trial. The God who was good in comfort remains good in grief. The God who was sovereign in peace remains sovereign in trouble.

Job said:

"Though he slay me, yet will I trust in him…" — **Job 13:15**

That is not shallow faith. That is trust under the blade.

Trusting God in suffering does not require pretending pain is small. Job did not pretend. The psalms do not pretend. Jeremiah did not pretend. Jesus Himself wept. Faith is not emotional numbness. It is clinging to God when emotion is raw and understanding is limited.

The believer may worship through tears because God's character has not failed.

Trusting God After Sin

Some of the hardest moments of trust come after personal sin.

The believer falls, and shame rises. He confesses, but the conscience still accuses. He wonders whether God will receive him again. He fears he has exhausted mercy.

In that moment, he must trust not his own worthiness, but God's character revealed in Christ.

John writes:

"If we confess our sins, he is faithful and just to forgive us our sins, and to cleanse us from all unrighteousness." — **I John 1:9**

Faithful and just.

God forgives the confessing believer not because sin is light, but because Christ is sufficient. The believer must not make his feelings stronger than the blood of Christ. He must not treat shame as more authoritative than the promise of God. He must not refuse mercy under the appearance of humility.

True repentance does not run from God. It returns to Him.

David prayed:

*"Have mercy upon me, O God, according to thy lovingkindness: according unto the multitude of thy tender mercies blot out my transgressions." — **Psalm 51:1***

He appealed to God's character.

That is what fallen believers must do. Not excuse sin. Not minimize guilt. Not hide. Come to God through Christ, trusting the mercy He Himself has revealed.

Trusting God for the Future

The future is one of the great testing grounds of trust.

We do not know what tomorrow holds. We do not know what losses, temptations, trials, duties, illnesses, opportunities, or sorrows may come. We do not know how long we will live. We do not know what will happen in the world. We do not know what burdens our children may carry. We do not know what the church may face before Christ returns.

But God knows.

Jesus said:

*"Take therefore no thought for the morrow: for the morrow shall take thought for the things of itself. Sufficient unto the day is the evil thereof." — **Matthew 6:34***

This is not a command to be careless. It is a command not to live under tomorrow's imagined burdens before tomorrow arrives. The Father feeds the birds. He clothes the lilies. He knows what His children need.

Trust receives today from God's hand and leaves tomorrow in God's hand.

This is difficult because fear wants control. It wants guarantees, details, timelines, and visible security. God often gives something better: Himself.

The believer can face an unknown future because it is not unknown to the God whose character cannot fail.

Trusting God When Obedience Is Costly

Trust is proven by obedience.

It is one thing to say God is faithful. It is another to obey Him when obedience costs reputation, comfort, money, relationships, opportunity, or safety. Yet true faith does not merely admire God's character. It acts upon it.

Abraham left his country because he trusted God's promise. Moses chose affliction with the people of God rather than the pleasures of sin for a season. Daniel prayed when prayer was outlawed. The apostles preached Christ after being commanded to stop. Faith obeys because God is trustworthy.

Jesus said:

"If any man will come after me, let him deny himself, and take up his cross daily, and follow me." — **Luke 9:23**

The call to follow Christ is not always easy. It may require denial of self, rejection by the world, suffering, and daily surrender. But the character of Christ makes obedience safe, even when it is costly.

The world may take much from the faithful believer. It cannot take Christ. It cannot take eternal life. It cannot take the Father's love. It cannot take the inheritance reserved in heaven.

Trust obeys because God is worth more than what obedience may cost.

Trusting God Together

Trust is personal, but it is also strengthened in the fellowship of God's people.

Believers help one another remember what is true. In weakness, another saint may speak the promise we are struggling to hold. In grief, the church may carry us when our own strength feels gone. In fear, a brother may remind us of God's faithfulness. In confusion, a pastor may bring the Word to bear.

The Christian life was never meant to be lived as solitary endurance.

Hebrews says:

"But exhort one another daily, while it is called To day; lest any of you be hardened through the deceitfulness of sin." — **Hebrews 3:13**

We need exhortation. Sin deceives. Fear distorts. Suffering narrows vision. Weariness weakens resolve. God uses His people to steady His people.

This is another mercy of the faithful God. He not only gives promises; He gives the church. He surrounds His children with voices that say, "Keep trusting Him. He has not failed. He will not fail now."

The God Who Cannot Fail

Trusting God is not trusting an idea.

It is trusting the living God whose character cannot fail.

- His goodness cannot turn sour.
- His wisdom cannot be mistaken.
- His faithfulness cannot break.
- His power cannot weaken.
- His love cannot be exhausted.

- His holiness cannot be corrupted.
- His mercy cannot be emptied.
- His truth cannot lie.
- His sovereignty cannot be overthrown.

This is why the believer can say with the psalmist:

"What time I am afraid, I will trust in thee." — **Psalm 56:3**

Not if I am afraid, but when. Fear may come. But fear does not have to rule. Trust answers fear by turning to God.

The Christian does not know everything God is doing.

But he knows God.

And because God's character cannot fail, trust is never wasted.

Chapter 47 — Fearing God Without Fleeing from Him

The fear of God is often misunderstood.

Some reject it because they think fear has no place in love. Others reduce it until it means little more than respect. Some speak of fearing God as though believers should live under constant dread of condemnation. Others speak of grace in a way that makes the fear of God sound like an old covenant idea no longer fitting for Christians.

Scripture does none of these things.

The Bible commands the fear of God. It praises the fear of God. It says the fear of the Lord is the beginning of wisdom. It tells believers to pass the time of their sojourning here in fear. It describes the early church walking in the fear of the Lord and in the comfort of the Holy Ghost.

Yet Scripture also tells believers not to flee from God as condemned enemies. In Christ, they are adopted children. They have boldness to enter by the blood of Jesus. They come to the throne of grace. They cry, "Abba, Father."

So the Christian must learn a distinction: we are to fear God without fleeing from Him.

That kind of fear is not the terror of a condemned sinner trying to escape judgment. It is the reverent trembling of a redeemed child who knows that his Father is holy, glorious, true, just, sovereign, merciful, and good.

The fear of God is not the enemy of assurance.

It is part of worship.

The Beginning of Wisdom

Scripture begins wisdom with the fear of the Lord.

Solomon writes:

"The fear of the LORD is the beginning of knowledge: but fools despise wisdom and instruction." — **Proverbs 1:7**

Again:

"The fear of the LORD is the beginning of wisdom: and the knowledge of the holy is understanding." — **Proverbs 9:10**

The fear of the Lord is not intellectual weakness. It is the foundation of true understanding. A man who does not fear God cannot see reality rightly. He may know facts. He may build systems. He may speak cleverly. But if God is not God in his thinking, his wisdom is already crooked.

The fear of the Lord puts the creature in his proper place.

God is not an idea to be managed. He is not a force to be used. He is not a projection of human desire. He is the Lord. He made us. He owns us. He judges us. He saves us. He speaks, and His Word stands. He commands, and His creatures are accountable.

A heart that does not fear God will eventually mishandle everything else.

- It will mishandle knowledge because it refuses the source of truth.
- It will mishandle morality because it rejects the holy Judge.
- It will mishandle freedom because it denies the rightful Lord.
- It will mishandle grace because it treats mercy lightly.
- It will mishandle worship because it has lost reverence.

The fear of God is not a small accessory to faith. It is foundational.

The Fear That Sinners Should Have

There is a kind of fear that belongs to the unrepentant sinner.

Jesus said:

"And fear not them which kill the body, but are not able to kill the soul: but rather fear him which is able to destroy both soul and body in hell." — **Matthew 10:28**

That is not merely reverence. That is warning. The sinner outside of Christ has reason to fear the judgment of God. He stands guilty before the holy Judge. He cannot save himself. He cannot hide. He cannot overpower death. He cannot escape the day when the books are opened.

This fear is appropriate.

A man sleeping in a burning house should be alarmed. A man standing in rebellion against God should tremble. A conscience awakened to judgment should not be quickly soothed with shallow words. The terror of the Lord is real.

Paul writes:

"Knowing therefore the terror of the Lord, we persuade men..." — **2 Corinthians 5:11**

The apostolic response to judgment was not embarrassment. It was persuasion. Men are in danger, and they must be warned.

But the warning is not meant to leave sinners fleeing blindly from God. It is meant to drive them to Christ. The same God who is to be feared has provided the Savior. The same Lord who warns of hell says, "Come unto me." The fear of judgment should make the sinner run to the refuge, not away from it.

The Fear That Believers Should Not Have

There is also a fear that believers should not live under.

John writes:

"There is no fear in love; but perfect love casteth out fear: because fear hath torment. He that feareth is not made perfect in love." — **I John 4:18**

This fear has torment. It is the fear of judgment, rejection, condemnation, and final wrath. The believer is not called to live in that fear because Christ has borne condemnation.

Paul says:

"For ye have not received the spirit of bondage again to fear; but ye have received the Spirit of adoption, whereby we cry, Abba, Father." — **Romans 8:15**

The Christian has not received the spirit of bondage again to fear. He has received the Spirit of adoption. He does not stand before God as a slave awaiting sentence, but as a child received in the beloved.

This must be protected.

Some preaching produces fear without gospel rest. It keeps tender believers in a constant state of uncertainty, as if assurance were presumption and every failure meant they may have fallen out of Christ. That is not the fear of God rightly taught. That is bondage.

The believer should fear sin, but he should not fear that Christ's blood is insufficient. He should tremble at God's holiness, but not doubt the Father's adoption. He should take obedience seriously, but not live as though condemnation remains over him.

The fear of God must never be used to undo the gospel.

The Fear That Believers Must Recover

If there is a fear believers should not have, there is also a fear they must not lose.

Grace does not make God less holy. Adoption does not make the Father less glorious. Boldness through Christ does not turn reverence into casualness. The veil has been opened by blood, but the One we approach is still God.

Peter writes:

"And if ye call on the Father, who without respect of persons judgeth according to every man's work, pass the time of your sojourning here in fear." — I **Peter 1:17**

Notice the balance. Believers call on the Father. Yet they are to pass the time of their sojourning here in fear. Fatherhood and fear belong together.

The next verses explain the cost of redemption:

"Forasmuch as ye know that ye were not redeemed with corruptible things, as silver and gold… But with the precious blood of Christ, as of a lamb without blemish and without spot." — **I Peter 1:18–19**

The fear of God is deepened, not weakened, by redemption. The blood of Christ does not make sin light. It shows how serious sin is. The believer fears God as one redeemed at infinite cost.

This fear is reverent, grateful, sober, and worshipful. It does not run from God. It bows before Him.

Fear and Love Together

Many errors come from setting fear and love against each other.

Human fear often drives out love. Sinful fear hides, distrusts, and flees. But biblical fear and holy love belong together because they are responses to the same God.

The psalmist says:

*"But there is forgiveness with thee, that thou mayest be feared." — **Psalm 130:4***

That verse is striking. Forgiveness does not remove fear. Forgiveness produces fear.

Why? Because forgiven sinners now see God more truly. They know the One who could have condemned them has shown mercy. They know sin required blood. They know grace was not cheap. They know the Holy One has received them. They know the Lord is both merciful and majestic.

A shallow heart says, "If I am forgiven, I need not fear." Scripture says, "There is forgiveness with thee, that thou mayest be feared."

Love draws near. Fear bows low. In the Christian life, these are not enemies.

The child who loves his father does not want to dishonor him. The servant who loves his master does not treat his commands lightly. The worshiper who loves God does not handle holy things carelessly.

Holy love has reverence in it.

Fear and Obedience

The fear of God produces obedience.

Moses told Israel:

"And now, Israel, what doth the LORD thy God require of thee, but to fear the LORD thy God, to walk in all his ways, and to love him, and to serve the

LORD thy God with all thy heart and with all thy soul." — **Deuteronomy 10:12**

Fear, walking in His ways, love, and service stand together. The fear of God is not a bare emotion. It moves the life. It teaches the feet to walk rightly.

A man who fears God cares what God has said. He does not treat commandments as suggestions. He does not measure obedience by convenience. He does not ask how close he can get to sin without consequence. He does not excuse secret rebellion because no human eye sees it.

Joseph feared God when he refused Potiphar's wife. He said:

"how then can I do this great wickedness, and sin against God?" — **Genesis 39:9**

That is the fear of God in action. Joseph knew the issue was not merely social risk. It was sin against God.

The fear of God makes private holiness matter because God is present when no one else is.

Fear and Speech

The fear of God also governs the tongue.

Men often speak too quickly about God, too casually about holy things, and too carelessly with Scripture. They joke about judgment, speak flippantly of demons, use God's name lightly, or handle doctrine as if it were debate material rather than divine truth.

The fear of God slows the mouth.

Solomon says:

*"Be not rash with thy mouth, and let not thine heart be hasty to utter any thing before God: for God is in heaven, and thou upon earth: therefore let thy words be few." — **Ecclesiastes 5:2***

God is in heaven. Thou art upon earth. That is enough to humble speech.

This does not mean believers should be silent about God. We are commanded to confess, teach, preach, sing, and bear witness. But we should speak as those who know we are handling holy truth.

Teachers especially must feel this weight. James says:

*"My brethren, be not many masters, knowing that we shall receive the greater condemnation." — **James 3:1***

The fear of God protects doctrine from prideful handling. A man may be bold and still reverent. He may speak clearly and still tremble. He may contend for truth without acting as though truth belongs to him.

Fear and Worship

The fear of God deepens worship.

Casual worship often comes from a diminished view of God. When people forget His holiness, glory, and majesty, worship becomes man-centered. It becomes performance, atmosphere, preference, or emotional experience detached from reverence.

Scripture calls for something weightier.

The psalmist says:

"O worship the LORD in the beauty of holiness: fear before him, all the earth."
*— **Psalm 96:9***

Fear before Him.

This does not cancel joy. The same psalms call us to sing, rejoice, clap hands, shout unto God, and bless His name. But biblical joy is not shallow noise. It is gladness before the Holy One.

The worship of heaven is filled with reverence. The living creatures cry, "Holy, holy, holy." The elders fall down. The redeemed sing of the Lamb who was slain. No one in heaven treats God casually.

The church should learn from that.

If our worship could continue unchanged whether God were holy or merely helpful, something is wrong. If our songs never tremble, never confess, never bow, never exalt, never declare His majesty, then our worship may be too small for the God of Scripture.

Fear and Comfort

The fear of God may sound severe, but it brings comfort.

That seems strange until we remember that fearing God frees us from fearing everything else wrongly. The man who fears God does not need to fear man as ultimate. He does not need to fear the world's disapproval as final. He does not need to fear circumstances as sovereign. He does not need to fear death as victorious.

Jesus said not to fear those who kill the body but cannot kill the soul. Fear God instead. That fear puts all lesser fears in their place.

Isaiah says:

*"Sanctify the LORD of hosts himself; and let him be your fear, and let him be your dread. And he shall be for a sanctuary…" — **Isaiah 8:13–14***

Let Him be your fear, and He shall be for a sanctuary.

That is beautiful. The One we fear becomes our refuge. When God is feared rightly, we stop treating lesser threats as though they were god. We remember who rules. We remember who judges. We remember who saves. We remember whose verdict matters.

The fear of God makes the soul brave.

Fear and the Church

The early church knew both comfort and fear.

Acts says:

"Then had the churches rest throughout all Judaea and Galilee and Samaria, and were edified; and walking in the fear of the Lord, and in the comfort of the Holy Ghost, were multiplied." — **Acts 9:31**

Fear of the Lord. Comfort of the Holy Ghost.

Not one or the other. Both.

This is a healthy church: reverent and comforted, serious and joyful, humbled and strengthened. The fear of the Lord did not crush the church. It helped build the church. The comfort of the Holy Ghost did not make the church casual. It strengthened them to walk rightly.

The church in every age needs this balance.

Without fear, churches become light, entertainment-driven, doctrinally loose, morally careless, and man-centered.

Without comfort, churches become harsh, fearful, suspicious, joyless, and exhausted.

The Spirit gives comfort. The Lord is to be feared. The two belong together in the life of God's people.

Fear and Final Accountability

Believers should also live with awareness that they will give account to God.

This is not condemnation. It is accountability.

Paul writes:

"For we must all appear before the judgment seat of Christ; that every one may receive the things done in his body, according to that he hath done, whether it be good or bad." — 2 Corinthians 5:10

The judgment seat of Christ should sober the believer. Our works matter. Our stewardship matters. Our words matter. Our motives matter. Our hidden life matters. The Lord will evaluate His servants.

Again, this does not overthrow justification. The believer's salvation rests on Christ. But grace does not erase accountability. The servant will stand before his Lord.

This should make Christians live carefully.

Not fearfully in the sense of dread of condemnation, but soberly. We should not waste life. We should not bury gifts. We should not excuse sin. We should not assume that hidden compromise is hidden from God. We should not treat the body as our own.

The fear of God makes life weighty.

The Guardrail for Doctrine

Fearing God without fleeing from Him protects several doctrines.

- It protects grace from becoming casual.
- It protects assurance from becoming presumption.
- It protects holiness from becoming harsh dread.

- It protects worship from becoming man-centered.
- It protects obedience from becoming optional.
- It protects pastoral care from crushing tender believers with condemnation.
- It protects evangelism from losing urgency.
- It protects the Christian life from both bondage and flippancy.

When the fear of God is lost, the church becomes shallow. When the fear of God is distorted, the church becomes fearful in the wrong way. But when the fear of God is held together with the love, mercy, holiness, and fatherhood of God, it becomes life-giving.

The believer fears God as Father, Lord, Redeemer, Judge, King, and Holy One.

He does not run away.

He bows and draws near through Christ.

Draw Near and Tremble

The Christian life is not the removal of reverence.

It is reverence brought near by blood.

- We come boldly, but not casually.
- We come loved, but not lightly.
- We come as children, but not as equals.
- We come forgiven, but not forgetful of the cost.
- We come to the Father, but the Father is holy.

The fear of God teaches us to tremble at His Word, obey His commands, confess our sins, worship with reverence, speak carefully, and live as those who will give account.

The love of God teaches us to draw near, trust His mercy, receive His forgiveness, rest in Christ, and cry, "Abba, Father."

We need both.

Fear without love flees from God.

Love without fear treats Him lightly.

But the gospel gives us something better.

We fear God without fleeing from Him because Christ has brought us near.

Chapter 48 — Becoming Like the God We Worship

Worship shapes the worshiper.

This is true whether the object of worship is true or false. A man becomes like what he reveres. His loves, fears, habits, speech, choices, and desires are formed by what he treats as ultimate. If he worships comfort, he becomes soft and self-protective. If he worships power, he becomes controlling. If he worships pleasure, he becomes enslaved. If he worships approval, he becomes fearful of man. If he worships a false god, he becomes conformed to the lie he adores.

Scripture shows this with idols.

The psalmist says of idols:

*"They have mouths, but they speak not: eyes have they, but they see not: They have ears, but they hear not: noses have they, but they smell not: They have hands, but they handle not: feet have they, but they walk not: neither speak they through their throat. They that make them are like unto them; so is every one that trusteth in them." — **Psalm 115:5–8***

They that make them are like unto them.

False worship deforms. True worship transforms.

The Christian life is not merely receiving correct information about God. It is being conformed to the God revealed in Christ. The full character of God is not only something to confess; it is something that begins to shape the people who belong to Him.

Peter writes:

*"But as he which hath called you is holy, so be ye holy in all manner of conversation; Because it is written, Be ye holy; for I am holy." — **1 Peter 1:15–16***

God's character becomes the pattern for His people.

The Image Restored in Christ

Man was created in the image of God.

That truth gives human life dignity, responsibility, and purpose. We were made to reflect God in the created order, to live under Him, to know Him, to obey Him, and to display something of His righteous rule.

Sin did not erase that image completely, but it corrupted man deeply. Instead of reflecting God rightly, man turned inward. He exchanged the truth of God for a lie. He worshiped and served the creature more than the Creator. His loves became disordered. His mind became darkened. His will became rebellious. His desires became corrupted.

Salvation restores what sin has ruined.

Paul writes that believers have:

*"put on the new man, which is renewed in knowledge after the image of him that created him." — **Colossians 3:10***

The new man is renewed after the image of the Creator. God is not merely forgiving sinners and leaving them unchanged. He is remaking them. He is conforming them to Christ, who is the perfect image of God.

Romans says:

*"For whom he did foreknow, he also did predestinate to be conformed to the image of his Son…" — **Romans 8:29***

That is the goal: conformity to Christ.

The Christian becomes like God by becoming like Christ. Not by becoming divine. Not by sharing God's incommunicable attributes. We do not become eternal, omnipotent, omniscient, or sovereign in the way God is. But we are made holy, righteous, loving, truthful, merciful, faithful, patient, and good according to the creaturely pattern God intends.

Christ is both Savior and pattern.

Holiness in the Whole Life

Because God is holy, His people are called to holiness.

This holiness is not limited to religious moments. Peter says, "in all manner of conversation." That means the whole conduct of life. Holiness touches speech, work, marriage, money, sexuality, entertainment, anger, forgiveness, ambition, truthfulness, and private thought.

A man cannot worship the Holy One on Sunday and make peace with uncleanness on Monday.

Paul writes:

"For this is the will of God, even your sanctification, that ye should abstain from fornication." — I Thessalonians 4:3

The will of God is not hidden here. Sanctification includes the body. It includes sexual purity. It includes refusing the sins the world excuses and the flesh desires.

Holiness also includes the inner life. Bitterness, envy, pride, lust, greed, deceit, and resentment may not always be visible to others, but they are visible to God. Becoming like the God we worship means sin must be dealt with where it begins, not merely where it becomes public.

This is not legalism. Legalism tries to earn favor with God through performance. Holiness is the fruit of belonging to God. The redeemed are called to live as those who have been bought with a price.

Holiness is not the enemy of grace.

It is one of grace's purposes.

Love That Reflects God

Because God is love, His people must love.

John writes:

"Beloved, if God so loved us, we ought also to love one another." — **I John 4:11**

The logic is simple and searching. If God has loved us in Christ, we ought to love one another. The love of God becomes the pattern and power of Christian love.

But again, this love must be defined by God, not by the age. Christian love is not mere niceness. It is not approval of sin. It is not emotional softness. It is not avoiding hard truth to preserve comfort. God's love is holy love, truthful love, sacrificial love, patient love, covenant love.

Paul writes:

"And be ye kind one to another, tenderhearted, forgiving one another, even as God for Christ's sake hath forgiven you." — **Ephesians 4:32**

The pattern is God's forgiveness in Christ.

This makes Christian love concrete. It forgives real wrongs. It bears burdens. It tells the truth. It refuses bitterness. It gives. It serves. It sacrifices. It keeps no selfish record for revenge. It seeks the good of others before self.

A man who claims to worship the God of love while remaining cruel, cold, harsh, selfish, or unforgiving is contradicting his worship with his life.

Love is not optional ornamentation in the Christian life.

It is family resemblance.

Mercy Toward the Needy and Guilty

Because God is merciful, His people must be merciful.

Jesus says:

"Be ye therefore merciful, as your Father also is merciful." — **Luke 6:36**

The command is direct. The Father's mercy becomes the pattern for His children.

This mercy must be more than a feeling. Biblical mercy moves toward need. It sees weakness and does not despise it. It sees misery and does not ignore it. It sees guilt and offers forgiveness where repentance is present. It sees brokenness and does not turn away in disgust.

The merciful Christian remembers that he lives by mercy.

This remembrance should soften pride. How can a man who has been forgiven much refuse mercy to others? How can one who stood guilty before God treat the repentant with contempt? How can one who has been helped in weakness despise the weak?

Jesus warned against a servant who received mercy but refused to show mercy. Such a man had not understood what had been done for him.

Mercy does not mean abandoning truth. It does not mean refusing discipline, justice, or correction. God's mercy is never lawless, and ours must not be either. But it does mean we should not be hard where God is tender. We should not be eager to condemn where God calls us to restore.

We should not treat others' weakness as though we ourselves were not dependent on grace.

The merciful Father forms merciful children.

Truthfulness in a World of Lies

Because God is true, His people must be truthful.

This applies to more than avoiding obvious lies. Truthfulness must mark the whole life. The Christian should be honest in speech, fair in business, faithful in promises, careful with Scripture, unwilling to manipulate, and quick to confess when he has spoken falsely.

Paul writes:

"Wherefore putting away lying, speak every man truth with his neighbour: for we are members one of another." — **Ephesians 4:25**

Lying is not merely a social flaw. It contradicts the God of truth and harms the body of Christ. A church cannot be healthy where deception is tolerated. Families cannot flourish where truth is bent. Doctrine cannot remain pure where Scripture is handled dishonestly.

Truthfulness also requires courage.

Sometimes truth costs. It may cost approval, comfort, opportunity, reputation, or peace with men. But the one who worships the God of truth must not become a servant of falsehood to avoid loss.

This does not excuse harshness. Truth must be spoken in love. But love does not make truth optional. God is both loving and true, and His people must learn to reflect both.

A truthful life is worship made visible.

Faithfulness in Small Things

Because God is faithful, His people must be faithful.

Faithfulness is not dramatic in the eyes of the world. It often appears in small, repeated acts of obedience. Keeping vows. Telling the truth. Showing up when tired. Praying when unseen. Providing for those entrusted to us. Finishing work honestly. Remaining loyal where covenant requires it. Holding to Christ when feelings fluctuate.

Jesus said:

"He that is faithful in that which is least is faithful also in much: and he that is unjust in the least is unjust also in much." — **Luke 16:10**

God cares about the least.

This rebukes the desire for visible greatness without hidden faithfulness. Some want public ministry but neglect private obedience. Some want to be trusted with influence but cannot be trusted with their speech. Some want spiritual reputation but fail in ordinary duties at home.

Faithfulness begins where God has placed us.

The faithful God forms faithful servants. They may not be famous. They may not be applauded. But they are steady because God is worthy. They keep going because His Word is true.

A faithful life may look small now, but it is precious before God.

Patience and Longsuffering

Because God is patient, His people must learn patience.

This is difficult because impatience feels natural. We want growth quickly, relief quickly, answers quickly, change in others quickly, victory quickly. When delays come, we become irritable, anxious, or demanding.

But God has been longsuffering toward us.

Paul writes:

"And the servant of the Lord must not strive; but be gentle unto all men, apt to teach, patient, In meekness instructing those that oppose themselves..."
— 2 Timothy 2:24–25

Patience is necessary in ministry, family, friendship, correction, and suffering. People do not always grow at the pace we prefer. Repentance may require careful instruction. Weak believers may stumble repeatedly. Children need repeated teaching. The suffering need endurance, not rushed answers.

Patience does not mean indifference. God's patience is purposeful. He calls sinners to repentance. He does not bless rebellion. But He is slow to anger, and His people must not be quick to wrath.

James says:

"Wherefore, my beloved brethren, let every man be swift to hear, slow to speak, slow to wrath." **— James 1:19**

A patient Christian reflects something of the God who has been patient with him.

Goodness in Action

Because God is good, His people should do good.

This goodness is practical. It is not vague pleasantness. It seeks what is right and beneficial before God. It blesses others. It resists evil. It gives, serves, protects, encourages, and acts with integrity.

Paul says:

"And let us not be weary in well doing: for in due season we shall reap, if we faint not." **— Galatians 6:9**

Weariness is real. Doing good can be tiring, especially when it is unnoticed, misunderstood, or repaid with ingratitude. But the call remains.

The Christian should not ask only, "What am I allowed to do?" He should ask, "What is good before God? What reflects His character? What serves my neighbor? What honors Christ?"

Goodness will affect how we use money, time, strength, speech, influence, and opportunity. It will move us toward the needy. It will make us dependable. It will restrain selfishness. It will make holiness visible in action.

God's goodness is not inactive. He does good.

So should His people.

Justice and Righteousness

Because God is righteous and just, His people must care about righteousness and justice.

This begins personally. A man who speaks loudly about justice in society while practicing unrighteousness in private is not reflecting God. Righteousness must begin in the heart, home, church, work, and daily conduct.

Micah says:

"He hath shewed thee, O man, what is good; and what doth the LORD require of thee, but to do justly, and to love mercy, and to walk humbly with thy God?" **— Micah 6:8**

Do justly. Love mercy. Walk humbly.

These belong together. Justice without mercy becomes harsh. Mercy without justice becomes morally weak. Both without humility become pride. The character of God holds them together, and His people must learn to do the same.

Christian righteousness includes honest dealings, fair judgment, protection of the vulnerable, refusal to show partiality, hatred of oppression, and personal obedience to God's commands. It does not adopt every slogan of the world, but neither does it ignore evil because confronting it is inconvenient.

The righteous God forms a people who love what is right.

Forgiveness and Peace

Because God forgives, His people must forgive.

This is one of the most searching applications of God's character. Many Christians are willing to praise forgiveness as doctrine while resisting forgiveness as obedience.

Paul writes:

"Forbearing one another, and forgiving one another, if any man have a quarrel against any: even as Christ forgave you, so also do ye." — **Colossians 3:13**

The standard is Christ's forgiveness.

This does not mean pretending wrong did not happen. It does not mean there are no consequences. It does not mean trust is instantly restored in every situation. It does not mean justice is irrelevant. But it does mean the Christian may not nurse bitterness, seek revenge, or withhold forgiveness from the repentant while claiming to live by grace.

Forgiveness is costly. It requires the death of pride, resentment, and the desire to make another pay emotionally. But forgiven people must become forgiving people.

The cross leaves no room for cherished bitterness.

Imitating God as Dear Children

Paul gives the command plainly:

*"Be ye therefore followers of God, as dear children; And walk in love, as Christ also hath loved us, and hath given himself for us an offering and a sacrifice to God for a sweetsmelling savour." — **Ephesians 5:1–2**

Followers of God. Dear children. Walk in love.

The Christian imitates God as a child imitates a father. Again, this is not imitation of God's infinite attributes. It is imitation of His moral character as revealed and commanded. Because we are His children, we should bear family resemblance.

The pattern is Christ's sacrificial love. He gave Himself.

This means becoming like God is not merely moral improvement. It is cross-shaped transformation. The believer dies to self. He learns to love when love costs. He serves when pride wants recognition. He forgives when bitterness wants revenge. He tells the truth when lying would be easier. He remains faithful when escape seems attractive. He pursues holiness when sin promises pleasure.

The life of God's child is formed under the shadow of the cross.

The Work of the Spirit

Becoming like God is not accomplished by human effort alone.

The believer must obey, but he does not transform himself by sheer willpower. Sanctification is the work of God in His people. The Spirit applies the work of Christ, renews the mind, convicts of sin, produces fruit, strengthens obedience, and conforms believers to the image of the Son.

Paul writes:

"But the fruit of the Spirit is love, joy, peace, longsuffering, gentleness, goodness, faith, Meekness, temperance…" — **Galatians 5:22–23**

These are not merely natural personality traits. They are the fruit of the Spirit.

This should give hope. The impatient man can grow in patience. The harsh man can grow in gentleness. The fearful man can grow in faith. The selfish man can grow in love. The undisciplined man can grow in temperance. Not because the flesh is strong, but because the Spirit is at work.

At the same time, the believer must not be passive. Paul also says to walk in the Spirit. The Christian must put off the old man and put on the new. He must mortify sin. He must obey the Word. The Spirit's work does not cancel human responsibility; it makes obedience possible.

Glory Will Complete What Grace Began

In this life, becoming like God remains incomplete.

Believers grow, but they do not become sinless. They love, but imperfectly. They obey, but with weakness. They worship, but with distraction. They repent, but often slowly. They reflect God's character, but not yet without distortion.

This should humble us, but not make us hopeless.

John writes:

"Beloved, now are we the sons of God, and it doth not yet appear what we shall be: but we know that, when he shall appear, we shall be like him; for we shall see him as he is." — **I John 3:2**

We shall be like Him.

The work will be finished. Sin will be gone. The image will be fully restored. Love will be pure. Holiness will be complete. Worship will be undistracted. Truth will be loved without resistance. The redeemed will reflect the glory of God as creatures made whole.

This future hope purifies the present life. John immediately adds:

*"And every man that hath this hope in him purifieth himself, even as he is pure." — **I John 3:3***

Hope does not produce laziness. It produces purification.

Because we will be like Him, we seek to become like Him now.

The Witness of a Godlike People

A people shaped by God's character becomes a witness in the world.

Jesus said:

*"Let your light so shine before men, that they may see your good works, and glorify your Father which is in heaven." — **Matthew 5:16***

Good works do not save, but they do testify. They show something of the Father's character. When Christians live with holiness, love, mercy, truth, faithfulness, patience, and goodness, the world sees a reflection of the God they confess.

This witness is often imperfect, and the church has too often contradicted its message by its conduct. But failure does not remove the calling. It calls us to repentance.

The world does not need Christians who merely argue well for God's character. It needs Christians whose lives have been marked by that character. Doctrine must become visible.

The truth we defend must shape the people we are becoming.

Beholding and Becoming

Paul writes:

*"But we all, with open face beholding as in a glass the glory of the Lord, are changed into the same image from glory to glory, even as by the Spirit of the Lord." — **2 Corinthians 3:18***

Beholding and becoming belong together.

We behold the glory of the Lord, and we are changed. Not all at once. From glory to glory. By the Spirit of the Lord.

This is why the full character of God matters for daily life. We become distorted when we behold a distorted god. We become shallow when we behold a shallow god. We become harsh when we isolate severity. We become casual when we isolate kindness. We become unstable when our doctrine is partial.

But when we behold the true God as He has revealed Himself in Scripture and supremely in Christ, we are changed.

- The holy God makes His people holy.
- The loving God makes His people loving.
- The merciful God makes His people merciful.
- The truthful God makes His people truthful.
- The faithful God makes His people faithful.
- The patient God makes His people patient.
- The good God makes His people do good.

We worship, and we are formed.

The Christian life is not merely knowing about God.

It is becoming like the God we worship.

Chapter 49 — Knowing God Is Eternal Life

The Christian life does not end with knowing about God.

It begins and ends with knowing God Himself.

Doctrine matters because God matters. Truth matters because God is true. Scripture matters because God has spoken. Worship matters because God is worthy. Obedience matters because God is Lord. Trust matters because God is faithful. Holiness matters because God is holy.

But all of these things are ordered toward communion with the living God.

Jesus prayed:

*"And this is life eternal, that they might know thee the only true God, and Jesus Christ, whom thou hast sent." — **John 17:3***

That sentence gathers the whole Christian life into one great reality: eternal life is knowing God.

Not merely knowing facts. Not merely belonging to a religion. Not merely affirming doctrines. Not merely avoiding judgment. Eternal life is the knowledge of the only true God through Jesus Christ.

This knowledge begins now and will be perfected forever.

The whole burden of this book has been that God must be known as He is. Not reduced. Not reshaped. Not divided. Not softened where Scripture is severe. Not made harsh where Scripture is tender. Not interpreted through human preference. Not confined to the attributes we find easiest to receive.

God must be known in the fullness of His revealed character.

And to know Him truly is life.

The Difference Between Knowing About God and Knowing God

There is a difference between knowing about God and knowing God.

A man may know many doctrines and yet remain far from God. He may define holiness, explain sovereignty, debate prophecy, defend orthodoxy, and recite confessions while his heart remains proud, cold, prayerless, and unrepentant.

Knowledge can become a dangerous thing when it is severed from worship.

Paul writes:

"Knowledge puffeth up, but charity edifieth." — **I Corinthians 8:1**

This does not mean knowledge is bad. Scripture commands us to grow in knowledge. False doctrine destroys. Ignorance is not spiritual maturity. But knowledge that only inflates the mind without humbling the heart has been mishandled.

To know God truly is not less than doctrinal knowledge, but it is more. It is doctrinal truth received in faith, love, reverence, repentance, obedience, and worship.

The demons know true things about God and tremble. The believer knows God as Father through Christ. That is not the same kind of knowledge.

The Christian does not merely know that God is merciful. He has fled to that mercy.

He does not merely know that God is holy. He has been undone and cleansed before Him.

He does not merely know that God is faithful. He trusts His promises.

He does not merely know that God is sovereign. He bows beneath His rule.

He does not merely know that God is love. He has received that love in the crucified and risen Christ.

True knowledge of God lays hold of the soul.

God Must Be Known Through Christ

No one comes to know God savingly apart from Christ.

Jesus said:

*"I am the way, the truth, and the life: no man cometh unto the Father, but by me." — **John 14:6***

That is exclusive, but it is not cruel. It is exclusive because Christ alone reveals the Father and reconciles sinners to Him. It is merciful because the way has been opened.

Sin has not merely made man ignorant. It has made him guilty, alienated, darkened, and rebellious. Man does not need only religious instruction. He needs redemption. He needs atonement. He needs forgiveness. He needs new birth.

Christ provides all of this.

John writes:

*"No man hath seen God at any time; the only begotten Son, which is in the bosom of the Father, he hath declared him." — **John 1:18***

The Son makes the Father known.

This means all true knowledge of God is Christ-centered. We do not know God by climbing up to Him through speculation. We know Him because the Son came down. We know Him because the Word was made flesh. We know Him because Christ died for sins, rose again, ascended, intercedes, and will return.

To know God, we must behold Christ.

He is not one revelation among many. He is the definitive revelation of the Father.

The Spirit Makes God Known

The knowledge of God is not produced by human intellect alone.

A man may read Scripture and remain blind. He may hear sermons and remain unchanged. He may study theology and remain unconverted. The mind must be illumined by the Spirit of God.

Paul writes:

*"But God hath revealed them unto us by his Spirit: for the Spirit searcheth all things, yea, the deep things of God." — **1 Corinthians 2:10***

The Spirit reveals what man could not discover by natural wisdom. He opens the eyes. He convicts of sin. He glorifies Christ. He bears witness with our spirit that we are the children of God. He sheds abroad the love of God in our hearts. He enables prayer, worship, obedience, and understanding.

This keeps the knowledge of God from becoming merely academic.

We need the Word of God, and we need the Spirit who opens the Word. We need doctrine, and we need life. We need truth, and we need the God of truth to make that truth living in us.

The Spirit does not lead us away from Scripture into private imagination. He leads us into the truth God has spoken. He does not reveal a different Christ. He glorifies the Christ of Scripture.

To know God truly, the sinner must be brought by the Spirit to the Son, and through the Son to the Father.

Knowing God and Loving God

To know God truly is to love Him.

This does not mean our love is perfect. It is not. Even the mature believer loves God with weakness, distraction, and need of growth. But where there is saving knowledge of God, love is born.

John writes:

*"We love him, because he first loved us." — **1 John 4:19***

God's love comes first. Our love answers His. We do not awaken love for God by our own strength. We love because He first loved us in Christ.

This love is not mere feeling, though it includes affection. It is not mere duty, though it obeys. It is the redeemed heart drawn to God Himself. The believer comes to see that God is not only necessary, but desirable. Not only true, but beautiful. Not only Savior, but treasure.

David says:

*"Whom have I in heaven but thee? and there is none upon earth that I desire beside thee." — **Psalm 73:25***

That is the language of a man who knows God as his portion.

The Christian must never be satisfied with a religion in which God's gifts are loved more than God. Forgiveness is precious because it brings us to God. Heaven is precious because God is there. Eternal life is precious because it is knowing Him.

God Himself is the reward.

Knowing God and Obeying God

The knowledge of God produces obedience.

John writes:

*"And hereby we do know that we know him, if we keep his commandments. He that saith, I know him, and keepeth not his commandments, is a liar, and the truth is not in him." — **I John 2:3–4***

These are strong words. Scripture does not allow a man to claim knowledge of God while living in settled rebellion against His commands.

Obedience does not earn eternal life. It is the fruit of knowing God. A man who knows God as holy cannot treat sin lightly. A man who knows God as Lord cannot treat His commandments as optional. A man who knows God as Father cannot be content to grieve Him. A man who knows Christ cannot be indifferent to following Him.

This does not mean believers obey perfectly. John also says that if we say we have no sin, we deceive ourselves. The Christian life includes confession, repentance, cleansing, and ongoing growth. But there is a difference between struggling against sin and making peace with it.

True knowledge of God changes the direction of life.

The man who knows God may stumble, but he cannot remain comfortable in darkness.

Knowing God in Weakness

God is often known deeply in weakness.

This is not the way we would naturally choose. We would prefer to know God through strength, success, ease, clarity, and visible blessing. Sometimes

He does make Himself known through those gifts. But often He reveals Himself to His people in suffering, need, loss, limitation, and dependence.

Paul pleaded for his thorn in the flesh to depart. The Lord answered:

"My grace is sufficient for thee: for my strength is made perfect in weakness." **— 2 Corinthians 12:9**

Paul then said:

"Most gladly therefore will I rather glory in my infirmities, that the power of Christ may rest upon me." **— 2 Corinthians 12:9**

Weakness became the place where Paul knew the sufficiency of grace and the power of Christ.

This does not make suffering pleasant. It does not make pain imaginary. But it means weakness is not wasted in the hands of God. The believer may come to know God's comfort in grief, His strength in frailty, His faithfulness in waiting, His nearness in loneliness, His mercy after failure, and His peace in uncertainty.

Some knowledge of God is learned only when every other support gives way.

The valley can become a classroom of glory.

Knowing God Through His Word

God is known through the Word He has given.

If we want to know Him as He is, we must be people of Scripture. Not merely occasional readers. Not merely collectors of verses that comfort us. Not merely debaters who use the Bible as ammunition. We must sit under the Word as those who need to hear God.

The psalmist says:

"Open thou mine eyes, that I may behold wondrous things out of thy law." — **Psalm 119:18**

That should be the prayer of every believer.

Scripture reveals God's works, words, promises, judgments, commands, mercy, covenant faithfulness, saving plan, and final purpose. It reveals Christ. It teaches us how to interpret the world, ourselves, history, sin, salvation, suffering, worship, and hope.

If our view of God is not continually corrected by Scripture, it will drift.

Experience alone cannot govern knowledge of God. Emotion alone cannot. Tradition alone cannot. Human reason alone cannot. Scripture must rule, because Scripture is the true witness God has given.

To neglect the Word is to invite a partial and distorted view of God.

Knowing God in Prayer

The knowledge of God also grows in prayer.

Prayer is not merely asking for things. It is communion with God. It is dependence spoken. It is worship, confession, thanksgiving, lament, petition, surrender, and trust before the face of the Father.

Jesus taught His disciples to pray:

"Our Father which art in heaven, Hallowed be thy name." — **Matthew 6:9**

The prayer begins with God: Father, heaven, holy name.

True prayer is shaped by God's character. We come because He is Father. We bow because He is holy. We ask because He is good. We confess because He is merciful. We trust because He is faithful. We submit because He is wise and sovereign.

A prayerless life cannot be a deeply God-knowing life.

A man may know theology and still avoid God. Prayer brings doctrine into direct address. It turns statements about God into speech before God. It exposes whether we really trust what we say we believe.

The believer who knows God will speak to Him.

Knowing God and Being Known by God

There is something even deeper than our knowing God: God knows His people.

Paul writes:

"But now, after that ye have known God, or rather are known of God…" — **Galatians 4:9**

That correction is precious. Yes, believers know God. But beneath that is the greater truth: they are known by God.

Jesus says of His sheep:

"I am the good shepherd, and know my sheep, and am known of mine." — **John 10:14**

The Shepherd knows His own. This is not bare awareness. He knows them in covenant love. He calls them by name. He gave His life for them. He keeps them. He will bring them home.

This gives deep comfort. Our knowledge of God is real but imperfect. It wavers in feeling. It grows slowly. It is sometimes clouded by fear, sorrow, confusion, and sin. But God's knowledge of His people does not waver.

The believer is not saved because he holds God with perfect strength. He is saved because God holds him.

We know God because He first knew us in love.

The Danger of Refusing to Know God

Scripture also warns of those who do not know God.

This is not a harmless condition. To refuse the knowledge of God is sin. Men are accountable for suppressing truth, rejecting light, despising the Son, and turning from the living God to idols.

Paul speaks of judgment:

*"In flaming fire taking vengeance on them that know not God, and that obey not the gospel of our Lord Jesus Christ." — **2 Thessalonians 1:8***

Not knowing God is not a neutral intellectual gap. It is bound up with disobedience to the gospel.

This should make evangelism urgent. Men do not merely need better values, improved circumstances, religious tradition, or moral encouragement. They need to know God through Jesus Christ. Without Him, they remain alienated, guilty, and under judgment.

The church must not be ashamed to say this.

There is one true God. There is one Mediator between God and men. Eternal life is found in knowing the Father and Jesus Christ whom He has sent.

To know Him is life.

To refuse Him is death.

Knowing God Forever

The knowledge of God that begins now will be perfected in glory.

Paul writes:

*"For now we see through a glass, darkly; but then face to face: now I know in part; but then shall I know even as also I am known." — **I Corinthians 13:12**

Now we know in part.

That is humbling. Even the best theology is partial. True, if governed by Scripture, but partial. We do not yet see as we will see. We do not yet know as we will know. Our worship is real, but incomplete. Our love is real, but imperfect. Our obedience is real, but mixed with weakness.

But then: face to face.

The redeemed will know God without the dimness of this present age. Not exhaustively, for creatures will never comprehend the infinite God fully. But truly, purely, joyfully, and without sin. There will be no unbelief clouding the mind, no fear twisting the heart, no sin dulling the affections, no suffering narrowing sight.

The knowledge of God will deepen forever because God is inexhaustible.

Eternal life will never become boring because God will never be exhausted.

The End for Which We Were Made

Man was made to know God.

Sin turned man away from that purpose. Redemption brings him back. Christ restores what was lost and brings His people into something even more glorious than Eden's beginning. The final state is not merely a return to innocence. It is communion with God through the crucified and risen Christ in a new creation where righteousness dwells.

This is the end for which we were made.

Not self-exaltation. Not comfort as the highest good. Not religious activity as an end in itself. Not knowledge for pride. Not morality without communion.

God.

To know Him, love Him, worship Him, trust Him, obey Him, enjoy Him, and dwell with Him forever.

Everything else must find its proper place beneath that.

The Full Character of God and the Life of the Soul

A partial god cannot give full life.

If we imagine God only as love without holiness, we will not know the true God.

If we imagine Him only as wrath without goodness, we will not know the true God.

If we imagine Him only as sovereignty without wisdom, we will not know the true God.

If we imagine Him only as mercy without justice, we will not know the true God.

If we imagine Him only as nearness without glory, or glory without tenderness, or truth without grace, or grace without truth, we will not know Him as He has revealed Himself.

The soul needs the whole God.

- The holy God who cleanses.
- The just God who justifies.
- The wrathful God who saves from wrath.

- The loving God who gives His Son.
- The merciful God who receives sinners.
- The gracious God who gives freely.
- The faithful God who keeps promises.
- The wise God who orders all things.
- The sovereign God who reigns.
- The truthful God who cannot lie.
- The good God who does all things well.
- The triune God—Father, Son, and Holy Ghost—blessed forever.

This is the God who gives life.

That They Might Know Thee

Jesus did not define eternal life first in terms of place, duration, or blessing, though all of those are involved. He defined it in terms of knowing God.

*"And this is life eternal, that they might know thee the only true God, and Jesus Christ, whom thou hast sent." — **John 17:3***

That is where the book must end.

With God Himself.

The believer will spend eternity knowing the One he has only begun to know here. Every promise will lead to Him. Every mercy will bring praise to Him. Every redeemed joy will be joy in Him. Every healed wound will magnify Him. Every song will rise to Him. Every doctrine will be seen in the light of His face.

The full character of God is not merely a subject to master.

It is the vision that saves us from falsehood, steadies us in suffering, humbles us in worship, guards us in doctrine, shapes us in holiness, and draws us into communion with the living God.

To know Him is eternal life.

And in Christ, that life has already begun.

Chapter 50 — Come to Jesus

There comes a point when study must become response.

It is possible to read about the character of God and remain at a distance. A person may consider His holiness, His justice, His mercy, His love, His wrath, His patience, His goodness, His faithfulness, and His grace, and still hold back from Him. He may understand more than he once did and yet remain unchanged. He may be interested, moved, even troubled, but not yet surrendered.

But the revelation of God is not given so that men may merely admire truth from afar.

God has made Himself known so that sinners may come to Him.

And sinners come to God through Jesus Christ.

The question at the end of this book is not merely, "Do you now understand the character of God more clearly?" That matters. But there is a greater question.

Have you come to Christ?

Jesus said:

"Come unto me, all ye that labour and are heavy laden, and I will give you rest." — Matthew 11:28

That is not a call to the strong. It is not a call to those who have mastered every doctrine. It is not a call to those who have cleaned themselves up enough to be worthy. It is a call to the weary, the burdened, the guilty, the broken, the sinful, the confused, the needy.

Come unto me.

That is the voice of Christ.

You Do Not Have to Understand Everything Before You Come

Many people hesitate because they think they must understand everything first.

They want every question answered, every doctrine settled, every confusion removed, every fear quieted, every mystery explained. They want to know how all things fit together before they surrender. They want full clarity before faith.

But Jesus does not say, "Understand all things, and then come unto me."

He says, "Come unto me."

This does not mean truth is unimportant. It does not mean doctrine can be ignored. It does not mean questions are wrong. God has spoken, and His Word matters. But a sinner does not need to comprehend the infinite God before coming to the Savior. If that were required, no one could come.

The disciples did not understand everything when they first followed Christ. They misunderstood much. They grew slowly. They were corrected often. They did not fully grasp the cross until after the resurrection. Yet they followed Him.

Peter did not have every answer, but he knew enough to say:

"Lord, to whom shall we go? thou hast the words of eternal life." — **John 6:68**

That is faith speaking.

You may not understand all things. But do you know this: that you are a sinner, that Christ is the Savior, that He died and rose again, and that there is no life apart from Him?

Then come.

Christ Will Teach Those Who Come to Him

Coming to Christ is not the end of learning. It is the beginning of true learning.

A man outside of Christ may study truth, but he remains spiritually blind until God opens his eyes. He may gather information, but he does not yet know God as Father. He may discuss doctrine, but he has not yet been brought into life.

Christ teaches His people.

He said:

"Take my yoke upon you, and learn of me; for I am meek and lowly in heart: and ye shall find rest unto your souls." — **Matthew 11:29**

Learn of me.

The one who comes to Christ becomes His disciple. Christ does not promise to answer every question at once, but He does promise Himself. He gives rest, and then He teaches. He corrects false ideas. He deepens understanding. He exposes sin. He strengthens faith. He reveals the Father. He opens Scripture. He leads His sheep.

There are things you may not understand now that will become clearer as you walk with Him.

There are truths that may seem distant now that will become precious later.

There are doctrines that may seem difficult now that will become worship as He opens His Word to you.

Do not wait until you know everything before you come.

Come to Him, and learn.

The God You Have Sinned Against Is the God Who Saves

The full character of God should make one thing unmistakably clear: sin is serious.

God is holy. He is righteous. He is just. He is true. He will not pretend evil is harmless. He will not call darkness light. He will not clear the guilty apart from the provision He Himself has made.

This means every person must face the truth about himself.

You have sinned against God.

Not merely against your own conscience. Not merely against other people. Not merely against society. You have sinned against the Lord who made you.

David prayed:

"Against thee, thee only, have I sinned, and done this evil in thy sight…" — **Psalm 51:4**

That confession is where mercy begins to be seen clearly. A man who hides his sin will not understand grace. A man who excuses his sin will not run to Christ. A man who thinks lightly of guilt will think lightly of the cross.

But the God you have sinned against is also the God who saves.

He is merciful. He is gracious. He is patient. He is full of compassion. He sent His Son. He provided the sacrifice. He opened the way. He calls sinners to come.

"But God commendeth his love toward us, in that, while we were yet sinners, Christ died for us." — **Romans 5:8**

While we were yet sinners.

Not after we became worthy. Not after we understood everything. Not after we repaired the damage. Christ died for sinners.

That is your hope.

Do Not Confuse Delay with Safety

One of the greatest dangers to the soul is delay.

Many people do not openly reject Christ. They simply postpone Him. They intend to think about it later. They plan to repent later. They assume there will be another opportunity, another sermon, another warning, another season when life is less busy and the heart feels more ready.

But Scripture does not speak that way.

"Behold, now is the accepted time; behold, now is the day of salvation." — 2 Corinthians 6:2

Now.

Not because God is impatient in a human sense, but because you do not own tomorrow. You do not know how long your heart will remain tender. You do not know how many times conviction may be resisted before the conscience grows dull. You do not know the day of your death. You do not know when Christ will return.

Delay feels safe because it avoids decision. But delay is not safety. It is danger disguised as control.

If Christ is calling, do not wait.

Come.

Do Not Try to Make Yourself Worthy First

Another person may say, "I know I need Christ, but I am not ready. I need to become better first."

But that misunderstands grace.

You do not come to Christ because you have made yourself clean. You come because you need cleansing. You do not come because you are strong. You come because you are weak. You do not come because you have conquered sin. You come because sin has conquered you and you need a Savior.

Jesus said:

"They that are whole need not a physician; but they that are sick." — **Luke 5:31**

Christ is the Physician. Sinners are the sick.

No sick man heals himself in order to become worthy of the doctor. He comes because he needs healing.

Do not dress up your soul before bringing it to Christ. Bring Him the truth. Bring Him your guilt, your shame, your confusion, your failure, your bondage, your fear, your pride, your emptiness. Bring Him the sins you are ashamed to name. He already knows. And still He says, "Come."

The blood of Christ is not for those who are almost clean.

It is for sinners.

Repent and Believe the Gospel

The call of Christ is not vague.

It is not merely "be religious." It is not merely "try harder." It is not merely "think positively about God." It is not merely "add Jesus to your life."

Jesus preached:

*"The time is fulfilled, and the kingdom of God is at hand: repent ye, and believe the gospel." — **Mark 1:15***

Repent and believe.

Repentance is turning from sin to God. It is not perfection. It is not payment. It is not cleaning yourself up before grace. It is the sinner agreeing with God about sin and turning to Him for mercy.

Faith is trusting Christ. Not merely agreeing that He exists. Not merely admiring Him. Not merely believing facts about Him while keeping your life for yourself. Faith receives Him, rests in Him, clings to Him, and trusts His finished work.

Paul told the Philippian jailer:

*"Believe on the Lord Jesus Christ, and thou shalt be saved…" — **Acts 16:31***

That is still the call.

Believe on the Lord Jesus Christ.

Christ Is Able to Save You Completely

Perhaps you fear that your sin is too great.

It is not.

Christ is greater.

Perhaps you fear that you have waited too long.

If you are still being called, come now.

Perhaps you fear that your faith is weak.

Then bring weak faith to a strong Savior.

Perhaps you fear that you will fail again.

You may. But Christ does not save only those who will never stumble. He saves sinners and then keeps, teaches, corrects, restores, and sanctifies them.

Hebrews says:

"Wherefore he is able also to save them to the uttermost that come unto God by him, seeing he ever liveth to make intercession for them." — **Hebrews 7:25**

He is able to save to the uttermost.

Not partly. Not barely. Not reluctantly. To the uttermost.

That means no sinner should despair who comes to God by Him.

Do Not Come to an Idea. Come to Christ.

Christianity is not merely accepting a system.

It is coming to a Person.

- Come to Christ crucified for sinners.
- Come to Christ risen from the dead.
- Come to Christ who reveals the Father.
- Come to Christ who gives rest.
- Come to Christ who forgives sin.
- Come to Christ who sends the Spirit.
- Come to Christ who keeps His sheep.
- Come to Christ who will return as King.

He is not merely a teacher of eternal life.

He is eternal life.

John writes:

*"He that hath the Son hath life; and he that hath not the Son of God hath not life." — **I John 5:12**

There is no life apart from Him.

Not because God is narrow in some petty way, but because Christ is the only Savior. He alone bore sin. He alone conquered death. He alone reconciles man to God. He alone is the way, the truth, and the life.

If you have Him, you have life.

If you do not have Him, you do not.

A Simple Prayer of Surrender

No prayer saves by its wording. There are no magic phrases. A person may repeat words and remain unchanged. Salvation is not in the formula of a prayer, but in Christ Himself.

But prayer can be the honest expression of faith and repentance.

If your heart is being drawn to Christ, you may come to Him simply. You may pray something like this:

Lord Jesus, I come to You as a sinner. I have sinned against God, and I cannot save myself. I believe You died for sinners and rose again. I believe You are the Son of God and the only Savior. Have mercy on me. Forgive me. Cleanse me. Save me. I turn from my sin and come to You. Teach me, lead me, and make me Yours. I do not understand everything, but I trust You. Lord Jesus, save me.

If that prayer is the true cry of your heart, do not look to the prayer as your Savior.

Look to Christ.

Begin Where Christ Tells You to Begin

If you come to Christ, do not remain alone and hidden.

Begin following Him.

Read His Word. Start with the Gospels and listen to the voice of Christ. Pray honestly. Confess sin quickly. Seek a faithful church where Scripture is preached and Christ is honored. Be baptized as a public confession of faith. Learn from mature believers. Do not expect instant understanding of everything, but do expect Christ to lead you.

The Christian life is not a moment of emotion only. It is a new life.

Jesus said:

*"If ye continue in my word, then are ye my disciples indeed; And ye shall know the truth, and the truth shall make you free." — **John 8:31–32***

Continue in His Word.

Christ will teach you. He will correct you. He will comfort you. He will expose what must die and strengthen what He has begun. He will not leave His own unfinished.

The Final Word Is Come

The full character of God is not meant to leave you standing at a distance.

- His holiness shows you your need.
- His justice warns you of judgment.
- His wrath tells you sin cannot be ignored.
- His mercy tells you sinners may be received.
- His grace tells you salvation is a gift.
- His love tells you He gave His Son.

- His faithfulness tells you His promise can be trusted.
- His power tells you He is able to save.
- His patience tells you He has not yet closed the door.
- His truth tells you not to delay.

And Christ says:

Come.

- Come with your sin.
- Come with your questions.
- Come with your fear.
- Come with your weak faith.
- Come with your broken past.
- Come with your need.

Do not wait until you understand everything.

Do not wait until you feel worthy.

Do not wait until your life is repaired.

Do not wait until conviction fades.

Come to Jesus Christ.

He will reveal what you do not yet understand.

He will teach what you do not yet know.

He will cleanse what you cannot cleanse.

He will save what you cannot save.

The door of mercy is open.

Come.

Jeff C. Edwards

www.ingramcontent.com/pod-product-compliance
Lightning Source LLC
Chambersburg PA
CBHW051457150726
47997CB00001B/4